Sustainable Modernity

In the 21st century, Norway, Denmark and Sweden remain the icons of fair societies, with high economic productivity and quality of life. But they are also an enigma in a cultural-evolutionary sense: though by no means following the same socio-economic formula, they are all cases of a "non-hubristic", socially sustainable modernity that puzzles outside observers.

Using Nordic welfare states as its laboratory, *Sustainable Modernity* combines evolutionary and socio-cultural perspectives to illuminate the mainsprings of what the authors call the "well-being society". The main contention is that Nordic uniqueness is not merely the outcome of one particular set of historical institutional or political arrangements, or sheer historical luck; rather, the high welfare creation inherent in the Nordic model has been predicated on a long and durable tradition of social cooperation, which has interacted with global competitive forces. Hence the socially sustainable Nordic modernity should be approached as an integrated and tightly orchestrated ecosystem based on a complex interplay of *cooperative* and *competitive* strategies within and across several domains: normative-cultural, socio-political and redistributive. The key question is: Can the Nordic countries uphold the balance of competition and cooperation and reproduce their resilience in the age of globalization, cultural collisions, the digital economy, the fragmentation of the work/life division and often intrusive EU regulation?

With contributors providing insights from the humanities, the social sciences and evolutionary science, this book will be of great interest to students and scholars of political science, sociology, history, institutional economics, Nordic studies and human evolution studies.

Nina Witoszek is a research professor at the Centre for Development and the Environment, Norway, and the Director of the Arne Næss Programme on Global Justice and the Environment at the University of Oslo, Norway.

Atle Midttun is a professor at the BI Norwegian School of Management, Department of Law and Governance, Norway; the Co-Director of the Centre for Corporate Responsibility, Denmark; and the Co-Director of the Centre for Energy and Environment, UK.

Routledge Studies in Sustainability

www.routledge.com/Routledge-Studies-in-Sustainability/book-series/RSSTY

Energy and Transport in Green Transition
Perspectives on Ecomodernity
Edited by Atle Midttun and Nina Witoszek

A Political Economy of Attention, Mindfulness and Consumerism
Reclaiming the Mindful Commons
Peter Doran

Sustainable Communities and Green Lifestyles
Consumption and Environmentalism
Tendai Chitewere

Aesthetic Sustainability
Product Design and Sustainable Usage
Kristine H. Harper

Stress, Affluence and Sustainable Consumption
Cecilia Solér

Digital Technology and Sustainability
Engaging the Paradox
Edited by Mike Hazas and Lisa P. Nathan

Personal Sustainability
Exploring the Far Side of Sustainable Development
Edited by Oliver Parodi and Kaidi Tamm

Sustainable Modernity
The Nordic Model and Beyond
Edited by Nina Witoszek and Atle Midttun

Sustainable Modernity
The Nordic Model and Beyond

**Edited by Nina Witoszek and
Atle Midttun**

First published 2018
by Routledge
2 Park Square, Milton Park, Abingdon, Oxon OX14 4RN

and by Routledge
711 Third Avenue, New York, NY 10017

Routledge is an imprint of the Taylor & Francis Group, an informa business

© 2018 selection and editorial matter, Nina Witoszek and Atle Midttun; individual chapters, the contributors

The right of Nina Witoszek and Atle Midttun to be identified as the authors of the editorial material, and of the authors for their individual chapters, has been asserted in accordance with sections 77 and 78 of the Copyright, Designs and Patents Act 1988.

All rights reserved. No part of this book may be reprinted or reproduced or utilised in any form or by any electronic, mechanical, or other means, now known or hereafter invented, including photocopying and recording, or in any information storage or retrieval system, without permission in writing from the publishers.

Trademark notice: Product or corporate names may be trademarks or registered trademarks, and are used only for identification and explanation without intent to infringe.

British Library Cataloguing-in-Publication Data
A catalogue record for this book is available from the British Library

Library of Congress Cataloging-in-Publication Data
A catalog record for this book has been requested

ISBN: 978-1-138-71821-0 (hbk)
ISBN: 978-1-315-19596-4 (ebk)

Typeset in Times New Roman
by Out of House Publishing

Contents

List of figures	vii
List of tables	viii
List of contributors	ix
Foreword	xi

1 Sustainable modernity and the architecture of the "well-being society": interdisciplinary perspectives 1
NINA WITOSZEK AND ATLE MIDTTUN

2 Cooperation, competition and multi-level selection: a new paradigm for understanding the Nordic model 18
DAVID SLOAN WILSON AND DAG O. HESSEN

3 Nordic humanism as a driver of the welfare society 36
NINA WITOSZEK AND ØYSTEIN SØRENSEN

4 Individualism and collectivism in Nordic schools: a comparative approach 59
KIRSTI KLETTE

5 Scaling up solidarity from the national to the global: Sweden as welfare state and moral superpower 79
LARS TRÄGÅRDH

6 Scandinavian feminism and gender partnership 102
CATHRINE HOLST

7 A welfare "regime of goodness"? Self-interest, reciprocity, and the moral sustainability of the Nordic model 119
KELLY MCKOWEN

8 Challenges to the Nordic work model in the age of
   globalized digitalization 139
   ATLE MIDTTUN

9 Between individualism and communitarianism: the
   Nordic way of doing politics 160
   NIK BRANDAL AND DAG EINAR THORSEN

10 Civilising global capitalism: aligning CSR and
   the welfare state 187
   ATLE MIDTTUN

11 Eco-modernity Nordic style: the challenge of aligning
   ecological and socio-economic sustainability 204
   ATLE MIDTTUN AND LENNART OLSSON

   *Afterword: lessons from the Nordic model –
   the US perspective* 229
   JEROME LIEBERMAN AND PAMELA IZVANARIU

   Index 237

Figures

1.1	Within-domain and across-domain sustainability	6
8.1	Disabled as a share of the population by age groups	149
8.2	Top income shares 1875–2011	150
8.3	Advanced functional flexibility and teamwork, by country	155
10.1	Government strategies to increase compatibility between CSR and advanced welfare states' policies	190
10.2	Cross-national CSR performance in 2007 and 2012	194
10.3	Partnered governance	196
11.1	Ecological footprints in 2013 of selected industrial countries (in global hectares)	209
11.2	Territorial emissions of CO_2 (tonnes/capita) of four Nordic countries and the EU from 1990 to 2014	210
11.3	CO_2 emissions from the four Nordic countries and the average of EU countries (tonnes/capita)	212

Tables

2.1	Eight Core Design Principles required for groups to function as collective units	27
4.1	How different aspects of deregulation have impacted on education in Nordic countries	67
8.1	Nordic performance	153
11.1	GDP per capita, 11 highest European countries	208
11.2	EU Member States' GHG reduction targets	213

Contributors

Nik Brandal is Assistant Professor in International Studies at Bjørknes University College, Oslo, Norway.

Dag O. Hessen is Professor of Biology, Dept of Biosciences, University of Oslo, Norway. He works primarily on evolution and ecology, from genes to ecosystem processes. He specializes in studying carbon cycling and climate, and his numerous publications focus on what can be labelled as "humans in nature – and the nature in humans".

Cathrine Holst is a professor at the Department of Sociology and Human Geography, University of Oslo, Norway. She is also connected to ARENA–Center for European Studies, University of Oslo, and CORE–Center for Research on Gender Equality at the Institute for Social Research in Oslo. She has published extensively on feminism and gender equality policy, democratic and political theory, the role of expertise in policy-making, European integration and the Nordic model.

Pamela Izvanariu is a legal scholar and practitioner and sociologist, who specializes in the nexus between labour, race and immigration. She has served as director of Florida International University's Research Institute for Social and Economic Policy, USA.

Kirsti Klette is a professor at the University of Oslo, Department of Teacher Education and School Research, University of Oslo, Norway. Her research interests include teaching and learning, teacher quality, classroom studies and comparative studies. She is currently the principal investigator in a project on Nordic Comparative Classroom Analyses (Justice through Education (JustEd)) and a large-scale classroom video study Linking Instruction and Student Achievement (LISA).

Jerome Lieberman is co-founder and secretary/treasurer of the Evolution Institute, an international science think tank. His studies and work have been focused on applying theory to practice for the purpose of improving quality of life, especially in communities and regions where inequality and social injustice remain prevalent.

Kelly McKowen is a PhD candidate in the Department of Anthropology at Princeton University, USA. His research focuses on the intersection of culture, morality and the welfare state in Scandinavia and the United States. At present, he is completing his dissertation project – an ethnographic study of unemployment and ethics in Norway.

Atle Midttun is a professor at the BI Norwegian Business School, Department of Law and Governance, Norway. He is co-director of two of the school's research centres: The Centre for Energy and The Centre for Corporate Responsibility. His teaching and research interests include economic regulation, innovation, energy, sustainability, corporate governance and CSR.

Lennart Olsson is Professor of Geography at Lund University, Sweden, and was the founding Director of LUCSUS 2000–2016. Current research focuses on the politics of climate change in the context of poverty, food insecurity and ill-health in sub-Saharan Africa. He was Coordinating Lead Author for the chapter on Livelihoods and Poverty in the IPCC's 5th Assessment Report 2011–2014, and the chapter on Land Degradation in the upcoming special IPCC report on Climate Change and Land (SRCCL), 2017–2019.

Øystein Sørensen is Professor of Modern History at the University of Oslo, Norway. He has published extensively on the history of political ideas and led an interdisciplinary research project The Development of Norwegian National Identity in the Nineteenth Century 1993–1997. His publications include The Cultural Construction of Norden (edited with Bo Stråth, 1997).

Dag Einar Thorsen is Associate Professor of Political Science at the School of Business, University College of Southeast Norway, Drammen.

Lars Trägårdh received his PhD in History from UC Berkeley, USA, and subsequently lectured at the Department of History at Barnard College, Columbia University, USA. He is currently professor of History and Civil Society Studies at Ersta Sköndal Bräcke University College in Stockholm, Sweden. He has written extensively on Sweden and the Nordic model.

David Sloan Wilson is President of the Evolution Institute (https://evolution-institute.org) and SUNY Distinguished Professor of Biology and Anthropology at Binghamton University in New York, USA. His most recent book is *Does Altruism Exist? Culture, Genes, and the Welfare of Others* (Yale/Templeton 2015).

Nina Witoszek is a research professor at the Center for Development and the Environment and the Director of the Arne Naess Programme in Global Justice and the Environment at the University of Oslo, Norway. Her research interests and publications include comparative Scandinavian history, environmental philosophy and ethics and the study of anti-authoritarian movements.

Foreword

This book is an experiment in several ways. It was born out of a dialogue with evolutionary scientists, who have inspired us to rethink the Nordic model as the result of an interplay between cooperation and competition at multiple levels in cultural, economic, political, and caring and redistributive realms. As an "interdisciplinary jamboree" – involving evolutionary thinkers, historians, anthropologists, pedagogues, sociologists, geographers and political economists – our project has invited scholars who rarely talk to one another to defamilarize the standard interpretations of the Nordic model. Needless to say, this exercise has been as exciting as it has been challenging.

The concept of the "Nordic model" deployed in this study has been contested, deconstructed and even exploded. Some scholars have objected to its use in the singular (we should rather talk about "Nordic models"), or pointed to potent differences between the Northern welfare states, which disable the concept or make it spurious. But, like many successful tropes, the "Nordic model" is as resonant as it is inaccurate, and it has become well established in both native and international discourse. In this volume we make an argument for a common cultural tradition as well as common ideas about political economy shared by most Nordic countries. To illustrate individual particularities, we navigate between the study of what is more appropriately called "Scandinavia" (i.e. Denmark, Sweden and Norway), making occasional forays into Finland, or focusing on *one* Nordic case which illustrates, in a nutshell, a more general Nordic trend or – in a poignant way – signals challenges faced by other Nordic countries. We apologize to our Icelandic colleagues for leaving them out of the analysis. Last time we engaged with Icelandic scholars, we learned that "Iceland, at its peak, before the financial crisis, had seen itself as moving beyond the Nordics, to become a unique synthesis of a welfare state and American turbo-capitalism": a fascinating development which deserves a separate study. However, both limited resources and the largely network-based character of our quest have prevented us from embarking on a more comprehensive survey.

We are grateful to the UiO: Nordic programme, which made our comparative symposia – and this volume – possible. We would also like to thank Mathew Little and Armando Lamadrid for their invaluable editorial interventions, and Knut Myrum Næss for his assistance in completing the book.

1 Sustainable modernity and the architecture of the "well-being society"
Interdisciplinary perspectives

Nina Witoszek and Atle Midttun

In 1914 Graham Wallas – the co-founder of the London School of Economics – published his influential *Great Society:* a study of the ways in which industrial revolution was transforming and distorting human relations. "If I try to make for myself a visual picture of the social system which I should desire for England and America," Wallas wrote, "it would be a harmonious society like the one in Northern Europe." In a rhapsodic exultation, he confided:

> There comes before me a recollection of those Norwegian towns and villages where everyone, the shopkeepers and the artisans, the schoolmaster, the boy who drove the post-ponies, and the student daughter of the innkeeper who took round the potatoes, seemed to respect themselves, to be capable of Happiness as well as pleasure and excitement, because they were near the Mean in the employment of all their faculties. I can imagine such people learning to exploit power from their waterfalls, and the minerals in their mountains, without dividing themselves into dehumanized employers or officials, and equally dehumanized 'hands'. But I recollect also that the very salt and savour of Norwegian life depends on the fact that poets, and artists and statesmen have worked in Norway with a devotion which was not directed by any formula of moderation.
> (quoted by Dahrendorf 1997: 39–40).

Wallas's pastoral vignette is arresting in a double sense. Though 21st-century Norway is the antithesis of the virtuous rural community he envisioned over a hundred years ago, some of its salient values – such as equality, reciprocity and basic humaneness – seem to live on. It is as if the spirit of the Norwegian harmonious, egalitarian village has been trapped, like a genie, in a capsule of time and guides the citizens of one of the richest and yet also most egalitarian democracies in the world.

But there is yet another dimension to Wallas's fascination with an exemplary society in the North. It belongs to an intriguing tradition of the outsiders' "romance" with Scandinavia, which has been a leitmotif of both early and late modernity. Already in the 19th century, romantic pilgrims – such as Mary Wollstonecraft and Maurycy Mochnacki – travelled to the North in search of a prototype of a free and egalitarian "nature tribe" (Witoszek 2013).[1] A century later, in the turbulent 1930s, with Marquis Childs's publication of his bestseller *Sweden: the Middle Way* (1936), the world would be galvanized again by a vision of a caring state and a cooperative national community on the margins of Europe. And in 2013, at the World Economic Forum in Davos, international economists and policy-makers set out to crack the code of the surprisingly affluent and altruistic modern "Vikings" mark 2.0.[2]

How is it that the Northern passage from rags to riches has resulted in societies that have managed to restrain the growth of Wallas's "dehumanized employers and [...] equally dehumanized "hands", and minimize the social distance between "shopkeepers, artisans and schoolmasters"? What have been the mechanisms – and who have been the actors – that have forged a seemingly non-hubristic Nordic modernity?

Three stages of Nordic modernization

One of the arguments of this book is that modern Nordic welfare societies owe their prosperity as much to their natural resources as to a cumulative build-up of cultural, value-charged, institutional and economic choices made at various stages of modernity,[3] each with its own gains and hazards. The first stage – that of techno-economic modernity – boasted spectacular technological innovation, industrial revolution and unprecedented productivity. The second stage – that of socially sustainable modernity – introduced the ethos of social care and partnership into the techno-economic dynamic. The third stage – what we call "eco-modernity" (Midttun and Witoszek 2016) – has emerged to address mounting environmental and climate challenges.

Needless to say that each stage of modernization had its liabilities tied to a progressive depletion of human and environmental resources. But one could also say that each subsequent phase was a corrective to the preceding one: the social excesses of early industrialization were tempered by socially sustainable modernity, while the dawn of eco-modernity has started adding environmental amendments to the carbon age. This endless process of self-correction has been a testimony to modernity's self-reflexivity; an attempt not to completely throw out the old "baby" of industrial and emancipatory modernity with the polluted bathwater, but to salvage some of the core achievements of human development.

As techno-economic modernizers at the periphery of Europe, the Nordics were relative latecomers, following the British first wave, and then the German and American second wave of industrialization. However, since the end of the 19th century, they were bold and precursory drivers of inclusive, socially sustainable modernity. This was due to a number of well known and well studied historical and political factors, such as the relative lack of feudal structures, a strong community of free peasants and fishermen, early literacy, and simultaneous modernization driven both by the grassroots and the elites (e.g. Østerud 1979; Seip 1997; Slagstad 1998; Sejersted 2011). This socio-cultural legacy was drawn upon by the labour movement, which, through confrontations and compromises with industry, co-created the welfare state.

But, as we argue in this volume, there are two, less explored drivers of the Nordic model in its current form. The first one is the shared Nordic humanism, which goes back to the 18th- and 19th-century founding tradition of a vibrant Christian Enlightenment, with its ideas of Samaritanism and social solidarity (see Chapter 3). The other derives from a cache of practical, local knowledge and "sustainability thinking", which – in Norway, Sweden and Finland in particular – constituted an inbuilt reflex and unwritten codex of prudent action. This storehouse of wisdom was especially relevant in regions whose citizens struggled, for a long time, to eke out a livelihood in the harsh environment – particularly along the rugged North Sea coast, and in barren, sunlight-starved agricultural terrains. There, a community's survival depended on an enduring tradition of social partnership and cooperation rather than unhinged competition. Long-term thinking, "ahead of a crisis", predisposed the expedient resolution of social conflicts, as well as the ability to live with – and adapt to – unpredictable elemental forces (Witoszek 2011).

This was an early industrial North, as portrayed by Wallas. In the second half of the 20th century, the Nordics underwent a rapid techno-economic transformation to make a quantum leap into successful, modern welfare states: a position that they have held rather consistently, in spite of numerous obituaries announcing their demise. Judged by international comparative indexes, the 21st century has marked their renaissance. Norway, Sweden, Denmark and Finland now rank on a par with the top drivers of techno-industrial modernity, while also scoring highest as exemplars of *socially sustainable* modernity. In the past ten years, the United Nations has ranked them as the "world's best countries to live in", the best countries for mothers and – if we are to believe the latest assessment of the Norwegian *via fortunata* – also places with a surprisingly high coefficient of gross national happiness.[4] This is a combination that few, if any, other countries can match.

It remains an open question whether the Nordics can equal their socio-economic success with a transition to eco-modernity. It is worth noting that, when the environmental sustainability agenda became a global programme, the Nordic countries were early pioneers, capitalizing on their "ecological" cultural memory and leading seminal initiatives advancing environmental concerns (see Chapter 11). In the 21st century, however, together with many other industrial nations, they have struggled to square the new climate objectives with economic growth. So far, they have certainly been impressive as modern myth makers. In Norway especially, the emergent, electrifying narrative of success – combined with prosperity and unspoiled beauty of nature – has been so potent, that even the country's high, oil-lubricated ecological footprint has been eclipsed by upbeat "green stories". One hears rhapsodies about Arne Naess's Deep Ecology and the Brundtland Commission's idea of sustainable development, not to mention the record number of peace missions and humanitarian initiatives in developing countries. As this volume will show, while the Norwegian economy has yet to live up to the country's green mythology, other Nordic countries, Sweden in particular, aim at climate front-runnership. The discovery of green growth heralds a new synthesis, where socio-economic sustainability is no longer a question of austerity, but an opportunity for novel business models.

Self-limiting modernity

In a panoramic take on Western modernity's central theme, Daniel Bell has pointed to the relevance of the word *beyond*: imagining a limitless world that was beyond nature, beyond culture, beyond humanity and God (Bell 1991: 353). The *beyondness* of modernity has been expressed in mobilizing stories and images, such as the powerful American frontier mythology, the British "civilizing mission" towards "savage species", German ideas of *Übermensch and Lebensraum* and the French Jacobin project of inventing a brave new world from scratch – without false gods and idols. In the Nordic countries, modernity's hubristic temptations seem to have been largely kept in check. As our volume will show, the Nordics are interesting examples of "self-limiting modernity": one, which has kept measure with regard to economic, social and ecological excesses. They have evolved gradually, through a *refolution* (a mixture of reform and revolution) rather than revolutionary change, and their most meaningful, world-changing texts, habits and routines show the workings of a pragmatic and cooperative ethos. This, we argue, is also the basis of the relative resilience of the Nordic model; the fact that its architects have managed to balance political and economic innovation with norms and values that have boosted community, identity, conciliatory ways of resolving conflicts and non-coercive strategies for monitoring human behaviour. In Chapters 3–7, we show how non-hubristic Nordic modernity has been supported by a set of strong behavioural and normative patterns. Here the capitalist *homo economicus* – a rational, profit-seeking protagonist – has been counterbalanced by strong educational ideals stressing public-mindedness and social cooperation. Interestingly, these ideals have tended to be oriented towards what is *achievable*, rather than wishful thinking. The overarching goal of the *homo nordicus* has never been to build an *ideal* society; rather, since the beginning of the 20th century, the Nordics have got on with the task of building what Peter Corning has called a "fair society", based on equality, equity and reciprocity (Corning 2011).

Evolutionary and socio-cultural underpinnings of the Nordic model

The strong tradition of teamwork which underlines the Nordic model has been the subject of numerous studies that focus on specific institutions, politics and industrial relations, (e.g. Sejersted 2011; Wahl, A. 2011, Dølvik et al. 2014; Engelstad 2015; Törnquist and Harriss 2016). We contend that these arrangements reflect deeper societal and behavioural principles that lie at the core of social and evolutionary theory. As Chapter 2 will show, by exploring the Nordic model through the combined evolutionary and socio-cultural lens, we are able to uncover novel facets of both the mainsprings and inner workings of Nordic sustainable modernity.

Our broad, inter-disciplinary approach has been inspired by a dialogue with evolutionary science and its findings on the role of multi-level selection and collaboration in human evolution. As opposed to the often crude and simplified Darwinism, "the third wave" of evolutionary biology has gathered evidence to the effect that collaborative behaviour may carry equal, if not stronger, weight than competition in forging resilience and adaptability in human evolution. Wilson and Wilson (2007), in their theory of multi-level selection, have shown how prosociality provides behavioural underpinnings for a doctrine of the competitive advantage of collaboration. There is evidence to the effect that, while unselfish individuals might be vulnerable to exploiters and free-riders within their own group, *groups* of individuals that behave prosocially will robustly outcompete groups handicapped by selfish exploitation and free-riding. The shortest rendition of this idea has been the legendary dictum: "Selfishness beats altruism within groups. Altruistic groups beat selfish groups. Everything else is commentary" (Wilson and Wilson 2007: 346). Translated onto the societal level, multiple-level selection theory implies that competitive advantage in the international economy can be fostered by collaborative behaviour at national and sub-national levels. But it also implies that the efficacy of domestic collaborative behaviour is critically dependent on external competition.

The evolutionary work on the efficacy of small prosocial groups chimes with the Nobel Prize winner Elinor Ostrom's studies of the mechanisms of governance for sustainable resource management. Ostrom explored communities that successfully managed to overcome the tragedy of the commons by a fair distribution of the pool of natural resources (Ostrom 1990). She singled out eight design principles of such efficacious management, including clearly defined boundaries and strong identity, collective decision-making, effective monitoring of group behaviour, graduated sanctions and swift and fair conflict resolution (Ostrom 1990; see also Chapter 2). While Wilson illuminated the basic evolutionary mechanisms of successful prosociality, Ostrom codified the governance conditions necessary to put this mechanism into practice in human societies. In a joint article, Wilson, Ostrom and Cox (Wilson et al. 2013) go as far as to argue that the design principles can be generalized and have the potential to explain the success or failure of social groups independent of their scale: a thesis which is tested and discussed in the successive chapters of this volume.

Applying multi-level selection to societal analysis involves scaling up from groups to large social systems.[5] Such systems typically involve specialization into social domains, including normative/cultural, socio-political, productive and redistributive/caring.[6] At this level, the dynamics of competition and collaboration become more complicated than in a small group. Overall societal

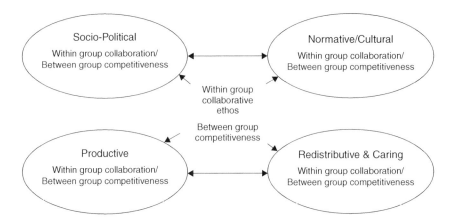

Figure 1.1 Within-domain and across-domain sustainability

efficacy now depends on the ability to strike a balance between competition and collaboration *within* the aforementioned domains as well as in relations *between* them (Figure 1.1). In this perspective, Nordic success (or efficacy) is predicated on the ability to forge a difficult, competitively challenged collaboration both *within* and *across* domains or realms.

Analysing the Nordics through the holistic lens of our evolutionary and socio-cultural perspective, we first argue that Nordic uniqueness is not merely the outcome of one particular set of historical institutional or political arrangements or sheer historical luck; rather it has to be approached as an integrated and tightly orchestrated ecosystem – a complex interplay of cooperative and competitive strategies *within* and *across* several domains: normative-cultural, economic, socio-political, economic and redistributive. In short, we contend that the basis of social sustainability of the Nordic countries has been a drive towards a balance of competition and collaboration in culture, economy and politics, both inside and outside national boundaries.

Inscribed into a project like ours is an inquiry into the eternal question of why nations fail or succeed. Acemoglu and Robinson (2013) believed they had solved the riddle by emphasizing the role of *social institutions* and underplaying cultural values, norms and taboos. Our research shows that that it is often uninstitutionalized, *cultural, value-charged innovation* – sparking new ways of seeing the world – that plays a vital role. In the chapters that follow we ask how the cooperative ethos has been established and solidified through Nordic cultural routines, religious beliefs, literature and schooling: the incubators of what Tocqueville called the "habits of the heart" and the "habits of the mind". It is these habits that have subsequently informed economic and political spheres and penetrated into gender relations.

What has been striking about the canonic, "sacred" texts and practices (*symbotypes*) in Danish, Norwegian and Swedish cultures is their consistent and strong advocacy of the ideal of a cooperative, tolerant and inclusive community, which is seen as superior to a competitive, hierarchic one (see Chapter 3). This ideal – replicated with great fidelity both in national literatures and in religious and secular pedagogy – has provided a blueprint for an imagined moral community that has valued teamwork and prosociality and, for a long time, looked down on selfishness, extravagance and explicit signs of individualist struggle for prestige and domination.[7] Witness the socio-political and economic consequences of the initially marginal Swedish feminist movement, which advanced the concept of the state as a "home", or the broad impact of Norwegian and Danish visions of alternative religiosity, which foregrounded cooperation, altruism and responsible entrepreneurship. As Chapter 3 demonstrates, *cultural innovation* – both top-down and grassroots – has had a pivotal impact on political and economic processes in Norway and Sweden. Though it has not eliminated conflict, it has discouraged disruptive, self-serving behaviours and reinforced symbiotic associations and collective work to achieve a common good. In addition, as argued in Chapter 6, it has had a bearing on the unique social democratic model of gender partnership, which – in contrast to a more self-centred, liberal feminism – seems to have yielded a more woman- and mother-friendly state and welfare system. The ideal of life as a cooperative effort to forge a common good has also affected social perceptions of the generous social benefits system. Contrary to the prevalent mythology, there is evidence to the effect that the so-called Norwegian "social clients" (or *NAVErs*) are far from relishing their *dolce far niente*; rather they deplore their status as beneficiaries of unemployment benefits and are troubled by the sense of not contributing to the welfare of others (see Chapter 7).

We argue that this strongly cooperative and pragmatic ethos, when transposed into economic and political realms, has yielded an "alchemical brew" of political cooperation, strong welfare provisions and a relatively prosocial model of capitalism. It has also solidified the deliberative aspect of the "Nordic way of doing politics" (Chapter 9); It has been pervasive in work life, where high unionization and tripartite negotiations between labour, industry and the state have produced agreements that allow the parties to pursue common interests in value creation in spite of diverse interests as to how that value is subsequently distributed; it has surfaced strongly in the leading role of Nordic companies as champions of corporate social responsibility (CSR); and, last but not least, it has featured in the self-imposed Nordic mission to support international institutions that promote human rights and "civilized capitalism" (Chapter 10).

We contend that it is the interplay of these diverse realms and their mutual cross-pollination with the ideal of prosociality that gives the Nordic model its regenerative potential, one that goes beyond *specific* institutions and domains. As in a "relay model" (Midttun and Witoszek 2016), if one institutional stronghold for social sustainability is overridden (e.g. by international regulation), other domains may step into the breach and generate new solutions, so that the prosocial, cooperative modus is reclaimed. What is also intriguing about the modern Nordic "regime of goodness" is not just its strong entrenchment in the national Bildung of the Nordic countries themselves, but the manifold attempts to export it abroad via either political or business initiatives. Such export, we argue, is not exclusively a sign of idealism; it is also part of a pragmatic calculus of small countries that stand to win more by nudging the world to adopt *their* cooperative norms than by shifting to a disruptive dog-eat-dog worldview.

The pragmatic basis of Nordic cooperation

While acknowledging that cooperation has been one of the strongest propellers of Nordic sustainable modernity, we take issue with Richard Sennett's (2013) tribute to the pivotal importance of teamwork and collaborative relations in fostering exemplary welfare states. Taking a more balanced view, our evolutionary socio-cultural perspective highlights the need to add the dynamic impulse from competition which prevents stasis. Thus, the high welfare creation inherent in the Nordic model has been predicated on a long and durable tradition of social cooperation, which has meshed with global competitive forces. Furthermore, being small, high-trust societies with strong states, the Nordics have ample organizational capacity for forging prosocial collective arrangements. This is exemplified in several chapters in this book (those on work life, eco-modernity and CSR engagement), which argue that Ostromian principles of a small-group self-governance appear to have been successfully scaled up to the welfare state. While scale, cohesion, trust and transparency facilitate Ostromian good governance and limit the erosion of prosocial arrangements from below, a strong focus on productivity has served to harmonize prosociality with international competitiveness – in most cases by finding win–win solutions, but sometimes, as in early-stage climate policy, by limiting collective responsibility until win–win solutions can be found.

To sum up: Nordic social sustainability is pragmatic through and through. It rests not just on the capacity to build welfare, but also on the ability to use welfare arrangements to enhance productivity. As Chapter 8 shows, the so-called flexicurity mechanism creates efficient human resource management to the benefit of industry (which gains flexibility), the worker (who gains security) and the state (which harvests benefits of increased productivity and competitiveness). A similarly pragmatic combination of prosociality and productivity can be observed in the Nordic endorsement of green growth in climate policy. In spite of their role as early advocates of environmental legislation, the Nordics started to embrace policy action to bring down CO_2 emissions only when it became clear that climate mitigation could be combined with continuous welfare and value creation through green growth. The 21st-century transition to eco-modernity has hardly been a "big-bang operation", especially in oil-rich Norway. On the contrary, it rests on a sober, business-like calculation which, in a malign interpretation, may appear as cold-hearted or hypocritical. But on closer inspection it shows traces of the Nordic "adaptive opportunism", which, paradoxically, has been as much part and parcel of a pragmatic peasant culture as the basis of a *socially sustainable* modernity.

The Nordic model on trial

Can the Nordic countries uphold the balance of competition and cooperation and reproduce their resilience in the age of globalization, cultural collisions, the digital economy, the fragmentation of the work/life division and often intrusive EU regulation?

In the 21st century, the egalitarian and cooperative ethos is increasingly under siege. It is challenged by the often sectarian values of immigrant communities, a predicament which leads to a cultural polarization among the indigenous population and the resurgence of populism. It is diluted by the ideal of individual excellence entering school programmes and subjugated to the tyranny of global educational rankings. It is diminished by outsourcing and digitalization in work and life, which pulverizes communities' coherence and individual responsibility. Last but not least, it is dismantled by the intrusion of the media logic and the technocratic mindset in political processes.

Our book explores the manifold ways in which the Nordic countries have responded and adjusted to these challenges. One of the most conspicuous attempts to *re-establish Nordicity* has occurred in the cultural sphere, where an ongoing debate in the mainstream and social media, framed in terms of the "battle" for Norwegian/Swedish/Danish values, points to signs of polarization of Nordic societies into "nationalist" and "cosmopolitan" camps. This debate has become especially vigorous in the second decade of the 21st century and illustrates the dilemmas faced by a region which has, for a long time, represented a constellation of small "Ostromian" communities. Increasingly, the design principles which made them efficacious are confronted by hybrid identities, dissolved boundaries and the clash of nationalist and cosmopolitan aspirations. While Denmark, Finland and Norway have been outspoken guardians of their national boundaries – both through their restrictive refugee policies and through the inclusion of the populist parties in political coalitions – Sweden was for a long time a warm defender of generous transnationalism and the "open door" policy. But even here, at the time this book is written, things are changing. The Swedish public sphere – for a long time incarcerated in the politically correct discourse of an inclusive and prosocial community – is coming to the realization that the ideal of the human rights-based identity has led to a split into "two Swedens" (Chapter 5). The challenge of reimagining and solidifying cultural-economic and political institutions under a cosmopolitan regime is accompanied by a set of new questions which have surfaced as a result of the massive cultural transformations of the last decades.

At the level of work life, the Nordic model has been challenged on several fronts: Chapter 8 illustrates how the Nordic collective wage bargaining and the exclusivity of welfare arrangements have been questioned, and in some cases eroded or rejected, in order to further a common European market. With the ascension of post-communist East European countries into the EU and the subsequent opening-up of free access to European labour markets, salaries less than one quarter of those in the North have posed a major challenge to egalitarian Nordic work life.

The Nordic model has been further exposed to new modes of commercial organization, capitalizing on a combination of technological innovation and new market-enhancing regulation. Many of these developments diminish labour's influence on strategic decision-making and dilute its bargaining power, thereby weakening one of the pillars of Nordic inclusive egalitarianism. This being said, while digitalization and the sharing economy have put the Nordic model under pressure, advanced segments of Nordic industry have thrived. This is partly due to the compatibility of Nordic work life organization and welfare arrangements with the need for flexible specialization in the context of the new innovation economy.

Eco-modernity, with its climate agenda, poses yet another challenge. As already mentioned, in the first decades of the 21st century, there has been a striking discrepancy between advanced Nordic environmental ideals and those countries' overall mediocre climate practice.[8] To the extent that environmental and socio-economic sustainability collide, the Nordics face a dilemma. Their inherent prosocial orientation allows for strong collective action in both domains, but when the pursuit of one is seen as undermining the other, it is socio-economic sustainability that prevails. However, Chapter 11 shows how the emergence of green growth opportunities has created greater potential for a broader synthesis of socio-economic and ecological sustainability. The increasingly accepted green growth agenda allows the Nordics to translate their environmental idealism into eco-modernity, where climate policy supports, rather than limits, their socio-economic endeavour.

Another challenge springs from the new modes of capitalism, which have increasingly included CSR in business and market agendas. Some have argued that the predominantly business-driven CSR platform is antithetical to the politically driven welfare state tradition of the Nordic countries. The Nordic welfare state tradition emphasizes universal rights and duties, extensive state engagement in the economy and negotiated agreements to regulate labour relationships. In contrast, the CSR tradition – with its neoliberal, Anglo-American dossier – emphasizes corporate discretion, voluntarism and market-based policy solutions. However, as shown in Chapter 10, the Nordic countries have managed to turn the challenge to their advantage. Here, CSR has become a joint project, promoted by industry and the state alike. Nordic companies, as well as governments, have pragmatically appropriated CSR in areas where traditional welfare state policies lack resources or outreach.

The quest for a good society

Modernity's potential as a locus of "good society" has been a subject of contention, and yielded dramatically opposing visions, where Pollyannas clash with Cassandras.

In 1992 Fukuyama published his scenario of the end of history and triumph of market economy and liberal democracy (Fukuyama 1992). This vision was part of a trend advocating market-based globalization by many Western mainstream economic and political elites. It was vigorously propagated by institutions like the OECD and IMF, and codified in GATT and the so-called "Washington Consensus". The promise was to deliver more wealth and welfare to ever more people through growth and innovation. There is even research to the effect that, in spite of terrorism and savage wars in the Middle East, the world is getting better educated, better fed, healthier and richer than ever before (Kenny 2015).

At the same time, however, at the end of the 20th century, a vocal Cassandric camp – with influential thinkers such as Zygmunt Bauman, John Gray and Naomi Klein – came to the fore with contrasting apocalyptic visions of soulless consumer democracy, "disaster capitalism" and the looming age of global anarchy. In John Gray's noir-voyant study *The False Dawn* (2015), social democracy is incompatible with global markets, ergo the project of forging a liberating and sustainable modernity is utopian. Free markets codified by the Washington Consensus and the IT revolution produce new transnational elites, but they also marginalize masses of redundant people. The outcome of this process, Gray concludes, is the awakening of the hinterland and the growth of populist, xenophobic, fundamentalist movements, which threaten retribalization of the world (Gray 2015: 20).

While we cannot entirely discount these dark prognoses, we take issue with their central premises. As we see it, market-based, globalized modernity has been over-hyped by both its proponents and its opponents. In fact, the modern global market economy combines extensive national and regional variation, as described in an extensive body of literature (Whitley 2000; Hall and Soskice 2001). In this perspective, various models of political economy, embedded in different cultural traditions, co-exist, clamour for space and mutually influence one another. In this global theatre, the Nordics position themselves as pragmatic dualists: ardent market-globalists when it comes to trade of goods, but proponents of national, collective prosociality when it comes to work conditions and welfare provision. This dualism, which is embedded in their culture, institutions and social organization, is more hospitable to the mixed – altruist and egoist, cooperative and competitive – potential of human nature. Thus the problem with both the Cassandras and the Pollyannas of our time is that, while sculpting their visions of social improvement or apocalypse, they overlook the inherent dualism of human nature. The dominant Cassandric projections tend to emphasize inherent selfishness and predatory competitiveness, and, predictably, are incompatible with the transition to a more sustainable future.

Is the Nordic model of a "well-being society" exportable?

Being an interdisciplinary exercise, this book gestures towards two different answers. On the one hand, historians and social scientists, focused as they are on difference and nuance, insist that the success of the Nordics is due to a combination of multiple factors, such as the common founding tradition of Christian Enlightenment, high state capacity and high trust, and relative homogeneity. The complex anchoring of productive prosociality in the interplay of several domains – culture, techno-economy, politics and welfare – would indicate that the Nordic model's replicability in other cultures should be treated with caution. On the other hand, the social scientists and historians agree with evolutionary scientists that the Nordic countries are cases of societies that have managed "a successful projection of the control mechanisms of a small village to the 'national village'" (Wilson and Hessen 2014). According to Wilson and Hessen, evolutionary theory casts new light on the Nordic countries as exemplars of good governance. "Norway and the other Nordic countries function as cooperators on the world stage providing a moral example for other nations [...] Any large-scale society, at any period of human history, functions well or poorly to the degree it succeeds at scaling up the Core Design Principles (CDP)" (Wilson and Hessen 2014). Even in large scale societies, good governance is possible once human groups are divided into small units according to the model of polycentric governance.

While this bold postulate is open to debate – and would need resources to replicate Ostroms's research programme – many of the chapters in our volume show the strength of CDP as one of the fundaments of the modern Nordic welfare state. There is yet another consideration. One of the advantages of globalization is the very velocity with which social ideals and blueprints are being circulated and shared. There is an ongoing diffusion and translation of innovative social visions and arrangements and, as the example of Bernie Sanders's America shows (see Afterword), the attraction of the social-democratic good society is unabated. The Nordic model itself has borrowed vastly from other traditions, including British Parliamentarianism, the ideals of the French Revolution and the visions of the American Founding Fathers. Even the green growth agenda, which the Nordic countries have taken on board in the 21st century, was first strongly advocated in South Korea before it was embraced in the global North.

When seen through a prism of evolutionary thought, the struggle for a good society springs from the unselfish and cooperative side of human nature and successful social organization. This means that, though the Nordic model is culturally specific, the dream of welfare, security and fairness is universal. Nations, regions and communities that have managed to get the "well-being formula" right will always be attractive role models.

And although they cannot be mechanically copied, the Nordic countries are compelling because they seem to have addressed the general condition of homelessness at the heart of modernity. This homelessness, as has been argued, springs from a triple alienation: from nature, history and community (Nisbet 1953 ix–xi). In the North this alienation seems to have been partly stymied by transposing the idea of "home" to the modern welfare state. Nowhere has this "domestication" of the state been more conspicuous than in modern Sweden, whose early 20th-century social democrats united the nation around the idea of Sweden as the "people's home" (*folkhemmet*). However ironized in the Age of Cynical Reason, the myth of the state as a fatherly protector of individual autonomy, and the perception of society as a "family", constitute a strong legacy, which tempers modernity's uprooting and disinheriting thrust.

In 1974, the German poet and writer Hans Magnus Entzensberger wrote an intriguing study, *Norsk utakt* (loosely translated as "Norway's Out of Stepness'"), where he claimed that the country was Europe's biggest folk museum, but also the biggest laboratory of the future. Its museum-like, anachronistic mien lay in its penchant for Spartan life in the bosom of nature, its dislike of extravagance and proclivity in favour of peasant frugality, and its premodern tradition of a community's *dugnad* (collective work for a public good). Its precursory, "futuristic" dimension stemmed from early peasant and workers' emancipation, its antecedent, "natural" feminism (as exemplified in Ibsen's plays), and its early versions of sophisticated, deliberative democracy (Entzensberger 1974).

The 21st century is a stress test for a model which has not quite broken its traditional moorings but rather has tried to tie them to a future-oriented, innovative thinking. The Age of Anthropocene and the array of swift, social and techno-economic changes mean that the Nordic home cannot survive in a cocoon of its own goodness; it has to renew itself in more dramatic ways than it has done so far. Its 20th-century version was designed to regulate and provide welfare under conditions of mass production in a mature industrial society. In the transition to the digitalized economy, with its more specialized and flexible work life, the Nordic model has to transform its architecture in tandem with the underlying techno-economy and socio-cultural innovation. The main challenge is thus to embark on regulatory and social innovation without losing social coherence and the potency of the Ostromian regulative principles. As we argue in this volume, one of the guarantors of this coherence are cultural norms, values and unifying stories replicated from generation to generation. It is the well entrenched ethos of fairness, care and prosociality that keeps being reactivated in situations where the IT economy's tax havens, or the sharing economy's insecure work relations, are in glaring breach of Nordic rules. Even a cursory glance at the ongoing value debates in the Nordic public sphere shows how scrupulously noted – and publicly condemned – is every case of industrial or political violation of the community's "sacred norms".[9] What is also interesting are public calls for visionary and creative ingenuity that address these issues "on Nordic terms" and "up to Nordic standards" in a globalized (or increasingly Europeanized) economy. At the 21st-century crossroads, culture strikes back – and often in unpredictable ways.

To sum up: One of the arguments in this book is that in the 19th and 20th centuries the Nordic welfare states – each of them in its own way – managed to organize and mythologize themselves as cooperative, inclusive families. The "Nordic homes" – with their norms, routines, taboos – are now disrupted by the metamorphosis of the world (Beck 2017), where change no longer happens in the world of certainties; rather it takes place in a maelstrom of ever new beginnings, where what was unimaginable yesterday becomes possible today. The Nordic welfare states are, not for the first time, at a critical juncture. Ultimately, their resilience is yet to be proven, but in the first decades of the 21st century they seem to be doing what they have always been rather good at: keeping a balance between the encroachment of a cosmopolitan, borderless *Zeitgeist* and the safeguarding of their identity as "fair societies".

What is intriguing is the degree to which modern Norwegians, Swedes and Danes have interiorized the image of their countries as the loci of good life, humanitarianism and well-being. Norway in particular, partly due to its extraordinary petroleum wealth and partly due to national skills in positive neuro-linguistic programming, boosts the image of itself as a "peace-and-nature tribe" amidst a world of upheavals, catastrophes and decline. In a 2008 study of the Norwegian idea of happiness (Hellevik 2008), a team of researchers concluded that the Norwegians, having obtained most things they desired, are now more aware of the colossal gap between their affluence and the genuine need and misery in other parts of the world. They feel moral discomfort, accompanied by concerns about climate change and environmental crisis. And though it is difficult to generalize from the virtual tsunami of debates in the mainstream media, there are indications that the majority of Norway's citizens are convinced that they have reached – at least in the current moment of history – a *eudaimonic condition:* the apex of human flourishing and happiness on earth. As one young journalist put it in 2008 (the year that Wall Street crashed):

> Thanks to good management and a great deal of good luck, Norway is the first society in the history of humanity which can afford a welfare system that can really make everybody free. Those of us who live today are closer than any previous generation to realizing our dreams. Our productivity exceeds anything the world has seen before. We have both more money and more spare time than our fellow brothers in the rest of the world. Why not take seriously the ideal of freedom linked to pleasant life?
>
> (Sandbu 2008)

And in 2017, Jan Egeland, secretary-general of the Norwegian Refugee Council, wrote the following words in the biggest national daily:

> There has never in humanity's history in or outside our country been a people that were richer, had more consumption goods and enjoyed more social security and personal safety. This should imply that the 2017 Norwegian election should focus less on increased consumption or purchasing power at home and more on the bottom billion whose lives have been wrecked by catastrophes and crises the likes of which we have not experienced for the past 70 years. This would be in line with the Norwegian ideals and interests we insist we stand for – and with our Christian, humanist legacy that we want to teach our new countrymen.
> (Egeland 2017)

Egeland's coruscating *cri de cœur* is not just an extended version of Norwegian prosociality and the call for a national *dugnad* to help the underdogs; it reveals glimpses of the old Lutheran guilt at being happier and better off than the rest of the world. And, although the scope of this study does not allow us to probe the subject, the half-euphoric, half-embarrassed awareness of one's own good fortune is typical of most middle-class Scandinavians. Whether Nordic modernity represents the peak of the well-being society, or only its beginning, remains to be seen. It is certainly a fragile construction, the catastrophists might say. And the ironists might add that it sometimes morphs into an unsavoury, narcissistic philanthropism, whose nature has been captured by W.H. Auden: "We are here on earth to help the others. What the hell the others are here for, God only knows."

Whatever the conclusion, the Nordic countries are an experiment – very much like this volume. But the book's radical interdisciplinarity invites us to look at the Nordic model telescopically, joining evolutionary insights with cultural, political and economic analysis. Like any experimental journey, our volume is explorative and tentative in its nature. It has been co-written by a group of scholars with widely divergent backgrounds and perspectives, and has fostered wide discussions and disagreements. The juxtaposition of studies of education and cultural history with business models and political analysis, as well as biology, involved a clash of languages, concepts and interpretations. However, we would like to believe that it has also fostered richer and broader insights than those ingrained within disciplinary silos. After all, in writing this book, we could not but follow Fridtjof Nansen's *bon mot*: "The difficult we do immediately. The impossible takes a little longer."

Notes

1 Madame de Staël, Herder, Heine and, later, Baudelaire were fascinated by the North as the quintessence of the Romantic idea of freedom and nature-inspired spirituality. For them, the true nature religion, hidden in mysterious runes, was to be found North of the *Mare Balticum*.

2 See the issue of *The Economist* from 27 April 2013, devoted to the Nordic model.
3 Following Eisenstadt (Eisenstadt 2000), we see Western modernity as stemming from an emancipatory cultural programme – with a salient ideal of individual autonomy and independent inquiry – which yielded scientific breakthroughs and the industrial revolution.
4 See UN Human Development Index: https://en.wikipedia.org/wiki/List_of_countries_by_Human_Development_Index; www.weforum.org/agenda/2017/03/why-norway-is-now-the-worlds-happiest-country; www.infoplease.com/world/health-and-social-statistics/ten-best-countries-mothers-5 (accessed 5 September 2017).
5 Human social systems are nested hierarchies of groups within groups within groups. The logic of relative fitness operates at every tier of the hierarchy: What's good for the family can be bad for the clan. What's good for the clan can be bad for the nation. The general rule is: "Adaptation at any level of a multi-tier hierarchy of groups requires a process of selection at that level and tends to be undermined by selection at lower levels."
6 A number of scholars have defined society as consisting of functional attributes, institutional or societal domains, with different goals, foci and logics (see e.g. Parsons (1964) and Luhman (1995)). The classification varies, and our domains represents an indicative typology that merely serves as a heuristic device.
7 The fate of Peer Gynt – an exemplary protagonist dreamt up by Henrik Ibsen – represents a cautionary tale of the nemesis that awaits those ruthless individualists who lust for fame, power and glory. As a result of his excesses, Peer lands in a mental asylum and finally returns home, where humility, equality and compassion prevail.
8 Sweden is an exception here. See Chapter 10 on "Eco-modernity Noridc style".
9 Examples abound: Corruption scandals in Telenor and Telia, worker safety in Hennes & Mauriz's supply chain, etc.

References

Acemoglu, D. and Robinson, J. A. (2013) *Why Nations Fail*. London: Profile Books.
Beck, U. (2017) *The Metamorphosis of the World. How Climate Change is Transforming our Concept of the World*. Cambridge: Polity Press.
Bell, D. (1991) *The Winding Passage. Sociological Journeys*. New Brunswick, NJ: Transaction.
Childs, M. W. (1936) *Sweden: the Middle Way*. Yale University Press.
Corning, P. (2011) *The Fair Society and the Pursuit of Social Justice*. Chicago: The University of Chicago Press.
Dølvik, E., Fløtten, T., Hippe, J. M. and Jordfald, B. (2014) Den nordiske modellen mot 2030. Et nytt kapittel? NordMod2030. Sluttrapport. Fafo-rapport 2014:46.
Dahrendorf, R. (1997) *After 1989: Morals, Revolution and Civil Society*. New York:St Martin's Press.
Egeland, J. (2017) Valgkamp anno 2017 bør handle om solidaritet med flyktninger, sultende og katastroferammede, *Aftenposten* 17 July.
Eisenstadt, S. (2000) *Multiple Modernities*. Special Issue of *Daedalus*.
Engelstad, F. (2015) *Cooperation and Conflict the Nordic Way: Work, Welfare and Institutional Change in Scandinavia*. London: Routledge.
Entzensberger, H. M. (1974) *Norsk utakt*. Oslo: Universitetsforlaget.
Fukuyama, F. (1992) *The End of History and the Last Man*. New York: The Free Press.

Gray, J. (2015 [1996]) *False Dawn: The Delusions of Global Capitalism*. New York: Granta Books.
Hall, P. A. and Soskice, D. (2001) *Varieties of Capitalism: The Institutional Foundations of Comparative Advantage*. New York: Oxford University Press.
Hellevik, O. (2008) *Jakten på den norske lykken*. Oslo: Universitetsforlaget.
Kenny, C. (2015) 2015: The Best Year in the History of the Average Human Being. *The Atlantic*, 18 December.
Luhman, N. (1995) *Social Systems*. Stanford: Stanford University Press.
Midttun, A. and Witoszek, N. (2016) *Energy and Transport in Green Transition: Perspectives on Eco-modernity*. London: Routledge.
Nisbet, R. A. (1962) *Community and Power*. New York: Galaxy Books.
Østerud, Ø. (1979) *Agrarian Structure and Peasant Politics, A Comparative Study of Rural Response to Economic Change*. Oslo: Universitetsforlaget.
Ostrom, E. (1990) *Governing the Commons*. Cambridge: Cambridge University Press.
Parsons, T. (1964) *The Social System*. Glencoe, IL: The Free Press.
Sandbu, M. (2008) Et uhørt forslag, *Aftenposten*, 21 July.
Seip, A. L. (1997) *Nasjonen bygges 1830–1870*. In: K. Helle et al. (eds), *Aschehoug Norgeshistorie*. Oslo: Aschehoug.
Sejersted, F. (2011) *The Age of Social Democracy: Norway & Sweden in the Twentieth Century*. Princeton: Princeton University Press.
Sennett, R. (2013) *Together. The Rituals, Pleasures and Politics of Social Cooperation*. New Haven, CT: Yale University Press.
Slagstad, R. (1998) *Nasjonale strateger*. Oslo: Pax.
Törnquist, O. and Harriss, J. (2016) *Reinventing Social Democratic Development: Insights from Indian and Scandinavian Comparison*. Copenhagen: Nordic Institute for Asian Studies.
Wahl, A. (2011) *The Rise and Fall of the Welfare State*. London: Pluto Press.
Whitley, R. (2000) *Divergent Capitalisms: The Social Structuring and Change of Business*. Oxford: Oxford University Press.
Wilson, D.S., and Hessen, D. (2014) A Blueprint for the Global Village. *Social Evolution Forum* https://evolution-institute.org/focus-article/blueprint-for-the-global-village/
Wilson, D. S., and Wilson, E. O. (2007) Rethinking the Theoretical Foundation of Sociobiology. *The Quarterly Review of Biology* 82: 327–348.
Wilson, D. S., Ostrom, E. and Cox, M. E. (2013) Generalizing Core Design Principles for the Efficacy of Groups. *Journal of Economic Behavior & Organization* 90/S: S21–S32.
Witoszek, N. (2011) *The Origins of the Regime of Goodness: Remapping the Norwegian Cultural History*. Oslo: Norwegian University Press.

2 Cooperation, competition and multi-level selection

A new paradigm for understanding the Nordic model

David Sloan Wilson and Dag O. Hessen

From Aristotle's *Politics* to Hobbes's *Leviathan* and the tradition of functionalism initiated by Emile Durkheim, the concept of society as comparable to a single organism has a long history in social thought. However, this holistic worldview has been eclipsed by more reductionist worldviews for over half a century. In biology, reductionism decomposes organisms to the molecular level. In the human social sciences, reductionism treats the individual as the fundamental unit of analysis, which is often called methodological individualism (Campbell 1990; Watkins 1957). The rational actor model in economics is one version of methodological individualism that has had a profound impact on the theory and practice of governance, especially in the United States and United Kingdom, but increasingly around the world (Beinhocker 2006; Jones 2012).

Theories of social evolution in the biological sciences have marched in step with methodological individualism in the human social sciences – so much so that one wonders if both areas of science were influenced by broader cultural trends. Group selection – the most straightforward way to explain how a society might evolve to function like a single organism – seemed to be decisively rejected in the 1960s in favour of what was called the Theory of Individual Selection (Williams 1966; Ghiselin 1974). Then Richard Dawkins (1976) used his considerable literary talents to portray everything that evolves as selfish at the genetic level. Historians will be needed to disentangle the cultural influences that led UK Prime Minister Margaret Thatcher to proclaim in the 1970s that "there is no such thing as society – only individuals and families."

Much has happened in evolutionary science since the 1970s that places the concept of society as an organism on a stronger scientific foundation than ever before in its long history. These developments have profound consequences for the theory and practice of human governance and cast new light on the Nordic countries as exemplars of good governance at the national scale. The following section will provide an overview of what has become known as Multi-level Selection (MLS) theory and its implications for governance at all scales, from single groups to the welfare of nations and to the global economy and environment.

A short history of Multi-level Selection (MLS) theory

The Christian worldview that preceded Darwin's theory of evolution assumed that God created a harmonious universe at all scales, from the tiniest insects to the stars in heaven. At first, Darwin thought that his theory of natural selection could explain all examples of design in the living world that had been attributed to a Creator. Upon further reflection, however, he came to a disturbing realization. If natural selection favours individuals that survive and reproduce better than other individuals, it would seem to select against traits that are regarded as morally virtuous, such as altruism, honesty and bravery, which almost by definition benefit others at the expense of the morally virtuous individual. Unless he added something to his theory, he could explain only the evolution of *individual-level* adaptations such as the sharp teeth of the tiger or the thick fur of the polar bear, not *group-level* adaptations such as individuals working together to produce a common good (Sober and Wilson 1998).

That "something" was not far to seek. Darwin realized that social behaviours are almost always expressed in groups that are small in comparison with the whole evolving population, such as a colony of bees, a flock of birds, a troop of primates or a human tribe. While it is true that benefiting others at the expense of oneself would be selectively disadvantageous within a single group, it is equally true that a group of cooperators would robustly outcompete a group whose members could not pull together. Natural selection can be imagined to operate at two levels: among individuals within groups, favouring self-serving behaviours in all their forms, and among groups in a multi-group population, favouring cooperative behaviours in all their forms.

Darwin's elaborated theory of two-level selection is easy to understand and has the potential to explain the evolution of group-level adaptations, but it also has some major limitations. First, not only is group-level selection required to explain the evolution of group-level adaptations, but it must also be strong enough to outweigh opposing selection within groups. Otherwise, selfishness prevails. Second, even when cooperation within groups does evolve by between-group selection, it can often be used in destructive competition with other groups. Group-level selection does not *eliminate* conflict so much as *elevate* it to the scale of between-group interactions, where it can take place with even more destructive force than before (Darwin was curiously silent on this implication in his own writing). The only solution to this problem would be to add another level of selection (among groups of interacting groups), turning two-level selection theory into multi-level selection theory (something that Darwin was also silent about). Given these limitations, Darwin's theory could explain the evolution of higher-level adaptations only when special conditions were met, which might be quite restrictive. There was still no warrant for the Christian worldview that harmony and order exists at all scales.

Important as these issues were, they did not occupy centre stage during the decades following the publication of *Origin of Species*, unlike such issues as the mechanisms of heritable variation (Provine 2001). Those who did think about social adaptations were not always as discerning as Darwin; some assumed that adaptations evolve at all tiers of a multi-level hierarchy without requiring special conditions. This could be called "The Age of Naïve Group Selection", which came to an end in the middle of the 20th century (Borrello 2010). The single most influential book of this period was *Adaptation and Natural Selection*, by George C. Williams (1966). Williams accepted the logic of MLS theory but argued as an empirical fact that lower-level selection almost invariably outweighs higher-level selection. As he put it (p. 90), "group-level adaptations do not, in fact, exist."

The widespread rejection of group selection, by others in addition to Williams (e.g. Maynard Smith 1964), challenged evolutionary biologists to explain how behaviours that *seemed* to be altruistic, and which had been attributed to group-level selection, could have evolved. A number of theoretical frameworks were developed to meet this challenge, including Inclusive Fitness Theory (Hamilton 1964), Evolutionary Game Theory (Maynard Smith 1982) and Selfish Gene Theory (Dawkins 1976). Inclusive Fitness Theory explains altruism as individuals helping their own genes in the bodies of others. Evolutionary Game Theory explains altruism as individuals benefiting others to obtain return benefits for themselves. Selfish Gene Theory explained altruism as a form of gene-level selfishness. In all cases, altruism was permuted into a form of lower-level selfishness that was only *apparently* altruistic. All three theoretical frameworks were regarded to be consistent with each other and collectively to provide a robust alternative to group selection. It became almost mandatory for authors to assure their readers that their theoretical model or empirical study did not invoke group selection.

Almost as soon as the ink was dry on the rejection of group selection, new developments began to prove otherwise. It must be remembered that the age of computer simulation models and desktop computing was only dawning during this period. The theoretical models that made group-level selection appear unlikely were mostly analytical models riddled with simplifying assumptions, such as behaviours coded directly by single genes, and random dispersal among groups. In addition, a subtle confusion crept in that Sober and Wilson (1998) called the Averaging Fallacy (see also Wilson 2015: ch. 3). To appreciate the Averaging Fallacy, imagine a situation (no matter how far-fetched) where between-group selection actually does outweigh within-group selection. The fact that altruism evolves in the total population means that the average altruist is more fit than the average selfish individual, all things considered. If you only take note of this fact, without comparing fitness differences within and between groups, it is easy to label fitness differences at the scale of the total population "individual-level" or "gene-level" selection, even though the selective disadvantage of these traits within groups is plain for anyone to see. In retrospect, it has become clear that all three theoretical frameworks that were developed as alternatives to group selection commit this fallacy. They all include the basic ingredients of a multi-level selection model: a total evolving population that is subdivided into groups, cooperative behaviours that are selectively disadvantageous within groups, and the most cooperative groups differentially contributing to evolution in the total population as a counterweight to within-group selection. This fact went unnoticed because the fitness of the lower-level entities (individuals or genes) was averaged across the higher-level entities (groups) and the net effect was called individual- (or gene-) level selection.

Ironically, it was W. D. Hamilton (1975), the originator of Inclusive Fitness Theory, who noticed his own mistake after encountering the work of another theoretical biologist named George Price in the early 1970s, an episode in the history of science well told by Oren Harman (2010) in his book *The Price of Altruism: George Price and the Search for the Origins of Kindness*. Price developed a statistical method that partitioned evolutionary change in the total population into within- and between-group components. When Hamilton translated his original formulation of Inclusive Fitness Theory into the Price equation, he realized that when social interactions take place among groups of relatives (for example, between siblings), selfish individuals have the advantage, just as for any other kind of social group (the within-group component of the Price equation is negative). The importance of genetic relatedness is that it clusters altruistic and selfish individuals into different groups. The higher the coefficient of relatedness, the more the clustering. In the extreme case of interactions among genetically identical individuals, there is no variation within groups and all of the variation is between groups. The Price equation revealed this to Hamilton in a way that his own equations had not.

Even though Hamilton (1975) was open enough to acknowledge his shift in thinking, which made Inclusive Fitness Theory an example of Multi-level Selection rather than an alternative to it, decades were required for the field of evolutionary biology as a whole to follow suit. Today, the consensus among authors of the peer-reviewed literature is represented by the following passage (Birch and Okasha 2014: 28):

> In earlier debates, biologists tended to regard kin and multi-level selection as rival empirical hypotheses, but many contemporary biologists regard them as ultimately equivalent, on the grounds that gene frequency change can be directly computed using either approach. Although dissenters from this equivalence claim can be found, the majority of social evolutionists appear to endorse it.

This passage represents a sea change in the acceptance of MLS theory compared with earlier decades, when authors felt compelled to say that they were not invoking group selection.

We have reviewed the history of thinking about MLS in a fair amount of detail because, while the issue is largely settled among authors of the peer-reviewed literature within evolutionary biology, there is still widespread confusion in the human social sciences and popular literature, where group selection is still often portrayed as heretical. For more on a "post-resolution" account of MLS theory, please consult Wilson and Wilson (2007) and Wilson (2015, 2017).

Major evolutionary transitions

Having set the stage, we can quickly show how MLS theory places the concept of a social group being like an organism on a stronger foundation than ever before in its long history. According to the concept of major evolutionary transitions, the balance between levels of selection is not static but can itself evolve. When mechanisms evolve that suppress the potential for disruptive competition within groups, then between-group selection becomes the dominant evolutionary force. The group becomes such a cooperative unit that it qualifies as a higher-level organism in its own right, as an analogue to the cooperation of specialized genes or cooperation between specialized cells that comprise a well functioning organism.

This concept was first proposed by the cell biologist Lynn Margulis (1970) in the 1970s to explain the evolution of nucleated cells (called eukaryotic), not by small mutational steps from bacterial cells (called prokaryotic) but from symbiotic associations of bacterial cells. It was radical at the time and would have been beyond the imagination of Darwin, but it has now become the accepted view. The concept was then generalized by the theoretical biologists John Maynard Smith (a former critic of group selection) and Eors Szathmary in the 1990s to explain other events such as the first cells, multicellular organisms, eusocial insect colonies and possibly even the origin of life itself as groups of cooperating molecular reactions (Maynard Smith and Szathmary 1995, 1999). These too have become widely accepted as cases of major transitions due to the evolution of mechanisms that suppress (although not entirely eliminating) the potential for disruptive competition within groups, so that between-group selection becomes the dominant evolutionary force. In other words, *every entity that is currently labelled with the word "organism" is in fact a social group that has evolved by between-entity selection to be so cooperative that the interactions among the parts only make sense in terms of the welfare of the whole*. In addition, eusocial insect colonies such as ants, bees, wasps and termites richly deserve their designation as super-organisms, i.e. as products of between-colony selection (Holldobler and Wilson 2008). If that is not a strong scientific foundation for the concept of a social group as being like an organism and an organism as like a social group, what would be?

Human genetic evolution as a major transition

Maynard Smith and Szathmary (1995, 1999) were somewhat timid in speculating about human evolution as a major evolutionary transition, confining themselves to the genetic basis of language. The work of Christopher Boehm

(1993, 1999, 2011) and others presents a much more solid case. In many non-human social species, including our closest ape relatives, between-group selection operates to a degree, but there is also intense and disruptive within-group selection. Even the cooperation that evolves often takes the form of small alliances that compete against other alliances within the same group (Waal 2013). What set our ancestors apart was the evolution of mechanisms that suppress the potential for bullying and other forms of disruptive competition within groups, so that cooperating as a group became the main strategy for survival and reproduction. Boehm calls this "reverse dominance" and it describes the kind of guarded egalitarianism found in most extant hunter-gatherer societies and many other small-scale traditional societies. It is the social organization that asserts itself in small group settings in modern life whenever there is a relatively equal balance of power among the group members. We will have much more to say about it in subsequent sections of this chapter. For now, it should be obvious that Boehm's concept of reverse dominance is nothing more or less than human genetic evolution as a major evolutionary transition.

Cultural multi-level selection

Cooperation in hunter-gatherer groups (both today and in the distant past) includes physical activities such as hunting, gathering, childcare, defence against predators and offence and defence against other human groups. Cooperation also includes mental activities, such as memory, decision-making, maintaining an inventory of symbols with shared meanings (including but not restricted to language) and the transmission of large amounts of learned information across generations. When we combine both physical and mental forms of cooperation, the concept of human genetic evolution as a major evolutionary transition has the potential to explain nearly everything that is distinctive about our species (Wilson 2009, 2015).

Our ability to transmit large amounts of learned information across generations became nothing short of an inheritance system in its own right that coevolved with the genetic inheritance system (Richerson and Boyd 2005; Henrich 2015; Paul 2015). This enabled our ancestors to adapt to their environments much faster than by genetic evolution alone, allowing them to colonize all habitable regions of the planet and dozens of ecological niches. It also led to a positive feedback loop between the production of resources and the scale of human society, leading to the mega-societies of today. This thesis has been developed in considerable detail by Peter Turchin (2015) in his book *Ultrasociety: How 10,000 Years of War Made Humans the Greatest Cooperators on Earth*. There are various ways by which human societies become well organized above the so-called Dunbar number of 150, which is the upper cognitive level for direct personal relations in a group (Dunbar 1996), such as social norms, formal and legal rules or the ability to construct imaginary commons (cf. Harari 2015). In the end, however, all very large aggregations or societies are susceptible to weathering from within.

According to Turchin and others, our genetic adaptations for suppressing disruptive self-serving behaviours, which evolved in the context of small groups, tend to break down in larger groups. This tendency resulted in phases where societies became despotic – ironically more like chimp societies than small-scale human societies. However, cultural evolution is a multi-level process no less than genetic evolution. In other words, sizable human groups varied in how well they functioned as cooperative units and the best replaced or were copied by the worst. (Imitating the best practices of a group qualifies as a form of cultural group selection.) Cultural group selection resulted in the evolution of cultural mechanisms that interface with previously evolved genetic mechanisms to regulate societies at ever larger scales. As Turchin puts it (p. 79):

> Such a multi-level nature of economic and social life has profound consequences for the evolution of human societies – just how profound we are only now beginning to understand, thanks to cultural evolution. The central theoretical breakthrough in this new field is the theory of Cultural Multi-level Selection.

As with genetic multi-level selection, special conditions are required for cultural between-group selection to prevail against within-group selection. There is also a back-and-forth quality to cultural multi-level selection, as Turchin (2005) identifies in the rise and fall of empires in his earlier book *War and Peace and War*. Empires tend to form in geographical regions with chronic between-group conflict, which acts as a crucible for the cultural evolution of cooperative societies. Once a highly cooperative society emerges (often with the help of new military technological innovations), it spreads to become an empire. Then cultural evolution takes place within the empire, favouring self-serving behaviours and factionalism in all their forms and ultimately leading to a collapse. This dynamic is eerily similar to cancer, which is a process of disruptive lower-level selection that takes place during the lifetime of multicellular organisms (Aktipis and Nesse 2013).

To summarize, the concept of a society as being like an organism stands on a stronger foundation than ever before in its long history. It should be seen not as entirely metaphoric, but as a result of similar evolutionary forces operating on a multi-tier hierarchy of units, which provides a theoretical framework for explaining both increases and reverses in the scale of human societies over the last 10,000 years. For the rest of this chapter, we will focus on the implications of this conclusion for contemporary governance at all scales, with special attention to Norway.

The many faces of competition and cooperation

MLS theory provides a paradigmatic alternative to free market perspectives in economics, which tend to regard competition as predominantly good for society. This is reflected in the metaphor of the invisible hand and its various mathematical formulations, such as the First Fundamental Theorem of Welfare Economics, which is often summarized in words as "Laissez faire leads to the common good" (Feldman 2008). Joseph Schumpeter's influential phase "creative destruction" emphasizes the creative aspects of competition. Hayek (1988) pioneered the interpretation of modern economics systems as products of cultural group selection. Friedman (1953) invoked competition among firms to explain why they behave as if the assumptions of rational choice theory are correct, even though the assumptions themselves are absurd (Wilson 2012).

MLS theory is far more nuanced in what it has to say about competition and cooperation. To begin with, it is essential to adopt relative fitness as a frame of comparison, rather than absolute fitness. From an evolutionary perspective, it does not matter how well an organism survives and reproduces; only that it does so better than other organisms in its vicinity. Examples abound in human life, as pointed out by the economist Robert Frank (2011) in his book *The Darwin Economy* and elsewhere. Yet, the prevailing assumption in mainstream economic theory, including the rational actor model, is that individuals strive to maximize their absolute utility (usually conceptualized as monetary wealth), as if they want to be as wealthy as possible in absolute terms without caring about their relative standing. Shifting the frame of comparison from absolute to relative fitness is a paradigmatic change for economic theory all by itself, even before we get to the nuances of partitioning fitness into within- and between-group components.

Once we start thinking in relative terms, it becomes clear and indisputable that competition within groups is primarily *disruptive* as far as the welfare of the group is concerned. This is due to the basic matter of tradeoffs. Working together as a group requires time, energy and risk on the part of individuals, which lower relative fitness within the group compared with free-riding or active exploitation. There might be exceptions to the rule, but there can be no doubt about the rule.

Competition *between* groups is a positive force for the evolution of within-group cooperation, as imagined by standard concepts of firm selection in economics, but it becomes more problematic as soon as we consider multi-tier hierarchies. A sizable firm is itself a multi-tier hierarchy, with individuals nested within teams, departments, divisions and so on. A classic ethnography of a corporation by the sociologist Robert Jackall titled *Moral Mazes* (2009) describes how between-group competition among middle-level units of the corporation disrupts the performance of corporation as a whole. The general rule is: "Adaptation at any given level of a multi-tier hierarchy requires a process of selection at that level and tends to be undermined by selection at lower levels" (Wilson 2015). Even if lower-level selection within firms can be suppressed, so that selection does act primarily at the level of firms, the outcome is likely to disruptive at the level of the multi-firm ecosystem (e.g. the global economy and environment). Against this background, the metaphor of the invisible hand, which portrays lower-level competition as robustly beneficial for the common good, is profoundly misleading.

To make matters more complex and interesting, some products of between-group selection that cause the group to function well as a unit look competitive in nature. A biological example is the adaptive component of the immune system, which is a carefully orchestrated competition among antibodies to select those that bind to antigens. The key phrase in the previous sentence is "carefully orchestrated". It is not a happy accident that the immune system is capable of producing approximately 100 million different antibodies and has a way of amplifying those that successfully bind to antigens. All of these mechanisms are products of between-organism selection. Individuals with faulty immune systems are not among our ancestors. By the same token, a human group might perform well by staging a competition among its members to select those who contribute most to the welfare of the group. This is a form of competition within groups, but it must be carefully orchestrated to result in group-beneficial outcomes. The orchestration is no more likely to be a happy accident than the orchestration of the immune system. Instead, it must be a product of group-level selection. This comparison highlights the utility of thinking of a human social group as like an organism.

To make matters still more complex and interesting, we must distinguish between cooperation and competition in terms of *actions* versus *thoughts and feelings*. Consider one group whose members are psychologically motivated to help each other, and another group whose members care only about their own reputations, which can be enhanced only if their actions benefit the group. If the latter group functions better as a group, then it will be favoured by group-level selection, even though its members are psychologically selfish. By the same token, psychological altruists can behave in ways that are pathological for the group as far as their actions are concerned (Oakley et al. 2011; summarized in Wilson 2015: ch. 9). These considerations fall under the heading of proximate vs. ultimate causation in evolutionary theory (see Wilson 2015: ch. 5 for a concise account).

The many faces of competition and cooperation might seem hopelessly complex, especially if the goal is to build analytic mathematical models of economic behaviour. One reason that orthodox economic theory makes assumptions such as absolute fitness maximization and self-regarding preferences is so that the mathematical equations can be tractable. But this only leads to the conclusion that a self-contained set of equations, which was originally inspired by Newtonian physics (Beinhocker 2006), is the wrong model for economic theory. Evolutionary theory is powerful and comprehensive, and makes use of analytic and computer simulation models, but in a different way – one that provides a better model for economics.

Governance at the scale of small groups

The work of Elinor Ostrom, a political scientist by training who received the Nobel Prize in economics in 2009, is central to a multi-level account of human society. Although she received their highest honour, Ostrom was largely unknown to economists at the time and her work still does not have the widespread recognition that it deserves. She studied groups that manage common-pool resources such as forests, pastures, fisheries and irrigation systems (Ostrom 1990). Conventional wisdom held that common-pool resources are invariably overexploited – Hardin's (1968) famous "Tragedy of the Commons" – unless they can be privatized or subjected to top-down regulation. Ostrom's great achievement was not only to show that groups can manage their common-pool resources, but also to identify eight core design principles (CDPs; shown in Table 2.1) that are responsible for their success.

Ostrom's most influential book was titled *Governing the Commons: The Evolution of Institutions for Collective Action*, published in 1990. At the time, she was using the word "evolution" in the colloquial sense (see Wilson 2011 for a short biography), but she increasingly adopted a more explicit evolutionary perspective, including evolutionary game theory, which was part of the revival of evolutionary thinking that began to take place in the social sciences at the end of the 20th century. One of us (DSW) was privileged to work with Ostrom and her associate Michael Cox for three years before her death in 2012, resulting in an article titled "Generalizing the Core Design Principles for the Efficacy of Groups" (Wilson et al. 2013). This article shows that the CDPs follow from the evolutionary dynamics of cooperation in all social species and our own evolutionary history as a highly cooperative species. For this reason, they should apply to all human groups, whose members must work together to achieve common goals. In a sense, cooperation is itself a common-pool resource vulnerable to the tragedies of disruptive within-group competition in all their forms.

Table 2.1 Eight Core Design Principles required for groups to function as collective units. They were derived for common-pool resource groups and are worded here to apply to all groups whose members need to work together to achieve common goals.

1. Strong group identity and understanding of purpose
2. Fair distribution of costs and benefits
3. Fair and inclusive decision-making
4. Tracking agreed behaviours
5. Graduated responses to transgressions
6. Fast and empathetic conflict resolution
7. Authority to self-govern
8. Appropriate relations with other groups

Source: Authors

The first design principle establishes the identity and purpose of the group as a socially constructed entity. Most of the other design principles make it difficult for members to succeed at the expense of other members, so that the only way to succeed is as a group. Stated in terms of Multi-level Selection theory, the CDPs suppress the potential for disruptive within-group selection, so that between-group selection becomes the primary evolutionary force. An intriguing way to put this is that the CDPs enable a major transition to take place within the group, as far as the expression of prosocial vs. contrasocial behaviours is concerned.

Since humans are genetically adapted to live in small, cooperative groups, we might predict that they instinctively adopt the CDPs at that scale. This is true to a degree, according to the work of Christopher Boehm and others described earlier. When people assemble in small groups, they do spontaneously share the work, make decisions together, monitor their behaviours and enforce norms, provided they have an equal balance of power. Nevertheless, that does not prevent groups in modern life from *varying* in their implementation of the CDPs. That is what Ostrom found for common-pool resource groups, which enabled her to identify them in the first place. A top priority should be to repeat Ostrom's research programme for other types of groups to confirm the generality of the CDPs.

One reason that some groups fail to implement the CDPs is because of competing narratives that make deviations from the CDPs appear to make sense. This is especially the case for business groups, where the influence of orthodox economic theory taught in business schools leads to flagrant violations of the CDPs. A great deal can be done to improve the quality of life at the scale of small groups, even before we consider governance at larger scales.

Scaling up governance

The eighth CDP is especially important for the subject of this book because it establishes that the CDPs are *scale-independent*. They are needed to govern relations among groups in a multi-group population, just as much as relations among individuals within groups. Ostrom and her colleagues, including her husband Vincent Ostrom, developed this concept under the term *polycentric governance* (Ostrom 2010a,b; McGinnis 1999), which notes that human life consists of many spheres of activity. Each sphere has an optimal scale, so good governance requires finding the optimal scale for each sphere of activity and coordinating the spheres. Thus stated, it can scarcely be otherwise, but it is not how most human societies are governed. From a multi-level evolutionary perspective, polycentric governance can be seen as a form of multi-cellularity. Just as a multi-cellular organism is composed of cells organized into various organs and physiological systems, a human society needs to be composed of small groups that function well as units in their own right and are appropriately organized to function well as a larger whole. A critical issue is to maintain identity and affinity beyond the local group (or Dunbar number), i.e. not to confine the feeling of "we" to the local community, the sports club, or the village, but also to maintain a sense of "we" at the nation level and beyond.

Insofar as large-scale human societies did not exist until about 10,000 years ago, their "anatomy and physiology" are products of cultural evolution. This leads to a testable empirical hypothesis. *Any large-scale society, at any period of human history, functions well or poorly to the degree that it succeeds at scaling up the CDPs.*

The Nordic model in an evolutionary perspective

The foregoing provides a new theoretical framework for examining variation in the quality of governance at the scale of whole nations, with Nordic countries consistently at the high end of the distribution. The chapters in this volume explore how both Multi-Level Selection theory and Ostromian core design principles have been reflected in the architecture of Nordic societies. Let us mention here some striking snapshots of the workings – and interaction between – different social domains. The first, and perhaps most conspicuous, are culture and education, which – in all Nordic countries – have been a reservoir of images, stories and norms (symbotypes) reinforcing a collaborative and prosocial ethos. As demonstrated in this volume, the Nordics share a common, value-charged tradition which has been a repository for collective action to balance the respective countries' strong exposure to international market pressures. Further, the culturally replicated model of inclusive and cooperative society is evident in a gender partnership that has not just strengthened social equality but also forged a higher level of productivity.

Interestingly, the cultural-historical analysis shows also the dual – both benign and pathological – side of altruism which we mentioned earlier in our chapter. As the example of Sweden shows, the ideal of human rights-based social solidarity with the whole suffering world on the run can lead to a deluge of immigration that seriously disrupts the country's carrying capacity. Moreover, as the chapter on education shows, the influx of large numbers of immigrants has undermined Swedish egalitarian ideals by generating new, subtle forms of social segregation expressed in the growing popularity of private schooling among the middle classes.

Another exemplification of MLS theory and Ostromian principles comes from Nordic politics and work life, where the Nordic societies have developed a tradition of negotiation, dialogue and compromise. In politics, they have a tradition of forging coalitions that generally make the countries governable in spite of political diversity and tensions. In work life, the flexicurity model represents a negotiated compromise whereby market dynamics are allowed to play out, while the welfare state guarantees family subsistence and the retraining of redundant employees. Another example is the "front industry model", whereby the Nordics allow internationally exposed sectors to set wages and then calibrate the wages of more protected sectors of the economy accordingly.

The management of the massive Norwegian petroleum resources provides an interesting case of multi-level selection with a productive mix of collaborative and competitive elements. On the one hand, the Norwegian regime has facilitated a collective appropriation of huge ground rent (super profits) for the benefit of the Norwegian society. On the other hand, it has also managed, through international market exposure, to secure a fairly competitive industrial performance. The public benefits are guarded by the establishment of one of the world largest sovereign wealth funds under democratic control, set aside for pensions and economic crisis management. In short, the competitiveness of the Norwegian petroleum industry is promoted by a mix of private and public ownership, a productivity-enhancing tax regime and a strategically oriented public administration. This provides a contrast with other petroleum nations – Angola or Venezuela, to mention but two – where either profits have been pocketed by the rulers, or highly inefficient and wasteful public monopolies have been created.

Admittedly, the socio-economic success of managing Norwegian petroleum resources does have an *ecological* downside. Due to its massive petroleum extraction Norway is a "selfish laggard" (in evolutionary terms) in climate-related greening.[1] Sweden, on the other hand, has succeded in playing a global ecological front-runner role.

Norway as an actor on the world stage

One outstanding example of national interests engaging in Tragedy of the Commons dilemmas is to be found in the international arenas for combating climate change by joint agreements for reducing CO_2 emissions. Just as there is a tragedy of the commons at the individual level (few will bear the costs of reducing their own emissions unless everybody else also does so), there is a corresponding tragedy operating at the international level. In a global economy, it is in each nation's interest to keep carbon taxing low and protect its own industries and capital interests, etc., and the outcome of these national self-interests is ever-rising CO_2 emissions and global temperature – a global Tragedy of the Commons. Norway's ability to act as a collective unit on a national scale in a climate change context is partly reflected not only by its role in these global negotiations to cut CO_2 emissions (while depending on income from fossil fuels), but also by its oil pension fund, which – amazingly for a nation of less than 6 million people – is the largest in the world. Many other nations have oil reserves equal to or greater than Norway's and have not used them for their collective good in the same way. In fact the fund itself is explicitly designed also to benefit coming generations. However, Norway's pension fund illustrates one of the most important principles of MLS theory – that cooperation at one level of a multi-tier hierarchy permutes to selfishness higher up the scale. Norway is faced with many investment options that would enrich the nation at the expense of other nations of the world and the global environment. It is faced with the temptation of becoming a selfish member of the global village and sometimes succumbs to the temptation. In other words, as with all investments there is often a conflict between short-term return and long-term benefits to other or future stakeholders. The former strategy adheres to the rationale of *Homo economicus*, while the latter is more concerned with ethical aspects or the greater good.

Despite the shortcomings of Norway in the context of sacrificing (some) national self-interest for the global and future good, the importance of acting for the global benefit is nevertheless well recognized at the political level, meaning that the ambitions to serve as a "nation of goodness" or behave like social democrats in the international arena should not be seen entirely as a hypocrisy or Machiavellian strategy. In many respects, Norway and the other Nordic countries function as cooperators on the world stage, providing a moral example for other nations. The fact that the CDPs are scale-independent means that the social interactions among nations and other leviathans (such as giant corporations) that inhabit the global village are essentially the same as among individuals in a real village. Cooperative leviathans are vulnerable to more self-serving leviathans but can still succeed to the degree that they confine their interactions to each other and implement the CDPs that hold all the leviathans in check. Implementing the CDPs at the scale of the global village is a daunting task, but it is the blueprint that must be followed (Wilson and Hessen 2014). To fail is to bequeath to our descendants a diminished existence at a planetary scale. No one will be exempt from the failure to cooperate.

Can Norway be copied?

Whenever the Nordic model is discussed, the question of whether the Nordic nations can be copied by other nations arises. An evolutionary perspective provides fresh insights in relation to this question. The Dutch biologist Niko Tinbergen, who received the Nobel Prize in physiology in 1973 for pioneering the study of animal behaviour (ethology), noted that four questions must be addressed for all products of evolution: What is their function? What is their mechanism? How did they arise as a historical process (phylogeny)? How do they arise during the lifetime of the organism (development)? (Tinbergen 1963; see Wilson and Gowdy 2013 for a discussion of Tinbergen's four questions in relation to economics and public policy). When we use this framework to ask whether the Nordic model can be copied by other nations, the answer depends upon which of the four questions we ask. In functional terms, not only *can* other nations copy the Nordic model, but they *must*, because the Nordic model succeeds only by implementing the CDPs. However, *how* a given nation implements the CDPs is likely to be highly contingent and path-dependent, based on the particular mechanisms of governance that have culturally evolved during its history. When it comes to the mechanism and development questions, each nation might need to follow its own path, although it would do well to borrow best practices from other successful nations as best it can.

When we examine other nations that function well through the same theoretical lens that we have applied to the Nordic model, they too can be understood in terms of the CDPs – that, at least, is our prediction. One example is the Polder model of consensus decision-making implemented in the Netherlands during the 1980s and 90s (Visser and Hemerijck 1997), which has been notably successful and can be easily interpreted in terms of the CDPs. A particularly interesting example is the United States of America, which has swung like a pendulum during its nearly 300-year history, as noted by Turchin (2016). During its most recent "Age of Well-being", the New Deal period, there was a balance of power and cooperation among the three major sectors of capital, labour and the state, much as in Norway. But this balance eroded during the Reagan era, to the point where capital now dominates both labour and the state, leading to its current "Age of Discord". The USA does not need to become more like Norway; it needs to become more like itself during a previous period of its own history.

Conclusion

In this chapter we have outlined a new paradigm for the study of governance at all scales that has emerged from evolutionary theory and provides a strong foundation for a venerable concept in the social sciences – of society as an organism. Most of the developments are so new, emerging only during the last 10 or 20 years, that they are known only to a relatively small community of scientists and scholars – although this community is growing and making solid progress in exploring the many implications of the new paradigm. Our own exploration has focused on Norway and the other Nordic countries as models of good governance, a topic that has already received a great deal of attention from a variety of perspectives. A dialogue between the human sciences and evolutionary theory will hopefully expand – and add new insights into – the exploration of the question of why societies fail or succeed.

Note

1 The Norwegians are trying to compensate for their high ecological footprint by using their financial muscle to invest in climate projects and protect rainforest abroad.

References

Aktipis, C. A. and Nesse, R. M. (2013) Evolutionary Foundations for Cancer Biology. *Evolutionary Applications* 6(1): 144–159. https://doi.org/10.1111/eva.12034

Beinhocker, E. D. (2006) *Origin of Wealth: Evolution, Complexity, and the Radical Remaking of Economics*. Cambridge, MA: Harvard Business School Press.

Birch, J. and Okasha, S. (2014) Kin Selection and Its Critics. *BioScience* 65(1): 22–32. https://doi.org/10.1093/biosci/biu196

Boehm, C. (1993) Egalitarian Society and Reverse Dominance Hierarchy. *Current Anthropology* 34: 227–254.

Boehm, C. (1999) *Hierarchy in the Forest: Egalitarianism and the Evolution of Human Altruism*. Cambridge, MA: Harvard University Press.

Boehm, C. (2011) *Moral Origins: The Evolution of Virtue, Altruism, and Shame*. New York: Basic Books.

Borrello, M. (2010) *Evolutionary Restraints: The Contentious History of Group Selection*. Chicago: University of Chicago Press.

Campbell, D. T. (1990) Levels of Organization, Downward Causation, and the Selection-theory Approach to Evolutionary Epistemology. In: G. Greenberg and E. Tobach (eds), *Theories of the Evolution of Knowing* (pp. 1–17). Hillsdale, NJ: Lawrence Erlbaum Associates.

Dawkins, R. (1976) *The Selfish Gene* (1st ed.). Oxford: Oxford University Press.

Dunbar, R. I. M. (1996) *Grooming, Gossip and the Evolution of Language*. Cambridge, MA: Harvard University Press.

Feldman, A. M. (2008) Welfare Economics. In: S. N. Durlauf and L. E. Blume (eds), *The New Palgrave Dictionary of Economics* (2nd ed.). New York: Palgrave Macmillan.

Frank, R. (2011) *The Darwin Economy: Liberty, Competition, and the Common Good*. Princeton: Princeton University Press.

Friedman, M. (1953) *Essays in Positive Economics*. Chicago: University of Chicago Press.

Ghiselin, M. T. (1974) *The Economy of Nature and the Evolution of Sex*. Berkeley: University of California Press.

Hamilton, W. D. (1964) The Genetical Evolution of Social Behavior: I and II. *Journal of Theoretical Biology* 7: 1–52.

Hamilton, W. D. (1975) Innate Social Aptitudes in Man, an Approach from Evolutionary Genetics. In: R. Fox (ed.), *Biosocial Anthropology* (pp. 133–155). London: Malaby Press.

Harari, Y. N. (2015) *Sapiens : A Brief History of Humankind*. New York: Harper & Row.

Hardin, G. (1968) The Tragedy of the Commons. *Science* 162: 1243–1248.

Harman, O. (2010) *The Price of Altruism: George Price and the Search for the Origins of Kindness*. New York: Norton.

Hayek, F. (1988) *The Fatal Conceit*. London: Routledge.

Henrich, J. (2015) *The Secret of Our Success: How Culture is Driving Human Evolution, Domesticating Our Species, and Making Us Smarter*. Princeton: Princeton University Press.

Holldobler, B. and Wilson, E. O. (2008) *The Superorganisms*. New York: Norton.

Jackall, R. (2009) *Moral Mazes: The World of Corporate Managers*. New York: Oxford University Press

Jones, D. S. (2012) *Masters of the Universe: Hayek, Friedman, and the Birth of Neoliberal Politics*. Princeton: Princeton University Press. Retrieved from www.amazon.com/Masters-Universe-Friedman-Neoliberal-Politics/dp/0691151571/ref=pd_sim_b_1?ie=UTF8&refRID=1ZMKMGNWTPZPQ2FBQHXV

Margulis, L. (1970) *Origin of Eukaryotic Cells*. New Haven: Yale University Press.

Maynard Smith, J. (1964) Group Selection and Kin Selection. *Nature* 201(March): 1145–1146.

Maynard Smith, J. (1982) *Evolution and the Theory of Games*. Cambridge: Cambridge University Press.

Maynard Smith, J. and Szathmary, E. (1995) *The Major Transitions in Evolution*. New York: W.H. Freeman.

Maynard Smith, J. and Szathmary, E. (1999) *The Origins of Life: From the Birth of Life to the Origin of Language*. Oxford: Oxford University Press.

McGinnis, M. D. (1999) *Polycentric Governance and Development: Readings from the Workshop in Political Theory and Policy Analysis*. Ann Arbor: University of Michigan Press.

Oakley, B., Knafo, A., Madhavan, G. and Wilson, D. S. (2011) *Pathological Altruism*. Oxford: Oxford University Press.

Ostrom, E. (1990) *Governing the Commons: The Evolution of Institutions for Collective Action*. Cambridge: Cambridge University Press.

Ostrom, E. (2010a) Beyond Markets and States: Polycentric Governance of Complex Economic Systems. *American Economic Review* 100: 1–33.

Ostrom, E. (2010b) Polycentric Systems for Coping with Collective Action and Global Environmental Change. *Global Environmental Change* 20 : 550–557.

Paul, R. A. (2015) *Mixed Messages: Cultural and Genetic Inheritance in the Constitution of Human Society*. Chicago: University of Chicago Press.

Provine, W. P. (2001) *The Origins of Theoretical Population Genetics*. Chicago: University of Chicago Press.

Richerson, P. J. and Boyd, R. (2005) *Not by genes Alone: How Culture Transformed Human Evolution*. Chicago: University of Chicago Press.

Sober, E. and Wilson, D. S. (1998) *Unto Others: The Evolution and Psychology of Unselfish Behavior*. Cambridge, MA: Harvard University Press.

Tinbergen, N. (1963) On Aims and Methods of Ethology. *Zeitschrift für Tierpsychologie* 20: 410–433.

Turchin, P. (2005) *War and Peace and War*. Upper Saddle River, NJ: Pi Press.

Turchin, P. (2015) *Ultrasociety: How 10,000 Years of War Made Humans the Greatest Cooperators on Earth*. Storrs, CT: Beresta Books.

Turchin, P. (2016) *Ages of Discord: A Structural-demographic Analysis of American History*. Storrs, CT: Beresta Books.

Visser, J. and Hemerijck, A. (1997) *A Dutch Miracle : Job Growth, Welfare Reform and Corporatism in the Netherlands*. Amsterdam University Press. Retrieved from http://pubman.mpdl.mpg.de/pubman/faces/viewItemOverviewPage.jsp?itemId=escidoc:2229759

Waal, F. B. M. De (2013) *The Bonobo and the Atheist : In Search of Humanism among the Primates*. New York: Norton.

Watkins, J. W. N. (1957) Historical Explanations in the Social Sciences. *British Journal for the Philosophy of Science* 8: 104–117.

Williams, G. C. (1966) *Adaptation and Natural Selection: A Critique of Some Current Evolutionary Thought*. Princeton: Princeton University Press.

Wilson, D. S. (2009) Multi-level Selection and Major Transitions. In: M. Pigliucci and G. B. Muller (eds), *Evolution: The Extended Synthesis* (pp. 81–94). Cambridge, MA: MIT Press.

Wilson, D. S. (2011) *The Neighborhood Project: Using Evolution to Improve My City, One Block at a Time*. New York: Little, Brown.

Wilson, D. S. (2012) A Tale of Two Classics. *New Scientist* 213: 30–31.

Wilson, D. S. (2015) *Does Altruism Exist? Culture, Genes, and the Welfare of Others*. New Haven, CT: Yale University Press.

Wilson, D. S. (2017) Reaching a New Plateau for the Acceptance of Multi-level Selection. Retrieved from https://evolution-institute.org/focus-article/reaching-a-new-plateau-for-the-acceptance-of-multi-level-selection/?source=tvol

Wilson, D. S. and Gowdy, J. M. (2013) Evolution as a General Theoretical Framework for Economics and Public Policy. *Journal of Economic Behavior & Organization* 90: S3–S10. https://doi.org/10.1016/j.jebo.2012.12.008

Wilson, D. S. and Hessen, D. (2014) Blueprint for the Global Village. Retrieved 4 September 2014 from https://evolution-institute.org/focus-article/blueprint-for-the-global-village/?source=sef

Wilson, D. S. and Wilson, E. O. (2007) Rethinking the Theoretical Foundation of Sociobiology. *Quarterly Review of Biology* 82: 327–348.

Wilson, D. S., Ostrom, E. and Cox, M. E. (2013) Generalizing the Core Design Principles for the Efficacy of Groups. *Journal of Economic Behavior & Organization* 90: S21–S32. https://doi.org/10.1016/j.jebo.2012.12.010

3 Nordic humanism as a driver of the welfare society

Nina Witoszek and Øystein Sørensen

Cultural evolution and symbotypes

Human goodness has not fared well as an emblematic virtue of late modernity. The dominant intellectual trend of the post-utopian era has been to cast altruism as a cover-up or camouflage of hidden agendas and selfish motives, from narcissism and megalomania to covert quests for profit and power. It is little wonder that the Nordic countries' success in international branding – as do-gooders, peace negotiators, gender champions and humanitarians – rouses a killer instinct in most practitioners of the hermeneutics of suspicion. It is enough to study the entrance door to the 'House of Sweden' in Washington – which advertises 'the Spirit of the Wild', 'Gender Equality', 'Human Rights' and 'Room for Children' – to see goodness in its postmodern form: more a constitutive part of the market of smart ideas than a disinterested moral aspiration.[1]

The Norwegian historian Terje Tvedt has coined the term "regime of goodness" (*godhetsregimet*), which has both codified and questioned moral and political ambitions of 21st-century Norway: not just the richest Nordic country but one of the most affluent liberal democracies on earth (Tvedt 2005, 2009).[2] The *regime of goodness* is an ironic trope: the concept of "regime" gives a technocratic, controlling ring to "goodness" – and thus both constructs and deconstructs Norway's achievements with a clever turn of phrase. According to Tvedt, the actual *regime of goodness* is a virtual "state within a state" which comprises countless NGOs and research institutions that have money, power and influence. Moreover, they actively promote an ostensible "illusion" about Norway's status as a humanitarian superpower. At the beginning of the 21st century, Tvedt argues, Norwegian "Samaritanism" has become so immune to outside criticism that the dirty deeds behind a glorious story are either ignored or dismissed (Tvedt 1995, 2005; Curtis 2009). True, Norway's booming arms exports, its business ties to tax havens and its oil fund investments in autocratic states such as Azerbaijan or Iran provoke occasional moral spasms in public debates. But the conviction that "it is typically Norwegian to be good" – going back to the former Prime Minister Gro Harlem Brundtland's famous declaration – is shared by most of the population, even if it is occasionally underpinned by "guilty irony".

Without discounting the delinquent side of Scandinavia, we wish to ask to what extent Norway, Sweden and Denmark are cases of moral communities that have invested in forging human goodness, decency and equality as their national aspirations. What is the relationship between their respective cultures and Scandinavian modernity, which seems less "disenchanted", and certainly more profitable, than many other modern experiment?

"Who prospers?" ask Harrison and Huntington, and propose: "The answer is cultural: Societies committed to the future, to education [...] to a better life for all, to community as well as to freedom and justice" (Harrison and Huntington 2004: 247). Though this cultural enthusiasm may be a bit farfetched, we argue that there is indeed a deep cultural, value-charged structure to Nordic welfare society. This structure has not emerged *ex nihilo*: it is a summary result of a journey of ideas, norms and patterns of action which, over time, have accreted to a *humanist habitus*.

In line with the evolutionary inspiration in our study, our idea of humanism assumes it not to be exclusively Western, Christian, post-Christian or modern. Instead, we see humanism as a permanent constitutive factor in our species' culture, a potential that has always been *latent in human nature* as a source of transcultural co-existence, communication and hybridization. Such humanism can be broadly defined as a mindset which respects human dignity, hospitality to the Other and the non-violent resolution of conflicts; and, in some societies, also includes a project of human emancipation through knowledge and social organization. This being said, humanism so conceived comes to us not in a monolithic form, but as a mosaic of culturally distinctive, symbolic elaborations.

To highlight the role of symbolic thought in transmitting both altruistic and selfish behaviour, evolutionary thinkers David Sloan Wilson and Yasha Hartberg have proposed the concept of the *symbotype*, which denotes repositories of cultural information that are replicated across generations and have a potent effect on social action, beliefs and values (Hartberg and Wilson 2016).[3] Symbotypes bear a superficial resemblance to Richard Dawkins's *memes* (Dawkins 1976). However, in contrast to memes – which refer to any cultural trait that spreads in an "epidemiological" fashion – symbotypes are the outcome of a long tradition: they are narratives, images, beliefs, rites and practices that have been reproduced over generations with relatively high fidelity and function as emblems of a community's identity.

Symbotypes are accessible to empirical inquiry: they figure in family stories, schoolbooks, models of cultural heroes, religious narratives, literature, architecture and the visual arts and media. On the one hand, they are like ancestral homes filled with memories, scripts and routines which the national community recognizes as "its own". On the other hand, they work like invisible "cultural mafiosi" in that they exert a constant moral blackmail on society, reminding it of "what we were, what we are, and what we should be". By being the markers of identity, symbotypes create heat waves in the citizens' brains and hearts. They may empower or disempower, foster competition or cooperation, generate change or cause stagnation. They are not limited to culture and religion; as semiotic and normative carriers of a community's founding traditions, they permeate political and economic realms. Thus, contrary to Acemoglu and Robinson's dismissive view of culture as a condition of societal success (Acemoglu and Robinson 2013), cultural symbotypes often *precede* institutional change. In short, they are society's adaptational tools: the ways to tackle new challenges, survive traumas and envision a better life.

Accordingly, what we propose in this chapter is a semiotic-evolutionary approach to those Scandinavian humanist symbotypes which, we argue, have contributed to the emergence of modern Scandinavian welfare societies. Drawing on our previous historical research and semiotic analysis of nation building in the North (Sørensen and Stråth 1997; Witoszek 1998; 2011), there are, we argue, three distinctive symbotypes. They can be called, respectively, the Norwegian *community of goodness*, the Swedish caring *people's home* (*folkhemmet*), and the Danish "*happy Christianity*" (with or without God). In what follows, we shall ask how they have emerged, who have been their catalysers, and in what ways they have moulded the distinctive Nordic humanism. In particular, we shall inquire to what extent the normative patterns they have prefigure the Ostromian-Wilsonian core design principles of efficacious groups. We shall examine them not as petrified texts and rites but as sites of cultural and political tensions. Last but not least, while reviewing an array of challenges to Nordic humanism in the 21st century, we shall point to the consequences of its amplification into a global and socio-environmental agenda. As we shall see, if visions of a good or better society have "worked" in Scandinavia, it is mainly because they have never been a chimerical dream of a perfect society. Nor have they been allowed to harden into complacent dogma. On the contrary, to this very day they have been subject to public debates and constant revisions.

Pastoral enlightenment revisited

While there is doubt that much of the Nordic countries' success as exemplary welfare states has been the result of: (i) pure chance and proverbial good luck; (ii) political and economic arrangements; (iii) socio-historical conditions – such as the relative absence of feudalism, the existence of a free and literate peasantry, especially in Norway and Sweden – and (iv) strong position of community law before the consolidation of the state, their status as loci of highly cooperative and humanitarian societies has been partially the result of moral imagination and cultural innovation. As David Landes puts it, "getting lucky isn't about culture, but staying lucky often is (Fukuyama 2008)."

As we have argued elsewhere (Sørensen and Stråth 1997; Witoszek 1998), Nordic countries, different as they are politically and economically, share a common cultural founding tradition which points to the values of a *Pastoral*

Enlightenment. This oxymoronic concept identifies both the pivotal role of 17th- and 18th-century priests – or rather pastors – as architects of national identity and the cultural elites' idealization of the peasantry as the carrier of Norwegianness/Swedishness/Danishness. We have also argued that the Nordic Christian Enlightenment – flaunting respect for the other social cooperation, pragmatic rationality, distrust of extravagance, and a focus on the future rather than a "golden past" – has effectively hijacked the agenda of Romanticism and toned down the often inflamed, dichotomizing nationalism that went with it in other parts of Europe (Sørensen and Stråth 1997; Witoszek and Trägårdh 2002).

Our contention is that it is largely thanks to the potency of the Christian-pastoral founding tradition that Nordic modernity has been a relatively socially sustainable formation; one that has honed the ideas of individual dignity and social justice and, at the same time, recognized the reality of human and environmental limits. We argue that this self-limiting, pro-social modernity has been the work of influential cultural innovators who succeeded in forging – and solidifying – narratives, norms and routines that promoted finding a middle way between the collectivist demands of a self-assertive, despotic *Volk* and the aspirations of the autonomous and altruistic individual.

Behind every symbotype there is an individual or a group of people that leaves a moral footprint on human evolution. Freya Mathews has alluded to a key role of *animateurs*, the "awakeners of slumbering creative potentials in both ourselves and the larger community of life to which we belong." (Mathews 2017: 228). Apart from helping a community to constellate and give expression to its latent aspirations, animateurs find ways of engaging others in novel creative projects which energize it, and even push it in a new direction. They come from both from the elite and the grassroots, and may be individuals or groups that coalesce into movements. In short, animateurs are cultural-evolutionary agents that combine a mythogenic (myth-making) talent with the practical ability to reimagine existing forms of social interaction. They are thus more than bearers of Bourdieu's *habitus*, or community's embodied knowledge (Bourdieu 1980); they are cultural innovators who manage to cut through social numbness, offer hope and create visions of a better and more meaningful life.

The scope of this chapter does not allow us to explore modern humanist symbotypes in Finland: a country whose traumatic modern history has yielded such thinkers and political leaders as Georg Henrik von Wright or the unique Mummiland feminism pervading the work of Tove Jansson. Neither do we have room to discuss the "searching humanism" informing the novels, poetry and journalism of the Icelanders, such as the Nobel Prize winner in literature Halldór Laxness. Here we have chosen to highlight those cultural animateurs whose work shaped sustainable modernity by either interacting with or infiltrating political and economic aspirations of national communities in Norway, Denmark and Sweden.

Hans Nielsen Hauge and the "Friends": Christian love and "clean profit" combined

There is evidence that, apart from the New Testament, one of Norway's most read religious texts is the sermons and revelations authored by the early-19th-century peasant preacher Hans Nielsen Hauge (1771–1824).[4] The conventional view is that Hauge was a *spiritus movens* of the 19th-century religoous revival, which empowered the peasantry and promoted Pietist values. The latest research, however, gives us a richer picture (e.g. Furre 1999; Bugge Amundsen 2007; Gundersen 2005; Ryland 2005; Ravnåsen 2002; Stibbe 2007). Hauge was not just a charismatic preacher and prophet but also an innovative social entrepreneur. His religious vision – which came to him in an epiphany while he was working on his farm – invoked a deeply personal and purified Christianity, which highlighted repentance, personal emancipation through education, and the ethos of "gain what you can, save all you can, and give all you can". His group of followers – who called themselves the "Friends" – were thus inspired to conduct an audacious, religious-moral-economic experiment on the margins of the dominant, Lutheran, culture. The Haugian *oppbyggelsesmøter* (edification meetings) took place outside church buildings or in people's homes, where the Friends abandoned the hierarchical seating plan: "People who usually sat apart by reason of social standing or gender now found themselves seated next to one another as a result of receiving the spiritual revelation"(Stibbe 2007: 288). They were a community of equals, reading the Bible, discussing the Lord's message – and designing new economic enterprises. True, the Pietist Haugianism had its shadowy side: it was low on carnival, alcohol and cholesterol. But what it lacked in hedonistic spirit, it more than made up for as a tool of peasant emancipation and a trigger for entrepreneurial vigour.

The meteoric rise of Haugianism is something of a puzzle, considering that between 1804 and 1813 Hauge was imprisoned in Christiania (modern-day Oslo) on account of breaking the so called *Konventikkelplakaten* – the law that banned religious gatherings and meetings organized outside the clergy's control.[5] And yet, in addition to the social hunger for an uplifting vision at times of crisis and Hauge's personal appeal, there were two pivotal drivers of the Friends' success. The first was their structure as a small group, which, we argue, shows clear parallels with the key Ostromian design principles: strong identity, clear boundaries, flat structure, inclusive decision-making, peaceful resolution of conflicts, social monitoring and the ethos of cooperation (Ostrom 1990).[6] In fact, cooperation permeated all Haugian projects: the paper mill at Eiker – the epitome of Haugian community enterprise – was cooperatively owed, the workers lived on the premises with their families, and provisions were made to employ those with disabilities and look after those who were either too ill or too old to work (Magnus 1978: 91ff.).

The second pillar of Haugianism's success was an alloy of word and action: reanimating existing Lutheran stories of Christian piety with an ideal of a caring fraternity that did not retreat from this world but contributed to a society's material wealth. Hauge's business projects – from brick and paper factories to iron and salt works – were joined with acts of philanthropy such as administering the poor fund, even providing financial support for the first University in Christiania. The emphasis on reading, writing and oratorical skills, perfected during religious deliberations, was a tool of both individuation and democratization (Bang 1910: 368). The more gifted peasant pupils quickly morphed into an extraordinarily vibrant and mobile social group, which included successful entrepreneurs, parliamentarians, the architects of the Norwegian Constitution of 1814, founders of the oldest publishing houses (Grøndahl and Dryer) and initiators of overseas religious missions.

What is interesting about Haugianism as an exercise in cultural innovation is that it did not break with the codex of Lutheran Christianity; rather, it energized it with ideas of social emancipation through education. It proposed a *refolution*[7]: a mixture of reform and revolution that let Lutheranism remain the imaginary centre that held the community together. We argue that it is this balance between the old and the new, between Christianity and successful prosocial enterpreneurship, that enabled Haugianism to shift from being a religious revival on the margins of the Norwegian culture to becoming a prefiguration of the economic and political architecture of the future welfare society.

The 21st century is anything but Pietist, though there are many Norwegians – including members of national elites – who openly boast of Haugian ancestors or personal elective affinity with the spirit of Haugianism. It would not be too much to say that the Haugian ethos of responsibility, cooperation and equality – replicated in school curricula and religious education well into the mid-20th century – has "civilized" the national brand of capitalism and informed political visions on the left and right. In the 21st century it is a *lieu de mémoire* that has not only generated contemporary institutions and regulations, but also shaped strong, culturally approved norms and standards which keep haunting even its staunchest opponents.

Norway reborn: Henrik Wergeland's vision of a "Republic of Goodness"

If Hauge was a master engineer of Norwegian pragmatic religiosity, Henrik Wergeland (1808–1845) was a poetic demiurge who sang of the soul of the newly born nation. Interestingly, although Wergeland's idea of national rebirth gestured towards medieval Norwegian society, this "ancient Norway" had little to do with heroic Viking terminators. On the contrary, it advocated individual freedom, wide-ranging social equality, justice, compromise and cooperation. These values, Wergeland argued, had to be rediscovered and harnessed in forging 19th-century society. In his speech "In Memory of the Ancestors" at Eidsvoll (1834), he deployed a strong and attractive metaphor of the old medieval state and the newly born Norwegian nation-state fitting together "as two parts of the same ring". Modern Norwegians were to be created by returning to their past, but a past which was about compassion and teamwork, and not vendettas and rivalry (Sørensen 1993: 26). As the heirs of "great and noble kings", Wergeland argued that Norwegians were naturally "great and noble": a democratic community of free peasants meeting at the *Ting*, discussing problems, and making just laws. In such a reimagined past, all challenges were tackled by way of deliberation and peaceful compromise. The national community's core virtue was freedom: a sacred site from which all other Norwegian virtues, such as desire for education and enlightenment and respect for the law, radiated (Sørensen 2001: 144). But it was not an unlimited freedom; it was liberty "bound by law", based on "reason and moral understanding" and "right before might" (Storsveen 1996: 85, Sørensen 2001: 144).

The founding myth of modern Norway was thus a result of Wergeland's imaginary dialectics: projecting contemporary values and aspirations – heavily inspired by Enlightenment ideas – into medieval society, declaring them ancient and sacred, and demanding their "rediscovery" in the present. That is how a mythical civilized past gave legitimacy to the Norwegian *via moderna*.

What was perhaps most striking about Wergeland's symbotype is that, at the time of frenzied and aggressive nationalism elsewhere in Europe, it flaunted an *enlightened* nationalism based on inclusive, tolerant communities. For many years Wergeland led a one-man campaign to repeal the infamous "Jewish clause" (*Jødeparagraf*) in the Norwegian 1814 Constitution, which denied Jews entry into the country (Storsveen 2008: 448ff.). He spoke through pamphlets – some of which were distributed among the members of the Norwegian parliament (1841) – and through his poetic masterpieces, such as *Jøden* (*The Jew*, 1842) and *Jødinden* (*The Jewess*, 1844). In his eyes, the infamous Jewish paragraph was not just an offence to the Christian principle of charity and tolerance; it clashed with the liberal-democratic aspirations of the Norwegian Constitution, making it intolerant and hence self-contradicting (Storsveen 2008: 454).[8]

While there is no doubt that Wergeland taught Norwegians a lesson of patriotism, he also taught them the value of transcultural humanism. His poems – obligatory reading for every Norwegian child as late as the 21st century – shine with empathy with, and support for, oppressed people and nations everywhere. They speak of outrage at bondage and tyranny and salute freedom fighters from North America, France and Poland – heroes as diverse as Washington, Lafayette, Kosciuszko, Dabrowski, Skrzynecki and O'Connell (Storsveen 2008: 154).[9] As "sacred texts" of Norwegian modernity, Wergeland's writings encode values which have been interiorized by every generation and recalled every year on Constitution Day, 17 May.[10] Apart from reminding the Norwegians of their shared moral patrimony, they perpetuate their self-perceptions (however deluded or problematic) as benevolent do-gooders in a world full of sound and fury. The modern "Norwegian regime of goodness" is thus not a calculated branding project invented by the Norwegian Ministry of Foreign Affairs as an emblem of Norwegianness; it is a deeply felt tradition which resonates with people at large.

N. F. Grundtvig: "First man, then Christian"

Among the various Danish animateurs there is one whose influence on Danish humanism has been indisputable: the theologian, poet and philosopher Nicolai Frederik Severin Grundtvig (1783–1872). Just like Hans Nielsen Hauge, Grundtvig was much more than a religious mentor of his time; his teachings have had an enduring impact on Danish and Norwegian models of education, perceptions of Christianity and even the relationship between the individual, society and the state (e.g. Skrondal 1929; Thorkildsen et al. 1996). As the author of poems and psalms, historical and philosophical works and polemical tracts, Grundtvig was not just widely read and taught for generations; "Grundtvigianism" remained a core concept in Danish culture and society throughout the 20th century.

The Grundtvigian ideal of a "good society" was partly rooted in core Enlightenment values – such as equality and individual liberty – and partly in a Romantic vision of national rebirth inspired by the New Testament's "love of the brother" and by Norse poetry and myths. By combining Christian and pagan traditions, Grundtvig challenged both the enthusiasms of Pietism and rationalism.[11] He preached a vision of a "happy, evangelical Christianity" (Witoszek 1998: 80), based on what Grundtvig called "the living word". His often quoted motto, "First man, then Christian"[12], captures the gist of his moral agenda: liberating the Church and Christians from religious dogma and freeing the secular elites from what he considered "rationalist oppression" (Bugge 2001). One of the pivotal Grundtvigian concepts was *folkelighed* – an ordinary people's culture, which, unlike the polarizing German *Völkischkeit*, rested on ideas of tolerance, social inclusion and individual liberty (Pedersen 2002). Needless to say, this gentle humanism – increasingly attractive both inside and outside the Danish State Church – earned Grundtvig many influential enemies. They made sure that, in spite of his prolific writings and broad social appeal, his rank in the Lutheran Church never went beyond that of a lowly parish priest.

What is interesting in our context is that Grundtvig's creative and prosocial pedagogy was found compelling not just in Denmark but also in Norway and Sweden, where the network of independent schools – or Grundtvig-inspired *folkehøyskoler* (folk high schools) – was established. The key objective of these schools was to equip youth with a common set of values and aspirations, such as tolerant, Other-oriented Lutheranism and the pursuit of independent inquiry.[13] For Grundtvig, education was only partly about imparting and popularizing scientific knowledge; it was just as much about creating emotional security. His pupils were considered not as competing individuals, but as members of a warm circle of the national community, where all that counted was fostering a happy life and good relations with the Other. Thus there were no exams in Grundtvig's ideal schools; the real exam, in his view, was life itself (Thorkildsen 1996: 51). Imagination, poetry and myths were put on an equal footing with rationality and science. Schoolbooks and religious texts were as important as legends, poetry and song: a source of moral reflection and deliberation in class.

Although the Grundtvigian symbotype of a "happy Christianity" evolved over time and lost its religious flavour, it has created a powerful and durable humanist legacy in both Danish and Norwegian *Bildung*. It is a normative codex which has both shaped generations of Scandinavian teachers, politicians and business leaders, and influenced institutional practice. As late as the 21st century, Grundtvigian humanism and its mutations constitute an ethical foundation of Danish and Norwegian self-perceptions and national aspirations. However challenged by global developments, it reminds modern Scandinavians of what they were, what they have learned, and what values they stand to lose if their symbotype is undone.

Sweden as a caring "people's home"

In 1928, the Swedish chairman of the Social Democrats, Per Albin Hansson, proposed a story which would consolidate and unify the nation at a time of social upheaval: the vision of the Swedish state as a caring *folkhemmet* (people's home) (Hansson 1928; 1982: 124). The metaphor of a people's home became not just a potent political trope; to this day it is one of the most successful mobilizing concepts in the history of European welfare states.

In the popular-wikipedic imagination, *folkhemmet* has been associated with social democratic discourse, or with the conservative political scientist and politician Rudolf Kjellén's vision of a corporatist-styled society based on class collaboration in the national interest. In this chapter we contend that the success of the trope of the Swedish state as a "people's home" was inspired by a powerful symbotype which had *preceded* the crisis in the 1930s and drew on the values of the Nordic Pastoral Enlightenment. As one of us has argued elsewhere, the mantra of the "carrying, good home" figured strongly already in 18th- and 19th-century Swedish literature and journalism (Witoszek 1998). The work of the greatest national bard, Erik Gustav Geijer, idolized family, independent peasant freeholders and the *odalshuset* (free peasant household) (Geijer 1849–1855: xxxii–xxxiii). Similarly the *prestegaards* (coffee-houses and salons) resounded with the rhetoric of "great family", where one could encounter "the feeling of home, goodwill and cordiality, happy kindness and understanding sympathy" (Melberg 1978: 56).

This early vision of Sweden as a warm and inclusive home was intriguing for two reasons: first it was forged in the age of selfish and aggressive nation-building elsewhere in Europe, and second, it countered the powerful national mythology of Swedish imperial greatness. Towards the end of the 19th century, the liberal daily *Aftonbladet* – the "bible of Swedish people"

(Tegner) – lampooned both muscular nationalism and the ideas of conquest marshalled by the glorious kings such as Gustavus Adolphus and Charles XII. The merciless scrutiny of Sweden's past imperial triumphs was brought to a climax by August Strindberg in his *Svenska folket i helg och söcken* (1881–1882), the first anti-heroic account of the Swedish Age of Greatness. Not only did it assault the wasteful – and murderous – virtues of previous rulers; it suggested that such virtues increased the misery and destruction of the Swedish people. What was needed was a country which was a happy home to its citizens.

Interestingly, at the end of the 19th and the beginning of the 20th century, the image of Sweden as a "good home" acquired a feminine – and then a feminist – ring to it. In Malla Silverstolpe's famous intellectual salon, the "family was holy" – a boundless source of *Gemenskap* (inclusive community). Fredrika Bremer asked: "Can you really be blind to this higher and nobler life which develops never more beautifully than in a tranquil home?" (Bremer 1848: 201). Last but not least, for early feminists such as Ellen Key, home was a "Fatherland in miniature" and a jumping board of women's emancipation (Key, 1903).

Interestingly, the most influential and precursory promoter of the metaphor of Sweden as a "caring home" was Sweden's own Nobel Prize Laureate in literature Selma Lagerlöf. In Lagerlöf's masterpiece, *Gösta Berling's Saga*, we find all the components of the home and nature mythology on display. The story concerns multiple expulsion from and returns to home. The finale radiates the ideals of reconciliation, atonement, compassion, building bridges and cancelling class boundaries and a strong belief in progress and the power of labour Lagerlöf 1891; 1982: 308).[14]

But the most explicit reference to the Swedish state as an inclusive home is to be found in Lagerlöf's groundbreaking address "Home and State", delivered at the Right to Vote Congress in Stockholm in 1915. Lagerlöf advocated women's emancipation and voting rights, but rather then embarking on a predictable tirade on the equality of men and women, she chose an intriguing reframing of her cause: she presented women's right to vote and work as a logical expansion of their traditional home tasks. Women had been experts in creating a good, caring home in the preindustrial household, Lagerlöf argued. Acting as custodians of family memory, maintaining values and rituals, and guarding peace at home, women were ecological actors: they had contributed to a more liveable earth. If they now aspired to emigrate from home, it was because they could help society to "build a bigger, caring home", which was the state. The key message was: "The really big masterpiece, the state, that has so far been created by men, deserves women's expertise and help in turbulent times".

The effect of Lagerlöf's rhetorical ploy was powerful and twofold: first, it reframed female voting rights from being a matter of emotions or competitive challenge to a Swedish male, to being a compelling agenda of gender partnership strengthening the national community; and second, it redefined the state from being an instrument of power, order and law, to being an institution of social well-being, security and moral upbringing. In short, bringing women into the labour market would benefit everybody by transforming the state into a better home for all citizens.

And so it became. When, in the late 1920s, the Swedish Social Democrats started talking about *folkhemmet*, the story was "new" only in the sense of being politicized by the government. In fact, it was a reformulation of the already entrenched national symbotype. In evolutionary terms, the Swedish Social Democrats were successful because they selected a potent trope which resonated with the people at large (many of them Lagerlöf's readers), inspired gender cooperation and reinforced social cohesion. In addition, *folkhemmet* softened the national self-image. It has been customary to associate Swedish social democracy with archetypally "masculine" aspirations such as bureaucratic prudence, pragmatism and scientific rationality. In contrast, the Lagerlöfian household mythology and ecology invoked values traditionally perceived as "feminine": survival, compromise, partnership, reconciliation, pacifism. From then on, modern Swedish society selected just these values as the foundation of their internal and external relations.

And thus, in his momentous speech in 1928, Albin Hansson insisted that "The basis of home is togetherness and a sense of belonging. A good home doesn't make a difference between privilege [and] backwardness, between darlings and stepchildren [...] In a good home equality, thoughtfulness and cooperation rule" (Hansson 1928: 124). If we further consider that many of the ideas running through this passage were also articulated in powerful social projects such as *Folkrörelse*, *Folkupplysning* and *Folkhögskola*, then it is clear that *folkhemmet* succeeded for the same reasons that Haugian fraternity succeeded in Norway: it was based on the already existing, familiar story reanimated with an emancipatory project, and it was replicated *ad infinitum* both in cultural texts and in the new forms of political and institutional praxis. In short, *folkhemmet*'s political and economic success was, in part at least, the result of cultural innovation: not a creative destruction but a creative amplification of the values of Enlightenment humanism.

A transcultural humanist agenda? Bjørnstjerne Bjørnson's and Fridtjof Nansen's prefiguration of humanitarian Norway

One of the intriguing features of modern Nordic humanism has been its missionary dimension: not just stabilizing the good society at home, but attempting to export it abroad. As we argued above, an aspiration to transnational humanism was already present in Wergeland's writing. But it gained national and international currency thanks to the work of three powerful Norwegian and Swedish animateurs: Bjørnstjerne Bjørnson and Fridtjof Nansen.

At the beginning of the 20th century, Bjørnson and Nansen were national heroes, celebrated by the world as Nobel Prize winners: Bjørnson for his literary opus (1903), Nansen for his peace initiatives and humanitarian work (1922). Both men had a knack for tackling "mission impossible": Apart from his attempt to "sing a better Norway" (*dikte et bedre Norge*), Bjørnson aspired to tame the belligerent German furies by forming a peaceful pan-Germanic League. In the very last article he wrote on the subject in 1908, he sharply distinguished what he called a "conquering Pan-Germanism" from a "serving Pan-Germanism" (Sørensen 1997: 204). He argued, almost clairvoyantly, that "the serving Pan-Germanism, one that seeks out Brothers on both sides of the Atlantic to make an end to all wars, and one that unites the different nations in voluntary cooperation – a Guardian Saint for all cultural purposes – is a blessing for Middle Europe" (Sørensen 1997: 204). As a humanist poet, thinker and doer, Bjørnson founded the first peasant bank, organized the teachers' fund, and kept sending money to his needy friends, strangers, even his enemies. He wrote long, warm, consoling letters to the imprisoned Dreyfus, and composed passionate appeals on behalf of oppressed minorities – Slovaks, Serbians, Croatians and Romanians. Admittedly, his philanthropy was not exactly a proof of sainthood – he was seen by many as a self-centred, poetocratic ass. In fact, he was a tormented soul who struggled to learn the art of transmuting his own countless errors and failures of judgement into feats of goodness. "As long as I live," he stressed, "I shall side with the party of the weak against the strong, and with the abused against the powerful ones" (quoted in Hagtvet 1998: 8). "*Jeg vil dø I den tro at de andre er god*" (I shall die believing that the others are good), he sang. Declarations like this were not just outpourings of poetic bathos; they were prefigurations of Norway's self-image and its foreign policy in the 21st century: a policy based on an open aspiration to become a humanitarian power.[15]

Bjørnson's somewhat younger contemporary Fridtjof Nansen was a Renaissance-like polymath: a man who was equally gifted as a scientist[16], Arctic explorer, artist, storyteller and humanitarian activist for whom what was difficult took a bit of time, and what was impossible took a little longer. As High Commissioner for Refugees at the League of Nations (1920–1930), Nansen transposed his expertise on his daring Arctic missions into the art of humanitarian assistance in crisis-ridden post-World War I Europe and starving Soviet Russia. He was an oddity in a world fascinated by violence, war and tribalism. His sporty Norwegian "ski-patriotism", to put it in the vernacular, and his continued appeals for international politics based on altruism seemed completely out of touch with the gruelling realities of civilizational breakdown in post-WWI Europe and Soviet Russia. Defying the general spirit of despondence and cynicism, he and Bjørnson persisted in their humanitarian quest. Bjørnson imagined Norway as a "holy ghost" of Europe, radiating human rights, natural beauty and peace to the outside world. Nansen – a staunch atheist – exemplified Christian *caritas* by trying to rescue millions of refugees and victims of famine. Four generations of Norwegians read them with red ears and foggy eyes. A procession of national icons, from ski-clad heroes of the Norwegian Resistance during World War II to humanist adventurers and national mentors – such as the legendary ethnographer and the leader of the KonTiki expedition, Thor Heyerdahl, and the ecophilosopher Arne Næss – tried to emulate them and thus revitalize their ethics of "thinking dutifully and acting beautifully". The "Bjørnsonian" and "Nansenian" symbotype and the accompanying litany of moral traits they encoded – reason, rights, concern for nature, equality, tolerance, science, progress – penetrated into the Norwegian mentality, creating what Alexis de Tocqueville meant by *moeurs*: "habits of the mind and the habits of the heart that make up the moral and intellectual state of the people" (Tocqueville 2000: 295). Most interestingly, very much like Wergeland, both national do-gooders attempted to amplify Nordic humanism into a transnational project: one that would become a universal moral codex. An interesting question is: have they initiated an alternative path to a sustainable modernity, or have they undermined the good society upon which such modernity has been founded?

Ambiguities of the universal "caring home"

The best way to assess the true function of a symbotype is by inspecting its potency and resilience in situations of crisis. By way of benchmarking, in the 1930s, the mythology which accrued around the modernizing process in Germany was intertwined with an anti-individualist, coral reef mentality, a story of Aryan superiority and looking backwards toward a splendid Teutonic past (Stern 1974; Witoszek and Trägårdh 2002). In contrast, the harmonizing Swedish *folkhemmet* had little to do with the integrationist vision of the German *Volksgemeinschaft*. In twentieth century Scandinavia, the visions of good society remained consistently affiliated with tolerant and egalitarian values and an anti-totalitarian mindset (Sejersted 2011: 103). The crucial questions to ask, thus, are: How do humanist ideas fare when they become translated into political ideologies? And, what becomes of humanist symbotypes when they are extended from national to universal agendas?

Sweden is a particularly interesting case, because it is here that the idea of the *state* as people's home became politicized from the start. In the first half of the 20th century, Swedish national strategists became fascinated with planning and rationality as the tools of improvement of the existing "core design principles" of *folkhemmet*. Two enthusiastic ideologues of the social engineering ideology, Gunnar and Alva Myrdal, insisted that the ongoing demographic, social and economic crisis in the 1930s could be solved only by a massive intervention of the "good state", acting on behalf of society as a collective (Myrdal 1936). To preserve the holy grail of *folkhemmet*, the Myrdals argued, the state should have both the right and the obligation to intervene in Swedish citizens' private sphere, overriding family and individual concerns (Sejersted 2005: 266).

Although this radical paternalism turned out to be a largely rhetorical exercise, it generated tensions within the Swedish public sphere. The leading social politician Gustav Möller managed to tone down the statist-technocratic aspects of the Myrdalian vision by reimagining the state as the protector of the autonomy and dignity of every citizen. But, for a while, there were hot disputes between the followers of what we may call the radical "Myrdal solution" and the more conciliatory "Möller solution" – debates which have only partly resolved the ambiguity inherent in the relation state–individual in the Swedish *folkhemmet* (Sejersted 2005: 267). Lars Trägårdh, in an attempt to create a *coincidentia oppositorum*, has nuanced the benign, Möllerian interpretation of people's home by proposing the concept of *statist individualism* (Trägårdh in Sørensen and Stråth 1997: 253ff.). In his reading, the state functions not just as the provider of social services, free, high-quality education and health care, but also as an agent of social emancipation and catalyzer of individual autonomy. In the modern Swedish welfare state, children and women are no longer dependent on their families or husbands. Instead, the caring state is the guarantor of their rights as individuals (Trägårdh 2013: 198; see also Chapter 5 in this volume). The question is: How does this moralization of the state fare with disadvantaged, subaltern groups or immigrant groups? Is it bound, as some critics suggest, to invite the state apparatus into the private sphere through the back door, thus violating the individual autonomy it is designed to safeguard?

The original ambiguity of the metaphor of the Swedish state as a caring home was exacerbated in the second half of the 20th century. The original *folkhemmet*, as envisioned by Per Albin Hansson and his successor Tage Erlander, was an expression of enlightened nationalism. The *folk* in *folkhemmet* had referred to the Swedish people: an inclusive Swedish family that was to be a blueprint for sustainable modernity. But in the 1950s, yet another, charismatic vision of *folkhemmet* humanism emerged: one which encompassed not just Sweden but the whole world. It was advocated by the Swedish UN General Secretary (1953–1961), Dag Hammerskjöld – a seemingly faceless and colourless bureaucrat, who made his reputation by boldly standing up to demands from the Soviet Union on the question of human rights. Hammerskjöld insisted that the UN should become an organization giving priority to the rights of individual citizens, even if this meant overriding national sovereignty. This project would have likely been forgotten as an example of harmless, utopian musing, were it not for Hammarskjöld's death in a plane crash in 1961.[17] The accident transformed him into the most prominent martyr in the history of UN peace operations – and into a new national hero of the *folkhemmet*. His legacy was given an additional lift through the publication of his posthumous papers, which he called "a sort of White Paper based on my negotiations with myself – and with God". Published in 1963 under the title *Markings* (*Vägmärken*), the diaries revealed a man who dreamt of the world as an extended *people's home* cultivating human rights and recognizing "mankind as a community of shared responsibility and shared guilt" (Lønning 2010: 19, 24, 36).[18]

In Hammarskjöld's biography, Mats Svegfors calls the former UN Secretary General the "first modern Swede" (Svegfors 2005). But the ambition to extend the Swedish *folkhemmet* from a national to a universalist project has not been unproblematic, as the ongoing refugee crisis in Europe has shown. In Elinor Ostrom's terms, the reasons for the Nordic model's efficacy is that, until the end of the 20th century, it evolved in relatively small and relatively homogeneous nations that observed norms and principles that sustained trust and reciprocity. How far – and by what means – these principles could be scaled up has been a subject of lively debate among the contributors to this volume (see Chapters 1 and 2). In the 21st century, Bjørnson's, Nansen's and Hammarskjöld's visions of transnational humanism, one where an ideology of human rights replaces *national* myths and values, may be attractive to cosmopolitan elites, but it is increasingly perceived as posing a threat to both national identity and polity.

Nordic humanism on trial

Does Scandinavian humanism – and humanism in general – matter? In the above, we have suggested that it does, for at least three reasons. One is cultural-evolutionary: humanism seems to increase the well-being of a society and its resilience in times of crisis. The second reason is political and economic: when the humanist agenda penetrates into political and economic models, it creates a relatively "civilized" capitalism, high-trust, cooperative politics and less-corrupt institutions. Third, and most importantly, the humanist agenda is a buffer against the totalitarian temptation.

This being said, humanism Nordic style – if not humanism *sui generis* – has never been a readily accepted mindset. As we have argued, with the possible exception of Selma Lagerlöf, each humanist animateur was perceived as a controversial – if not downright dissident – individual by many of his contemporaries. Hans Nielsen Hauge was imprisoned for nine years for his non-Orthodox Christianity. Henrik Wergeland was widely detested by Norwegian bureaucratic and political elites and scorned by the literary establishment. N. F. S. Grundtvig was never given the high position in the Danish Church he was entitled to. Bjørnstjerne Bjørnson's sharp political attacks on the Swedish–Norwegian Union earned him the reputation among Norwegian and Swedish conservatives of being a dangerous political extremist. Fridtjof Nansen's polemical tirades against the rhetoric of class struggle and the ostensible threat of a Marxist revolution were enough to get him branded as a "fascist" in the Norwegian socialist press.

This being said, the humanist symbotypes were in the end appreciated and included among the "sacred texts and rites" in Scandinavian countries. What is also important to note is that all controversies and conflicts ignited by humanist innovators were peacefully resolved. Hauge's followers gained their religious freedom. Wergeland's humanism and poetic genius were recognized – if only post mortem – even by his former enemies. Bjørnson was given the Nobel Prize in literature by his former enemy, King Oscar II, and the union between Sweden and Norway was dissolved in a peaceful way. Last but

Nordic humanism   51

not least, nearly all of Nansen's former political enemies stopped believing in revolutionary ideas and embraced a liberal, parliamentarian democracy.

The contention of this chapter has been that, for all the internal strife, modernity as filtered and disseminated by the Scandinavian *humanist symbotypes* has yielded more cooperative societies and less rigid, centralized structures, and has been less bedevilled by social inequality than many other Western countries.

However, at the beginning of the 21st century, the legacy of Nordic humanism is as much contested as it is potent. In this section, we shall touch on some of the pivotal cultural challenges.

First, Ostrom's design principles point to the importance of strong identity and well defined boundaries as conditions of a sustainable community's success. As we have argued, it is in large part thanks to culturally transmitted humanist symbotypes operationalized *within* small, "Ostromian" national communities that the Nordic productive welfare societies have emerged and solidified. For a long time, this process has been undisturbed, forging a relatively homogeneous and cooperative *Gemeinschaft* with a strong prosocial identity. The questions are, however: What are the limits to extending the boundaries of the Nordic communities, and what is the ceiling for expanding their identity and their binding, cooperative ethos in a multicultural world? One way to address this question –has been through further cosmopolitization of Nordic humanism – a project that has gathered the intelligentsia's support in Sweden. But this cosmopolitization – inspired by Dag Hammarskjöld's universalist human rights approach – has a downside. Sweden shows that the human rights-based humanism cultivated by post-national elites encounters a growing sense of outside threat to a shared cultural patrimony. There is a widespread sense of a cooperative and altruist modus at a higher level being undermined by the increasingly selfish lower level – a sense exemplified by the popularity of the anti-immigration party, Sweden Democrats. In the eyes of the latter, the vision of a society which considers that its duty is to take care of, and integrate, every individual who aspires to join the *folkhemmet* has a dystopian ring to it, especially if the newcomers refuse to share the social norms that made *folkhemmet* possible in the first place. The elite-driven ideal of human rights as the foundation of an ever expanding and generous *folkhemmet* not only has underplayed ongoing national tensions and social unrest but, paradoxically, may also have propagated a cosmopolitan homelessness rather than a sense of belonging.[19] The 2015 refugee crisis, during which the Swedish Prime Minister was compelled to recant his proud motto "My Europe does not build walls", illustrated the insurmountable nature of the problem (see Chapter 5 in this volume).

The second, much discussed, *cultural* challenge to the Nordic humanist symbotypes comes from the narratives that extol the ideal of a competitive, knowledge-based society. There is an interesting tension between the rhetoric of cooperation – still pervasive in Nordic children's books[20], school curricula (see Chapter 4) and political discourse – and the competitive, stardom-orientated mindset peddled by the media and demanded by the tyranny of international rankings. The Norwegian Parliamentary Report on the *School of the Future* (NOU 2015) is an example of the resulting *doublethink and doublespeak*: although the report alludes to the *paramount importance* of international competition in the introduction, in the over 100 page-long text, the concepts of competitiveness and competition appear six times *in total* (on pp. 19, 20, 21, 24, 31 and 57), while the idea of cooperation and its derivatives (cooperative processes, collaboration, co-action/*samhandling*, interaction, etc.) are repeated over 250 times. In short, in spite of the growing authority and influence of the competitive mindset and practice, Norwegian educators stubbornly remain faithful to their original egalitarian values and aspirations, at least at the level of official rhetoric. But practice on the ground points to two clashing visions of Norway: one which reasserts the ideal of an ordinary, prosocial and happy citizen, and the other which promotes stressful individual exceptionality, mastery and excellence.[21] If, up till the second decade of the 21st century, the Nordic model has balanced competition with cooperation, the increasingly commodified society is producing a different character type conditioned by a consumer and stardom culture. Not only does it de-skill people in practising cooperation; it also increases social segregation and devalues decency and goodness as outmoded and futile virtues.

Another – largely under-researched – cultural challenge to Nordic humanism has to do with the North becoming part of an increasingly disembodied, IT-fuelled commons. As has been argued, modernity today is not just about the quest to overcome diverse constraints of living processes, but about the increasing intrusion of technology into human relations, making them more and more virtual and disembodied (Gare 2014: 331). Until the 21st century, social organization through commodification, via the alliance of bureaucracies and markets, was relatively weak in Scandinavia. The basic, underlying humanism in politics and the economy rested on *embodied* personal relations in communities that cherished a cooperative ethos and practised efficacious control mechanisms. How will the Facebook animateurs of the Nordic model manage to sustain an embodied, earth-bound democracy?

One thing is certain: in order for humanism – whether Nordic or universal – to remain a potent driver of moral communities, its symbotypes need to be reimagined as sources of local and national empowerment. This involves not just institutional and political innovation, but also *cultural innovation* in forging the future of the Nordic model. Admittedly, the most demanding challenge is the Bjørnsonian-Nansenian-Hammerskjöldian idea of making transcultural humanism into a viable project. Apart from the necessity to imagine new institutions and redefine the social contract, Nordic societies will need both to rethink their *educational* strategies and to find ways to expand the Ostromian core design principles into a caring, multi-ethnic "home" that will reinvigorate the humanist norms and values which have constituted the backbone of sustainable modernity in the North.

Conclusion: towards eco-modernity as a cultural programme?

While discussing Bjørnson, Wergeland or Lagerlöf as the founding fathers – and mothers – of Norwegian and Swedish humanism, we have highlighted their social visions, featuring inclusive and tolerant communities. But, in most of the cases under scrutiny, we are talking about an "amplified humanism", one which also includes strong connections with the natural environment. As one of us has suggested elsewhere (Witoszek 1998, 2011), what gives the 19th-century modernization of Norway and Sweden its ideological and mythological coherence and integrity is a philosophical tradition which might be tentatively described as "ecohumanist".[22] Ecohumanism refers to a cosmology based on humanist ideals, but one in which the symbolic referents of identity derive from nature imagery and from a particular allegiance to place. The basic premise of humanism, the recognition of the inherent dignity of the human species, is here modified by values springing from man's experience of nature. The ecohumanist tradition of knowledge has been forged less by the lore of the city and more by the "wisdom of the open air": it has promoted frugality rather than extravagance, equality rather than hierarchy and, though it launched holistic perceptions of nature, it has measured the value of the environment and culture in pragmatic rather than romantically idealist terms. In this pragmatic cosmology, values are resilient under stress; flexibility is the key to successful adaptation. After all, pragmatism, as William James remarked, "means the open air and the possibilities of nature, as against […] dogma, artificiality and the preference of finality in truth" (James 1975). Ecohumanism is the art of the *via media* and *via activa*, based on the knowledge of nature's ways and moderated by the awareness of limitations inherent both in nature and in society. The "eco-" prefix, we may say, protects humanism from its own excesses.

The most outspoken advocates of Scandinavian ecohumanism, such as Henrik Wergeland, Bjørnstjerne Bjørnson, Selma Lagerlöf and Fridtjof Nansen, linked the malady of modern civilization to people's withdrawal from their original home. But it is especially Selma Lagerlöf's *Nils Holgerssons underbara resa genom Sverige* (1906–1907)[23] – a canonic text in Scandinavia – that captures the deeply felt, ancestral dimension of the Northern environment. It tells a story about a boy who soars on the back of a goose and talks to animals and plants; it broadens the scope of human empathy with the natural world, tying it to a biotic imaginary. The Swedish community is presented here as not just national; it is ecological, including nature that has a voice.

Though the scope of this chapter does not allow us to elaborate on the role of the ecohumanist aspect of the Nordic cultural legacies, there is ample evidence that it has informed a plethora of texts and practices, from national literatures, folklore and children's art and stories to the idea of sustainable development advocated by the Brundtland Commission (1987) and Arne Naess's ecophilosphy (Witoszek 1998; Midttun and Witoszek, 2011). As Chapter 10 in this volume shows, Nordic countries were early drivers of international initiatives and conferences on the environment, which gave an impetus to green transition. It is indeed puzzling that, in trying to address the climate agenda, they have not mobilized their strong and shared ecohumanist traditions. Certainly in Norway, Sweden and Finland, national mythologies are as humanist as they are ecological: a potential springboard for launching eco-modernity as not just an economic project, but a civilizational agenda..

From such an eco-modern perspective, a positive scenario of 21st-century modernization in Scandinavia would include solidifying, and further refining, the unique Nordic balance between traditionally opposing values, such *culture* and *nature*, *communitarianism* and *individualism*, *cooperation* and *competition*, *religion* and *scientific progress*. But, in the last instance, facing the assorted challenges of late modernity – from the climate shift to the refugee crisis – requires the safeguarding and balancing two pivotal and strong cultural ideals of the Nordic countries: individual freedom and inclusive community. For, as Zygmunt Bauman has put it eloquently, "community without freedom is a project as horrifying as freedom without community" (Bauman 1996: 79–90).

Notes

1 www.houseofsweden.com (accessed September 2017).
2 Tvedt's metaphor was seemingly inspired by the claim of former Prime Minister Gro Harlem Brundtland, that "It is typically Norwegian to be good."
3 "Symbotype" plays on "genotype", denoting culturally significant information replicated via a multitude of symbolic forms generated by education, religion, the arts, folklore, etc.
4 Research shows that at least 100,000 people read Hauge's books between 1796 and 1801. See Thorvaldsen (1996); Stibbe (2007).
5 The *Konventikkelplakaten* was imposed by the Danish King Christian VI in 1741.
6 Cooperation is implicit rather than explicit in Ostrom's eight core design principles, but it is an inseparable condition of a sustainable community.
7 The term was coined by Timothy Garton Ash to refer to the 1989 revolution in East Central Europe (Ash 1990).
8 The Jewish paragraph was finally repealed in 1851, six years after Wergeland's death. Norwegian Jews still honour Wergeland in an annual ritual ceremony on Norwegian National Day, when the Mosaic Society puts flowers on Wergeland's grave.
9 After the defeat of the Polish uprising against Czarist Russia, Wergeland became disappointed and enraged. He wrote the poem "Cæsaris", a thinly disguised attack on the Czar. The protagonist is presented as a character of pure evil – a Satan's representative on Earth. The poem is packed with bloody and morbid metaphors, and is evidence of how strongly Wergeland identified himself with the struggle of the oppressed Polish nation.
10 One of modern testimonies to the enduring strength of Wergelandian humanism was the unanimous protest by Norwegian teachers against the "Nazification" of school curricula during the German occupation. The teachers argued that Teutonic

ideas of racial superiority clashed with their conscience and their Christian and humanist values (Slagstad 1998: 107–108).
11 Interestingly, Grundtvig's youth was conservative and his mature age progressive: from being a supporter of enlightened absolutism, he became an advocate of democratic ideas later in life.
12 "First Man and then Christian" was the title of a Grundtvig poem, which was published posthumously (Bugge 2001).
13 The Folk High School movement played an especially important part in the left-liberal political movement in Norway in the second half of the 19th century, a movement that won political power in the 1880s.
14 When the protagonist, the Major's Wife, lies on her deathbed, Gösta Berling, a colourful villain who has dispossessed her, makes his peace with her while invoking a vision of a happy home: "Don't you hear what the hammer says? [...] Your work shall continue. That farm shall always be a home for great and true labour." I quote from a rather poor English translation (Lagerlöf 1891; 1982: 308).
15 See, for example, one of the speeches of the Norwegian Minister of Foreign Affairs Jonas Gahr Støre, *Norge som fredsnasjon- myte eller virkelighet?* ("Norway as a Peace Nation: Myth or Reality?" 24 April 2006 (available at: www.regjeringen.no/nb/dep/ud/aktuelt/taler_artikler/utenriksministeren/2006/norge-som-fredsnasjon--myte-eller-virkel.html?id=273461) (accessed 17 September 2017).
16 According to Huntford, "He passed his doctoral exam – rather controversial and ahead of its time – thanks to his examiners' charity. It was generally believed that he was heading for disaster and was unlikely to return form his expedition to the North Pole" (Huntford 1971 76).
17 Hammarskjöld was killed in a plane crash in Ndola on 18 September 1961, while he was negotiating a peaceful solution to the ongoing crisis in Congo. The circumstances of his death remain unclear and controversial: was it an accident or was he deliberately killed by a bomb, and if so, by whom?
18 One might argue that Hammarskjöld was the very person who redefined the United Nations, by giving it an ethical dimension. In the introduction to a collection of Hammarskjöld's speeches, *Att fora världens talan. Tal och uttalanden av Dag Hammarskjöld* (2004), Kaj Falkman points out that a surprisingly substantial number of high-ranking UN officers had a portrait of Hammarskjöld in their offices.
19 Both Norway and Denmark curbed the implosion of their "models" by instituting much more restrictive immigration policies.
20 The canonic masterpieces of children's literature in the Nordic countries – *Pippi Langström, Rovere i Kardemommeby* and *Mummibokene* – all feature altruistic, socially sensitive and reformable individuals.
21 In 2016 and 2017 the Norwegian public sphere exploded with debates on the negative influence of Pisa tests on pupils' psychic condition. Many teachers and researchers refer to the growing "performance anxiety" among the students: a prize which is too high according to many, and reduces the quality of everyday life and a sense of personal identity. For a summary of the latest research see Røed Skårderud, "Elever sliter i Pisa skolen" ("Pupils struggle with Pisa test in schools"), *Klassekampen*, Saturday 26 August 2017.
22 The concept of "ecohumanism" is used here in a metaphorical sense; it designates a set of phenomena which predated the proper discovery of the environment and the establishment of the science of ecology. As such it is a result of a struggle to

name, and thereby come to terms with, a distinctive tradition of knowledge which has been heavily influenced by the dynamics of man's relationship to nature.
23 The title of the English translation (by Velma Swanston Howard) is *The Wonderful Adventures of Nils* (illustrated by Mary Hamilton Frye. New York: Doubleday, Page & Company, 1922).

References

Acemoglu, D. and Robinson, J. A. (2013) *Why Nations Fail*. London: Profile Books.

Ash, Timothy Garton (1990) *The Uses of Adversity*. New York: Granta. www.nybooks.com/articles/1985/06/27/poland-the-uses-of-adversity/ (accessed 5 September 2017).

Bang, A. (1910) *Hans Nielsen Hauge og hans samtid*. Et tidsbillede fra omkring aar 1800 (Hans Nielsen Hauge and his Times. Picture of the Period from the 1800s). Oslo: Christiania.

Bauman, Zygmunt (1996) On Communitarians and Human Freedom: Or How to Square the Circle. *Theory, Culture and Society* 13(2): 79–90.

Bourdieu, P. (1990) *The Logic of Practice*. Pao Alto: Stanford University Press.

Bremer, F. (1848) *Syskonlif*. Stockholm.

Brundtland Commission (1987) *Brundtland Report. Our Common Future*. Oxford: Oxford University Press.

Bugge, K. E. (2001) "Menneske først" – Grundtvig og hedningemissionen. *Grundtvig Studier* 1/2001. https://tidsskrift.dk/grs/article/view/16400

Bugge Amundsen, Arne. (2007) Books, Letters and Communications. Hans Nielsen Hauge and the Haugean Movement in Norway 1760–1849. In: *Revival and Communication. Lunds universitets kyrkohistoriska arkiv.*

Curtis, Mark (2009) Norway's Dirty Little Secrets. *The Guardian*, 24 September. www.theguardian.com/commentisfree/cif-green/2009/sep/24/norway-ethical-oil-environment-arms

Dawkins, R. (1976) *The Selfish Gene*. Oxford: Oxford University Press.

Falkman, Kai (ed.) (2004) *Att föra världens talan. Tal och uttalanden av Dag Hammarskiöld*. Stockholm: Atlantis.

Fukuyama, Francis (2008) Wealth and Culture. A Conversation with David Landes. *The American Interest,* September/October. www.the-american-interest.com/article.cfm?piece=464 (accessed 13 December 2017).

Furre, Berge (1999) Hans Nielsen Hauge: Stats- og samfunnsfiende. In: S. A. Christoffersen (ed.), *Moralsk og Moderne? Trekk av den kristne moraltradisjonen fra 1814 til i dag* (Moral and modern?: Features of the Chrsitian moral tradition from 1814 until today) (pp. 80–101). Oslo: Ad notam.

Gare, A. (2014) Speculative Naturalism: A Manifesto. *Cosmos and History: The Journal of Natural and Social Philosophy* 10 (2): 300–323.

Geijer, E.G. (1849–1855) Samlade Skrifter I. Stockholm.

Gundersen, Trygve Riiser (2005) "Jeg troer derfor jeg taler": Forfatterfunksjon i Hans Nielsen Hauges forfatterskap. (I think, therefore I talk. The function of the writer in Hans Nielsen's Writings). *Norsk Litteraturvitenskapelig Tidsskrift* 8: 33–52.

Hagtvet, Bernt (1998) *Bjørnstjerne Bjørnson, de intellektuelle og Dreyfus–saken*. Oslo: Aschehoug.

Hansson, Albin (1928) Folkhemmet, medborgarhemmet. (People's home, co-citizen's home) In: *Från Fram till folkhemmet*. Stockholm: Metodica Press.

Harrison, L. and Huntington, S. (2001; 2004) *Culture Matters. How Values Shape Human Progress*. New York: Basic Books.
Hartberg, Yasha and Wilson, David Sloan (2017) Sacred Text as Cultural Genome: An Inheritance Mechanism and Method for Studying Cultural Evolution. *Religion, Brain and Behavior* 7 (3): 11–13. www.tandfonline.com/doi/abs/10.1080/2153599X.2016.1195766 (accessed 5 September 2017).
Huntford, Roland (1971) *New Totalitarians*. London: Allen Lane.
James, William (1975) *Pragmatism*. Cambridge, MA: Harvard University Press.
Key, Ellen (1898) *Tankebilder*. (Thought Images) Stockholm: Bonnier.
Key, Ellen (1903) *Kärleken och äktenskapet* (Love and Marriage). Stockholm: Bonnier.
Lagerlöf, Selma (1891; 1982) *The Story of Gösta Berling*, trans. Robert Bly. Karlstad: Karlstad Press.
Lønning, Inge (2010) *Politics, Morality and Religion – The Legacy of Dag Hammarskjöld*. Uppsala: Dag Hammerskjöld Foundation.
Magnus, Alv Johan (1978) *Vekkelse og Samfunn. En undersøkelse av Haugevekkelsen og dens virkninger for det norske samfunnet i det 19. århundre magistergrads avhandling i sosiologi* (Religious Awakening and Society. An exploration of the Haugean Movement and its Impact on Society in the 19th Century). Master's thesis in sociology. Oslo: University of Oslo.
Mathews, Freya (2017) Come with Old Khayyam and Leave the Wise to Talk. *Worldviews* 21(3): 218–234.
Melberg, Arne (1978) *Realitet och utopi*, Stockholm: Rabén & Sjögren.
Midttun Atle and Witoszek, Nina (2011) Nordic model: Is it Sustainable and Exportable? Report. Norwegian Business School and SUM, Oslo University. www.ceres21.org/media/UserMedia/Nordic%20model_original%2020110309.pdf
Myrdal, Alva and Myrdal, Gunnar (1934) *Kris i befolkningsfrågan*. Oslo: Tiden Norsk Forlag.
Ostrom, Elinor (1990) *Governing the Commons*. Cambridge: Cambridge University Press.
Pedersen, Kim Arne (2002) Grundtvig på anklagebænken. Grundtvig Studier 1. http://ojs.statsbiblioteket.dk/index.php/grs/article/view/16429 (accessed 10 October 2017).
Ravnåsen, Sigbjørn (2002) *Ånd og Hånd: Hans Nielsen Hauges etikk for ledelse og næringsliv* (The Spirit and the Hand: Niels Hauge's Ethics for Leadership and Business). Oslo: Luther Forlag.
Ryland, Glen Peter (2005) *Peasant Radicalism in Early Nineteenth Century Norway: The Case of Hans Nielsen Hauge (1771–1824)*, unpublished MA dissertation in Liberal Studies, Burnaby, Surrey and Vancouver: Simon Fraser University. http://ir.lib.sfu.ca//handle/1892/2407 (accessed 10 October 2017).
Sejersted, Francis (2011) *The Age of Social Democracy: Twentieth Century in Sweden and Norway*. Princeton: Princeton University Press.
Skrondal, Anders (1929) *Grundtvig og Noreg. Kyrkje og skule 1812–1872* (Grundtvig and Norway: the Church and the School). Bergen: Lunde & Co.
Slagstad, R. (1998) *De Nasjonale strateger*. Oslo: Pax.
Sørensen, Øystein (ed.) (1993) *Nordic Paths to National Identity in the Nineteenth Century*. Oslo: KULTs skriftserie.
Sørensen, Øystein (1997) *Bjørnstjerne Bjørnson og nasjonalismen*. (Bjørnstjerne Bjørnson and Nationalism) Oslo: Cappelen.
Sørensen, Øystein (2001) *Kampen om Norges sjel*. (The Struggle for Norway's Soul) Oslo: Aschehoug.

Sørensen, Øystein and Stråth, Bo (eds) (1997) *The Cultural Construction of Norden.* Oslo; Oxford: Scandinavian University Press.

Stern, F. (1961; 1974) *The Politics of Cultural Despair: A Study in the Rise of the Germanic Ideology.* Berkeley: University of California Press.

Stibbe, Alison Heather (2007) Hans Nielsen Hauge and the Prophetic Imagination. PhD thesis, University of London. http://discovery.ucl.ac.uk/15430/1/15430.pdf

Storsveen, Odd Arvid (1996) *Henrik Wergelands norske historie.* Oslo: KULTs skriftserie.

Storsveen, Odd Arvid (2008) *Mig selv. En biografi om Henrik Wergeland.* Oslo: Cappelen.

Svegfors, Mats (2005) *Dag Hammarskiöld. Den förste moderna svensken.* Stockholm: Norsteds.

Thorkildsen, Dag et al. (1996) *Grundtvigianisme og nasjonalisme i det 19. århundre.* Oslo: KULTs skriftserie.

Thorvaldsen, Steinar (1996) Visjonen bak plogspissen: Om Hans Nielsen Hauge ved hans 200-års jubileum. Visjon 1–2. www.hitos.no/fou/kristendom/hauge/htm

Tocqueville, Alexis de (1835; 2000) *Democracy in America.* Trans. and ed. Harvey C. Mansfield and Delba Winthrop. Chicago: Chicago University Press.

Trägådh, Lars (2013) The Historical Incubators of Trust in Sweden: From the Rule of blood to the Rule of Law. In: Marta Reuter, Filip Wijkström and Bengt Kristensson Uggla (eds), *Trust and Organizations. Confidence across Borders.* New York: Palgrave Macmillan.

Tvedt, Terje (1995) *Den norske samaritan.* Oslo: Gyldendal pamflett.

Tvedt, Terje (2005) Det nasjonale godhetsregimet: om utviklingshjelp, fredspolitikk og det norske samfunn. In: Ivar Frønes, Lise Kjølsrød (eds), *Det norske samfunn.* Oslo: Gyldendal.

Tvedt, Terje (2009) *Utviklingshjelp, utenrikspolitikk og makt : den norske modellen.* Oslo: Gyldendal.

Witoszek, Nina (1998) *Norske naturmytologier: fra Edda til økofilosofi.* Oslo: Pax.

Witoszek, Nina (2011) *The Origins of the Regime of Goodness: Remapping of the Norwegian Cultural History.* Oslo: Norwegian University Press.

Witoszek, N. and Trägårdh, L. (2002) *Culture and Crisis: the Case of Germany and Sweden.* Oxford: Berghahn Books.

4 Individualism and collectivism in Nordic schools

A comparative approach

Kirsti Klette

Introduction

In Nordic countries, education is a basic right of citizens, as outlined in their respective constitutions. Education is, likewise, considered a key vehicle for forging a fair and equal society supporting democracy, participation, welfare and life-long learning. The key elements of the Nordic education model include: (a) a non-tracked and non-streamed model for K-9 education, providing all students, irrespective of social, economic and geographical background, the same educational opportunities; (b) a focus on inclusion and integrated solutions (e.g. consideration of students' social and ethnic diversity, an adaptive model of education and a unified syllabus); (c) national curricula; and (d) instructional practices that balance individualism and collectivism, emphasizing collaboration and active learning on the part of the student.

Despite these common characteristics, however, interesting differences emerge in the Nordic countries, especially with regard to issues of individualism and collectivism. Recent policies in the Swedish educational system, for example, have put emphasis on individual competition and school choice, giving parents the right to choose their preferred school using a voucher system. This has led to more than 40 per cent of pupils in Swedish urban areas like Stockholm and Gothenburg enrolling in private schools, or "free schools". Generally, this refers to children in grades 1–9, but it sometimes also refers to students at the high school level. A similar trend is identified in some urban areas in Finland. In Norway, the proportion of private schools is relatively stable (3 per cent), and children are, as a rule, enrolled in their neighbourhood school.

In this chapter, I investigate and compare the ideas of individualism and collectivism as they are represented in the respective national curricula and key legislative texts, governing policies, and school/classroom policies across the Nordic countries. The three levels – national curricula, governing policies, and school/classroom policies – could also illustrate how shifting between *macro*, *meso*, and *micro* approaches generates different conclusions with regard to individualism and collectivism in Nordic schooling.

The chapter discusses how the merging of new models of individualism and the encroachment of the ethos of competition in both private and state schools may pose a challenge to education as a foundation for a cooperative and fair society in the Nordic countries – with different implications at different levels. Two main questions will be addressed:

1. *To what extent can we talk about shared educational values among the Nordic countries?*
2. *To what extent does the Nordic education model balance stability and renewal, individualism and collectivism?*

As indicated, the three analytical lenses – curricula policies, governing policies and classroom policies – will provide the point of departure for the exploration of developments and trends in 21st-century Nordic schooling.

Theoretical framing

A range of researchers from different academic disciplines have homed in on a Nordic or social-democratic welfare model in the post-war period, commonly as a comparison with other welfare regimes (Esping-Andersen 1996; Hort 2014; Kuhnle 1998, 2000). The social-democratic welfare regime has been characterized by extensive economic re-allocation and high taxation levels, generating universal policies covering, for example, pensions, health insurance, child allowances, comprehensive cost-free education and extensive childcare (Hort 2014). Four of the Nordic countries were among the five ranked highest in the UNICEF evaluation of child well-being in rich OECD countries (UNICEF 2013), and they clearly stand out among the OECD countries as having continuous and strong support for families with young children (Thévenon 2011).

Similarly, scholars have debated distinctive features of a Nordic model of education (Dovemark et al. 2018; Lundahl 2002, 2016; Telhaug et al. 2004). Education has been an important part of the Nordic welfare system (Esping-Andersen 1996; Hort 2014; Telhaug et al. 2004) and has been generally regarded as a crucial instrument for creating social justice and security by providing schooling of high and equal quality to all citizens regardless of social class, gender or geographic origin and location. A joint model of schooling, known as *A School for All*, has been seen as a means to build social cohesion and a sense of belonging and social community, especially after World War II. Telhaug and colleagues (2004) distinguish between a *recruitment* motive and a *social* motive when renewing and redesigning the Nordic educational model in the post-World War II period. The social motive contains perspectives on recruitment, the main emphasis of which is on the school and the classroom as forging an "all-embracing social community bringing together students from different backgrounds" (Telhaug et al. 2004: 143). Conversely, the recruitment perspective focuses on equal access to education, thus ensuring that the full potential of human resources is exploited. Some have argued that the experience of being on the margins of society would be replaced by solidarity and a sense of belonging and that emphasis on social justice and equal access to education would benefit especially children from remote, rural regions, and would result in a stronger nation: The school as a social community should serve nation building because it develops a sense of belonging, respect, and mutual understanding between students representing different social classes (Telhaug et al. 2004: 143). After World War II and up to the late 1980s, common ideas about the rationale and organization of education framed the development of the school systems in all Nordic countries, and this was especially relevant for the framing of primary and lower secondary education. Compulsory education was reformed in all the Nordic countries during the 1960s and 1970s so that there was little or no streaming, starting in Sweden. In both Sweden and Norway, a 10-year experimental period in the 1950s preceded the final decision on the nine-year compulsory schooling decision made in 1962 for Sweden, in 1969 for Norway, in 1972 for Finland and Iceland, and in 1975 for Denmark. Telhaug and colleagues (2004: 142) show how representatives of the Nordic social democratic governments developed an idea to design a *joint* Nordic school system in the 1960s, the Norwegian Minister of Church and Education, Helge Sivertsen (1960–1965), being one of their most enthusiastic advocates (Telhaug 1966). The idea was never realized, but the fact that it was seriously debated at the intergovernmental level illustrates the wide support for a general educational reform involving all Nordic countries.

The existence of exceptionally strong social democratic parties in most of the Nordic countries was crucial to launching the extensive school reforms during this post-World War II period. Other political controversies notwithstanding, most of the reforms were based on broad agreement *across* the political spectrum. This stands in sharp contrast to many other European countries, where the idea of universal education was severely debated and resisted by opponents (Wiborg 2004). Despite prior differences in educational policies – for example, the strong tradition of parental involvement and school choice in Danish education policies (e.g. the presence of state-supported free schools in Denmark from the 19th century) – we could argue that a distinct Nordic model of education existed for much of the post-war period. Telhaug and colleagues (2004: 204) call this period the "heyday of a joint Nordic model". This early phase of the Nordic model was dependent on a strong state as the key provider and facilitator of education, providing regulations but also resources for a unified, un-streamed comprehensive model. Throughout the 1970s and early 1980s, this top-down and centralized way of governing came under pressure and was criticized for being undemocratic, rigid and obsolete (Lundahl 2002; Simola et al. 2013; Telhaug et al. 2004).

In the late 1980s and particularly the 1990s, decentralization reforms were introduced in all Nordic countries,[1] giving the municipalities and local school authorities a greater degree of autonomy and freedom in implementing national education objectives and allocating resources to fit local circumstances and requirements.[2] From the late 1980s, the political discourse on social justice and equality was complemented by values such as competition, freedom of choice and accountability (Dovemark 2004; Englund 1996; Telhaug and Tønnesen 1992; Varjo 2007). While deregulation policies materialized in all Nordic countries, Sweden took these reforms to their utmost, giving municipalities responsibility for school governance and recruitment as well as for curriculum design and implementation. The Swedish National Curriculum from 1994 illustrates this change of policy when it comes to curriculum design, paying attention to overarching goals and objectives, rather than contents and teaching methods (Carlgren and Klette 2009). While Norway, Finland and Denmark redesigned their policies in the direction of deregulation during this period, they balanced this with a focus on state mandatory regulations (Dovemark et al. 2018). In Sweden, deregulation efforts were followed by an emphasis on free schools and the entitlement of parents to choose which school they wanted to send their children to.[3] Since the turn of the millennium, we have seen a rapid growth of fully tax-funded and voucher-based free schools and the number of children attending them (Gustafsson et al. 2016; Lundahl et al. 2013), especially in urban areas. By 2017, as many as 15 per cent of Swedish children attended free schools; in urban areas, such as Stockholm and Gothenburg, up to 40 per cent of children were enrolled in non-public schools. Although parental involvement and individuals' right to choose have been underscored in decentralization efforts in the other Nordic countries, these efforts have not been linked to an increase in private schooling and, again, the proportion of private schools in Finland and Norway has been pretty stable (3 per cent).

In summary, a thread in Nordic compulsory schooling dates back to Grundtvig and his ideas about schooling as part of building citizenship, democracy and the "whole human" (Korsgaard and Wiborg 2006), and equal access to education has been a normative foundation of this development. Since the end of World War II, equal opportunities for all has been one of the cornerstones of the Nordic education model (Esping-Andersen 1996), which emphasizes the following:

- An absence of streaming and tracking that ensures equal opportunities and access regardless of social, geographical, and ethnic background;
- A strong focus on education as community building and as a glue for social cohesion, paying attention to international and universalistic ideas and values such as citizenship building and democracy.
- Participation and democratic values both at the level of norms and overarching ideas and as a guideline for concrete school and classroom practices.

Based on this review, the following four aspects will serve as analytical dimensions (Arnesen and Lundahl 2006) when reviewing the Nordic educational model:

a) Access to education and related resources;
b) Differentiation of education (integrated versus differentiated solutions);
c) Emphasis on democratic values and compulsory schooling; and
d) Community and equality versus individualism and competition.

I will use these dimensions when addressing (a) educational values and overarching discourses in national curricula and key national texts, (b) meso-level educational policies such as the degree of school choice and governing, and (c) educational practices in schools/classrooms. The three levels of analysis provide different views on the balance between stability and renewal when it comes to the Nordic education model.

Educational values and discourse: national curricula and priority texts

Telhaug and colleagues (Telhaug et al. 2004; Telhaug et al. 2006) identify some key values that underscore the educational discourse and narratives of Nordic curricula (see also Sivesind and Wahlström 2016 Zilliacus et al. 2017). These values include *equality* in terms of equal access and opportunities; *participation* and schooling as a means of fostering democratic values; and schooling as a means of *social mobility* and *student-centred* pedagogy. These rather stable values have survived across shifting political regimes and periods. Analysing education reforms in the Nordic countries over a period of 60 years, Telhaug and colleagues, for example, underscore the dominance of the basic ideas of social democratic progressivism emphasizing equality, solidarity and individual emancipation (Telhaug and Volckmar 1999), without underestimating interesting periodical shifts and transformations towards economic liberalism (Telhaug et al. 2006). Providing equality in terms of *equal access and opportunities* seems to be a stable key value in the Nordic discourses about education. It has been a key value in the overarching part of the respective national curricula since the late 1960s; and, whenever new national curricula are introduced, providing resources and accessibility for all regardless of social and cultural background is a key aspect. In analysing new curricula reforms in Finland (Finnish National Board of Education 2014) and Sweden (Swedish National Agency for Education 2015), Zilliacus et al. (2017) underscore how curriculum-making in the Nordic countries emphasizes equality, providing education for all, and minimizing social differences. This emphasis is still present, they argue, "even if more individualistic views and neo-liberal reasoning have gained pace since the 1990s" (p. 167).

In the early phase of Nordic "comprehensivism" (1960s–1980s), special attention was paid to equality and access irrespective of social and geographical background. For example, in the late 1970s and early 1980s, the debate focused on how key values of Nordic schooling should reflect diversity in terms of geographical and regional knowledge (Broady 1980; Høgmo et al. 1981) and how schooling should serve as a means of social mobility and not preserve existing social inequalities linked to cultural (Bourdieu 1984; Hoem 1978) and social (Bernstein 1975; Bourdieu and Passeron 1977) capital. Equal opportunities and the idea of *A School for All* have in recent years been framed in terms of providing equal access despite differences in cultural and ethnic backgrounds. Globalization, immigration and the refugee situation in Europe have issued new challenges for Nordic values of tolerance and universalism as well as the idea of schooling in the Nordic countries as a means of community building and creating a shared sense of identity and belonging. In the recent curriculum in Finland (Finnish National Board of Education 2014), for example, "cultural identity" is strongly emphasized, both in the general part of the curriculum and in the subjects of mother tongue and literature, second national language instruction, and foreign languages (Zilliacus et al. 2017). The focus is on students' ability to develop active citizenship and identity, thus not seeing cultural identity as something that is fixed, predefined and permanent, but rather seeing multicultural identities as relevant to all students despite their ethnic background. Compared with the previous curriculum, there is less reference to Finnish national identity and heritage (Zilliacus et al. 2017). Instead, global identity through world citizenship is increasingly present, and "the goal is to support all students to develop a multilingual and multicultural identity" (Zilliacus et al. 2017: 172). Cultural diversity is less present in the new Swedish curriculum (Swedish National Agency for Education 2015), and Zilliacus et al. (2017) argue that cultural diversity is framed within the context of increased internationalization, while cross-border mobility places high demands on the ability of people to live with, and appreciate, the values inherent in cultural diversity. Awareness of one's own cultural origins and sharing in a common cultural heritage are introduced as a solution (Swedish National Agency for Education 2015), as is the idea that it is "important to develop the ability to understand and empathize with the values and conditions of others" (Swedish National Agency for Education 2015: 7). In the Norwegian White Paper *Framtidens Skole*[4] (The School for the Future; NOU 2015/8), issues of migration and cultural diversity are only briefly touched upon in connection with bilingualism and multilingualism and are discussed rather superficially (NOU 2015/8: 21).

Participation and democracy have also survived as key ideas of Nordic schooling. While these ideas were largely linked to education in basic literacy (the ability to read and write), education in a participatory democracy and social science education as a subject area in the early phase (1960s and 1970s), a renewed interest in participatory democracy and literacy skills has materialized since the turn of the millennium, linked to an emphasis on generic skills and key competences for a globalized world (see DeSeCo framework; e.g. Rychen and Salganik 2003; OECD 2016). The new national curriculum in Sweden (Swedish National Agency for Education 2015) underscores students' ability to participate in informed discussions as a key target for their schooling. Goal attainment (*måloppnåelse*) in Swedish writing is, for example, defined as forging

[s]tudents' capacity to discuss and be familiar with key knowledge areas throughactive listening and communicative engagement, including ways of posing and responding to questions, and to be explicit in their recommendations and epistemological positions. Students should engage in, and demonstrate skills in *different* types of discourses and communication genres.[5]

Similar formulations are recognized in both Finnish curricula (Finnish National Board of Education 2014) and Norwegian curricula (Norwegian Ministry of Education 2006) and white papers (NOU 2105:8).

Education as a means of *social mobility* was stressed in the national policy texts and white papers during the 1970s (Broady 1980; Hernes and Knudsen 1976) but less so in recent years. Instead, we see an increased focus on the individual and how schooling should offer opportunities so that human resources are exploited to their full potential (e.g. the knowledge economy argument; Carlgren et al. 2006; Telhaug et al. 2006).

Student-centred pedagogy and educational progressivism have been strong across all Nordic curricula, especially in Sweden and Norway. Student-centred ways of working and the active involvement of students in learning have been key ideals in all Norwegian curricula since 1974. They are seen as a prerequisite for students' engagement and motivation as well as a component in fostering democratic citizenship. Active learning is less present in the Finnish and Danish curricula, and key policy texts in these countries are reluctant to interfere with teachers' professional judgements and decisions at the classroom level. In the case of Denmark, for example, Danish school authorities are not expected to intervene in schools. Telhaug and colleagues (2004: 146) report: "Their job descriptions (e.g. state and municipality levels) clearly stated that it was not among their duties to press new methods upon teachers or to criticize them".

To summarize, the overarching ideas about education as a means of social cohesion and community building are still key values in the Nordic schools (witness national curricula and legislation), and equal opportunities in terms of enrolment and access to an un-streamed, non-tracked model for compulsory schooling are the cornerstone. However, *A School for All* has been questioned over the last decade, not least due to the arrival of a large number of immigrant students. Additionally, universal ideas about schooling as community- and identity-building have been put under pressure.

Education policies

Education policies in the Nordic countries were for a long time closely linked to the overarching values and key ideas as outlined in the national curricula and supported by strong state legislation. In the 1990s, deregulation reforms and criticism of a too inflexible, rigid state combined with the drive for local initiatives and solutions and a transition towards curricula focused on governing by objectives rather than governing by specifying content (Carlgren and Klette 2008; Jóhannesson et al. 2002). As a result, national policies have taken different forms in the Nordic countries. As I will argue, this has especially affected integrated versus differentiated divisions of education (e.g. the degree of private versus state schooling) and issues of individualism, collectivism and community features in the case of Swedish schooling. I will also briefly touch upon how a deregulated order between the state and the municipalities/schools impacts on national assurance and accountability systems.

As mentioned earlier, deregulation systems in Sweden entail the funding of free schools through general taxation without tuition fees and an opportunity for private corporations to make a profit from their investment in education. This regime has made free schools attractive for private owners, stakeholders and investors (Lundahl 2016). Starting out in early 2000, and with huge expansion between 2006 and today, one-fourth of all compulsory students and 40 to 55 per cent of upper secondary school students have been enrolled in free schools. The numbers are even higher for urban areas like Stockholm, Malmø and Gothenburg. At present, one-third of the youth in urban areas in Sweden commute to a municipality and free school other than their own neighbouring school (Lundahl 2016: 10). The last decade has seen the emergence of free schools characterized by aggressive marketing, profit making and the involvement of venture capitalists (Erixon Arreman and Holm 2011; Lundahl et al. 2013).

In contrast, Finland, Norway and Iceland have a small and stable degree of private schooling (2–4 per cent) and, notably, do not allow private owners to make profits from their education activities. In Norway, for example, private schooling is allowed only on the basis of religious and/or pedagogical arguments. This means that Norwegian private schools are either framed within alternative pedagogical platforms (e.g. Waldorf and Montessori schools) or are religious schools providing an enhanced degree of religious education compared with regular state schools. Both types of school are required, however, to be run within the framework of national curricula and legislation.[6] In Finland, as in Norway, the proportion of private schools has been stable (3 per cent). However, in urban areas of Finland (e.g. Helsinki, Tampere), we see an increased degree of school choice linked to "specialized schools" or schools with specific subject profiles such as music, foreign languages or STEM education (Arhonen 2014), as well as a tendency to recruit students from highly educated families (Kosunen and Seppänen 2015; Varjo et al. 2015). The 1990 Iceland Education Act allowed school choice towards the end of the decade, but this has been realized only to a limited degree (Sigurðardóttir et al. 2014). Denmark, in contrast, has historically had a greater number of free schools than the other Nordic countries, based on a long-lasting ideology emphasizing parents' rights to choose education for their children. Legislation on private schooling was introduced as early as 1855[7] (Reeh 2008), in line with a political tradition of limiting the power of the state over citizens, especially in questions of religion and ideology. This model has ensured that parents and

Table 4.1 How different aspects of deregulation have impacted on education in Nordic countries (see also Lundahl 2016: 6)

	Denmark	Finland	Iceland	Norway	Sweden
Decentralization of governance to municipalities and schools	Yes	Yes	Yes	Yes	Yes
Extent of private schools	High	Low	Low	Low	High
Promotion of school choice	Extensive	Local only	Local only	Local only	Extensive
Tuition fees for private schools	Yes	No	Yes	No	No
Profit-making allowed	No	No	No	No	Yes
National quality assurance system	Yes	No	No	No (soft)	Yes

students have had the opportunity to choose schools based on different ideological platforms (Dovemark et al. 2018). Just as in Sweden, private schools in Denmark are nevertheless obliged to teach according to national curricula and legislation; however, unlike the Swedish case, it is not possible for private school-owners to use education activities for financial gain.

With regard to differentiation in education, segregation between state and private schools, and community solutions versus individual solutions, Sweden has gone much further than any of the other Nordic countries (see Table 4.1 above). It is thus debatable whether we can still talk about a joint Nordic model when it comes to the level of policies, school choice and school competition.

Accountability systems

Deregulation also involved changes in accountability systems and quality assurance mechanisms in the Nordic countries. Until the 1990s, quality assurance was seen primarily as a part of governance throughout the national curricula, which prescribed the content and subject knowledge the students were supposed to learn. With deregulated systems, where the municipality is in charge of schooling, new quality assurance mechanisms were introduced. Hogan et al. (2015) call this "evaluation-based governance", while others refer to it as outcome-based governance (Whitty et al. 1998). In Sweden and Denmark, deregulation from the state level to the municipality level was accompanied by school inspections. Neither Finland nor Norway introduced an inspection corpus for schools; however, Norway, after a heated debate (Mølstad and Karseth 2016), introduced national tests in mathematics, reading and English language learning for grades 5, 8 and 9 as a part of its national quality assurance system in 2007. Finland never introduced national tests but continued to use optional tests (*utvalgsprøver*) as a part of what might be described as a "soft monitoring" system (Lawn 2006). In summary, Finland – and to some degree Norway – continues to have a soft monitoring system as its basic quality assurance mechanism, while Denmark and Sweden have combined new regulation forms with predefined and harder governing tools. Table 4.1 summarizes how different aspects of deregulation (private versus state schools, level of school choice, the role tuition fees and profit making, and accountability systems) have impacted on schooling in the Nordic countries.

To sum up, education policies show resemblances both at the level of policies and at the level of value-charged rhetoric, which emphasizes democracy, active student engagement, equality and access to education/educational resources. However, different Nordic countries show contrasting levels of differentiation and school choice. Norway, Finland and Iceland are at one end of the continuum, with restricted options regarding school choice and individualized solutions, as well as a rather stable percentage of private schools (3 per cent). Denmark and, especially, Sweden represent the other extreme, with an increasing number of free schools, which have dramatically changed state schooling and access to a 'School for All'.

Education practices

As indicated earlier, active learning on the part of the student has been a part of the curriculum tradition in the Nordic countries, especially Sweden and Norway. The active involvement of students when it comes to teaching and learning (labelled under the umbrella of educational progressivism (Dewey, 1963) in its early phase), while often framed within constructivist or social constructivist theories of learning today (Bransford et al. 2000), has a long tradition in the Nordic countries. For example, the Norwegian framework curriculum, dating back to 1939 (see Framework plan 1939), underscored how teaching methods should contribute to the active involvement and engagement of students as opposed to transmissive ways of teaching. Alongside this, a strong tradition of classroom studies (i.e. studies of teaching, learning and interaction in the classroom) has been implemented, especially in Denmark (Projegt Skolesprog 1979), Sweden (Callewart and Nilsson 1974; Lindblad and Sahlström 1999), and Norway (Bjerrum Nielsen 1985; Klette 1998). Reports from Nordic classrooms portray strong similarities across the classrooms in terms of instructional repertoires: teacher-led whole-class instruction dominates, supported by individual work and group work, while providing ample room for students to raise their voices and contribute to the classroom conversation. Several studies (Bergem and Klette 2010; Emanuelsson and Sahlström 2008; Klette and Ødegaard 2015) show that Nordic classrooms provide more opportunities for students to contribute than do those in other countries (see also Alexander 2006).

However, while student engagement and active learning might be key features of Nordic classrooms, we also recognize some interesting differences within and across the Nordic countries. Simola (2005) and Simola et al. (2013) describe Finnish classrooms as highly individualized and with few opportunities to talk. Conversely, Bergem and Klette (2010) argue that Norwegian classrooms support student questioning and engagement; however, students' contributions are often practical and procedural questions rather than cognitively demanding enquiries (Klette and Ødegaard 2015). Analysing Swedish classrooms, Emanuelsson and Sahlström (2008) use the term "the Price of Participation" to discuss the cognitive and communicative challenges presented by classroom learning that includes a high degree of student involvement. Recent comparative analyses from mathematics classrooms in Finland, Sweden and Norway (Klette et al. 2018) suggest strong similarities when it comes to pedagogical practices at the classroom level where teacher-led instruction and individually focused seat work still dominate. Targeted analyses indicate a larger degree of student engagement, or opportunities for students to talk with their peers/or in small groups, in Swedish and Norwegian classrooms than in Finnish classrooms. Students' access to their supervising teacher is similar in all three countries, where the relation between adults and students is described as engaging and supportive. This is also the case for classroom management (e.g. order and discipline in the classroom), although Swedish classrooms have a slightly higher tendency to experience interruptions and disruptive behaviour.

As previously mentioned, teacher-led instruction together with individual seat work dominates in all three countries. Typically, whole-class instruction follows a discourse format consisting of three stages: initiation (often via a teacher question), student response, and teacher evaluation or follow-up. This format is commonly referred to as the IRE/F format (Mehan 1979) and typically features a pattern where the teacher asks an information-seeking question (Initiative) that requires a predetermined short answer (Response). The teacher then praises correct answers and corrects those answers that are wrong (Evaluation), offering follow-up or feedback (Feedback). Several studies have prescribed the prevalence of this structure of classroom interaction – often also referred to as the "grammar of schooling" (Tyack and Tobin 1994). More than Norwegian or Finnish teachers, Swedish teachers encourage their students to engage in discussions with their peers; however, these teachers often lack the tools for making these conversations cognitively demanding (Klette et al. 2018).

Individualized and/or adaptive teaching has been promoted in Norwegian and Swedish classrooms. During the late 1990s and early 2000s, individualized teaching methods were implemented, often linked to the use of "own work" (*eget arbete*) (Österlind 1998) in Swedish classrooms and in individualized "work plans" (Klette 2007) in Norwegian classrooms. Both instructional formats list students' required tasks and assignments for a certain period (often a week) but leave it up to the students to decide when and where to perform the different assignments. The instructional format was designed to allow students more autonomy and choice with regard to content, materials, learning resources and pace of learning. In these classrooms, teacher-led whole-class instruction was reduced to a minimum and, in principle, students might work on different tasks and assignments during their time in class.

Österlind (1998) shows how instructional practices such as work plans are better adjusted to high-achieving students than to low achievers. While high-achieving students frequently seek advice from teachers when they need assistance and manage to finish the plan in time, low-achieving students rarely ask teachers for help, and fail to finish in time. Observations from Norwegian primary (Haug 2006) and secondary classrooms (Klette 2007) support these findings and show how low-achieving students attend lessons devoted to work plans without doing any of the required schoolwork. Klette (2007) discusses whether individualized teaching methods, like the use of work plans, put too much burden on the students, thus implying that low achievers, often boys, are put in a position in which they become responsible for "regulating their own failure in school" (p. 352). Österlind (1998) demonstrates how individualized teaching methods in Swedish classrooms increase the individual student's influence (pacing and rhythm of schoolwork) – but at the cost of the class as a shared community and with severe implications for community building and solidarity in the classroom.

Discussion and concluding remarks

A School for All, a highly unified, non-streamed, non-tracked model of universal schooling, has a long tradition in the Nordic countries. This tradition has been the subject of transformation and developments since its heyday in the 1970s (Telhaug et al. 2004). For example, in the 1990s, Nordic welfare policies (e.g. constitutional state power and comprehensive regulation) were combined with a high degree of decentralization and local autonomy. This shift reflects similar policy developments in other sectors as well as in international policy trends (Whitty et al. 1998).

From an international point of view, the Nordic model emphasizes features that are acknowledged as critical qualities of education, such as the high prioritization of education, sufficient funding and resources, and the delaying of tracking/streaming for as long as possible (Antikainen 2006; Darling Hammond 2017; OECD 2014; UNESCO 2016). The Swedish political scientist Esping-Andersen (1996) calls the Nordic welfare model a "gift to the modern world". The question is: Can we still talk about a shared Nordic model in education – one that forges a community embodying the Ostromian core design principles? (Wilson et al. 2013). In other words, how much of the Nordic model must remain in place for it still to be termed comprehensive and thus *A School for All*?

In this chapter, I have used three analytical approaches to the Nordic model: (a) overarching values and discourses (as envisioned in national curricula and priority texts/legislative texts); (b) education policies (such as governing mechanisms, school choice and integrative mechanisms, and quality assurance systems); and (c) educational practices and interaction at the classroom level. The main findings from these analyses suggest that, depending on the analytical approach different conclusions can be drawn.

If we use overarching values and discourse as our analytical approach, similarities are more striking than differences. National curricula and legislative texts in all countries underscore shared and rather stable values linked to equal opportunities and access to a non-differentiated and inclusive model of schooling. The Nordic education model of curriculum-making emphasizes equality, providing the same education for all and minimizing social differences, with a set of clear guidelines in for the structuring of each curriculum (Blossing et al. 2014). This emphasis is still present, even if more individualistic views and neo-liberal reasoning have gained pace since the 1990s (Arnesen and Lundahl 2006; Isopahkala-Bouret et al. 2014). However, all countries have updated their national curricula to respond to increasing cultural diversity, and all curricula texts now include migration issues and a wide definition of cultural identity and belonging as part of a Nordic *School for All* (Zilliacus et al. 2017). Curricula aims and goals were for a long time defined through general aims and accompanying content areas. Recent, redesigned curricula point, however, to a more differentiated Nordic landscape. Targeted analyses of the formulation of aims and goals (see, for example, Sivesind and Wahlström 2016) suggest a shift from competence-based curricula to performance-based goals in the Swedish curricula texts (Wahlström 2016) and a move to a more content-driven orientation in the Finnish curricula (Sivesind and Wahlström 2016). Norway, as a third example, is currently positioned in the middle, emphasizing competence aims, which cover all elements without any particular focus on content, performance or results (Mølstad and Karseth 2016). However, despite some analytical and more detailed differences, the overall message is clear: The Nordic countries demonstrate strong shared values when it comes to the overall mission of schooling.

Education practices in the classrooms also point to strong similarities across the Nordic countries. This is not surprising, as substantial research points to enduring and stable classroom practices – the so-called "grammar of schooling" (Tyack and Tobin 1994) around the world (see, for example, Alexander 2000; Cohen 1988; Cuban 1993). Using educational practices in classrooms as an analytical lens, and judging from the level of progressivism and the extent of student involvement, the Nordic countries show a family resemblance. Students in Nordic classrooms are encouraged to raise their voices and formulate arguments within the classroom context, thus elaborating on their understanding and testing out possible hypotheses. This is especially prevalent in Norwegian and Swedish classrooms.

Both Sweden and Norway have aspired to differentiated and individualized teaching methods. In both countries, individualized learning plans (called "work plans" in Norway and "own work" plans in Sweden) have been introduced. Research into instructional practices using these ways of organizing classroom work shows that individualized work increases the individual student's influence and autonomy regarding their classroom work (Österlind 1998). However, this happens at the cost of the classroom as a community (Carlgren 2005; Klette 2007) and a shared space for learning. Furthermore, individualized teaching methods reinforce the individual background of the student (e.g. academic, socio-economic) and thus produce less equality in the classroom (Österlind 2005). To sum up, despite some minor but interesting differences across Nordic classrooms, comparative classroom analyses suggest the prevalence of shared key features when it comes to Nordic classroom teaching and learning practices.

Educational polices, or the principles for governance and the degree of school choice and integrated versus differentiated solutions, represent yet another approach for analysing the Nordic education model. As indicated above, policies of governance went through a major shift during the 1990s, when a highly centralized system was replaced by a decentralized model in which municipalities became the key providers of education (see e.g. Simola et al. 2013). These changes took place in all Nordic countries during the 1990s. However, Sweden combined this "municipalization process" (*kommunaliseringen*) with a new regulation between public schools and private schools, opting for fully tax-supported free schools, providing all parents with a voucher, and allowing parents and students to choose between state schools and different free schools. Since the beginning of the 2000s, we have seen an explosion of free schools in Sweden. Gustafsson et al. (2016) argue that the "municipalization process" in Sweden can be described in terms of "marketization" because the responsibility for education has moved, in effect, from the state to the municipalities as a consequence of the various free school choice reforms.

Deregulation processes and shifts in the state's role from being a provider of education to being a regulator of education (Beach 2010) have required new quality assurance systems. In Sweden and Denmark, curricula reforms focusing on goals (and later on competences and performances) have been supported by the creation of inspection corpuses, together with national tests and final exams. Neither national tests nor inspections or exams were introduced in Finland, but Norway introduced national tests in 2007, thus solidifying Norway's middle position in the continuum. Regarding policy reforms for Finland and Norway, the egalitarian ideology is still widely upheld (Simola et al. 2013; Sivesind and Wahlström 2016), and marketization efforts have so far been modest.

In the case of educational policies, the deregulation reforms in the 1990s and 2000s created distinct differences between the Nordic countries. Lundahl (2016) and others (Dovemark et al. 2018); Rinne et al. 2002) ask if we can still talk about a joint education model given the case of Sweden: "In essence then, and especially when considering the development in Sweden, it is [...] highly doubtful if one may still speak of a Nordic model of education" (Lundahl 2016: 9). Although beyond the scope of these analyses, the growth of Swedish private schooling raises questions and calls for explanations. The thorough municipalization process (*kommuninaliseringen*), occurring at a level where it is hard to reverse it, might offer one possible reason behind the popularity of free schools. Similarly, school choice as a privilege and parental right – once introduced and implemented – may be difficult to change.

In summary, depending on analytical approaches, different conclusions can be drawn. On the one hand, there is evidence to the effect that, rather than *one* Nordic education model, we should start talking about different Nordic models. On the other, the overarching ideas and values understood at the macro levels point to strong and enduring normative similarities across the Nordic countries. Similarly, on the one hand, micro-level practices such as activities in the classroom give rise to strong similarities, but meso-level analyses that follow the implementation at district and school level reveal a somewhat different picture. When summarizing all these analytical positions, it seems fair to conclude that Sweden has gone the farthest in departing from the Nordic model of schooling in the 21st century.

Notes

1 In Norway, Sweden, Denmark and Finland, these regulatory reforms were introduced in the 1990s (Lgr 1994, L1993/97), and in Iceland in 1996.
2 *Den som har skoen på, vet hvor den trykker* ("those who have their shoes on, know where they are too tight") was the saying.
3 In Denmark, parental rights in terms of school choice have been a part of the education system since the late 19th century. By 1855, 17 per cent of Danish schools were free schools.
4 To be followed up with a revised national curriculum during 2017/18.
5 Requirement for grade "A" for students at level 6 (Swedish National Agency for Education 2015: 6, my translation).
6 For several years, Muslim communities in Oslo have tried to establish Muslim schools in the capital area, but failed due to their inability to define how the schools would follow the requirements of the national curriculum in Norway. A similar discussion has taken place in the Drammen region outside the capital area, where leaders of a Muslim school were accused of disciplining their students in a way that conflicted with the legal requirements for schooling in Norway.
7 By the late 1880s, 17 per cent of Danish students attended private schools after new legislation was introduced in 1855.

References

Alexander, R. (2000) *Culture and Pedagogy: International Comparisons in Primary Education*. Oxford: Blackwell.
Alexander, R. (2006) *Towards Dialogic Teaching: Rethinking Classroom Talk*. Cambridge: Dialogos.

Antikainen, A. (2006) In Search of the Nordic model in Education. *Scandinavian Journal of Educational Research* 50 (3): 229–243.

Arhonen, S. (2014) A School for All in Finland. In: U. Blossing, G. Imsen and L. Moos (eds), *The Nordic Education Model. "A School for All" Encounters Neo-liberal Policy* (pp. 77–93). Dordrecht: Springer.

Arnesen, A.-L. and Lundahl, L. (2006) Still Social and Democratic? Inclusive Education Policies in the Nordic Welfare States. *Scandinavian Journal of Educational Research* 50 (3): 285–300.

Beach, D. (2010) Identifying and Comparing Scandinavian Ethnography: Comparisons and Influences. *Education and Ethnography* 5 (1): 49–63.

Bergem, O. K. and Klette, K. (2010) Mathematical Tasks as Catalysts for Student Talk: Analysing disCourse in a Norwegian Mathematics Classroom. In: Y. Shimizu, B. Kaur, R. Huang and D. Clark (eds), *Mathematical Tasks in Classrooms around the World* (pp. 35–62). Rotterdam: Sense Publishers.

Bernstein, B. (1975) *Class, Codes and Control, Vol. 3: Towards a Theory of Educational Transmission*. London: Routledge and Kegan Paul.

Bjerrum Nielsen, H. (1985) Pedagogiske hverdagsbeskrivelser – et forsømt område pedagogisk forskning (Pedagogical Everyday Classroom Description). *Tidsskrift for nordisk forening for pedagogisk forskning* 2: 27–42.

Blossing, U., Imsen, G. and Moos, L. (eds) (2014) *The Nordic Education Model. "A School for All" Encounters Neo-liberal Policy*. Dordrecht: Springer.

Bourdieu, J. P. (1984) *Distinction: A Social Critique of the Judgement of Taste*. London: Routledge.

Bourdieu, J. P. and Passeron, J. C. (1977) *Reproduction in Education, Society and Cultures*. London: Sage.

Bransford, J. D, Brown, A. L. and Cocking, R. (eds) (2000) *How People Learn: Brain, Mind, Experience, and School*. Washington, DC: National Academy Press: Committee on Developments in the Science of Learning.

Broady, D. (1980) Den Dolda Läroplanen (The Hidden Curriculum). *Kritisk Utbildnings Tidsskrift (KRUT)*. 16: 8.

Callewart, S. and Nilsson, B. A. (1974) *Samhället, Skolan och Skolans Inre Arebete* (Society, Schooling, and the Inner Workings of Schooling). Lund: Lunds Bok och Tidsskrift.

Carlgren, I. (2005) Konsten att sätta sig själv i Arbete [The Art of Putting Oneself into Work]. In: E. Österlind (ed.), *Eget arbete – en kameleont i klassrummet. Perspektiv på ett arbetssätt från förskola till gymnasium* (Own Work – a Chameleon in the Classroom?) (pp. 11–38). Lund: Studentlitteratur.

Carlgren, I. and Klette, K. (2008) Reconstruction of the Nordic Teachers: Reform Policies and Teachers' Work during the 1990s. *Scandinavian Journal of Educational Research* 52 (2): 117–133.

Carlgren, I., Klette, K., Myrdal, S., Schnack, K. and Simola, H. (2006) Changes in Nordic Teaching Practices: From Individualised Teaching to the Teaching of Individuals. *Scandinavian Journal of Educational Research* 50 (3): 301–326.

Cohen, D. K. (1988) Teaching Practice Plus: Ça Change. In P. Jackson (ed.), *Contributing to Educational Change*. Berkeley: McCutchan.

Cuban, L. (1984; 1993) *How Teachers Taught. Constancy and Change in American Classrooms 1880–1990* (2nd ed.) New York: Teachers College Press.

Darling-Hammond, L. (2017) Teacher Education around the World: What CAN we Learn from International Practice? European Journal of Teacher Education 40 (3): 291–309. DOI 10.1080/02619768.2017.1315399

Dewey, J. (1938; 1963) *Experience and Education*. New York: Collier Books.

Dovemark, M. (2004) Ansvar, flexibilitet och valfrihet. En etnografisk studie om en skola I förändring (Responsibility, Flexibility and Freedom of Choice. An Ethnographic study of a School in Transition). Dissertation. Gothenburg: University of Gothenburg.

Dovemark, M., Kosunen, S., Kauko, J., Magnúsdóttir, B. and Hansen, P. (2018) Deregulation, Privatisation, and Marketisation of Nordic Comprehensive Education: Social Changes Reflected in Schooling. Education Inquiry.

Emanuelsson, J. and Sahlström, F. (2008) The Price of Participation: Teacher Control Versus Student Participation in Classroom Interaction. *Scandinavian Journal of Educational Research* 52: 205–223.

Englund, T. (ed.) (1996) *Utbildningspolitiskt systemskifte?*[Change of the Education Policy System?] Stockholm: HLS Förlag.

Erixon Arreman, I. and Holm, A.-S. (2011) Privatisation of Public Education? The Emergence of Independent Upper Secondary Schools in Sweden. *Journal of Education Policy* 26 (2): 225–243.

Esping-Andersen, G. (1996) *The Three Worlds of Welfare Capitalism*. Cambridge: Polity Press.

Finnish National Board of Education (2014) Core Curriculum for Basic Education [Grunderna för läroplanen för den grundläggande utbildningen]. Helsinki: National Board of Education.

Framework plan (1939) Normalplanen av 1939 [Framework plan from 1939]. *National Curriculum, Norway 1939*. Oslo: Aschehough Publishing.

Gustafsson, J.-E., Sörlin, S. and Vlachos, J. (2016) *Policyidéer för svensk skola*. (Policy Ideas for Swedish Schools). Stockholm: SNS Förlag.

Haug, P. (ed.) (2006) *Kvalitet i opplæringa: arbeid i grunnskulen observert og vurdert* (Quality in Norwegian Primary Education – Observed and Assessed). Bergen: Caspar Publishing.

Hernes, G. and Knudsen, K. (1976) Utdanning og Ulikhet (Education and Inequalities). Oslo: Norges Offentlige Utredninger.

Hoem, A. (1978) *Sosialisering* (Socialization). Hamar: Opplandske Bokforlag.

Hogan, A., Sellar, S. and Lingard, B. (2015) Commercialising Comparison: Pearson Puts the TLC in Soft Capitalism. *Journal of Education Policy*. Published online.

Hort, S.-E. (2014) *Social Policy, Welfare State, and Civil Society in Sweden. Volume II. The Lost World of Social Democracy 1988–2015*. Lund: Arkiv Förlag.

Høgmo, A., Solstad, K. J. and Tiller, T. (1981) *Skolen og den lokale utfordringen* (Schooling and the Local Challenge). Tromsø: University of Tromsø.

Isopahkala-Bouret, U., Lappalainen, S. and Lahelma, E. (2014) Educating Worker-Citizens: Visions and Divisions in Curriculum Texts. *Journal of Education and Work* 27: 92–109. doi:10.1080/13639080.2012.718745

Jóhannesson, I. A., Lindblad, S. and Simola, H. (2002) An Inevitable Progress? Educational Restructuring in Finland, Iceland and Sweden at the Turn of the Millennium. *Scandinavian Journal of Educational Research* 46: 325–339. doi:10.1080/0031383022000005706

Klette, K. (1998) *Klasseromsforskning på Norsk* (Classroom Research in Norway). Oslo: Ad Notam Gyldendal.

Klette, K. (2007) Bruk av arbeidsplaner i skolen – et hovedverktøy for å realisere tilpasset opplæring? (Use of Work Plans in the Classroom – A Tool for Individualized Teaching?). *Norsk pedagogisk tidsskrift* 91 (4): 344–358.

Klette, K. and Ødegaard, M. (2015) Instructional Activities and Discourse Features in Science Classrooms: Teacher Talking and Students Listening or …? In: K. Klette, O. K., Bergem and A. Roe (eds), *Teaching and Learning in Lower Secondary Schools in the Era of PISA and TIMSS* (pp. 17–31). Dordrecht: Springer.

Klette. K., Sahlström, F., Blikstad-Balas, M., Luoto, J. M., Tanner, M., Tengeberg, M. and Roe, A. (2018) Justice through Participation: Student Engagement and in Nordic Classrooms. *Education Inquiry*.

Korsgaard, O. and Wiborg, S. (2006) Grundtvig – The Key to Danish Education? *Scandinavian Journal of Educational Research* 50 (3): 361–382.

Kosunen, S. and Seppänen, P. (2015) The Transmission of Capital and a Feel for the Game: Upper-class School Choice in Finland. *Acta Sociologica* 58 (4): 329–342.

Kuhnle, S. (1998) The Nordic Approach to General Welfare. Available at: www.nnn.se/intro/approach.htm (accessed 15 November 2015).

Kuhnle, S. (ed.) (2000) *Survival of the European Welfare State*. London: Routledge.

Lawn, M. (2006) Soft Governance and the Learning Spaces of Europe. *Comparative European Politics* 4 (2/3): 272–288. http://dx.doi.org/10.1057/palgrave.cep.6110081

Lindblad, S. and Sahlström, F. (1999) Gamla mönster och nya gränser. Om ramfaktorer och klassrumsinteraktion (Classroom Interaction in Swedish Classrooms). *Pedagogisk Forskning i Sverige* 4(1): 73–92.

Lundahl, L. (2002) Sweden: Decentralization, Deregulation, Quasi-markets – And Then What? *Journal of Education Policy* 17 (6): 687–697.

Lundahl, L. (2016) Equality, inclusion and marketization of Nordic education: Introductory notes. Comparative and International Education 11 (1): 3–12. DOI: 10.1177/1745499916631059

Lundahl, L., Erixon Arreman, I., Holm, A. et al. (2013) Educational Marketization the Swedish Way. *Education Inquiry* 4 (3): 497–517.

Mehan, H. (1979) *Learning Lessons: Social Organization in the Classroom*. Cambridge, MA: Harvard University Press.

Mølstad, C. E. and Karseth, B. (2016) National Curricula in Norway and Finland: The Role of Learning Outcomes. *European Educational Research Journal* 15 (3): 329–344.

Norwegian Ministry of Education (2006) *Kunnskapsløftet. Læreplanen for grunnskolen* (National Curriculum, Norway). Oslo: Ministry of Education.

NOU:8 (2015) School of the Future – Renewal of subjects and competences. Official Norwegian Reports NOU 2015:8. Oslo: The Ministry of Education and Research.

OECD (2014) *Education at a Glance 2014: Highlights*. Paris: OECD Publishing.

OECD (2016) *Global Competence for an Inclusive World*. Paris: OECD Publishing. Available at: www.oecd.org/education/Global-competency-for-an-inclusive-world.pdf

Österlind, E. (1998) Disciplinering via frihet: elevers planering av sitt eget arbete. Doctoral dissertation, Uppsala University.

Österlind, E. (2005) En skräddarsydd skola för alla? (A Tailor-made Education for All?) [in Swedish]. In: E. Österlind (ed.), *Eget arbete – en kameleont i klassrummet. Perspektiv på ett arbetssätt från förskola till gymnasium* (Own Work – A Chameleon in the Classroom. Perspectives on a Method of Work from Preschool to High School) in Swedish. Lund: Studentlitteratur.

Projegt Skolesprog (1979) Skoledage. Copenhagen: GMT, Unge Pædagoger.
Reeh, N. (2008) Den danske stat og de frie skolers frihed – i 1855 og 2005 (The Danish State and the Freedom of the Free School – in 1855 and 2005). In: *Uddannelseshistorie* (History of Education) (pp. 82–98). Århus: Selskabet for Skole- og Uddannelseshistorie.
Rinne, R., Kivirauma, J. and Simola, H. (2002) Shoots of Revisionist Education Policy or Just Slow Readjustment? The Finnish Case of Educational Reconstruction. *Journal of Education Policy* 17 (6): 643–658.
Rychen, D. S. and Salganik, L. H. (eds) (2003) *Key Competencies for a Successful Life and a Well-functioning Society*. Paris: OECD.
Sigurðardóttir, A. K., Guðjónsdottir, H. and Karlsdóttir, J. (2014) The Development of a School for All in Iceland: Equality, Threats and Political Conditions. In U. Blossing, G. Imsen and L. Moos (eds), *The Nordic Education Model. "A School for All" Encounters Neo-liberal Policy* (pp. 95–113). Dordrecht: Springer.
Simola, H. (2005) The Finnish Miracle of PISA: Historical and Sociological Remarks on Teaching and Teacher Education. *Comparative Education* 41 (4): 455–470.
Simola, H., Rinne, R., Varjo, J. and Kauko, J. (2013) The Paradox of the Education Race: How to Win the Ranking Game by Sailing to Headwind [sic]. *Journal of Education Policy* 28: 612–633.
Sivesind, K. and Wahlström, N. (2016) Curriculum on the European Policy Agenda: Global Transitions and Learning Outcomes from Transnational and National Points of View. *European Educational Research Journal* 15 (3): 271–278.
Swedish National Agency for Education (2015) Läroplan för grundskolan, förskoleklassen och fritidshemmet 2011, Reviderad 2015 (Curriculum for the Compulsory School, Preschool Class and the Recreation Centre 2011, Revised 2015). Stockholm: Swedish National Agency for Education.
Telhaug, A. O. (1966) Er vi på vei mot en felles nordisk skoleordning? (Towards a Joint Nordic School System?). *Prismet* 7: 193–201.
Telhaug, A. O. and Tønnesen, R. T. (1992) *Dansk utdanningspolitikk under Bertel Haarder 1982–1992. Nyliberalistisk og nykonservativ skoletenkning* (Danish Education Policy under Bertel Haarder 1982–1992. A Neo-liberal and Neo-conservative School Philosophy). Oslo: Universitetsforlaget /Oslo University Press.
Telhaug, A. O. and Volckmar, N. (1999) Norwegian Education Policy Rhetoric 1945–2000: Education Philosophy in the Political Party Platforms. *Scandinavian Journal of Educational Research* 43 (3).
Telhaug, A. O., Aasen, P. and Mediås, O. A. (2004) From Collectivism to Individualism? Education as Nation Building in a Scandinavian Perspective. *Scandinavian Journal of Educational Research* 48: 141–158. DOI:10.1080/0031383042000198558
Telhaug, A. O., Mediås, O. A. and Aasen, P. (2006) The Nordic Model in Education: Education as Part of the Political System in the Last 50 Years. *Scandinavian Journal of Educational Research* 50: 245–283. DOI:10.1080/00313830600743274
Thévenon, O. (2011) Family Policies in OECD Countries: A Comparative Analysis. *Population and Development Review* 37 (1): 57–87.
Tyack, D., Tobin W. (1994) The Grammar of Schooling: Why Has it been so Hard to Change? *American Educational Research Journal* 31 (3): 453–579.
UNESCO (2016) Measures of Quality through Classroom Observation for the Sustainable Development Goals: Lessons from Low- and Middle-income Countries. Available at: http://unesdoc.unesco.org/images/0024/002458/245841e.pdf

UNICEF (2013) *Child Well-being in Rich Countries: A Comparative Overview*. Florence: UNICEF Office of Research.

Varjo, J. (2007) Kilpailukykyvaltion koululainsäädännön rakentuminen. Suomen eduskunta ja 1990-luvun koulutuspoliittinen käänne (Drafting Education Legislation for the Competitive State. The Parliament of Finland and the 1990s Change in Education Policy). Department of Education. Research Report 209. Helsinki: University of Helsinki.

Varjo, J., Kalalahti, M. and Lundahl, L. (2015) Recognizing and Controlling the Social Costs of Parental School Choice. In G. W. Noblit and W. T. Pink (eds), *Education, Equity, Economy: Crafting a New Intersection* (pp. 73–94). Dordrecht: Springer.

Wahlström, N. (2016) A Third Wave of European Education Policy: Transnational and National Conceptions of Knowledge in Swedish Curricula. *European Educational Research Journal* 15 (3): 298–313.

Whitty, G., Power, S. and Halpin, D. (1998) *The School, the State and the Market*. Milton Keynes: Open University Press.

Wiborg, S. (2004) Education and Social Integration: A Comparative Study of the Comprehensive School System in Scandinavia. *London Review of Education* 2 (2): 83–93.

Wilson, D. S., Ostrom, E. and Cox, M. E. (2013) Generalizing the Core Design Principles for the Efficacy of Groups. *Journal of Economic Behavior & Organization* 90: 21–32.

Zilliacus, H., Paulsrud, B. and Holm, G. (2017) Essentializing vs. Non-essentializing Students' Cultural Identities: Curricular Discourses in Finland and Sweden. *Journal of Multicultural Discourses* 12 (2): 166–180. Available at: https://doi.org/10.1080/17447143.2017.1311335

5 Scaling up solidarity from the national to the global
Sweden as welfare state and moral superpower

Lars Trägårdh

Introduction

The "Swedish model" has for a long time intrigued scholars and politicians struck by Sweden's capacity to sustain a social contract that seemed to have achieved a productive and sustainable balance between imperatives that have often been conceived as opposites in a permanent and fatal conflict: a society infused with strong social values that inspire cooperation and compromise, yet also a society that celebrates and promotes individual autonomy to an extreme extent; a socio-economic and political order that has become known as the prototypical social democratic "regime", yet also an order that is profoundly committed to the primacy of private property rights and the magic of the market, and is in this guise celebrated as a "supermodel" by capitalist-friendly institutions like *The Economist*. As Marquis Childs summed it up as early as 1936, Sweden had somehow managed a compromise between communism and capitalism, becoming, as he put it in the title of his book, *Sweden – The Middle Way* (Childs 1936).

In many regards Sweden is but the first and historically most prominent exemplar of the "Nordic" model, which is the focus of this book. But, I will argue, to this day, Sweden remains perhaps the most interesting Nordic country from the point of view of a key question for this book: In so far as the Nordic countries have managed to achieve a "sustainable modernity" at the level of the nation-state, is it possible to move even further up the ladder from the local tribe to the global village, to scale up such "well-being societies" to a higher, ultimately global level in an age of migration and economic globalization? Or is the Nordic model doomed to remain a strictly national project, dependent on the supposed homogeneity and small size of its populations and, most crucially, on "clearly defined boundaries", as suggested by Wilson et al. (2013). Sweden sticks out here, since, while Norway, Denmark and Finland have chosen to remain in, or retreat into, the comforts of the walled-in nation-state, Sweden has chosen a different route, embracing more open borders and a politics of multiculturalism, becoming a Nordic version of the famed Anglo-Saxon immigrant societies like the United States, Canada, Australia, New Zealand and, to a lesser extent, the United Kingdom.

Indeed, Sweden has long been known for both for its domestic welfare state and its advocacy of international, humanitarian ideals. For many years, expansive social investments in Sweden and ambitious development projects across the globe seemed to be part and parcel of a unified commitment to solidarity and equality at home and human rights and development aid abroad. In this chapter, I will explore the historical roots of these two – sometimes competing, sometimes converging – conceptions of Swedish national identity and also consider the contemporary challenges facing Sweden as it seeks to live up to these ideals.

Both ideals, which constitute two competing versions of the "Swedish model", have strong historical roots and enjoy considerable popular legitimacy. While they have peacefully co-existed for a long time – thought of not only as compatible but even as synonymous – they are in fact based on fundamentally divergent solidarity ideals and "rights logics". One is profoundly national, bounded and informed by nitty-gritty Realpolitik centred on the sovereign nation-state; the other is explicitly internationalist, unbounded and informed by the sometimes starry-eyed idealism that envisions a world without borders.

Since for many decades the ideals were, in practice, projected onto two separate stages – social rights for citizens at home and development aid for needy foreigners in their own far-away countries – the tensions between solidarism based on citizenship, on the one hand, and solidarism based on human rights ideals, on the other, remained largely hidden. However, the strains between the two became brutally apparent during the refugee crisis of 2015, the consequences of which are still a salient feature of Swedish political and social life. Even so, it is clear that in Sweden there is a will – if at times naïve and not particularly well thought through – to scale up solidarity, cooperation and reciprocity from the national to the global level; a project eagerly watched by observers both abroad and at home, both by those who appear to wish for it to fail (perhaps to justify their own isolationist positions) and by those for whom the experiments carried out by Sweden – as well as by Germany – are pregnant with hope.

The "fall" of 2015

One of the great puzzles of the refugee crisis during the autumn of 2015 was the abrupt reversal of Sweden's policy from an initial embrace of open borders to the resurrection of border controls in early January 2016. Only weeks separated a brave and morally charged claim by Prime Minister Stefan Löfvén on 6 September that "my Europe does not build walls" and a tearful press conference on 24 November, when the government was forced to back down in the face of chaotic conditions and increasing popular resistance, expressed not least in rising support for the anti-immigration party, the Sweden Democrats.

The reversal was signalled less than two weeks before, on 11 November 2015, when the Swedish government, under pressure from the Swedish

Migration Agency, decided to set up provisional border controls, most dramatically along the border with Denmark, across which Swedes and Danes had enjoyed passport-free travel since the 1950s. These controls were extended on 24 November to include requirements that all individuals who passed the border must show passports or other approved ID documents. These new rules took effect on 4 January 2016 and, although they were meant to be temporary, they were in effect as late as December 2017.

A law was also passed that limited the entitlement of refugees to obtain residence permits in Sweden (SFS 2016: 1242). Legislation was also introduced that restricted the previously liberal rules with respect to family reunion as well as the right to housing and financial aid for refugees whose asylum applications had failed. Furthermore, the Swedish Migration Agency was given the authority to remove such refugees from their housing by force. With respect to children, who carried special rights under the Convention of the Rights of the Child (CRC), the Swedish government clamped down on what had previously been a broad and generous interpretation. A special assignment was given to the Swedish National Board of Forensic Medicine to develop a more reliable method for determining the age of individuals claiming to be under age, procedures that earlier had been considered an undue violation of the individual refugee's personal integrity.

How are we to understand this turn of events? One simple explanation is that the number of asylum applicants during 2015 – 162,877 in total, 2 per cent of the total population and the equivalent of some 5 million arriving in the United States during one year – simply overwhelmed the capacity of the Migration Agency, the police, and local and national government to handle, in an orderly fashion, their needs for housing, schooling and social services. However, while this may indeed help us to understand why the governing alliance, including the Green Party and many pro-immigration Social Democrats, chose reluctantly to reverse course and to close the borders it explains neither the deep divisions nor the confusion that characterized both the political debate and the response by citizens acting in civil society. On the one hand, there were those, like the human rights organization Civil Rights Defenders, who claimed that Sweden had now reneged on its obligations under what they claimed to be legally binding international conventions, in effect breaking international law by violating fundamental human rights principles. On the other hand, there were those who argued that the needs of Swedish citizens had become secondary to those of refugees and that it was time to recognize that there is a fundamental difference between the responsibility that the Swedish state has towards, for example, a Swedish pensioner living in poverty and a Syrian refugee. In one case it was a matter of binding duties and rights, in the other it was more a question of charity and voluntary aid.

A related debate also erupted concerning the actual costs and benefits of immigration, pitting those who viewed immigration chiefly as a positive phenomenon in terms demographic renewal, increased economic growth and added national income from taxes against those who argued that immigration, and especially refugee immigration, in the short and medium term would constitute a major burden on the national economy (Scocco and Andersson 2015; Sanandaji 2017).

The argument of this chapter is that the crisis was about much more than numbers of refugees and the cost of handling them. Rather, it struck at the very heart of Swedish national identity and ultimately expressed the unsolved challenge of scaling up to the global level a politics of solidarity and cooperation that has worked well at the national level. What the refugee crisis of 2015 exposed in dramatic fashion were the tensions and contradictions that exist between national and global solidarity; between the rights of citizens and human rights. In what follows I will try to lay bare the historical roots and contemporary consequences of this internal contradiction, the overcoming of which would have to be central to any project devoted to scaling up the architecture of the Nordic well-being society.

The Swedish model 1.0: National democracy and welfare state nationalism

The Swedish social contract is at heart rather straightforward: an alliance between state and citizens, whereby citizens work, pay taxes and earn their fundamental social rights. It is a combination of a national solidarity project, an egalitarian social investment scheme, and a giant insurance company. In this guise Sweden became famous as the quintessential welfare state; as early as the 1930s both Swedish politicians and foreign journalists began to promote Sweden as a "model" with global, universal claims. To this day Swedish politicians from the left to the right remain eager to claim ownership of "the Swedish model". It is also a social contract that enjoys great popularity and legitimacy among the citizens of Sweden. To grasp this commitment to the national welfare state, one must understand how Swedes have come to understand the proper relationship between state, society, nation and people. That is, Swedish national identity has come to be tightly linked to the welfare state, understood not simply as a set of institutions, but as the realization of *folkhemmet*, the central organizing slogan of the Social Democrats, the party which has dominated Swedish politics since 1933.

As I have argued elsewhere in more detail, it is this combination of a positive view of the state, common institutions, the rule of law and an emphasis on individual freedom that is the linchpin in a social contract that has fostered the development of a high-trust society (Trägårdh 2013). Crucial here is to understand that this has entailed a particular form of trust, what is usually called "generalized" trust, a form of trust that includes "most people" in a society. This form of trust is to be contrasted with "particularized" trust, which is the trust a person has for family, kin, clan, tribe and religious or ethnic community. In a country with a high degree of generalized trust, the trust radius is long and the trust is "cool" and rooted in the primacy of law. In a society dominated by particularized trust, the trust radius is short and the trust is "hot" and based on relations of honour and the rule of blood (Trägårdh et al. 2013).

Central to the success of this political project has been the ability of the Swedish Social Democrats to dominate what we can call the politics of national community. Historically speaking this was by no means a given. During the 1920s and 1930s struggles took place throughout Europe over who would write the national narrative and thus be able to tap into the potent power of nationalism. In general, it was right-wing parties who won out, offering up visions of national community that were cast in the language of xenophobia and ethnic solidarity.

The political left's anxiety-ridden relationship with the idea of the nation, national solidarity and nationalism has a long history dating back to Marx and the old ideals of the International and the notion that workers have no fatherland. In most countries, the parties of the left were hampered by their attachment to an internationalism that was linked to a Marxian conviction that both the nation and the state were destined for the dustbin of history. Their preferred mode of political rhetoric was instead one that emphasized a global class struggle in which they joined hands across national borders under the banner of the red flag. This left them open to attack from parties to the right, who accused them of being unpatriotic and lacking a sense of national solidarity.

The hopes that socialist internationalism would overcome supposedly backward allegiances to nation and state were largely buried in 1914. In the trenches of World War I German and French workers abandoned the red flag in favour of their national banners. But unease with the nation remained in many leftist and social democratic parties. The Social Democrats in Sweden and the other Nordic countries were in this regard exceptionally successful in bucking the general trend that favoured the victory of right-wing nationalism. By fusing nationalist and socialist ideals they laid, during the 1920s and 1930s, the groundwork for the social-democratic welfare state.

This national turn by the Swedish Social Democrats came in two phases. During the first phase, in the early 1920s, the Social Democrats, influenced by Austro-Marxists like Karl Renner and Otto Bauer, accepted the centrality and legitimacy of the nation-state, breaking with classic Marxist anti-national and anti-statist dogma. The growing realization among leading Swedish Social Democrats that the nation was enduring and that nationalism was a potent political force led them in turn, in a second phase that culminated during the 1930s, to discover the potential of the existing Swedish national narrative. Thus they gradually abandoned the divisive language of class and class struggle in favour of the language of "folk", which served to create political bridges to both the rural peasantry and the urban middle classes (Trägårdh 1990).

Thus, by 1933, the year that Hitler came to power in Germany under the banner of *Volksgemeinschaft* ("People's community"), the Swedish Social Democrats had already formed the first of many governments in the name of *folkhemmet* ("the people's home"). Both slogans celebrated national community, solidarity and welfare, but while in the German case the ideal was *ethnos*, seeking ethnic purity under authoritarian leadership, it was in the Swedish case as much a matter of *demos*, connoting social equality and democracy. Indeed, the extraordinary and lasting potency of the *folkhem* concept derived from the seamless way in which the two concepts of "the people" – those of *demos* and *ethnos* – were fused into one coherent whole. That is, it is not simply that in Sweden the democratic-Jacobin notion of the people won out over the ethnic-cultural reading associated with, most infamously, the German experience; rather, the Swedish concepts of *folk*, *folklighet*, and *folkhemmet* are all part and parcel of a national narrative that has cast the Swedes as intrinsically democratic and freedom-loving; as having democracy in the blood. Thus, since to be a Swedish nationalist meant perforce that one embraced democratic values, it was possible in the 1930s for the Social Democrats to successfully harness the power of national feeling, to become "national socialists", and fight off the challenge from domestic wannabe Nazis (Trägårdh 2002).

The national narrative that undergirded the social contract and the values associated with it revolved around ideas and practices that focused on the positive role of the state and the primacy of the rule of law over the rule of blood. Most influential in constructing this narrative was the famous Swedish 19th-century historian and poet Erik Gustaf Geijer, who celebrated what he called the two Swedish freedoms, the independence of the state and the freedom of the peasants. These were themes that turned out to be highly compatible with Social Democratic ideals and goals, stressing on the one hand the power of the state, on the other the freedom of the individual.

According to this national narrative, part concrete facts, part romantic fiction, the Swedish peasants had retained their personal, legal and economic freedoms to an extent unheard of in the rest of Europe, where most peasants had lost both their property and their civil and political rights during the feudal era. By contrast, the Swedish peasantry never lost their representation as one of the estates in the parliament alongside the nobility, the clergy and the bourgeoisie. They also retained their civil rights and a great deal of political power at the local level and, not least, they kept ownership of their land to such an extent that, by the end of the 18th century, peasants owned some 50 per cent of the land in Sweden. This legacy of freedom of "the people" was, in turn, tied to a sense that the King – the State – was allied with the peasantry, having a common enemy in the nobility, which tended to want both to undermine royal power and to enserf the peasants. Connected to this positive view of the state was the high status of the rule of law, which to this day underpins the high degree of social trust and confidence in public institutions in Sweden. Constructing a romantic historical vision that celebrated "Swedish" freedoms, in terms of both personal freedom and national independence, leading Swedish historians like Geijer created a national narrative that was potentially compatible with more modern political notions, fusing liberal ideas about personal freedom with socialist ideals celebrating equality and solidarity.

It was the embrace of this national narrative that encouraged and allowed the Social Democrats to adopt and adapt the originally conservative notion of *folkhemmet*, which, as we noted above, catapulted the Swedish Social Democrats into enduring political power. And, by abandoning the rhetoric of class struggle, they also placed themselves in a position to build ties with the Swedish industrial elite, finding legendary expression in the so-called Saltsjöbaden agreements of 1938, which set in place a corporatist order of peaceful and constructive relations between labour unions and big business.

In this national turn, the Social Democrats managed to fuse notions of individual freedom, social equality and national community, harking back to the slogan of the French Revolution (freedom, equality, fraternity), but also looking forward by embracing modern notions that stressed individual autonomy and gender equality. In this way, the "Swedish model" came to be characterized by an extreme form of statism even as it involved a rejection of traditional socialist goals such as the nationalization of banks and industries. Instead, it opened up a new arena for radical social transformation, particularly in the realm of family and social policy, organized around a social contract between a strong and good state, on the one hand, and the emancipated and autonomous individual, on the other.

I have described and analysed this order of things elsewhere, coining the concept of "statist individualism" to capture this alliance between state and individual (Trägårdh 1997; Berggren and Trägårdh 2010, 2015). Through the institutions of the state the individual, so it was thought, was liberated from the institutions of civil society that fostered inequality, patriarchal gender relations and relations of dependency – such as the patriarchal family and charity organizations. These institutions were replaced by an egalitarian social order characterized by state-sponsored gender equality, children's rights and individual autonomy in general. At the same time, this Swedish ideology, with its dual emphasis on social equality and individual autonomy, was understood to be distinctly modern and highly efficient; the "welfare" of the welfare state implied not just solidarity and equality but also prosperity and progress.

By institutionalizing the moral logic of this social contract, the modern welfare state further entrenched Sweden as a society characterized both by social values, favouring cooperation and trust, and by individualistic values, enabling autonomy and freedom.

The Swedish model 2.0: Sweden as moral superpower

While support for the welfare state remains strong in Sweden, the idea of national community and a solidarity limited to citizens has nonetheless become controversial. Herein lays a paradox. A tension has emerged between ideals focused on human rights and those that centre on the principle of national citizenship. This has particularly affected the Social

Democrats and other parties on the left, which vacillate between a traditional commitment to a national social contract and an internationalist vision that involves a positive view of the United Nations and the European Union, and a commitment to provide asylum to refugees. By shifting the boundaries for the reach of community, solidarity and welfare, a political vacuum has been created, resulting in the emergence of the Sweden Democrats, a right-wing party that embraces welfare state nationalism along explicitly ethno-nationalist lines, and is hostile to immigration as well as sceptical of the EU and globalism more broadly. This brings us to the second ideal that informs contemporary Swedish national identity, namely Sweden as especially devoted to internationalism, the UN, development aid and human rights.

Again, to understand this new turn towards internationalism, it is necessary to make a historical detour. Starting with the Stockholm Exhibition of 1930, and accelerating after WWII, the historical dimension of Swedish national identity was complemented and eventually overwhelmed by a focus on Sweden as the "prototypical modern society". The deemphasizing of overt nationalism was also a consequence of the horrors of WWII and especially the example of Nazi Germany. It was also, arguably, a consequence of Swedish neutrality during the war, which initially involved rather close relations to Germany, including trade in iron ore and the granting of permission for German troops to transit through Sweden to northern Norway. Swedish post-WWII internationalism, moralism and devotion to foreign aid can be viewed as a prolonged *mea culpa* for its wartime behaviour.

At any rate, after the Second World War, human rights and UN-inspired internationalism became increasingly important to Swedish international politics and national identity. Not least Dag Hammarskjöld, the second Secretary-General of the UN, and the prominent Social Democratic Prime Minister Olof Palme came to symbolize Sweden's special role in this regard. As the commitment to foreign aid and the political support of "third world" countries grew, the idea emerged that Sweden was a country especially devoted to peace and international solidarity. If the United States was the ultimate military power, Sweden was the "moral superpower". The headquarters of SIDA – the Swedish Development Agency – was Sweden's answer to the Pentagon.

Thus "conservative" and "capitalist" Europe was contrasted with a Sweden that was imagined to be more "moral" in its behaviour, not only at home, but also in its foreign policy. While others – especially the Great Powers – conducted themselves in a manner more befitting a Bismarck or a Metternich, the Swedes ostentatiously rejected the amoralism of *Realpolitik*. From Dag Hammarskjöld and Folke Bernadotte to Olof Palme, and indeed including even Carl Bildt, the Swedish way has been one of whole-hearted support of binding international law, expressed in a language steeped in a deeply moralist vision of a new world order, one fashioned in the image of Swedish rationality, democratic values and benign social engineering.

By the early 1960s Swedish intellectuals were seriously debating the rather self-satisfied notion that Sweden was the "world's conscience". In an attempt to deepen the discussion, the prominent author Lars Gustafsson argued that in fact Swedish "Third Worldism" should be understood as a new and central aspect of Swedish national identity (Ruth 1984: 71). That is, as Arne Ruth summarized, internationalism acquired the status of national ideology: "Equality at home and justice abroad have come to be regarded as complementary and mutually supporting values" (Ruth 1984: 71).

This conception of a special Swedish gift for handling international conflicts in a rational, lawful and peaceful manner was fuelled partly by what was widely seen as a wise settling of two potentially explosive conflicts: the first in 1905, when Norway separated from the union with Sweden, and the second during the 1920s, when the question arose of what to do with the Finnish islands of Åland, whose population is Swedish-speaking. In both cases, Sweden acted in a manner that has been perceived as giving priority to lawful and peaceful conduct, even if that meant giving up what many might have thought to be a legitimate claim from a strictly national point of view, especially in the case of recognizing Finnish sovereignty over the Åland islands.

This vision of Sweden as particularly adept at handling potentially explosive situations has underpinned and inspired many ambitious initiatives when it comes to foreign aid, peace-keeping missions and disarmament schemes. The most eloquent and well known proponent of this ideology was Olof Palme, whose passion for foreign policy in this spirit became legendary. The most dramatic example was possibly his trenchant critique of the United States' war in Vietnam, but the same line of thinking was evident in his equally strong condemnation of the Soviet invasion of Czechoslovakia.

Still, a strong emphasis on national sovereignty remained during the postwar period, expressed both in the support of the rights of small states, including the struggle for national liberation in the Asian and African countries under Western Imperial rule. In an essay from the early 1980s on "Sweden's Role in the World", Palme summed up his view of the goal of Swedish foreign policy as befitting a developed and non-aligned nation:

> To secure in all situations and in the ways we choose ourselves, our national freedom of action in order to preserve and develop our society within our frontiers and according to our values, politically, economically, socially and culturally; and in that context, to strive for international détente and peaceful development. The realization that durable peace and détente are possible is a concept fundamental to social-democratic foreign policy since the beginning of the 1920's [...] The same concept has guided us as we have shaped our foreign policy with regard to the Third World in the 1960s and 1970s. We have taken a stand for national freedom and independence [...] As a small state we have as our goal a world in which the principles of sovereignty and non-intervention are

fully respected. This has also made it possible for Sweden, albeit to a modest extent, to build bridges between South and North in a period marked by crisis and the risk of polarization.

(Palme 1982: 244–45)

This quote makes clear the connection between "national freedom" and the preservation of "our values" on the one hand and the support for "small states" in general and Third World countries in particular on the other. In both cases the fundamental principle is that of respect for national sovereignty. The "internationalism" of Palme was not a matter of collapsing the world of nation-states into a World Federation, but rather a vision of a global order based on the right of all nations to create their own "people's home", broadly understood.

This attitude found expression in a preference for, at the one extreme, a global approach when it came to trade and supra-national organizations: GATT and the UN were frameworks within which Sweden found its place with natural ease. At the other extreme, this global perspective was complemented not by only an insistence on the sanctity of neutrality and the sovereignty of the nation-state, but also by a fondness for various Nordic – usually failing – cultural, economic and security arrangements. Indeed, the Nordic countries appeared as less problematic and more "natural" partners because they were perceived as culturally and ethnically close. Europe did not figure in this scheme of things, being simultaneously too close and too different. As the historian Mikael af Malmborg summarizes the debate over European integration between 1945 and 1959: "Norden, the world, and nothing in between" (Malmborg 1994).

This sceptical attitude towards continental Europe shaped the long-standing suspicion of the emerging European Union (at that time the EEC) and would remain salient well into the debates over EU membership in the 1990s. It took the form of a left-wing welfare-state nationalism that saw Europe south of the Nordic region as a backward bastion of the so-called 4 Ks: *Kolonialism, Kapitalism, Konservatism, Katolicism* (Colonialism, Capitalism, Conservatism, Catholicism). With its reluctant accession to the EU in 1994 – against the background of deep economic crisis – Sweden entered, however, a new phase in which both the centre-right and the left began to take post-national positions. This created an opportunity for new parties to appeal to the enduring attachment to national identity and nationalism, creating a political space for the Sweden Democrats – a party that was founded as late as 1988 and did not enter parliament until 2010, but by the elections of 2014 had grown to be the third largest party in Sweden.

Citizenship vs. human rights

In one sense it is not surprising that the ideals of citizenship and human rights become confused with each other. In fact, the idea of citizenship shares a common history with the notion of human rights. Both are pillars of modern political theory as it came to challenge the *ancien régime*, replacing a feudal and pre-democratic order, with its primacy of family, clan and estate, with a liberal political order based on the notion that all individuals are of equal value. The connection between civil rights – the rights of citizens – and human rights are clearly expressed in the founding documents of both the American and the French revolutions. In the French case this is obvious from the very title of the document: Declaration of the Rights of Man and the Citizen (1789). At the same time the tension between the rights of citizens and human rights is there from the outset. While the first paragraph of the French declaration proclaims that all "men are born and remain free and equal in rights", the third paragraph introduces a crucial limiting principle, namely that "the principle of any sovereignty resides essentially in the Nation. No body, no individual can exert authority which does not emanate expressly from it."

The close historical connection between citizenship-based rights and human rights was reasserted after the establishment of the Universal Declaration of Human Rights (UDHR) in 1948. While the UDHR stopped short of listing positive rights that would entail a global responsibility to provide services such as schooling and healthcare to all human beings, it did – especially in articles 22–26 – oblige the signatories to provide a certain level of social welfare to all members of each given society. Human rights have since increasingly become integral parts of the very concept of democracy (Keane 2009). But in practice rights have developed within sovereign states, where they have achieved legal status and become enforceable, a principle which was also enshrined in the UDHR. It was understood to be the responsibility of each particular state to realize these principles within its borders. As Hannah Arendt famously argued (1951), citizenship became "the right to have rights". Thus the logic suggested in the Declaration of the Rights of Man and the Citizen has held fast, tying enforceable rights to the power and sovereignty of states and assigning such rights primarily or even exclusively to citizens.

As suggested by T. H. Marshall in his seminal work *Citizenship and Social Class* (1950), rights have developed in stages, and the social rights typical of an evolved welfare state such as Sweden represent the third stage in a historical development towards a rights-based citizenship, where the first stage was the establishment of civil rights (individual legal rights) in the 18th century, and the second stage was the enshrining of political rights (universal suffrage), which gradually developed in the 19th century and were established more generally in the early 20th century. Social rights were, in Marshall's description, introduced to mitigate the inherent conflict in capitalist society between equal political and legal citizenship and an unequal distribution of material wealth.

The social rights of a welfare state are manifested through social policies that provide all citizens with a certain level of basic resources, such as education, health care, pensions and elderly care, regardless of wealth and income level. Social rights are, like the civil and political, meant to promote equal citizenship. But whereas political and civil rights by and large do not involve the transfer of large sums of money through taxation and government expenditure, social rights have become very costly and for that reason also controversial and subject to political conflict. For the promoters of social rights, the aim was to offer a vision of economic democracy and socio-economic fairness as well as to forge a sense of social cohesion in society (Dwyer 2010). Marshall himself never stated exactly which services should be considered as the basis of social rights, but he seems to have limited them to a basic standard of living and education. Furthermore, he also listed a number of obligations that citizens should adhere to in return for the social rights. These were to pay taxes, undergo schooling, serve in the military and generally be a good, trustworthy, civic-minded citizen (Johansson 2008).

The emphasis on this connection between rights and duties has endured, underlining the extent to which the modern welfare state at heart is an expression of a social contract characterized by mutual obligations between citizen and society within a bounded political community (Mead 1997). One might say that this social contract exhibits traits that places it midway between a legal contract, such as one might have in relation to an insurance company, and the solidaristic logic typical of families, clans and ethnic or religious communities. Many social rights in modern welfare states are conditional and contractual, assuming civic-minded, hard-working citizens who pay taxes and a trustworthy state that supplies social insurance benefits in return. Other rights, such as healthcare for all, education of children, care for the elderly and the protection of the disabled, assume a politics of solidarity and social investments within the framework of national community that go beyond the insurance logic. This second type of rights is, as scholars like Lister (2007) have argued, unconditional in the sense that the logic of private insurance, which depends on the insured paying a fee, is missing. Still, these rights are reciprocal and conditional in that they assume a link across generations and within the national community; the rights do not apply to children, the sick, the elderly or the disabled in general but specifically to those that belong to the nation-state in question.

In this context it is also important to note that to be deemed a worthy member of society, both employment and good behaviour are essential. It is sometimes claimed that the Nordic countries, like Sweden, with "social democratic welfare regimes" (Esping-Andersen 1990) offer social rights based on citizenship, in contrast to "liberal" regimes, such as the US, which provide benefits on the basis of need, and "conservative" ones, such as Germany, which grant rights based on work (the Bismarckian model). Similarly, the Swedish model of social rights is sometimes described as being "universal" or "general" rather than "selective" or "residual", that is, equal for all citizens rather than limited, in a stigmatizing way, to the poor and needy (Rothstein 2010). However, this is a distinction that dramatically underplays the extent to which, in fact, social rights in Sweden are often directly tied to employment status and income level, for example unemployment insurance, sick-leave insurance, parental leave insurance and pensions. Indeed, there is a clear historical legacy here that ties rights to obligations and the expectation that each adult and able-bodied citizen works and behaves well. Hence the well known figure of the "wholesome worker" – *den skötsamme abetaren* – central to the culture of the Swedish popular movements, which equally emphasized the duty of each member of society to accept individual responsibility and show "character", and the requirement to work collectively to improve society through civic engagement in social movements and political parties (Ambjörnsson 1988). Finally, it should be noted that a key manifestation of a social contract of the kind typical of the Nordic countries is the positive view of the state and the legitimacy of taxes. Taxes and trust are two sides of the same coin, expressing the mutual confidence between citizens and the state and the shared sense of a social contract institutionalized and made concrete through extensive social rights.

Human rights, on the other hand, are the inherent rights each human possesses simply by virtue of being a human being, regardless of either citizenship in a state or national belonging, including a range of freedoms, such as freedom of expression and worship, and freedom from need and fear. According to Amartya Sen, human rights can primarily be seen as ethical demands, rather than legal rights (Sen 2004). Indeed, the notion of "rights" has from the beginning created confusion, inviting interpretations that link human rights to law, rather than to morality or ethics. Indeed, as Sen points out, the rights claims made in American Declaration of Independence (1776) and the French Declaration of the Rights of Man and the Citizen (1798) were swiftly dismissed by critics like Jeremy Bentham (1792, cited in Sen 2004), who sought to debunk any talk of "natural" or "inalienable" rights as "nonsense", since they lacked legal foundation.

The complex relationship between ethics and law has continued to complicate theories of human rights to this day, especially since the establishment of UN conventions and treaties with a legal or quasi-legal standing, such as the UDHR in 1948, the International Covenant on Economic, Social and Cultural Rights (ICESCR) in 1966/1976 and the Convention on the Rights of the Child (CRC) in 1990. The trend towards greater emphasis on law is also related to what Charles Epp and others have called the "rights revolution" and the "juridification" of politics, which has spread from the United States to the rest of the world, entailing a challenge to majoritarian, democratic politics in the name of minority and individual rights, which occupy a position of higher law that can trump ordinary politics (Epp 1998; Trägårdh and Delli Carpini 2004). In the United States, this political strategy was central to the Civil Rights movement, which sought to undo the legacy of slavery and the enduring discrimination of blacks. A similar approach has been pursued by other groups – women, gays, disabled – who have sought to gain through courts what they have been unable to achieve through ordinary, majoritarian, democratic politics centred in elected parliaments.

Furthermore, with the general decline of international socialism after 1989, human rights have emerged as the new ideological basis for idealistic movements with global reach and claims (Moyn 2010). But it has also come to influence the political idiom in nation-states. In this spirit, modern welfare states, notably including Sweden, have come to refer not only to social rights tied to citizenship but also to human rights and UN conventions, such as the CRC. This complex interplay between national social rights and global human rights notwithstanding, the tension between social rights tied to taxation and state budgets and human rights, largely taking the form of unfunded mandates, can be observed in many countries. However, it has become especially acute in Sweden, a country with, on the one hand, an unusually comprehensive system of social services (schools, healthcare, elderly care, disability rights, parental insurance, pensions, and so on), which are provided according to a social rights logic, and, on the other hand, explicit ambitions to live up to human rights ideals and human rights conventions, of which Sweden historically has been a strong advocate.

One can also observe a trend in the other direction, namely in the way notions of social rights begin to influence the way human rights are conceived of and thought about – what Davy (2013) refers to as "social citizenship going international". As Sen (2004) has noted, seeing social (or welfare) rights as part of human rights is a profoundly controversial question, since the inclusion of these kinds of rights would, as he put it, "vastly expand the claimed domain of human rights" (Sen 2004). These rights are "positive" rights, which cost money, as opposed to the "negative" (civil and political) rights that he describes as the "classical" human rights. Thus, social rights are sometimes referred to as "second generation rights", which involve the globalization of social citizenship and invoke the utopia of a global welfare state. As Davy (2013) notes, influential scholars writing about human rights, such as Sam Moyn and Lynn Hunt, have largely bypassed this recent turn towards global social rights, which Davy argues only emerged in earnest after 1993. This development is tied to the passing of the ICESCR, noted above, a UN covenant that, to date, 164 countries have signed. The impact of the ICESCR is relatively understudied but, like other UN conventions, its focus has been on nudging countries to provide basic services in their own state, with a primary goal of alleviating poverty, rather than on requiring a full-fledged welfare state along Nordic lines. As with other UN conventions, the ICESCR is global in scope, but implementation is still assumed to be carried out by and taking place in each separate state. That is, the ICESCR is not primarily constructed to address the consequences of migration and refugee flows – which recently have become the focus of the increasingly obvious problem associated with extending tax-funded rights to non-citizens following a human rights logic.

Migration, the paradox of national democracy and the promise of post-national citizenship

The tensions between tax-based social rights and boundless human rights, between national and cosmopolitan ideals, have long been a concern for academic research, not least in the context of migration to and within Europe.

European integration fuelled more rapid migration within the EU at the same time as globalization increased flows from the outside world into the EU in the context of large gaps in economic wealth and political stability. This exposed the European countries to an increasing in-flow of political and economic refugees from the global South, creating new classes of "denizens"; non-citizens who could lay claim to some but not all of the rights associated with citizenship (Soysal 1994). Since both national community and democratic citizenship were historically linked to the emerging global dominance of the nation-state, and rested fundamentally on boundaries that excluded at the very same time as they included, the increased volume and speed of migration has tended to expose, on the one hand, a profound challenge to national sovereignty (Ruggie 1993; Wæver 1995; Sassen 1995) and, on the other hand, what scholars refer to as the "paradoxes" or "contradictions" of (national) democracy. Thus, the political philosopher Seyla Benhabib (2004) has argued that national democracies are intrinsically exclusionary, since they offer full rights and privileges only to members, i.e. citizens. In spite of the fact that they speak internally in a universalist language rooted in notions of equal democratic rights, this is a bounded universalism that distinguishes between national citizenship and universal personhood (Bosniak 2008).

In the context of migration this contradiction translates into differential treatment of persons on the basis of legal rules shot through with political and moral claims that demonstrate the persistence of racialized hierarchies and notions of ethnic-cultural membership. This raises the question whether it is possible to simultaneously promote societal bonds of national citizenship and accommodate ethnic and religious diversity (Barker 2013). The attempts by the EU and its Member States to stem the flow of migration and reassert boundaries have led concretely to brutal border controls, detentions and deportations of "aliens", and more broadly to a moral and political crisis. The contradictions between universal moral rules founded in notions of human rights, and nationally bounded claims derived from the idea of citizenship in particular nation-states, have thus become ever more clear. One line of inquiry in this field of scholarship has become known as "crimmigration" – the study of how the challenge of migration is handled as a crime issue rather than as a question of how to extend democracy and alleviate suffering (Stumpf 2006). One recent contribution to this body of research is the work by the sociologist Vanessa Barker, including a book with the telling subtitle "*Walling the Welfare State*" (2017), in which she highlights how Sweden, a self-proclaimed "good society", subjects refugees who have committed no crimes to harsh measures such as imprisonment and enforced deportation (Barker 2015, 2017).

The politics of 2015: nationalism vs. globalism and the collision of the two Swedish models

Both of the Swedish models of solidarity and rights described above – one national, the other international – enjoy deep historical roots and strong popular legitimacy. But, as noted at the outset of this chapter, while these two models have peacefully co-existed for a long time – thought of not only as compatible, but even as synonymous – the tensions and contradictions between them have now become evident. What makes the current dilemma poignant is that both ideals are so central to Swedish national identity. While many countries in the West can sport welfare states, albeit of varying reach and ambition, few countries have staked their reputation so tightly on the welfare-state idea. Similarly, many countries engage in foreign aid, but outside the Nordic region few have been as vocal in proclaiming as their national mission such a strong commitment to foreign aid efforts and human rights ideals.

This makes it all the more important to lay bare the contradictions between these two models and their internal rights logics and solidarity ideals. So let us try to boil down these differences to a limited set of contrasts.

First, one model gives primacy to the nation-state and citizenship and presupposes borders and differences. Social rights are limited to those who are citizens or enjoy legal residence in the country. Furthermore, many of those rights are tied to work, income, taxes and the national budget. The primary rights logic is *conditional reciprocity* tied to employment and earned income (pensions and unemployment-, parental leave- and illness-insurance); the secondary rights logic is *solidarity within the nation-state*, covering those who cannot yet, any longer or ever work: the young, the elderly, the infirm and the disabled (healthcare, obligatory schools, higher education, elderly care and disability benefits). The other model – human rights – invokes a borderless universalism. Human rights are unconditional and are derived from quasi-religious ethics with roots in natural law ideals. The primary rights logic is *altruism and compassion*. Rights are intrinsic to every human being, not earned through work or contributions, nor limited by citizenship. Indeed, modern human rights doctrine developed as a reaction to the atrocities and discriminatory policies carried out in the name of the nation before and during the Second World War.

The two models differ in another crucial regard. The social rights that constitute central parts of the Swedish welfare state are ultimately products of national, democratic and political processes characterized by a rather crass and cold-hearted concern for money and keeping within budget. Even though one often talks of "rights", these are not rights in a strict legal sense that would be claimable in a court of law. Rather they take the form of legislation through which the state takes a broad but unspecified responsibility for providing certain collective goods, such as healthcare, on equal terms for all citizens and legal residents. These rights are at heart political and collective rights, rather than juridical and individual rights. Human rights, on the other hand, are fundamentally different in this regard. Indeed, they are meant to serve as trump cards that protect individuals and minorities from abuse and arbitrary decisions made by politicians, not just in authoritarian regimes but also in majoritarian democracies. Thus, constitutional amendments detailing individual and minority rights at the national level, as well as international conventions that seek to protect human rights globally, express attempts to nudge governments to respect universal human rights and to counteract discrimination against minorities. International conventions establishing human rights catalogues are thus, as argued above, examples of the juridification of politics and the challenge by lawyers, judges and courts to the primacy of politicians, parliaments and the sovereignty of the nation-state. Human rights are, to summarize, to be thought of as a juridified secular religion, decoupled both from the nation-state and from the mundane concerns with budgets and popular legitimacy that characterize ordinary democratic politics.

In other words, global human rights ideals stand as a matter of both legal principle and moral logic in conflict with the idea of national citizenship. The Swedish refugee crisis of 2015 exposed this latent conflict. In official Swedish policy it was expressed by sudden shifts between open and closed borders; between high-strung human rights rhetoric and defensive references to the primacy of citizenship; between appeals to the idea of national sovereignty on the one hand, and to international conventions that challenge that very sovereignty on the other. These contradictions were apparent also in civil society. Even as thousands of citizens volunteered to welcome and assist refugees under the banner "Refugees Welcome", an increasing number of (other) citizens joined or otherwise supported the anti-immigration Sweden Democrats in their critique of Swedish immigration policy.

Left and right critiques of the nation-state

Enthusiasm for post-national visions can be found across the political spectrum in Sweden, among politicians, journalists and academics as well as among ordinary citizens. "Nationalism" and "Swedishness" have become dirty words for the media elite and the mainstream parties. Conversely, human rights ideals have become trump cards in the political debate, played against those who are accused of being "nationalists", a label that is often is associated with other pejoratives such as "populist", "xenophobic" or "racist". The twin ideas of national community and citizenship, historically central to both modern democracy and the sense of solidarity without which the welfare state would not be possible, have increasingly given way to a new language that stresses cosmopolitan ideals at the expense of national democracy. The human rights left and the neo-liberal centre-right have united in their shared abhorrence of borders and "excluding" nation-states that embrace what is sometimes called, disdainfully, "welfare chauvinism". The centre-right has come to imagine that we now live in a global market society, while the left prefers a post-national rhetoric that speaks in the language of "no borders" and human rights.

The critique of the nation-state has been directed at both components: the *state* as well as the *nation*. But notably the *nation* is primarily the target of the post-national left, which sees it as excluding and xenophobic, whereas the *state* is more likely the bête-noire of the liberal right, which sees the state as an obstacle for free enterprise. In the one case, a vision of a solidaristic and equal world without borders beckons at the horizon; in the other, a global market society without annoying, politically motivated regulations and taxes is the ideal. Together these anti-nationalists and anti-statists constitute an unholy but very powerful alliance: a perfect storm that from two directions undermines the legitimacy of the nation-state.

The allure of post-national utopias creates problems for both the Swedish centre-right alliance, on the one hand, and the Social Democrats and their coalition partner, the Greens, on the other. On the political right, the vision of a global market society in which we ride an "urban express" (Schlingmann and Nordström 2014) towards an exciting future designed by destructively creative entrepreneurs, is not always shared by the centre-right's voters – who at times take a rather sceptical view of their leaders' enthusiasm for free trade and immigration. In this regard Sweden is by no means unique. On both sides of the Atlantic the political debate during 2016 and 2017 has been dominated by anxiety and anger. To some extent this is a consequence of the fact that the current economic order has pitted the winners of globalization against the losers. While economists in general insist that immigration and free trade in the long term have positive, aggregate effects, many citizens in Western countries apparently feel – in an era of increasing inequality and declining social mobility – that these rather abstract advantages by no means compensate for their own immediate and highly concrete losses and sufferings. This angry gap between elites and people characterizes politics throughout the West; from the vote in favour of "Brexit" in the UK to the election of Donald Trump as the new US president, populist right-wing politicians favouring nationalism over globalism have successfully channelled popular revolt while casting the opponents as beholden to urban, cosmopolitan elite interests.

But cosmopolitan internationalism is above all a challenge for the parties to the left, not least the Swedish Social Democrats, whose ideals and historical legacy are so intimately tied to the idea of national democracy and the vision of a solidaristic "people's home". Indeed, the democratic welfare state has been the chief instrument for the political left throughout the Western world in its mission to tame capitalism and create a balance between politics and market. This project, anchored in the nation-state's promise of a civic social contract through which citizens pay taxes in exchange for social rights, is now challenged not only by neo-liberal globalization at the material level, but also ideologically by a cosmopolitan internationalism in which human rights have come to be pitted against citizenship and national belonging.

This turn towards internationalism is directly linked to the decline of the old socialist left after the fall of the Berlin Wall. With the collapse of communism and socialism as a serious alternative to liberal democracy, a political vacuum developed on the left that was filled by human rights idealism, attracting young people and finding expression both in academic programmes and in a variety of political initiatives spearheaded by organizations like the Ford Foundation, Amnesty International and Human Rights Watch, as well as by environmental organizations with global ambitions, such as Greenpeace. Common to these professional, elite-driven organizations was a post-national and even post-democratic stance that tended to stress the role of global civil society, international conventions and juridified rights rather than that of the democratic nation-state. By betting on law over politics, these organizations risk finding themselves in the same situation as the US Civil Rights movement; by overinvesting in lawsuits and court action and neglecting ordinary politics the latter came face to face with a political backlash that still defines American political culture and politics today. Indeed, with the election of Trump as President this backlash has now reached a new level of vengeance.

In this perspective, the current crisis in Europe and the West more broadly is primarily a crisis of social democracy. The post-national turn of the left has to grapple with the fact that the nation-state refuses to disappear in spite of all the rhetoric about globalization. Indeed, while economic globalization continues to make headway, political globalization seems to be stuck or even in retreat, as the current crisis of the EU shows. Thus all democratic politics remains national at a time of a growing gap between elites who can more easily imagine being or becoming world-citizens and the many who continue to live local, national lives. And this tension characterizes the left as much as the right. For each Donald Trump, there is a Bernie Sanders; both criticize free trade and defend the primacy of the nation-state and its borders.

In spite of these similarities, the undermining of the nation-state is uneven in its effects. For the winners in the global market economy, de-nationalization and post-democratic tendencies result in more freedom from troublesome politicians and social movements that demand regulations of the market and tax-based social investments in the name of social justice. That the liberal right has a critical perspective on the classical nation-state makes sense, but for those who have historically fought for equality, solidarity and an extensive welfare state, the demise of the moral logic of the nation-state would appear far more problematic.

Of particular concern is the tendency to reduce all resistance to post-national visions to a question of xenophobia, ethnic nationalism and racism. Linked to this is the equally problematic turn towards identity and group politics, whereby the supposedly anti-racist left paradoxically affirms group and community identities along racial, ethnic, gender, sexual and religious lines. This contemporary political style, characteristic of the post-modern left, tends to deepen divisions in society and cloud the vision of a common interest uniting all citizens as individuals. What is in danger of getting lost here is what I call "civic statism", that is a preference for the nation-state rooted in an enduring commitment to the traditional social contract that allies the individual citizen and the state through the elaborate system of taxes paid and social rights earned.

Conclusions

Now the question beckons of how Sweden in years ahead is to balance its dual commitments to the national welfare state and to international solidarity and, thus, to reconcile the growing tensions between the two Swedish models. This is a challenge that is generally shared by many if not all democratic nation-states, but which is perhaps posed in a particularly dramatic way in Sweden. Indeed, it is in Sweden that the question of whether it is possible to scale up the politics of solidarity and cooperation is posed most sharply. Is it possible to "go Nordic" beyond the national level? Can a similar approach be realized at the European or global level? Is it possible for reciprocity and cooperation, as social, economic and political practices, to develop at levels above that of the nation-state?

One answer is that the Swedish social contract has been based on reciprocity and conditions, not on altruism or unconditional love. The rather stern moral principles that have informed this social contract require of each person not simply to demand rights or expect compassion, but to perform duties and uphold their own end of the contract. Above all it is a social contract based on institutions, taxation, borders and a common legal space. The hallmark of a high-trust society, Nordic style, is the acceptance of high taxes, which in turn are linked to social rights that are earned; not charities that are given for free out of the goodness of the (state's) heart.

In contrast, as argued above, the politics of solidarity that has been projected, so far, onto the global stage has followed a different logic. It has revolved around unconditional altruism rather than conditional reciprocity; it has operated in an institutional and legal vacuum, rather than being firmly grounded in a democratic institutional structure – the nation-state – where reciprocal rights and duties are tightly linked to taxes, the legitimacy of which is itself the ultimate expression of both social trust and confidence in common institutions. It has celebrated a no borders vision, in sharp contrast to the Swedish and Nordic social contracts, which are profoundly predicated on stable borders and zero-sum budgets.

One starting point for a project aiming to scale up solidarity would be the reconstruction of the EU as (or if) it learns its lessons from Brexit. It is becoming clear that the problem with the EU is the mismatch between a unified market, on the one hand, and a political system plagued by a democratic deficit, on the other. While there is talk of "European citizenship", this is to a great extent a matter of rhetoric since the fundamentals of a social contract are missing. There are neither taxes nor social rights; the borders are fluid and largely unprotected; there is no unified army, nor European conscription; there is no president or otherwise elected executive power. As Thierry Baudet has pointed out, the EU is currently "stuck somewhere halfway between a federation and mere intergovernmental cooperation" (Baudet 2012).

In order to overcome this unstable situation, the fundamental choice is between moving towards a true European nation-state and de facto absorption of the Member States, or to retreat into a less ambitious but possibly more realistic option of a European free trade zone, which, of course, was the principle that guided the European project to begin with. The third option would be to refine the current EU by building a federal order that aims to create a clearer balance with respect to sovereignty between the different levels of community without bypassing the lower levels. As both Baudet and Wilson have argued, it is questionable whether this splitting of sovereignty is workable. For Wilson and his colleagues, the core principles for the efficacy of groups concerned the centrality of "clearly defined boundaries" and the importance that the group can negotiate both costs and benefits, i.e. taxes and social rights, within those boundaries (Wilson et al 2013). Thus we again find ourselves with the basic choice of either retreating into smaller groups or nation-states or expanding the nation and the polity to embrace a larger and perhaps more diverse demos. The latter option may entail a social contract that is centred less in the dense, substantive democracy of the Nordic welfare states than in a "thinner" social contract in the form of a procedural republic along US lines, or an even more minimalist, libertarian "night-watchman" state.

For Sweden – and the EU – to reconcile its internal contradictions, national and global principles must be brought into better harmony. This means for Sweden that it must recognize the legitimacy of the nation-state while rethinking its global ambitions. One option is to think in terms of a division of labour between state and civil society. The Swedish state would focus on the national social contract and the logic of a high-trust society: high taxes paid by citizens in exchange for extensive social rights. Swedish civil society, on the other hand, could carry out the task of providing assistance on a global scale in the spirit of humanity and human "rights". However, this must entail the de-juridification of human rights, returning them to their proper domain of moral values, rather than legal claims. Then the principles of voluntariness and charity could replace the notions of legally binding rights and duties, eliminating the current political tensions that follow from the confusion of the rights of citizens with the wish to assist non-citizens in need and despair. History can, in fact, provide examples. During the First World War, Sweden received tens of thousands of children from war-torn Austria, but the sole role of the state was to provide legal entry into Sweden; all financial burdens and legal responsibilities were borne by civil society organizations like Save the Children and the Red Cross, and, principally, by the foster families that volunteered to receive the children. In this way (some, maybe many) Swedes could, as global civil society actors, reconstitute Sweden as a moral superpower in the realm of global civil society, while the Swedish State would concentrate on its primary task of fostering and protecting the "home of the citizens".

References

Ambjörnsson, R. (1988) *Den skötsamme arbetaren*. Stockholm: Carlsson.
Arendt, H. (1951) *The Origins of Totalitarianism*. London: Deutsch.

Barker, V. (2013) Democracy and Deportation: Why Membership Matters Most. In: K.F. Aas and M. Bosworth (eds), *Borders of Punishment: Migration, Citizenship and Social Exclusion*. Oxford: Oxford University Press.

Barker, V. (2015) Border Protest: The Role of Civil Society in Transforming Border Control. In: L. Weber (ed.), *Rethinking Border Control for a Globalizing World*. Abingdon, UK: Routledge.

Barker V. (2017) *Nordic Nationalism and Penal Order: Walling the Welfare State*. Abingdon, UK: Routledge.

Baudet, T. (2012) *The Significance of Borders: Why Representative Government and the Rule of Law Require Nation States*. Leiden: Brill.

Benhabib, S. (2004) *The Rights of Others: Aliens, Residents, and Citizens*. New York: Cambridge University Press.

Berggren, H. and Trägårdh, L. (2006; 2015) *Är svensken människa? Gemenskap och oberoende i det moderna Sverige* (2nd ed.). Stockholm: Norstedts.

Berggren, H. and Trägårdh, L. (2010) Pippi Longstocking: The Autonomous Child and the Moral Logic of the Swedish Welfare State. In: Helena Matsson and Sven-Olov Wallenstein (eds), Swedish Modernism: Architecture, Consumption and the Welfare State. London: Black Dog.

Bosniak, L. (2008) *The Citizen and the Alien: Dilemmas of Contemporary Membership*. Princeton: Princeton University Press.

Childs, M. (1936) *Sweden: The Middle Way*. New Haven, CT: Yale University Press.

Davy, U. (2013) The Rise of the "Global Social": Origins and Transformations of Social Rights under UN Human Rights law. *International Journal of Social Quality* 3 (2): 41–59.

Dwyer, P. (2010) *Understanding Social Citizenship: Themes and Perspectives for Policy and Practice* (2nd ed.). Bristol: Policy.

Epp, C. R. (1998) *The Rights Revolution: Lawyers, Activists, and Supreme Courts in Comparative Perspective*. Chicago: University of Chicago Press.

Esping-Andersen, G. (1990) *The Three Worlds of Welfare Capitalism*. Cambridge: Polity.

Johansson, H. (2008) *Socialpolitiska klassiker*. Malmö: Liber.

Keane, J. (2009) *The Life and Death of Democracy*. London: Simon and Schuster.

Lister, R. (2007) Inclusive Citizenship: Realizing the Potential. *Citizenship Studies* 11 (1): 49–61.

Malmborg, M. (1994) *Sverige och den västeuropeiska integrationen 1945–1959*. Lund: Lund University Press.

Marshall, T. H. (1950) *Citizenship and Social Class, and Other Essays*. Cambridge: Cambridge University Press.

Mead, L. M. (1997) Citizenship and Social Policy: T. H. Marshall and Poverty. *Social Philosophy & Policy* 14 (2): 197–230.

Moyn, S. (2010) *The Last Utopia: Human Rights in History*. Cambridge, MA: Harvard University Press.

Palme, O. (1982) Sweden's Role in the World. In: B. Rydén and W. Bergström (eds), *Sweden: Choices for Economic and Social Policy in the 1980s*. London: Allen and Unwin.

Rothstein, B. (2010) *Vad bör staten göra? Om välfärdsstatens moraliska och politiska logik*. Stockholm: SNS Förlag.

Ruggie, J. (1993) Territoriality and Beyond: Problematizing Modernity in International Relations. *International Organization* 47 (1): 139–174.

Ruth, A. (1984) The Second New Nation: The Mythology of Modern Sweden. *Dædalus*, 113 (1): 53–96.
Sanandaji, T. (2017) *Massutmaning: Ekonomisk politik mot utanförskap och antisocialt beteende*. Stockholm: Kuhzad Media.
Sassen, S. (1995) On Governing the Global Economy. Draft of the 1995 Leonard Hastings Schoff Memorial Lectures, 34. [Later published as part of *Losing Control? Sovereignty in an Age of Globalization*. New York: Columbia University Press, 1996].
Schlingmann, P. and Nordström, K. (2014), *Urban Express*. Stockholm: Forum.
Scocco, S. and Andersson, L. (2015) *900 miljarder skäl att uppskatta invandring*. Stockholm: Arena Idé.
Sen, A. (2004) *Elements of a Theory of Human Rights*. Princeton: Princeton University Press.
SFS 2016:1242 Lag om ändring i lagen (2016:752) om tillfälliga begränsningar av möjligheten att få uppehållstillstånd i Sverige
Soysal, Y. N. (1994) *Limits of Citizenship: Migrants and Postnational Membership in Europe*. Chicago: University of Chicago Press.
Stumpf, J. (2006) The Crimmigration Crisis: Immigrants, Crime, and Sovereign Power. *Am Univ Law Review* 2: 367–420.
Trägårdh, L. (1990) Varieties of Volkish Ideologies. In: Bo Stråth (ed.), *Language and the Construction of Class Identities*. Gothenburg: Gothenburg University Press.
Trägårdh, L. (1997) Statist Individualism: On the Culturality of the Nordic Welfare State. In: Bo Stråth and Øystein Sørensen (eds), The Cultural Construction of Norden. Oslo: Scandinavian University Press.
Trägårdh, L. (2002) *Sweden and the EU: Welfare State Nationalism and the Spectre of "Europe"*. London: Routledge.
Trägårdh, L. (2010) Rethinking the Nordic Welfare State through a neo-Hegelian Theory of State and Civil Society. *J of Political Ideologies* 15 (3): 227–239.
Trägårdh, L. (2013) The Historical Incubators of Trust in Sweden: From the Rule of Blood to the Rule of Law. In: M. Reuter, F. Wijkström and B. Kistersson Uggla (eds), *Trust and Organizations: Confidence across Borders*. New York: Palgrave Macmillan.
Trägårdh, L. and Delli Carpini, M. (2004) The Juridification of Politics in the United States and Europe: Historical Roots, Contemporary Debates and Future Prospects. In: Lars Trägårdh (ed.), *After National Democracy: Rights, Law and Power in America and the New Europe*. Oxford: Hart Publishing.
Trägårdh, L., Wallman Lundåsen, S., Wollebaek, D. and Sverdberg, L. (2013) *Den svala svenska tilliten: Förutsättningar och utmaningar*. Stockholm: SNS Förlag.
Wæver, O. (1995) Identity, Integration and Security: Solving the Sovereignty Puzzle in EU Studies. *Journal of International Affairs* 48 (2).
Wilson, D. S., Ostrom, E. and Cox, M. E. (2013) Generalizing the Core Design Principles for the Efficacy of Groups. *Journal of Economic Behaviour & Organization*.

6 Scandinavian feminism and gender partnership

Cathrine Holst

The Scandinavian region is maybe not a feminist "nirvana" (Lister 2009), but compared with most other regions its gender equality credentials are extraordinary. Undoubtedly, Sweden, Denmark and Norway are in several respects "woman-friendly societies" (Hernes 1987), or have at least come a long way towards becoming so. The Scandinavian countries' effective inclusion of women in paid work is well known, but the contemporary international gender equality indexes which regularly rank these countries on top (see Elias 2013; Liebowitz and Zwingel 2014) measure gender gaps in employment and earnings, but also in education types and levels, political representation, health, and time spent on house work, leisure and volunteering.[1] The consistently high scores of the Scandinavian countries, Finland and Iceland on these rankings solidly confirm Gösta Esping-Andersen's (1999) influential diagnosis of "liberal" and "conservative" welfare states as less gender equal than the Nordic "social democratic" types.

And clearly, the Scandinavian/Nordic region stands out not only when we look at gender equality performance, but also, and unsurprisingly per haps, when we look at gender equality policies. Since the 1960s, a significant increase in female labour participation has gone hand in hand with welfare state expansion through public care for children and the elderly. Not least, Scandinavian family policy (extensive public subsidization of parental leave schemes and childcare arrangements) has seemingly been beneficial to the inclusion of women in public life and the labour market (Ellingsæter and Leira 2006; Leira 2012; Ellingsæter 2014). All the Scandinavian countries have, moreover, established both gender equality legislation that combines protection against discrimination with a duty for public authorities and employers to promote equality, as well as gender quotas to promote representation and participation in both political parties and corporate boards.

This is not to deny the non-trivial variation within the region. A recent in-depth mapping of Nordic gender gaps places Denmark consistently below the other Nordic countries on most indicators, and pinpoints Sweden as the front-runner (Skjeie and Teigen 2016). On the policy level, there are also considerable differences, for example in gender quota arrangements. Sweden and

Norway have political party quotas and parental leave schemes with quotas for fathers, while Denmark has none. Meanwhile, the Nordic front-runner, Sweden, still lacks quotas for corporate boards (Teigen 2015). Moreover, as we will see towards the end of this chapter, some noteworthy gender gap challenges remain in this region – and to be sure, even a relatively "women-friendly" political culture and citizenship ideal may have blind spots.

However, compared with the outside world, Scandinavian gender equality scores are close to one another and consistently high. This gives rise to a certain "social hope"[2] (Rorty 1999) in a world where campaigners for gender equality seem widely to be on the defensive (Walby 2011; Fraser 2013).[3] A complex question, naturally, is how the Scandinavian region – internal variation and limitations aside – has become so successful in gender equality terms. This chapter will not provide anything close to a full answer, but will take as its point of departure the core design principles for successful groups devised by Elinor Ostrom (1990) and later developed, applied more widely and given a grounding in evolutionary theory by David Sloan Wilson and colleagues (for example Wilson et al. 2013). In short, Ostrom and Wilson predict that socially and evolutionary viable groups are relatively clearly delineated and regulated by cooperative orientations and arrangements, consensus-inducing procedures, effective but graduated sanctions and conflict-resolution mechanisms, cost–benefit proportionality, and subsidiarity norms. Applied on our case, the prediction is that the Scandinavian region's successes and societal achievements[4] in the gender arena are interlinked with cultural schemes and institutional arrangements that inhabit and contribute to, but also give flesh and local colour to, the consolidation of something similar to the "core design" ethos. More concretely, this essay will provide a test of this hypothesis, by scrutinizing and providing examples of how the historical and contemporary expressions of feminism – be they cultural, political or intellectual – resonate with such an ethos in the case of Norway.[5] Specifically, it is suggested that the limited influence of Anglo-American style liberal feminism; a strong, but in the end reform-oriented tradition of "feminism of difference"; a social-democratic-tempered approach to radical feminist ideas and patriarchy conceptions; a firm egalitarian embedding of feminist claims across the political spectrum; Norwegian feminism's strong emphasis on political representation and participation; its pragmatic outcome, negotiation and compromise orientation and focus on piecemeal progress; and, finally, its stress on shared values and community ideals, are all characteristics that could be considered conducive to group success (Wilson et al. 2013).

Norwegian feminism seems also to have characteristics that distinguish it from feminism in Sweden or Denmark – and this internal pluralism of Scandinavian feminism will be addressed only superficially in this short chapter. Norwegian/Scandinavian feminism will furthermore be casually contrasted with "Anglo-American feminism", and occasionally with other feminisms, such as "French feminism", to show how these branches of feminism seem less Ostromian-Wilsonian in spirit. Such an endeavour is obviously risky, given not only the internal richness but also the contradictions of feminist theory and practice in France and the US. Not least in the US there is a glaring discrepancy between the many innovative and progressive contributions to our intellectual understanding of gender relationships and gender equality on the one hand, and the much more meagre results in terms of societal progress and gender equality in practice on the other hand. Yet this comparative approach, even if sweeping and full of limitations, reflects the underlying conviction of this contribution: namely, that there are some region-specific cultural patterns to the ways in which gender relations are approached, talked about, reflected upon and institutionalized that deserve more scholarly attention.

Finally, it should be stressed that the questioning of some of Norwegian feminism's characteristics at the end of this chapter does not cast doubt on the many gender equality achievements of the Scandinavian societal model. However, it is a reminder that no real-world society can serve as a fully fledged blueprint for other societies, that not all good things necessarily go together, and that the more detailed criteria of "successful groups" are not beyond reasonable controversy.

In Anglo-American feminist debate there is often talk of a "liberal hegemony". This hegemony is both embraced and opposed, but few would deny that feminist liberalism constitutes a vital part of this region's feminist reflection. Liberal ideology comes in several versions, including "social", "democratic" and even "multicultural" variants (see Kymlicka 1995), but individuals' right to non-interference, private autonomy and freedom of choice belong to its normative core. Anglo-American feminist liberals have typically tacked their emancipatory projects onto this core, while at the same time advancing liberal thinking and exposing the patriarchal blind spots of mainstream liberal thinkers (for example Okin 1989; Phillips 1992; Nussbaum 1999; Cornell 1998, 2009; Hampton 2002). In sharp contrast to this state of affairs, there can be no talk of a dominant liberal branch in Norwegian feminism: this feminism *lacks a liberal hegemony*.

During the first wave of feminism in the 19th century, the standard liberal argument of equal rights for all was less pronounced and important in the struggle for women's right to vote and other political rights than the instrumental argument that women had the proper moral constitution, national sentiments and loyalty and so should be considered as responsible political subjects (Danielsen et al. 2015).

During the second-wave revival in the 1960s and 70s, liberal feminism was more or less absent from the intellectual and political discourse of Norwegian feminism (Holst 2000). Unsurprisingly, there was a Marxist renaissance in this period. Accordingly, there was vivid controversy between proponents of different approaches within socialist ideology, Marxism and critical theory – and in particular between socialists, on the one hand, and so-called radical feminists, on the other. Whereas the latter considered "patriarchy" and not "capitalism" to be the fundamental cause of women's oppression and emphasized the emancipatory potential of women's culture, the more orthodox socialists saw in this culture primarily a culture of the oppressed and as a perverted creation of capitalism and/or patriarchy. There was certainly also an older generation of feminists with experience from the post-war civil rights, peace and environmental movements who were socialized into the pre-second-wave vocabulary of "gender roles" (see Holter 1970 for a classical exploration). They were also more reluctant to adopt the Marxist and radical feminist approach of the "new" women's movement. However, "the feminist liberal" was not really a relevant figure in these debates.

A similar pattern occurs when we move to the legislative sphere and the discussions and mobilization among Norwegian feminists leading up to the watershed 1979 Gender Equality Act. The dominant controversy concerned whether this act was really "women-centred" enough. To what extent should feminist legislation be stated in gender-neutral terms? To what extent should it not only allow, but also serve women's interests and emancipation? Was the need a "women's law", or rather legislation that symmetrically ensured anti-discrimination and equal opportunities for all? Standard themes in feminist liberal jurisprudence – whether the new law adequately ensured equal treatment, negative freedoms, limitations on illegitimate state intrusion, etc. – were not an issue in the internal feminist debates and struggles around the legislation. Instead, this issue remained in the margins of deliberations over feminism and what feminists should care about (contrast here with liberal feminist approaches, for example Cornell 1998; Cohen 2002).

From the 1990s and into the new millennium, Norwegian feminist thinking – along with much Western feminism – entered a phase of intense self-reflection and even self-criticism spurred by globalization and new class inequalities, multicultural and postcolonial critiques, poststructuralist doctrines of "deconstruction" and radical social constructivism. Once more, and in sharp contrast to Anglo-American debates, this period of reflexivity in the Norwegian feminist intellectual and academic field had few, if any, pronounced liberal feminist voices (Holst 2005: 269–271). What we saw instead was the rise of an even more accentuated and fine-grained critique of liberalism and liberal philosophy; of its abstract, reductive, contract-based approach to human relations and society; its anti-social, anti-relational idea of human agency; its sharp, misleading distinction between private and public issues; its universalist pretentions – inevitably ending up in "false universalisms"; and its rationalistic bias and misconception of the role of sentiments.

Examples of how liberal assumptions and predictions fall short in the case of Norwegian feminism could be multiplied. Consider the story of women's shelters. Such shelters were established across the country during the second-wave period and onwards, and were initiated and run by a strong branch of the Norwegian women's movement – the women's shelter movement – on the basis of radical feminist platforms and sisterhood slogans: Women help and protect one another and stand together against patriarchal violence. Consequently, and until only recently,[6] these shelters, and their funding and services, were not a responsibility assumed by the government. For a long time then, the handling of a core liberal concern – the right to exit from abusive relationships – was delegated to civil society organizations dependent on women's solidarity and community spirit, and unequipped to give the abused any legal guarantees. In the exact same period – and this is the paradox from a liberal perspective – the welfare state developed to ensure that women in Scandinavia received unprecedented levels of economic and social welfare. The liberal narrative would, of course, rather have it that the state should ensure minimal liberal rights – such as basic shelter rights – before it develops ambitious welfare legislation and policies.[7] However, dominant political conceptions in Scandinavia and a range of real events tend to turn this order of things upside down: a vast, women-friendly welfare state has developed relatively smoothly, whereas core liberal guarantees, including what could arguably pass as fundamental night-watchman state requirements, have actually been more controversial or added later.

We see this in the women's shelter case, but also in the rather mediocre speed of the development of basic anti-discrimination laws and sanctions. Norwegian feminist scholars, activists and "femocrats" have pushed for advanced work–family balance policies, state feminist gender machineries – including a separate Ministry of Children and Equality, an Equality Ombudsman and an Equality Tribunal – and laws obliging both the public sector and private enterprises to promote gender equality. Norwegian anti-discrimination laws still fail, however, to be fully in accordance with UN and EU recommendations (Blaker Strand and Hellum 2017; Skjeie et al. 2017), and, despite recent amendments, basic legal-aid schemes for discrimination complainants are lacking. To be sure, the Norwegian women's movement has welcomed recent revisions to strengthen anti-discrimination legislation and citizens' access to justice, but legislative reforms along these lines have arguably not been so high on the agenda, and the normative significance of such reforms in a rule of law perspective has been toned down and overshadowed by the women's organizations' grievances with other parts of the law.[8]

At the same time, and comparatively speaking – and this must be emphasized – the Norwegian gender equality and anti-discrimination legislation and apparatus in its current shape undoubtedly ensure citizens an advanced protection of civil and political rights. At a time when we see "illiberal democracies" rise in Europe, the Scandinavian region's consolidated consensus-oriented liberal democracies offer some consolation: there is no doubt that liberal legislative and constitutional requirements and even a relatively well developed liberal political culture have been gradually and firmly established and made a part of Scandinavian governance and citizenship ideals. Yet what we have seen very little of is conscious application and institutional design on the basis of liberal philosophy and principled liberal feminist arguments. It is symptomatic that the political scientist Helga Hernes (1987: 138), in her authoritative portrayal of the "women-friendly Scandinavian social democracy", depicts the "social democratic citizenship ideal", with its emphasis on participatory rights, social equality and community, as the antidote to the typical liberal political imaginary concerned with the interests of "the part-time citizen" and his/her right to "personal integrity of body and mind", private autonomy and "self-realization".

To be sure, there is intra-Scandinavian variation in how liberalism and liberal culture is perceived and interpreted. In Denmark, there is a tradition of liberal argument that has resulted in a more pronounced critical approach both to gender quotas and to sex buyer laws (Borchorst 2014; Siim et al. 2017). The Danish approach on these points resonates better with Anglo-American feminist liberalism in its reluctance to interpret equal opportunities as a requirement of *parité* – 50/50 distributions of positions between women and men, as well as its inclination to regulate prostitution under social and labour law, as opposed to criminal law (Cornell 2000; Nussbaum 2010). Symptomatically, in Sweden and Norway there is currently a ban on buying sex, while in Denmark, sex work has been progressively decriminalized. Yet, even in Denmark, liberal negative-right arguments tend not to come from within the feminist camp.

Another question is what this all means from the Ostromian-Wilsonian perspective of effective groups. Are Scandinavian societies successful gender equality champions because liberalism has played a limited role among feminist thinkers, policy-makers and activists? And if so, should we conclude that a liberal ethos is incompatible with cultivating the norms that seem to make societies work well? Surely, the implications of this finding must not be overstated or taken the wrong way. Scandinavian culture, law and politics have developed clear liberal features, and generally there is no reason why groups cannot be cooperative, consensus-oriented or proportional in cost–benefit assessments within the frames of a broadly speaking liberal culture and institutions that protect fundamental rights.

At the same time, strong versions of normative individualism and the typical liberal emphasis on negative freedoms – on upholding a sharp distinction between private issues and public concerns, and on the limited scope of legitimate state intervention – can arguably complicate the cultivation of core design principles. Generally, it is harder to succeed with negotiations across dividing interests and differing values for piecemeal, proportional reform if actors bring absolutes to the table. Yet this is exactly what liberals tend to do: they defend their ideas of privacy and the role of the state as "right" and "just", and their claims easily take the shape of unconditional and unnegotiable claims. It will also undoubtedly be more challenging to develop collectivity and effective groups if the primary focus is on what serves the individual and ensures the individual's sphere of freedom against efforts to ensure cooperation and community relations. In brief: liberal negative-right arguments and core design principles should not be perceived as inevitable opposites, but they do seem to pull in somewhat different directions.

We must be similarly wary when reading an Ostromian-Wilsonian spirit into the *Scandinavian style "feminism of difference"*. Closely connected to liberal feminism in Anglo-American feminist discourse is the notion of an "equality feminism"; that is, a feminism that concentrates on ensuring women's equality in terms of rights, treatment, opportunities, etc. Equality feminism has certainly played a central role in Norwegian discourse, although with a less pronounced liberal framing, and from the 1980s onwards it was part of the social democratic ideology celebrating social and political equality and women's inclusion in all societal arenas on a par with men. A feminism of difference, emphasizing women's distinctive "culture" (Ås 1974), "dignity" (Holter 1996), "lifeworld" (Fürst 1995), "experiences" (Widerberg 1994), "rationality of care" (Wærness 1984) and "responsibility" (Ve 1999), has, however, been key during all waves. The contention of the Norwegian "difference feminists" has been that women should strive not only to become equal to men, but also to cultivate and pursue their own particular orientations, values and morality as women, and to "feminize" public institutions and struggle for gender equality, but from a "women's perspective". Several of the most profiled 19th-century suffragettes were of this conviction, and "the rhetoric of difference" (Skjeie 1991; see also Solheim 1998) in debates on women's right to political participation and representation has persisted. The most recent example is the process leading up to gender quotas for corporate boards, where the central argument was not one of women's equal opportunities, but rather that "pluralism", and the difference women would make to corporate decision-making, is good for enterprises, economic growth and corporate responsibility (Øyslebø Sørensen 2013).

The mainstream of Scandinavian-style feminism of difference is, however, strikingly different from the more renowned French feminism of difference, where "the feminine" is depicted as the ultimate and essential "other", and women are regarded as "abjects" (Kristeva 1980), unable to speak "as women" within the confines of Western patriarchal culture and the current social and political system (for a discussion, see Moi 1985). The Norwegian feminism of difference similarly stresses female commonality and collectivity, but is at the same time framed and defined as a basis for pragmatically intervening in and reforming existing institutions. Once more, this is not to say that figures such as Julia Kristeva, Luce Irigaray and Helen Cixous somehow contribute to blocking the development of cooperative principles and effective groups – this chapter explores suggestive affinities; it does not aim at identifying causal relationships.[9] Yet, unquestionably, the Norwegian reception, interpretation and implementation of difference arguments have been distinctively and comparatively pragmatic.

We see something similar in the "*patriarchy modified*" approach that is arguably characteristic of Norwegian intellectual and political feminist culture. An innovation of Anglo-American second-wave feminism was radical feminist theories of patriarchy: the idea that there is a gender hierarchy where men have more power than women and power over women because they are men (and women are women) (for example Millett 1970; Firestone 1970; Pateman 1988; Walby 1990). The notion of patriarchy has always been part of Norwegian feminism, even during the 1970s. A review of a selection of dissertations and central anthologies published in this period shows that theories of patriarchy are a key backdrop to feminist exchange and research (Holst 2000). However, confrontational variants of radical feminism in which gender relations are regarded as a zero-sum game and women's and men's interests as starkly opposed in the end gained little support – opening up a space for gender partnership and the cultivation of core design norms that a more purist and less adaptive patriarchy approach could easily have restricted. We see this in the way Norwegian feminists have typically embraced the social democratic welfare state and regarded it as a hallmark of "women-friendliness" (Hernes 1987; Leira 2012). A striking contrast is the Anglo-American "New Left" feminist criticism of the welfare state as a "public patriarchy" paternalistically patronizing women and reducing them to clients (Young 1997; Pateman 1998; Fraser 2013; for a criticism, see Hernes 1987).

A somewhat different accentuation in Sweden and Norway on this point should surely be recognized. More confrontational variants of radical feminism seem to have played a more significant role in Swedish feminist discourses and scholarship. A prominent example is Yvonne Hirdman's (1988) analysis of Swedish society in terms of a "genus system" (*genussystemet*) in her contribution to the Swedish Power and Democracy Study, and how this notion later became a central framing of Swedish policymaking in the area of gender. Similarly, if we compare Swedish and Norwegian third-wave statements – for example the Swedish anthology *Fittstim* (1999), which set the stage all over Scandinavia for a feminist revival amongst younger generations, with Norwegian follow-ups – the Swedish original is more strongly defined by radical feminist parameters running in parallel with the narrative of a more "individualist" post-second-wave feminism. Furthermore, even the landscape in Norway is varied, from Hanne Haavind's (1982) critique of Scandinavian gender equality as an "ideology" masking gender hierarchy, to more recent system-oriented analyses of gender power. Yet in the end old and new variants of gender/sexual system analyses have had limited effects both on scholarly discourse and on popular debates, as well as on policy-making.

Norwegian feminism has, moreover, been a distinctive *social feminism*. To be sure, in academic and intellectual debates, not least in the period of self-reflection and after, Scandinavian social democracy has been under both scrutiny and fire for being ethnocentric and heteronormative: it fails, it is argued, to take cultural pluralism and colonial heritages properly into account, and it tends to idealize heterosexual intimacy and family life. Moreover, the "feminism of difference", also so pronounced in this region, implies a strong critique of mechanical equality-thinking and a one-eyed focus on redistribution, technocratic rationality and materialism.

However, Scandinavian feminism is in the end robustly embedded in arguments of social equality. Postmodern, radical feminist and difference-oriented critics are typically not in favour of "less" redistribution or welfare, but rather articulate demands for a welfare state that is better adapted to the fact of sexual, ethnic and religious pluralism. Importantly, the social democratic welfare state so far receives support across the left/right continuum. Historically, there has been broad consensus around its development and central features (Hatland et al. 2001; Barth et al. 2003), and all in all this consensus remains. This is not to deny the existence of considerable controversy, for example around recent New Public Management reforms, taxation levels and family policy. But in short, and in particular if compared with other countries and regions, Norwegian conservatives have a relatively egalitarian orientation.

This also goes for non-left-wingers among Norwegian feminists. Historically, some campaigners of women's issues have come from the conservative party, and in the aftermath of the third wave, starting from around the turn of the millennium, a new generation of "bluestockings" stepped forward with the ambition of formulating a feminism for liberal conservatives. However, the disagreements they have with the left-wing feminists are in the end rather modest. There is no question of rolling back the welfare state. The Norwegian bluestockings oppose, for example, the ban on buying sex and are sceptical of earmarking parts of parental leave exclusively for fathers. However, in both instances the proposed alternatives are firmly social liberal or social democratic: the ban is to be replaced by social and educational policies; the one-year parental leave scheme is to be kept and remain publicly funded, but families should be granted "freedom of choice" to organize family life and their everyday schedules as they deem fit. In other words, the Norwegian "blue" feminism is, in the end, very far from the free-market equal treatment arguments for women's civil and enterprise rights that are found in corners of American feminist debates.[10]

Scandinavian feminism's rock solid defence of a "social" democracy and a redistributive welfare state, together with the broader culture of egalitarian sentiments in this region, are, obviously, likely to be conducive to the consolidation of a core design ethos of collectivity and community. Furthermore, and peculiarly, this welfare orientation is combined with firm measures against welfare dependency. The Scandinavian welfare model is often depicted as a model in which the protection of universal social rights is key. This is true, but universal arrangements are in the end combined with a strong "workfare" orientation and a reciprocity norm (Kildal and Kuhnle 2005). In other words, the size of welfare benefits depends significantly on labour market participation, and it has been argued that the basic social democratic moral code is less "claim your rights" than "do your duties, then claim your rights". The same goes for feminists, who have mostly subscribed to the workfare approach and its persistent focus on how to get women into employment. Once more, we see how Scandinavian cultures and feminisms seem to resonate with fundamental preconditions for the development of effective groups and group interaction.

Workfare, and not only "welfare", and the more general emphasis on rights–duties reciprocity sit well with ideas of graduated sanctions and cost–benefit proportionality.

With all this in mind, some contemporary interventions in Anglo-American feminist debates make less sense on Scandinavian soil. One such intervention is Nancy Fraser's (2013) call for a feminism that is less enmeshed in identity politics and once more engages with redistributive issues. Clearly, within Scandinavian feminism, redistribution has been relatively high on the agenda all along. Another such intervention is Anne Phillips's (1998) call for a feminism that focuses more strongly on the "politics of presence", to quote the title of one of her books; a feminism with a concern for the recognition of cultural identities and redistribution of material goods, but also for representation in political processes and decision-making. Once more, this is arguably what Scandinavian feminism has very much been about. The objective, at least since the 1970s, has been *to make feminism participatory*. The "women-friendly" welfare state and gender machineries are maybe not without technocratic features but, all along, a clear anti-technocratic tenet has clearly run in parallel: in Scandinavia, state feminism "from above" is combined with feminism "from below". This amounts to the inclusion of civil society, stakeholders and the women's movement in political life and policy-making, as Helga Hernes notes (1987: 153). Hence, there is in this regime, she says, potential for a fruitful "alliance" between women and the welfare state (Hernes 1987: 162).

The participatory ambition is reflected in the high legitimacy of gender balance parameters and quota policies. Norwegian corporate boards and public commissions are required to have at least 40/60 distributions between women and men, and many other organizations, in both the public and the private sectors, have introduced measures to achieve the prescribed balance of the sexes. Such measures generally have high support, also among many groups of men (Skjeie and Teigen 2003), and worries such as those typically found in Anglo-American contexts about how quotas, affirmative action and descriptive representation compromise equal treatment requirements and meritocracy, are seldom raised in Norwegian debates.

Even more significant is the Scandinavian-style idea of democracy that goes beyond parliamentarian institutions and national elections (Engelstad et al. 2017), in which the social democratic ambition is "democratization of all areas of social life" (Hernes 1987: 144). A prerequisite for this is the historical development of "institutional interdependence and a public-private mix, rather than a public-private split. Such a mix results in the absence of clearly-defined institutional boundaries" (Hernes 1987: 153), leading to the more concrete development of consensus-making institutions that catalyse negotiations and consensus-reaching where a diversity of interest groups, civil society organizations and experts are brought around the same table. One prominent example of such a consensus-making institution is the centralized tripartite corporate bargaining system, where the national unions, employers and the government negotiate on wages, pensions and working life regulations. Other interesting examples are the Scandinavian systems of public inquiry commissions – *Norges offentlige utredninger* (NOU), *Statens offentliga utredningar* (SOU), etc. – deliberative advisory committees composed of civil servants, academic researchers and/or interest group representatives mandated to analyse the state of affairs, define problems and formulate policies in areas of concern (Christensen and Holst 2017).

As expected perhaps, given this institutional context, Scandinavian feminism stands out as relatively *pragmatic as well as compromise- and reform-oriented.* Exaggeration and caricature on this point must, however, be avoided. Reformism and a practical approach is, of course, not the full story of feminist intellectual and artistic life in this region. Also in Scandinavia there are independent feminist artists, writers and intellectuals that care less about applicability, consensus-making and broad societal impact. Arguably, a certain radicalism and individualism lie at the heart of true intellectual and artistic life, irrespective of cultural and institutional contexts. Furthermore, the more practically inclined among Scandinavian feminists have taken issue with aspects of how the contemporary consensual decision-making systems tend to work. Specifically, the centralized collective bargaining system has been accused of working in favour of male-dominated unions and men's economic interests (Skjeie and Teigen 2003).

At the same time, there is a long and influential tradition among feminist activists, professionals and scholars of effectively utilizing all the available channels and consensus-making mechanisms. An example is the role of public commissions in the gender equality and anti-discrimination area. Only during the 2000s did such commissions prepare new legislation on discrimination based on ethnic and religious (2005) and disability (2009) grounds and prepare legislation (2009) on a general yet comprehensive equality act. A commission on Equal Pay (2008) preceded the Gender + Equality Commission (2010–2012) with a mandate to investigate gender equality status and policies broadly. All these commissions involved gender experts and femocrats among the commission members and/or in the secretariat, and invited detailed reports from stakeholders, including women's organizations. Once more, we see a clear parallel with Ostrom's and Wilson's framework of effective groups: the core design ethos essentially prescribes negotiation, inclusion and piecemeal problem-solving, and this remains very much the *modus operandi* of Scandinavian feminism.

Finally, this feminism is unusually hospitable to the specific core design principle of subsidiarity: the idea that decisions should be made on the most local level possible. For one thing, a branch of Norwegian feminism from the second wave onwards has been eager to explore and engage with women's situation and gender relationships in different sub-national regions and local communities (Engelstad and Gerrard 2005; Valestrand and Gerrard 1999). Underlying these enquiries and interventions is the idea that local communities are immensely valuable and need to be sustained both culturally and politically. Inspiration is drawn from recent postcolonial literature, but first and foremost, we see a feminist variant of a distinctively Norwegian periphery mobilization against the perceived cultural hegemony of and oppression from the centre.

However, the most important frame of reference for Norwegian feminist thinking and implementation is no doubt the nation-state and national community. Hernes captures yet again the feminist spirit of Scandinavia quite precisely. Here, the nation-state is not simply a constitutional, legislative and political unit; it is also "an ethical community with shared meanings, identities and symbols" and the basis for "the altruistic impetus" that is a precondition and characteristic for Scandinavian social democracy, its egalitarianism and "women-friendliness" (Hernes 1987: 141, 161).

To believe that gender equality and women's emancipation in accordance with social democratic standards require the cultivation of a thick *national ethos, shared values and a feeling of community* across strata and segments is to give feminism a so-called "communitarian" embedding (Holst 2005: 302–304). On the one hand, this should come as no surprise. The nation-state and women's partnership with the state and national community have served the women of this region well; no wonder national sentiments have a good reputation among many Scandinavians and are considered essential for the making of good societies. On the other hand, Scandinavian countries are internationally oriented: they have open economies, they have ratified international conventions and recognized international courts, they participate actively in international organizations, and they are donors of substantial amounts of humanitarian aid. To be sure, Scandinavian feminists both are included in and push for such international engagement, and so, to the extent that their feminism has a communitarian orientation, it is no doubt combined with a commitment to transnational dialogue, solidarity and institution-building.

However, if we look once more at the Norwegian feminist discourse more specifically, cosmopolitan visionaries are extremely hard to find. In Anglo-American feminist debates from the 1990s onwards, issues of transnational democracy and cosmopolitan justice have been key points of feminist reflection and theorizing. What we do see also among Norwegian feminists in this period is a stronger interest in how international human and women's rights conventions shape Norwegian law and policy-making among scholars of women's law and political science, in the state feminist apparatus and in some civil society organizations. There is, however, no question of a cosmopolitan wave of any sort. Instead, we often see the role of international organizations and commitments in the gender equality area toned down: standards and policies are framed as homegrown, "Norwegian", "Scandinavian" or "Nordic", even when they are national adaptions of UN conventions or EU laws (Skjeie et al. 2017). The reason for this is likely the high trust in national political institutions both in the general citizenry and among feminists, and a commitment in large parts of Norwegian society to small-scale government and nation-state democracy. The sceptical attitude towards the European

Union among many Scandinavian feminists is illustrative in this respect, and very different from the EU-friendliness found among feminist scholars and activists in many non-Nordic European countries.

All in all, then, it seems reasonable to conclude that Scandinavian feminism is hospitable to the development of a core design ethos in a range of ways. Scandinavian feminism is social, democratically inclined, consensus-oriented, pro gender partnership, ambivalent to cosmopolitanism, and not very hospitable to negative-right arguments. Furthermore, the contention of this chapter has been that the Ostromian-Wilsonian spirit of this region's feminism presumably has contributed to the success of the struggle for Scandinavian gender equality.

Such a conclusion raises, of course, several and quite fundamental questions: Is what we have before us unequivocally a success story? Could things not be better, even in Sweden, Norway and Denmark, and could they not be better even in the realm of gender equality? We have already noted how Denmark falls behind its Nordic partners on international gender gap indexes. In addition, despite high overall rankings on these indexes for countries in this region, some gender gaps remain relatively high (Skjeie and Teigen 2016). Gender segregation within labour markets is, for example, strong and stable: women tend to crowd in female-dominated occupations within the public sector that are on relatively low pay scales. A considerable gender pay gap remains as a result of this gender segregation, but also because about one-third of employed women work part time. Furthermore, there are comparatively few Scandinavian women in senior executive positions in enterprises. They achieve top positions in other arenas – politics, civil service, civil society – but not so often in economic decision-making.

Maybe there are also connections between these less celebrated facets of Scandinavian society and its feminist reflection, approaches and discourses. Commentators have, for example, pointed to the likely linkages between the relatively strong feminism of difference tradition and a resistant gender segregation in the labour market (Solheim 2007).

Furthermore, whether something is a success or not depends, of course, on the assessment parameters applied. Human and social progress, and even "women-friendliness", seem in the end to amount to something more than just sustaining even distributions of positions and resources between women and men. Arguably, individual freedom in all its facets, and respect for minority views and ways of living are goods for all, women and men, and we should remember that gender gap indexes do not count them in. Similarly, whether all the identified features of Norwegian and Scandinavian feminism that have been highlighted here should be regarded as beneficial in all respects also depends on perspective. Where some see freedom from liberal dominance, others find more of a liberal deficit; where some see a vital tradition of feminism of difference, others see a feminism that reproduces stereotypes of women's commonalities; where some identify a sensible defence of subsidiarity, others see a cosmopolitan deficit; etc.

In short, modern societies are, as John Rawls (1971; 1999) famously put it, characterized by "the fact of reasonable pluralism". Obviously, people can hold illegitimate views and sustain indefensible norms and practices – there are "primary goods" that all should cherish regardless of whatever else they cherish. But just as often, people disagree or act and socialize in different and even conflicting ways because they quite reasonably interpret and rank social values, norms and principles differently.

A crucial question is what this state of affairs implies for how we are to understand and use the Ostromian-Wilsonian idea of effective groups. Maybe we should interpret the idea literally and strictly, and consider the cultivation and consolidation of such groups as valuable beyond disagreement; as not up for grabs for evolutionary reasons. But more likely – and more in accordance with what evolutionary thinkers themselves prescribe for their approach – the idea of effective groups is to be understood in more Rawlsian terms, as a more general framing of what we should aim for evolutionarily, giving considerable scope for reasonable interpretation and contestation. If so, there is also plenty of leeway to assert both that Scandinavian feminism and gender partnership ideas inhabit a significant core design spirit that has been conducive to gender equality successes in the region, and that reform and critical debate remain both sensible and important.

Notes

1 The EU Gender Equality Index includes the widest set of dimensions of the international indexes. Among its indicators are gaps between women and men: in overall employment rates; in the education, human health and social work sectors; in job quality and mean monthly earnings; among graduates of tertiary education; in participation in caregiving and educational activities outside work, cooking and housework, sports, cultural or leisure activities outside the home, voluntary or charitable activities; among Ministers, members of Parliament, and in company boards; and in life expectancy, healthy years lived, and unmet medical needs. Sweden, Denmark and Finland top the ranking, and estimates by Skjeie and Teigen (2017) show that EU non-members Norway and Iceland generally score similarly to the Nordic EU members.
2 Rorty reminds us that social hope depends less on the state of affairs than on our ability to make inspiring and mobilizing "redescriptions". The path to a "less painful future where men do not thank God [...] they were not born women" lies in the "creative use [...] of language" in ways that that "change instinctive emotional reactions" (Rorty 1998). Accordingly, what is central is not, or at least not only, this or that score on welfare indicators, but how we conceptualize, interpret, explain and assess what this means for us. Broadly speaking, this chapter is part of such an endeavor, with feminism and gender equality in Scandinavia as a point of departure.
3 A recent expression of this is the collapse of the global UN Beijing +20 Women's Conference in 2015 after obstruction from an alliance ranging from conservative Muslim states to Russia and the Vatican.
4 See Knutsen 2016 for overviews of the characteristics and merits of the Nordic/Scandinavian societal model in a range of domains.

5 I rely here on my previous studies of feminism in Norway (Holst 2000, 2005, 2017).
6 In legislation from 2009, the shelters were officially made a public responsibility and so transformed into a service of the welfare state.
7 See Rawls' (1999: 63) so-called lexical ordering of principles. Rawls himself did not spell out the implications of his first prioritized freedom principle for women, but this is spelled out by Cornell (1995), Okin (2002) and Hampton (2002).
8 In a spring 2017 amendment, the conservative government initiated a set of legislative changes, including loosening the private sector's duty to promote gender equality.
9 This is also not to deny that French feminism and deeper articulations of "the feminine" and difference feminism have influenced figures in the Norwegian intellectual field (for example, see Mortensen 1994, 2002).
10 Consider, for example, Ellen Frankel Paul's (1993) argument against market regulation: since discrimination decreases productivity, unregulated markets and basic rule of law standards are sufficient to protect women against wage discrimination over time.

References

Ås, B. (1974) Om kvinnekultur. In: *Kvinnens årbok 1974*. Oslo: Pax.
Barth, E., Moene, K. and Wallerstein, M. (2003) *Likhet under press. Utfordringer for den skandinaviske fordelingsmodellen*. Oslo: Gyldendal Akademisk.
Blaker Strand, V. and Hellum, A. (2017) Solbergregjeringens forslag til reformer på diskrimineringsfeltet. *Kritisk juss* 53 (1): 4–34.
Borchorst, A. (2014) Fortrop og bagtrop i ligestillingspolitikken. *Social Politik* 2: 24–28.
Christensen, J. and Holst, C. (2017) Advisory Commissions, Academic Expertise and Democratic Legitimacy: The Case of Norway. *Science and Public Policy*. https://doi.org/10.1093/scipol/scx016
Cohen, J. (2002) *Regulating Intimacy. A New Legal Paradigm*. Princeton: Princeton University Press.
Cornell, D. (1995) *The Imaginary Domain. Abortion, Pornography & Sexual Harassment*. New York: Routledge.
Cornell, D. (1998) *At the Heart of Freedom. Feminism, Sex, and Equality*. Princeton: Princeton University Press.
Cornell, D. (ed.) (2000) *Feminism & Pornography*. Oxford: Oxford University Press.
Cornell, D. (2009) *Moral Images of Freedom*. New York: Rowman and Littlefield.
Danielsen, H., Larsen, E. and Owesen, I. W. (2015) *Norsk likestillingshistorie*. Oslo: Fagbokforlaget.
Elias, J. (2013) Davos Women to the Rescue of Global Capitalism. *International Political Sociology* 7(2): 152–169.
Ellingsæter, A. L. (2014)Nordic Earner-Carer Models – Why Stability and Instability? *Journal of Social Policy* 43(3): 555–574.
Ellingsæter, A. L. and Leira, A. (2006) *Politicising Parenthood in Scandianvia: Gender Relations in Welfare States*. Bristol: The Policy Press.
Engelstad, E. and Gerrard, S. (eds) (2005) *Challenging Situatedness: Gender, Culture, and the Production of Knowledges*. Delft: Eburon.
Engelstad, F. et al. (eds) (2017) *Democracy and Institutional Change*. De Gruyter Open.

Esping-Andersen, G. (1999) *The Three Worlds of Welfare Capitalism*. Princeton: Princeton University Press.
Firestone, S. (1970) *The Dialectics of Sex: The Case for Feminist Revolution*. New York: Farrar, Straus and Giroux.
Fraser, N. (2013) *Fortunes of Feminism: From State-managed Capitalism to Neoliberal Crisis*. New York: Verso.
Fürst, E. L. (1995) *Mat – et annet spark. Rasjonalitet, kropp og kvinnelighet*. Oslo: Pax.
Haavind, H. (1982) Makt og kjærlighet i ekteskapet. In: R. Haukaa et al. (eds), *Kvinneforskning. Bidrag til samfunnsteori*. Oslo: Universitetsforlaget.
Hampton, J. (2002) Feminist Contractarianism. In: L. M. Antony and C. E. Witt (eds), *A Mind of One's Own*. Cambridge: Westview Press.
Hatland, A., Kuhnle, S. and Romøren, T. I. (2001) *Den norske velferdsstaten*. Oslo: Gyldendal.
Hernes, H. (1987) *Welfare State and Woman Power: Essays in State Feminism*. Oslo: Scandinavian University Press.
Hirdman, Y. (1988) Genussystemet – reflexioner kring kvinnors sociala underordning. *Tidsskrift för genusvetenskap* 3: 49–63.
Holst, C. (2000) *Sosiologi, politikk og kvinnelighet*. Bergen: SVT Press.
Holst, C. (2005) *Feminism, Epistemology & Morality*. Saarbrücken: VDM Dr. Müller Verlag.
Holst, C. (2017) *Hva er feminisme*. Oslo: Universitetsforlaget.
Holter, H. (1970) *Sex Roles and Social Structure*. Oslo: Universitetsforlaget.
Holter, H. (1996) *Hun og han. Kjønn i forskning og politikk*. Oslo: Pax.
Kildal, N. and Kuhnle, S. (2005) *Normative Foundations of the Welfare State*. London: Routledge.
Knutsen, O. (2016) *The Nordic models in Political Science: Challenged, but Still Viable?* Oslo: Fagbokforlaget.
Kristeva, J. (1980) *Powers of Horror. An Essay of Abjection*. Colombia: Colombia University Press.
Kymlicka, W. (1995) *Multicultural Citizenship: A Liberal Theory of Minority Rights*. Oxford: Oxford University Press.
Leira, A. (2012) Omsorgens institusjoner, omsorgens kjønn. In: A. L. Ellingsæter and K. Widerberg (eds), *Velferdsstatens familier*. Oslo: Gyldendal Akademisk.
Liebowitz, D. J. and Zwingel, S. (2014) Gender Equality Oversimplified? Using CEDAW to Counter the Measurement Obsession. *International Studies Review* 16 (3): 362–389.
Lister, R. (2009) Nordic Nirvana? Gender, Citizenship, and Social Justice in the Nordic Welfare State. *Social Politics* 16 (2): 242–278.
Millett, K. (1970) *Sexual Politics*. Colombia: Colombia University Press.
Moi, T. (1985) *Sexual/Textual Politics: Feminist Literary Theory*. New York: Routledge.
Mortensen, E. (1994) *The Feminine and Nihilism: Luce Irigaray with Nietzsche and Heidegger*. Oxford: Oxford University Press.
Mortensen, E. (2002) *Touching Thought: Ontology and Sexual Difference*. Lanham: Lexington Books.
Nussbaum, M. (1999) *Sex & Social Justice*. New York: Oxford University Press.
Nussbaum, M. (2010) *From Disgust to Humanity*. Oxford: Oxford University Press.
Okin, S. M. (1989) *Justice, Gender, and the Family*. New York: Perseus.
Okin, S. M. (2002) "Mistresses of Their Own Destiny": Group Rights, Gender, and Realistic Rights of Exit. *Ethics* 112 (2): 205–230.

Ostrom, E. (1990) *Governing the Commons: The Evolution of Institutions for Collective Action*. Cambridge: Cambridge University Press.
Øyslebø Sørensen, S. (2013) *Likestilling uten kjønn?* Trondheim: Norges teknisk-naturvitenskapelige universitet.
Pateman, C. (1988) *The Sexual Contract*. Stanford: Stanford University Press.
Pateman, C. (1998) The Patriarchal Welfare State. In: J. Landes (ed.), *Feminism, the Public & the Private*. Oxford: Oxford University Press.
Paul, E. F. (1993) *Equity and Gender. The Comparable Worth Debate*. London: Transaction Publishers.
Phillips, A. (1992) Must Feminists Give Up on Liberal Democracy? *Political Studies* 40 (1): 68–82.
Phillips, A. (1998) *The Politics of Presence*. Oxford: Oxford University Press.
Rawls, J. (1999 [1971]) *A Theory of Justice*. Oxford: Oxford University Press.
Rorty, R. (1998) Feminism and Pragmatism. In: *Truth and Progress: Philosophical Papers. Volume 3*. Cambridge: Cambridge University Press.
Rorty, R. (1999) *Philosophy and Social Hope*. London: Penguin.
Siim, B. et al. (2017) Gender Equality without Gender Quotas: Dilemmas in the Danish Approach to Gender Equality. In: E. Lepinard et al. (eds), *Transforming Gender Equality*. Cambridge: Cambridge University Press.
Skjeie, H. (1991) The Rhetoric of Difference: On Women's Inclusion into Political Elites. *Politics and Society* 19 (2): 233–263.
Skjeie, H. and Teigen, M. (2003) *Menn imellom. Mannsdominans og likestillingspolitikk*. Oslo: Gyldendal Akademisk.
Skjeie, H and Teigen, M. (2016) The Nordic Gender Equality Model. In: O. Knutsen (ed.), *The Nordic models in Political Science: Challenged, but Still Viable?* Oslo: Fagbokforlaget.
Skjeie, H., Holst, C. and Teigen, M. (2017) Benevolent Contestations: Mainstreaming, Judicialisation and Europeanization in Norwegian Gender+ Equality Debate. In: H. MacRae and E. Weiner (eds), *Towards Gendering Institutionalism*. London: Rowman & Littlefield International.
Solheim, J. (1998) *Den åpne kroppen*. Oslo: Pax.
Solheim, J. (2007) *Kjønn og modernitet*. Oslo: Pax.
Teigen, M. (2015) The Making of Gender Quotas for Corporate Boards in Norway. In: F. Engelstad et al. (eds), *Cooperation and Conflict the Nordic Way*. Berlin: De Gruyter Open.
Valestrand, H. and Gerrard, S. (1999) Mellom Harvard, Honningsvåg og Coto Sur. Kvinneforskning 1: 89–107.
Ve, H. (1999) *Rasjonalitet og identitet*. Oslo: Pax.
Wærness, K. (1984) The Rationality of Caring. *Economic and Industrial Democracy* 5 (2): 185–211.
Walby, S. (1990) *Theorizing Patriarchy*. London: Basil Blackwell.
Walby, S. (2011) *The Future of Feminism*. Cambridge: Polity Press.
Widerberg, K. (1994) *Kunnskapens kjønn*. Oslo: Pax.
Wilson, D. S., Ostrom, E. and Cox, M. E. (2013) Generalizing the Core Design Principles for the Efficiency of Groups. *Journal of Economic Behavior & Organization* 90: 21–32.
Young, I. M. (1997) *Intersecting Voices. Dilemmas of Gender, Political Philosophy, and Policy*. Princeton: Princeton University Press.

7 A welfare "regime of goodness"?
Self-interest, reciprocity, and the moral sustainability of the Nordic model

Kelly McKowen

Introduction

In contemporary Norway, there is perhaps no greater symbol of moral decay than the *"naver"*. A *naver* is someone who refuses to work or go to school, instead living on benefits and services provided by the Norwegian Labour and Welfare Administration (NAV). Public concern about *naving* arose in the wake of the far-reaching 2005 administrative reform that created NAV and initiated its national roll-out between 2006 and 2011. The NAV reform took what had been three separate public agencies – municipal social assistance services, Aetat (employment services) and the National Insurance Service – and amalgamated them into a one-stop shop. The new super-organization, NAV, would, its proponents believed, prevent people with complex needs from being bounced around different agencies, streamline the sizeable welfare state bureaucracy, and offer its "users" (*brukere*) – the choice was consciously made to drop the term "client" (*klient*) – holistic assistance that would protect their well-being while actively assisting them to re-enter the labour market (Reegård 2008; Andreassen and Aars 2015). *Flere i arbeid, færre på trygd*, policymakers said – "More in work, fewer on welfare."

What nobody anticipated was that NAV's name would become slang for some of the very problems the reform was designed to combat. In March 2012, the Norwegian Broadcasting Corporation (NRK) reported that employees at a NAV office in Hedmark county, just north of the capital, had observed that high school students were talking about using their eligibility for social assistance (*økonomisk sosialhjelp*) – a comparatively meagre, means-tested benefit – to take a year off school.[1] The teenagers referred to this legal but unethical practice, much to the consternation of the local NAV office, as *"naving"* (Rikvoll and Wold 2012). This introduced *naving* to the public discourse and catalysed an impassioned debate about dependency on the internet and in the pages of the country's daily newspapers. By the end of year, *"å nave"* – "to nav" – had so firmly entrenched itself in the Norwegian lexicon that the National Language Council recognized it as its new word of the year (Rostad 2012).[2] Since then, public interest – and anxiety – about *naving* has hardly abated. A selection of headlines from the past few years reflects the desires to understand the phenomenon and to stop it: "Earning more from NAV than from work"; "*Navers* Have Status"; "NAV Director Wants an End to '*Naving*'"; "Don't Want Youth to *Nav*"; "Stringent Requirements to Get Young *Navers* out of NAV".

The *naver* disrupts the otherwise flowery image of Norway as a "great and good place on earth" (Witoszek 2011: 14). This image dominates both domestic and international representations of contemporary Norway – a country conceived of as "good" in a double sense. On the one hand, Norwegian goodness is associated with the quality of the country's economic, political and social institutions: Norway's oil and gas sector has made it one of the richest countries in the world. Its democracy is stable, transparent and active. And along with its Nordic peers, it ranks at or near the top of the world in terms of socio-economic equality, gender equality, social mobility, work–life balance and transparency. On the other hand, Norway's reputation for goodness stems from the perceived moral superiority of the Norwegian people. Internationally, they are lauded as humanitarians and peace-builders (Skånland 2010). At home, they have constructed their own version of the famed "Nordic model", a distinctive political economic formation that joins an export-driven liberal market economy to a tax-funded, cradle-to-grave welfare system (Dølvik et al. 2014; Dølvik 2016). This welfare system, which Esping-Andersen (1990) cites as an example of a "social democratic welfare regime", is distinguished from the "liberal" welfare regimes of the Anglo-American world and the "conservative" welfare regimes of continental Europe by both the generosity of its benefits and services and their "universal" provision on the basis of citizenship or legal residence.[3] In short, with regard to both quality and morality, the Norwegians, to repurpose a felicitous concept coined by Tvedt (2003), have erected a "regime of goodness".

How, then, to make sense of Norway's alleged *naving* problem? The issue of *wilful* dependency in Norway is worth investigating not only because it subverts romantic representations of the Nordic country but because it suggests that the Nordic model, despite its notable achievements and long tenure, may be "morally unsustainable". More specifically, the *naver* allows one to ask fundamental questions about the extent to which the Norwegian – and, more broadly, Nordic – welfare state affects its own viability through the encouragement of free-riding, rent-seeking and fraud. These latter practices are animated by the "antisocial" norm of material self-interest, and involve maximizing individual return without a corresponding contribution to the shared pool from which resources are distributed. By contrast, "prosocial" norms reinforce practices that entail matching or exceeding one's individual material gain with contributions to the shared pool of resources. A morally unsustainable welfare state arrangement is thus one that undermines its own functionality via the inculcation of antisocial norms through economic incentives or the suppression of prosocial norms. Given the international interest in the Nordic model (Pontusson 2011), particularly in the wake of the recent global financial and Eurozone crises, understanding its effect on norms is critical to determining both how it functions and whether it should be seen by others as a standard to which to aspire.

This chapter aims to contribute to the broader study of the moral sustainability of the Nordic model with a close examination of one antisocial pattern of welfare-claiming, *naving*, in contemporary Norway. In the first part, I specify the nature of the Nordic model and describe why widespread *naving* would constitute an existential threat to Norway's version of it. I then briefly review two scholarly accounts of the Nordic model that provide separate frameworks for understanding the unique institutional conditions under which antisocial patterns of welfare-claiming like *naving* might arise. These accounts set the stage for a closer look at the Norwegian case. Here, I turn to comparative statistics and my own ethnographic research among the unemployed in Oslo in 2015–2016. In a particular, I draw on data from "unemployment life histories" collected from 30 individuals, including 4 non-immigrant women, 12 non-immigrant men, 8 immigrant women (2 from Lithuania and 1 each from Serbia, Latvia, China, Switzerland, Poland and Dubai), and 6 immigrant men (2 from Chile and 1 each from Romania, Portugal, Poland and Somalia). While the perspectives of this group are not representative of those of the Norwegian population as a whole, they nevertheless gesture toward shared experiences, practices and interpretations that unsettle received ideas about the lives – and motivations – of the unemployed. Using their accounts in tandem with comparative statistics, I cast doubt on *naving* as a pervasive empirical phenomenon and sign of moral climate change among users of the Norwegian welfare state. Instead, I offer a counter-interpretation that emphasizes the productive role that the *naving* discourse may play in promoting prosocial patterns of welfare-claiming. I conclude the chapter by suggesting that the greatest moral threat to Norway's welfare state – and, by extension, its iteration of the Nordic model – is the possibility that *naving* will be uncritically accepted by elites or the public as incontestable evidence of either weak work ethics or rampant material self-interest and calculating behaviour among some or all users of the welfare system. Such a reductive "folk anthropology", I argue, could justify reforms toward a more restrictive, more punitive – indeed, less "good" – welfare state.

The moral architecture of the Nordic model

To much of the world, the Nordic model is an unlikely thing – a *happy* marriage between capitalist productivity and socialist egalitarianism.[4] Unfortunately, public interest in the Nordic model has left both its admirers and detractors with a rather simplistic understanding of what it is and how it functions. Often, the Nordic model – or narrower "Scandinavian model" – is used to refer to what is more accurately called the "universal welfare state". This welfare state arrangement features an extensive public sector that provides a suite of tax-funded benefits and services during different phases of the life-cycle, primarily as a condition of citizenship, legal residence or labour market participation. The conflation of the Nordic model and the Nordic countries' universal welfare states, while not entirely incorrect, obscures the fact that the Nordic model encompasses a range of institutions which include but are not limited to those associated with individual and social welfare. Dølvik et al. (2014: 18–19) suggest envisioning the Nordic model as a "triangle" with three "institutional pillars" at its vertices. At one vertex is "economic governance", characterized by "an active, stability-oriented economic policy, international free-trade, and coordinated wage-formation in order to promote growth, full employment, and social leveling". At another vertex is organized labour–capital relations, comprising centralized collective bargaining based on export industries, as well as active labour market policy. The triangle is completed by a "public welfare" system – the universal welfare state – where, among other things, "universal schemes for income and standard maintenance facilitate high labor force participation and mobility". Working in combination, these three pillars support a democratic corporatist system (Katzenstein 1985) characterized by relatively high macroeconomic flexibility and adaptability (Dølvik et al. 2015), a compressed wage structure and comprehensive social citizenship for a broad swathe of the population.

Note that these pillars are interdependent – a wobble in one could, at least in theory, topple the model as a whole. Previous scholarship has primarily focused on exogenous "wobbles", including immigration (Brochmann and Hagelund 2010; Brochmann and Grødem 2013; Djuve 2016), Europeanization and globalization (Jæger and Kvist 2003) and the vicissitudes of global finance (Dølvik et al. 2015). Endogenous challenges, particularly those pertaining to the Nordic model's vulnerability to the effects of the universal welfare state on individual behaviour, have received less attention. Nevertheless, the need for such studies is clear. Scholars agree that through the institutionalization of incentives, the universal welfare state – or any welfare state arrangement, for that matter – has the potential to impact individual motivations and behaviour at different points in the life-cycle. According to Lindbeck (1995: 490), "The basic dilemma of the welfare state is that it partly disconnects the relationship between effort and reward by creating disincentives to work, saving, asset choice, and entrepreneurship." Some argue that these disincentives, which can result in antisocial norms that reinforce practices of free-riding, rent-seeking and fraud, are so significant that they hamper welfare states' capacities to reduce poverty and social exclusion, augmenting suffering for people on the margins of society (Murray 1984; Mead 1986; Lindbeck et al. 1999, 2003).

Beyond stifling policymakers who want to solve social problems, however, antisocial patterns of welfare-claiming may actually undermine the functionality of a particular welfare state arrangement. They do so in two ways. First, free-riding, rent-seeking and fraud weaken a welfare state arrangement's popular legitimacy. This legitimacy is predicated on voter self-interest, as well as ideological-normative considerations (Rothstein 2001), such as shared norms of exchange and reciprocity (Mau 2003, 2004), fairness and justice (Rothstein 1998; 2015). This point is made persuasively by Rothstein (1998: 141–143), who argues that for a given welfare state configuration to be viewed as legitimate, it must conform to a shared standard of "substantive justice" – that is, the distribution of social goods must be viewed as fair. Governments that fail to meet this standard will find that the public will make their desire for redistribution felt at the ballot box. Further, the system must reflect what the public views as a "just distribution of burdens". This means that voters want to know that others are also contributing to the pool of resources doled out in cash and in kind. Free-riding delegitimizes the welfare state and may cause people to withdraw their support. Last, the system must meet the public's criteria for "procedural justice". Even a welfare state arrangement that achieves substantive justice and a just distribution of burdens risks losing support if the system of allocation is corrupt. Antisocial patterns of welfare-claiming like *naving* represent a threat to the legitimacy of the universal welfare state because they signal that some members of society are unwilling to do their bit, skewing the distribution of burdens. In theory, the universal welfare state is designed so that able-bodied people work and pay the taxes that make the provision of goods and services possible. Rothstein's conception of welfare state legitimacy posits that if the contributors perceive that their peers are capable of working but have chosen not to in order to live on publicly funded benefits, they will eventually withdraw their support by voting for parties promising reform.

Second, antisocial patterns of welfare-claiming undermine the sustainability of welfare state arrangements by eroding their economic bases. In Norway, the universal welfare state is funded by taxes – primarily on income and consumption – and depleted by social expenditures. The common pool of resources into which taxes are paid, and from which social expenditures are drawn, constitutes a "fiscal commons" (Jakee and Turner 2002), which, like the communal meadows, irrigation systems, fisheries and other "common pool resources" famously studied by Elinor Ostrom (1990), is susceptible to overuse and thus depletion. On the use side, though welfare states have extensive rules that stipulate who is eligible to receive a given benefit and for how long, users are afforded variable amounts of discretion when it comes to claiming, depending on the scheme in question and personal circumstances. Just because one is jobless and eligible to receive unemployment benefits for two years, for instance, does not mean one ought to leave the labour market for that long. Indeed, social expenditures would no doubt increase markedly if everyone claimed all the benefits to which they were legally entitled. In addition to legal use, social expenditures also reflect illegal utilization, as less scrupulous users claim benefits to which they are not entitled by misrepresenting their situations. On the funding side, the fiscal commons of the welfare state is depleted by tax avoidance and evasion, both of which decrease the store of resources from which social expenditures are drawn. Both overutilization and underfunding create pressure on policymakers to enact either entitlement reform (e.g. reducing payments, shortening duration, tightening eligibility) or tax reform. Neither is likely to be popular with the public. It is more prudent to safeguard the financial health of the universal welfare state by ensuring that those who are capable of working and paying taxes do so.

The two dimensions of welfare state sustainability – popular legitimacy and financial viability – highlight the threat posed by *naving* to the universal welfare state in Norway. On the one hand, voluntary dependency has ideational effects. To the extent that it fosters the impression that burdens are not fairly distributed and contributions are not reciprocated, it weakens the legitimacy of the welfare system and diminishes its popular support. On the other, *naving* has material effects. Subsisting on benefits provided by the state when one could otherwise work and pay taxes reduces the universal welfare state's financial fitness, compelling policymakers to raise additional revenues or restrict access to current benefits and services. In short, the universal welfare state is viable only insofar as it induces its users to reciprocate via the symbolic and material contributions associated with labour market participation.

But why should there be *naving* in the first place? Explanations for the origin of antisocial patterns of welfare-claiming in the Nordic countries are furnished by two scholarly accounts, each of which argues that the Nordic universal welfare states are uniquely configured to fail without drastic modifications. The first, a synoptic essay by Danish politician and social scientist Bent Rold Andersen (1984), explains that the universal welfare state was never intended to function in a society of rational actors. Prior to the social democratic *Gesellschaft* of the universal welfare state, he argues, there was a distinctive Nordic *Gemeinschaft* consisting of face-to-face community ties and networks. These traditional ties and networks suppressed material self-interest, enabling politicians and bureaucrats to erect a massive system of social protection and redistribution. But as the universal welfare system expanded, it absorbed functions that had once fallen within the domain of the family, the church, the friendly society and so on. Through the colonization of the community, the state broke the personal ties and social networks that had for so long effectively stifled free-riders, rent-seekers and fraudsters. Community, Andersen contends, forced people to act "irrationally", putting the collective good above private interest. The bureaucratic, impersonal welfare state thus unbridled the "rationality" of the public. Without the invention of some way "to restore a clear psychological connection between rights and duties", perhaps by "reintroducing ties between contributions and eligibility [...] or by confining the major responsibility of solidarity to smaller units of social formations" (p. 137), rational actors will eventually destroy the universal welfare state through demanding as much, and contributing as little, as possible.

A similarly pessimistic account, albeit with very different emphases, is offered by Danish sociologist Aage Sørensen (1998), who traces the development of the Nordic welfare states beyond the social democratic breakthrough of the 1930s often cited by scholars to the 18th century. Sørensen argues that this was a formative moment, as relations between the governing

Self-interest, reciprocity, sustainability 125

and the governed were fundamentally renegotiated amidst the "conflation of absolutism with Pietism", and regulated by a unique ethos of "obedience and respect" (p. 364). This meant that the sovereign could implement relatively generous aid schemes, as was done in the 1799/1802 Danish "poor plan", without having to worry about rent-seeking. Sørensen writes:

> The 18th-century project was based on a political culture of obedience to the paternalistic ruler and his good intentions. Absence of this culture will expose the welfare system to rent-seeking, that is, obtaining benefits by breaking rules or changing behaviour to obtain benefits rather than being self-supporting.
>
> (Sørensen, 1998: 373)

In Scandinavia, the 20th century brought the construction of more – and more elaborate – schemes to protect individual and social welfare against the vicissitudes of health and the industrial economy. Contemporaneously, however, the ethos of obedience and respect was gradually eclipsed by an ethos of individualism. This latter ethos, which is today hegemonic, is anathema to the universal welfare state, the reach, generosity and open accessibility of which require subjects be obedient, moderate and self-effacing. "The crisis of the modern Scandinavian welfare states", Sørensen writes, "does not reflect the contradictions of capitalism [...] but the contradiction between traditional society, with actions controlled by norms and authority, and modern capitalism, with actions controlled by self-interested rationalism" (p. 365). Like Andersen, Sørensen divines the crisis of the universal welfare state in a moral decay that coincides with the very inconvenient breakthrough of *homo economicus* in Scandinavian society.

In the Hall of the Welfare King

Naving is a practice that symbolizes to its critics not only the unleashing of material self-interest and rent-seeking but also the erosion of an ethical commitment to work for its own – or society's – sake. It would therefore represent strong evidence for the kinds of moral decay in the universal welfare state described by Andersen and Sørensen. Indeed, both scholars furnish compelling frameworks with which to understand what *naving* is and where it comes from. Following Andersen, for instance, one might interpret *naving* as a symptom of the underlying, perhaps terminal, disease of a society purged of its personal ties and social networks by the bureaucratization of care. From this viewpoint, the wilful avoidance of work and education through welfare-claiming is indicative of the user's rationality when confronted with a beneficent welfare system in the absence of institutions able to impose adequate restraints or costs on that claiming. Or consider a reading in the Sørensenian mode: *naving* is the result of a moribund ethos of obedience and respect, causing the public – or segments of it – to choose between work or school and applying for benefits based on a simple cost–benefit analysis. From either perspective, *naving* is material self-interest run amok in Norwegian society. It is bad news for a welfare state arrangement seemingly predicated on, if not the altruism of its users, then at least their willingness to contribute what they can and take only what they must.

Still, before *naving* can be declared a threat to the popular legitimacy and financial viability of the universal welfare state, and treated as evidence corroborating the pessimistic accounts sketched above, one must look beyond sensationalistic media coverage – which takes *naving*'s existence for granted – to substantiate the *naver* as an empirical phenomenon. There is no question that Norway may have its share of able-bodied shirkers. Nevertheless, the size and significance of this population is unclear. That is, public fixation on *naving* may exceed the extent of the demonstrable problem. And if this is so, what might this tell us about the moral sustainability of the universal welfare state in Norway and the Nordic countries more generally?

When one digs into the quantitative data, the picture which emerges hardly supports the notion that *naving* is pervasive. In fact, comparatively, the Norwegians come out looking favourably.[5] A comprehensive report by the OECD (2014), for example, found that among OECD countries Norway has maintained one of the lowest unemployment and highest employment rates during recent decades. Further, both the youth unemployment and NEET ("neither in employment nor in education and training") rates – both critical indicators, given the common association of *naving* with young people – are among the lowest in the OECD.[6] At the same time, Norway boasts both the OECD's highest rate of disability pensioning and sickness absence incidence. Further, the Norwegians that are employed rank toward the bottom of the OECD in terms of average annual hours worked, clocking 1,419 per person against the OECD average of 1,765. Also, while youth unemployment is relatively low, it is heavily segmented by skill and education. Moreover, as of 2014, the Norwegian upper secondary graduation rate fell just short of the OECD average of 85 per cent (OECD 2016: 46).[7] Finally, there are striking differences between non-immigrant and immigrant employment and unemployment rates, particularly if the immigrants come from Asia or Africa (OECD 2014).[8] In their own comparative study of labour market outcomes and welfare state use, Barth et al. (2015: 168–169) weigh the evidence and characterize the Norwegian situation, in comparison with that of other OECD countries, as follows:

> Norway has generous social security schemes [*trygder*], many on disability pensions, but a lower proportion of the population on benefits all in all. We do not have a particularly high number outside of work or education among vulnerable groups with low education, modest skills, and poor health – neither in the population as a whole nor among the youth. On the contrary, we have high employment and labor force participation in the vast majority of groups. The experiences of the Nordic countries

seen in relation to the experiences of the rest of the OECD shows that the most generous social security schemes are not associated with having the most people outside of work or education.

(translation mine)

With the accommodations for disabled and sick individuals aside, as well as the low employment rates of some immigrant groups, this hardly suggests that Norway is in the throes of the kinds of existential moral crises described by Andersen and Sørensen, or suggested by the more alarmist commentary on *naving*. Further, the notion that the universal welfare state is uniquely vulnerable due to flawed incentive architecture lacks a strong empirical basis and inadequately accounts for the complex effects on labour market participation and retention of benefit schemes based on social insurance principles (Pedersen et al. 2015). Supplemented by other studies that show Norwegians – and Scandinavians generally – to be strongly committed to work (Svallfors et al. 2001; van der Wel and Halvorsen 2015), the statistical evidence for widespread *naving* seems inconclusive at best and somewhat unsupportive at worst.

Nevertheless, this is only part of the story. After all, what distinguishes *naving* as a genre of welfare-claiming is not so much the practice but the motive. *Naving* is understood as the *deliberate* avoidance of employment and education through the exploitation of one's legal entitlement to social assistance, unemployment benefits, sick pay, temporary rehabilitation benefits or disability benefits. This perception was confirmed during my own field-based qualitative research on the experiences of the unemployed in Oslo between August 2015 and August 2016. During that time, I spent a six-month period as a regular participant observer in state-funded job-seeker courses for the unemployed and collected "unemployment life histories" via in-depth interviews with 30 current and former jobless individuals.[9] Interviewees were recruited through snowball and convenience sampling, and interviews were recorded for analysis. Though the views of my interlocutors cannot be treated as representative, the recurrence of particular themes, terms and tropes indicates that, despite the idiosyncrasies of individual experience and interpretation, there are distinctive ideas about *naving* that circulate in Norwegian society and are held in common across generational, gender and ethnic lines.

One of these ideas is that *naving* is distinguished from "normal" welfare state use by motivation and job-seeking effort. Hans Magnus, a 26-year-old Norwegian who recently returned from business school in London and is looking to work in finance, explained the difference:

AUTHOR: *Å nave* – can you tell me what that is?
HANS MAGNUS: Well, I think the expression is a – I don't really know how it became an expression, but the truth is that it means simply not having a job and receiving money from NAV because you don't want to work.

And I think it's a very misused expression because obviously the key phrase is the not wanting to work. I think, like, if you're injured or if you're let [sic] off, you cannot claim that someone is *naving*.

This view was broadly shared by the other interviewees, though some implied that because others do not know the circumstances of a person's joblessness, they might assume – mistakenly – that one is a *naver*. This misrecognition is frustrating and even painful because *naving*, they explained, is shameful. When asked why he sought support from NAV instead of his parents, for example, Emil, a 21-year-old would-be retail associate from Hamar, stated that he did not want to be a burden on his family, who he believed had little money themselves. He nonetheless carefully accounted for the social costs of that decision:

EMIL: I don't know. It's maybe a little better to get support from my parents than to be a "*naver*" – with how society, Norwegian society, sees *navers*. And so, I never say that I'm a *naver* when I come into the city and meet people, and [they] ask, "What are you up to?" "No, I *nav*".
AUTHOR: You say that?
EMIL: No, I say: "I am doing self-work." I never say NAV because NAV has – it's a very negatively loaded word. People will get a very negative view of you if the first thing when you meet [is] "Hi, I am a *naver*". I don't want to say it. People will look very condescendingly on it. It is definitely not a comfortable [feeling].

Emil expressed a common view, one held also by some of the jobless immigrants I interviewed in Oslo. Martim, for instance, a Portuguese man who had lost his engineering job in the oil and gas sector, said that one hears talk of *naving* as soon as one is unemployed:

AUTHOR: Do you feel like there's a stigma attached to being unemployed in Norway?
MARTIM: I mean, one of the first words that I heard when I found out that I was being unemployed [sic] – everyone told me that you're going to be a "*naver*". That was the first thing that I heard, so yeah, I think so.
AUTHOR: When you heard that, what did you think it meant?
MARTIM: It's like a bum that gets money to live from the benefits that other people pay. So, yeah, to be a *naver* is really, really bad.

The stigma experienced by some jobless individuals is so intolerable that it seemingly compels them to draw very clearly the difference between themselves and the stereotypical *naver*. When asked how she would react to being called a *naver*, Ida, a 24-year-old Norwegian woman struggling to find any position after losing her job as an activity coordinator, was unambiguous about how it would frustrate her:

IDA: I would be very dissatisfied. Yes, right now [that is the case], but I don't want to be that because there's so much talk about those [people] who exploit the system and cheat the system and use other people's tax money and whatnot. And it's not because I want to, it's because I have to! So, that's the most important thing if someone calls me a "*naver*" […] It is not something I want myself or do because I want to. It is something I have to do in order to survive.

Hans Magnus was similarly defensive:

AUTHOR: Do you know *navers*?
HANS MAGNUS: No, no one […] in Oslo, I've never really met someone who didn't have a job. I mean, I may be the worst one I've met. I've gone without employment for a year and that's –
AUTHOR: But you don't feel like you're a *naver*?
HANS MAGNUS: No, I don't really feel like it. I admit that I'm probably the closest I've come to one. But I don't feel like I'm exploiting the system because it's not like I write the five obligatory applications and then sit back and relax. I feel like I'm in a constant battle for jobs in Oslo and London, and that I do a lot of learning basically about myself and about the job market. So, I don't feel like the typical "*naver*".

These selections, which reflect views that were largely shared among my interlocutors, signal the need for an alternative interpretation of *naving*. Neither the statistical evidence nor my ethnographic data substantiates the idea that *naving* – the willful avoidance of employment or education to live on benefits – is a widespread empirical phenomenon. Interestingly, however, its existence as part of everyday discourse is incontrovertible, and it is in this form that I argue its impact on the Norwegian welfare state is most profound. Above, I asserted that the cultivation of antisocial patterns of welfare-claiming would represent an existential threat to the universal welfare state because of the incompatibility of these patterns with the reciprocity that undergirds both the welfare state's popular legitimacy and its financial viability. In the light of this, I contend that the *naving* discourse, which is invariably pejorative, deprecates free-riding and rent-seeking behaviours, implicitly promoting the prosocial norm of contributing what one can and taking only what one must. It does so through first allowing for the collective representation of practices that are inimical to the functionality of the welfare state, and second, stigmatizing them. The result is an imagined welfare-claimant, a trope that looks like the photographic negative of the kind of good, ethical NAV user on which the universal welfare state – and, more broadly, Norway's version of the Nordic model – depends.

One may interpret the deployment of this fictive entity as serving as an informal moral check on transgressive behaviour – a collective means of monitoring and sanctioning (Ostrom 1990; Wilson et al. 2013) antisocial practices. In Norway, the moral code with respect to the use of benefits and services is given a certain structure and visibility through formal conditions enshrined in law and policy. Breaking these conditions has material consequences, such as the termination of benefits. There are also conditions, however, which are not enshrined in law or formalized in policy. These conditions, as articulated in the flow of everyday life and interaction, constitute an informal and dynamic guide to the ethical use of welfare benefits and services. *Naving* unambiguously violates this code, and thus to be seen as a *naver* is in most cases a shameful thing. Even if one would prefer to passively receive benefits instead of work or go to school, the social and psychological costs associated with being a *naver* are in some cases, my interlocutors suggest, a non-negligible deterrent to free-riding. Contrary to what one would expect from hyperbolic accounts of *naving*, as well as the pieces by Andersen and Sørensen, jobless individuals in contemporary Norway do not seem like self-interested rent-seekers. Rather, they approach welfare-claiming and job-searching with various and shifting motives, including material self-interest, the perception of reciprocal obligations (e.g. giving back, doing one's bit, contributing to society) and, importantly, constitutive goals. That is, they wish to be something: a good citizen, a good employee, a good social democrat, a good parent – anything but a *naver*.

Naving, knaves and welfare queens

While the invocation of *naving* plays a part in promoting sustainable patterns of welfare state use, it may also have understudied pernicious effects. There are at least three ways in which the *naving* discourse could be used to justify the implementation of more restrictive social policy that is antithetical to the universal welfare state. First, to the extent that it fosters the perception that NAV users are motivated by material self-interest and engage in calculating, rent-seeking behaviour, the *naving* discourse could nurture the idea that protecting the common good can be achieved only by harnessing or taming private interest through the manipulation of economic incentives. All social policy reflects "folk anthropologies", or shared beliefs and assumptions about the fundamental nature of human motivation and behaviour (Grand 1997; Deacon and Mann 1999). Let us imagine, for instance, that policymakers believe that the public is motivated by a deep-seated goodness and behaves, on the balance, altruistically. Given that users of publicly funded benefits and services would be most concerned about others or the sustainability of the welfare system itself, policymakers would be able to develop schemes that promote user autonomy via extended periods of eligibility and substantial benefits and services without having to worry that these schemes would be exploited or overutilized. On the other hand, if policymakers saw the public as full of self-interested utility-maximizers, or "knaves", as Hume (1987) famously put it, the aforementioned policy would be both ineffective and reckless. To these users, work and welfare would be interchangeable means to the same outcome (i.e. money), and their participation in the labour market would be entirely dependent on whether employment or unemployment was more lucrative. For the knavish/*nav*-ish public, policymakers would be more likely to use economic incentives, surveillance and control "to induce self-regarding individuals to act in the common interest when market competition alone would fail to accommodate this" (Bowles 2008: 1605).

Norwegian policymakers would not be the first to succumb to this misleading view of human nature. In an analogous context, Dubois (2014) shows that French bureaucrats rationalize greater surveillance and control of poor social assistance recipients by invoking a dogmatic understanding of the typical claimant as a rational actor who will, if permitted, wring as much money from the state as possible. Whatever certainty this dogma provides to policymakers, however, it does so at the expense of radically simplifying and distorting representations of the poor and the decisions that shape their approach to welfare-claiming. Dubois calls this dogma an "economic vulgate" and warns that it "partly causes the symbolic violence that delegitimizes entire segments of the population" (S146).

The embrace of this vulgate by elites in Norway could lead to the adoption of social policies that restrict or strongly disincentivize welfare-claiming. This would be problematic because while restrictions and disincentives – e.g. work-for-your-welfare schemes – would spur some recipients to return to the labour market, they would harm those with no or diminished work capacity (Molander and Torsvik 2015). For these users, generous benefits are not a deterrent to work but rather the means to participate in society on equal or near-equal terms with their peers who can work. Further, social policy that aims to influence the behaviour of rational actors through the use of economic incentives may actually achieve the exact opposite of what it intends. This occurs because of the flawed assumption that economic incentives and moral imperatives are separable and additive – they are not (Bowles 2008, 2016). If they were separable and additive, appeals to a user's material self-interest – say, through minor fines for undesirable behaviour – would incentivize desired behaviour without reducing or distorting the efficacy of parallel appeals to a user's ethical and constitutive commitments be a certain kind of – good – person. In Norway, the embrace of social policy that reflects the rational actor view and its attendant fondness for the manipulation of economic incentives could diminish the various – and variously felt – moral imperatives that already deter *naving*. The result would be more behaviour that resembles *naving*, engendering the perception that what is needed is more restrictive policy and manipulation of economic incentives, and so on. The *naving* discourse, in sum, could ease the identification of knavishness with human nature, and thus risks both limiting and distorting the imaginative universe of social policy.

The second way in which the *naving* discourse might result in significant modifications to the universal welfare state pertains to its effects on voter support. Recall that the legitimacy of the welfare system is in part contingent on its achieving what the public sees as the "just distribution of burdens". According to Rothstein (1998), people will not endorse a system they feel is exposed to widespread free-riding – why give if others only take? In Norway, regardless of how burdens are actually distributed, the *naving* discourse suggests that a segment of the population is happy to live off public largesse without doing their share. It reinforces the impression that others – particularly young people and foreigners – are lazy and parasitic. Following Rothstein's reasoning, the spread of this belief among voters could lead to the withdrawal of the public support necessary for the relatively high taxes that allow the universal welfare state to operate.

Third, it is not difficult to imagine the *naving* discourse facilitating the deeper convergence of scepticism toward the distribution of burdens with scepticism toward immigrants. After all, it is already somewhat common to hear Norway's growing immigrant population associated with *naving*. In a 2015 hit song by Norwegian hip-hop duo Karpe Diem, for example, the voice of an imagined Norwegian native shouts at an immigrant, "You'll never be Scandinavian, *naver, naver, naver, naver, naver!*" (*Du blir aldri skandinaver, naver, naver, naver, naver, naver*!). The mapping of ethnic division onto patterns of welfare-claiming suggests that, given the growing diversity of Norwegian society, along with the aforementioned disparity in employment rates between different ethnic groups in Norway, the *naver* discourse has the potential to join simplified understandings of welfare-claiming and dependency to pernicious stereotypes, stigmatizing the former and reifying the latter. In turn, this could augment support for welfare chauvinist and right-wing populist politicians, who do not hesitate to call for more restrictive forms of social policy aimed at ending the alleged voluntary dependency of the Other.

On this point, the American case is an instructive analogue. During the Great Depression, the Roosevelt administration implemented an array of progressive reforms as part of the New Deal. Among them was Aid to Dependent Children (ADC). ADC, later Aid to Families with Dependent Children (AFDC), was originally intended to provide support for destitute single mothers, and for decades the programme was a mostly uncontroversial part of the American social safety net. But as the demographics of AFDC use shifted, popular sentiment toward the benefit soured. Increasingly, people believed AFDC caused dependency and discouraged marriage. By the 1980s, a growing share of Americans associated the typical AFDC beneficiary with the stereotyped, racialized and gendered imagery of the "welfare queen" (Hancock 2004; Soss et al. 2011). In 1996, under pressure to solve the perceived problem with the welfare state, the Clinton Administration passed the Personal Responsibility and Work Opportunity Reconciliation Act, dissolving AFDC and creating Temporary Assistance for Needy Families, a more restrictive, time-limited benefit. Though initially praised for trimming the welfare rolls, Clinton's welfare reform has been directly and indirectly condemned by subsequent studies that have told a darker story of life for the

American poor in the post-reform era (Morgen et al. 2010; Soss et al. 2011; Edin and Shaefer 2015; Desmond 2016).

The American case should indicate to Norwegian and other Nordic policymakers that interpreting the lower employment rates and disproportional benefit-dependency of some groups through the moralized – and sometimes racialized – lens of *naving* undermines the case for the universalism that is a constitutive part of the universal welfare state. If this case were to be further weakened, resulting in the increased use of means-testing or the restriction of benefits and services to particular groups, it would represent a significant institutional and discursive departure. Selective policy follows a different moral logic, and with it a different way of talking about social problems and solutions. In countries where selective policy is the norm, such as the United States, policymakers ask "how shall we solve *their* problem?" more often than "how shall we solve *our common* problems with social insurance?" (Rothstein 2001: 224–225).

Conclusion

There is widespread agreement that the universal welfare state associated with the Nordic model has been successful at limiting socio-economic inequality, reducing poverty and promoting gender equality (Kvist et al. 2012). But to what extent have these gains been made at the expense of growing the public's appetite for social support and promoting practices that ultimately undermine both its popular legitimacy and its financial basis? A satisfactory answer would necessitate fine-grained empirical research on the decision-making processes of the people for whom welfare schemes are designed and by whom they are utilized. This chapter constitutes a first step and invitation for future study. Rooted in ethnographic investigation of the experiences of the unemployed, it has cast doubt on the idea that *naving* – as practice – is either a significant threat to the viability of the welfare state or unambiguous evidence of moral decay in contemporary Norway, while highlighting the important role the *naving* discourse plays in allowing people to collectively represent and stigmatize antisocial patterns of welfare-claiming. If the universal welfare state is a common pool resource, this discourse is a tool people use to informally monitor and sanction one another – and themselves. It is a sign of the system's moral sustainability.

This functionalist interpretation of the Norwegian fixation on *naving* should not obscure the discourse's more nefarious potential, however. In this chapter I have made the case that the popular tendency in Norway to use *naving* as a lens through which to grapple with human nature, the distribution of burdens in society and the welfare-claiming patterns of the Other has potentially serious consequences for the universal welfare state moving forward. What these applications share is an inevitable discrediting of the idea that one's peers, who have received support, can be trusted to reciprocate. In promoting this belief, the *naving* discourse may erode the sense of obligation to give, upon which the universal welfare state rests. I have thus argued that the greatest moral threat to the universal welfare state – and thus the Nordic model in Norway – as we have known it is not *naving* per se, but the unreflexive deployment of the *naving* discourse. One need look no further than the American case to see what monumental effects the marriage of anxious resentment and a stereotype can have on social policy – and thereby on the lives of society's most vulnerable groups. Recalling the constitutive role played by the "welfare queen" on the American road to Bill Clinton's 1996 welfare reform should give Norwegian policymakers pause. By casting all or some users as weak-willed layabouts or pursuers of short-term self-interest, the *naving* discourse has a similar potential to justify the turn toward residual and ineffectual social policies that would fail to uphold the values of equality, material security and individual autonomy enshrined in the universal welfare state.

Like any another welfare state arrangement, the Norwegian welfare state is rooted in reciprocity. Both its popular legitimacy and its fiscal viability require that the distribution of benefits and services to the public be supported by contribution in the form of labour market participation, which results in higher tax revenues and lower social expenditures. Labour market participation is shaped by many factors, including both economic incentives and moral imperatives. The challenge for those who would replicate the successes of the Nordic model is to construct institutions that perpetuate themselves through incentivizing labour market participation and cultivating prosocial norms that lead people to identify sustainable practices – e.g. contributing what one can and taking what one must – with the "good" and "desirable". That the discourse of *naving* appears to be more widespread than the behaviours associated with *naving* suggests that in Norway there are both formal and informal mechanisms that undergird that identification. It is when the public stops despising *naving* and instead praises it – that is, when practices animated by antisocial norms are admired – that one can declare the universal welfare state morally unsustainable. At least for now, that appears unlikely.

Notes

1 In 2015, the latest year for which statistics are available, the average social assistance payment per month was 8,975 kr, or approximately $1,050 (Statistisk sentralbyrå 2016).
2 Curiously, this is not the first time a neologism for jobless dependency has been so recognized in Europe. For its 2009 "Youth Word of the Year" (*Jugendwort des Jahres*), German publisher Langenscheidt chose "*hartzen*", a term which takes its name from Germany's 2000s Hartz reforms of the labour market and welfare state.
3 It is critical to note that this description is valid only as it pertains to the ideal type of the social democratic welfare regime. In reality, many of the benefits and services provided by the Norwegian welfare state, including unemployment insurance, sick pay and paid parental leave, are contingent on labour market participation. Kolm and Tonin (2014) argue convincingly that income equality and favourable labour market outcomes in the Scandinavian countries are in part attributable to the institutionalization of work-conditionality.

4 It should be noted that while the Nordic countries – Norway, Sweden, Denmark, Finland and Iceland – share numerous political, economic and socio-cultural features, there is no single Nordic model. For this reason, it is better to conceive of the Nordic model as either "a model with five exceptions" (Christiansen et al. 2006) or as an ideal type derived not from identical institutions in the Nordic countries but from those sharing Wittgensteinian "family resemblances".

5 As do the other Nordics. Unsurprisingly, on a variety of measures, Norway, Sweden, Denmark, Finland and Iceland tend to cluster. For the sake of the current discussion, it is relevant to note that as of 2007 the Nordics – along with the Netherlands and Germany – had the highest proportions of their population in either employment or education. Conversely, the Nordics all have relatively high shares of those outside employment and education on disability benefits. From this, as well as the fact that countries with *more* people outside employment and education tend to have *fewer* recipients of disability benefits, it appears that the NEET rate and the proportion of the population on disability benefits are inversely correlated (Barth et al. 2015).

6 The data, from 2012, show that Norway's youth unemployment rate was 8.6 per cent, nearly half the OECD average of 16.3 per cent (OECD 2014: 80).

7 Norway is not alone among its Nordic peers in this regard. Sweden's upper secondary graduation rate is also below the OECD average. The good news for Norway is that recent data indicates that a growing share of students are completing high school within five years (Statistisk sentralbyrå 2017). Between 2011 and 2016, 73 per cent of students finished within five years. This represents an increase of 4.5 percentage points when compared with the five-year completion rates for the period 1994–1999.

8 In 2012, for instance, the employment rate for non-immigrants was 69.7 per cent, while for African immigrants it was 42.5 per cent. It is worth noting that the non-immigrant employment rate is not actually the highest in Norway. In 2012, the most-employed group was immigrants from the other Nordic countries, 76.1 per cent of whom were working. The native population was also less employed than migrants from EU countries in Eastern Europe, 73 per cent of whom were employed. The extreme differences between the employment rates of various migrant groups reflects not only demographic factors and the circumstances under which group members came to Norway, but the nature of the labour market, the distribution of skills and education within the migrant population, and labour market discrimination. For the full breakdown of 2012 migrant employment rates, see OECD (2014: 125).

9 To protect the privacy of my interlocutors, their actual names have been replaced by pseudonyms.

References

Andersen, Bent Rold (1984) Rationality and Irrationality of the Nordic Welfare State. *Daedalus* 113(1): 109–139.

Andreassen, Tone Alm and Aars, Jacob (2015) *Den store reformen: Da NAV ble til.* Oslo: Universitetsforlaget.

Barth, Erling, Moene, Kalle and Pedersen, Axel West (2015) Trygd og sysselsetting i et internasjonalt perspektiv. In: Ann-Helen Bay, Anniken Hagelund and Aksel Hatland (eds), *For mange på trygd? Velferdspolitiske spenninger* (pp. 153–170). Oslo: Cappelen damm akademisk.

Bowles, Samuel (2008) Policies Designed for Self-Interested Citizens May Undermine "the Moral Sentiments": Evidence from Economic Experiments. *Science* 320 (5883): 1605–1609.

Bowles, Samuel (2016) *The Moral Economy: Why Good Incentives Are No Substitute for Good Citizens.* New Haven; London: Yale University Press.

Brochmann, Grete, and Grødem, Anne Skevik (2013) Migration and Welfare Sustainability: The Case of Norway. In: Elena Jurado and Grete Brochmann (eds), *Europe's Immigration Challenge: Reconciling Work, Welfare and Mobility* (pp. 59–76). London: I. B. Tauris.

Brochmann, Grete and Hagelund, Anniken (eds) (2010) *Velferdens grenser: Innvandringspolitikk og velferdsstat i Skandinavia 1945–2010.* Oslo: Universitetsforlaget.

Christiansen, Niels Finn, Petersen, Klaus Edling, Nils and Haave, Per (eds) (2006) *The Nordic Model of Welfare: A Historical Reappraisal.* Copenhagen: Museum Tusculanum Press.

Deacon, Alan and Mann, Kirk (1999) Agency, Modernity and Social Policy. *Journal of Social Policy* 28(3): 413–435.

Desmond, Matthew (2016) *Evicted: Poverty and Profit in an American City.* New York: Crown.

Djuve, Anne Britt (2016) *Refugee Migration – A Crisis for the Nordic Model?* Berlin: Friedrich Ebert Stiftung.

Dølvik, Jon Erik (2016) Welfare as a Productive Factor: Scandinavian Approaches to Growth and Social Policy Reform. Oslo: Fafo.

Dølvik, Jon Erik, Fløtten, Tone Hippe, Jon M. and Jordfald, Bård (2014) *Den nordiske modellen mot 2030: Et nytt kapittel?* Oslo: Fafo.

Dølvik, Jon Erik, Andersen, Jørgen Goul and Vartiainen, Juhana (2015) The Nordic Social Models in Turbulent Times: Consolidation and Flexible Adaption. In: Jon Erik Dølvik and A. Martin (eds), *European Social Models from Crisis to Crisis: Employment and Inequality in the Era of Monetary Integration* (pp. 246–287).

Dubois, Vincent (2014) The Economic Vulgate of Welfare Reform: Elements for a Socioanthropological Critique. *Current Anthropology* 55(S9): S138–146.

Edin, Kathryn J. and Shaefer, H. Luke (2015) *$2.00 a Day: Living on Almost Nothing in America.* Houghton: Mifflin Harcourt.

Esping-Andersen, Gøsta (1990) *The Three Worlds of Welfare Capitalism.* Princeton: Princeton University Press.

Grand, Julian Le (1997) Knights, Knaves or Pawns? Human Behaviour and Social Policy. *Journal of Social Policy* 26 (2): 149–169.

Hancock, Ange-Marie (2004) *The Politics of Disgust: The Public Identity of the Welfare Queen.* New York: New York University Press.

Hume, David (1987) *Essays Moral, Political, Literary.* Edited by Eugene F. Miller. Indianapolis: Liberty Fund.

Jæger, Mads Meier and Kvist, Jon (2003) Pressures on State Welfare in Post-industrial Societies : Is More or Less Better? *Social Policy & Administration* 37 (6): 555–572.

Jakee, Keith and Turner, Stephen (2002) The Welfare State as a Fiscal Commons: Problems of Incentives Versus Problems of Cognitions. *Public Finance Review* 30 (6): 481–508.

Katzenstein, Peter J. (1985) *Small States in World Markets: Industrial Policy in Europe.* Ithaca: Cornell University Press.

Kolm, Ann Sofie and Tonin, Mirco (2014) Benefits Conditional on Work and the Nordic Model. *Journal of Public Economics* 127: 115–126.

Kvist, Jon, Fritzell, Johan Hvinden, Bjørn and Kangas, Olli (2012) Changing Social Inequality and the Nordic Welfare Model. In: Jon Kvist, Johan Fritzell, Bjørn Hvinden, and Olli Kangas (eds), *Changing Social Equality: The Nordic Welfare Model in the 21st Century* (pp. 1–22). Bristol: Policy Press.

Lindbeck, Assar (1995) Welfare State Disincentives with Endogenous Habits and Norms. *The Scandinavian Journal of Economis* 97 (4): 477–494.

Lindbeck, Assar, Nyberg, Sten and Weibull, Jörgen W. (1999) Social Norms and Economic Incentives in the Welfare State. *The Quarterly Journal of Economics* CXIV (1): 1–35.

Lindbeck, Assar, Nyberg, Sten and Weibull, Jörgen W. (2003) Social Norms and Welfare State Dynamics. *Journal of the European Economic Association* 1 (2–3): 533–542.

Mau, Steffen (2003) *The Moral Economy of Welfare States: Britain and Germany Compared*. London; New York: Routledge.

Mau, Steffen (2004) Welfare Regimes and the Norms of Social Exchange. *Current Sociology* 52 (1): 53–74.

Mead, Lawrence (1986) *Beyond Entitlement: The Social Obligations of Citizenship*. New York: Free Press.

Molander, Anders and Torsvik, Gaute (2015) Kan tvungen aktivering forsvares? In: Ann-Helén Bay, Anniken Hagelund and Aksel Hatland (eds), *For mange på trygd? Velferdspolitiske spenninger* (pp. 38–60). Oslo: Cappelen damm akademisk.

Morgen, Sandra, Acker, Joan and Weigt, Jill (2010) *Stretched Thin: Poor Families, Work, and Welfare Reform*. Ithaca: Cornell University Press.

Murray, Charles (1984) *Losing Ground: American Social Policy, 1950–1980*. New York: Basic Books.

OECD (2014) *OECD Skills Strategy Diagnostic Report: Norway*. Paris: OECD Publishing.

OECD (2016) *Education at a Glance 2016: OECD Indicators*. Paris: OECD Publishing.

Ostrom, Elinor (1990) *Governing the Commons: The Evolution of Institutions of Collective Action*. Cambridge: Cambridge University Press.

Pedersen, Axel West, Finseraas, Henning and Schøne, Pål (2015) Økonomiske insentiver i trygdesystemet. In: Ann-Helen Bay, Anniken Hagelund and Aksel Hatland (eds), *For mange på trygd? Velferdspolitiske spenninger* (pp. 78–106). Cappelen Damm: Akademisk.

Pontusson, Jonas (2011) Once Again a Model: Nordic Social Democracy in a Globalized World. In: James E. Cronin, George W. Ross and James Shoch (eds), *What's Left of the Left: Democrats and Social Democrats in Challenging Times* (pp. 89–115). Durham; London: Duke University Press.

Reegård, Kaja (2008) Historien om Nav-reformens unnfangelse: Om idéleverandører bak reorganiseringen av aetat, trygdeetaten og sosialtjenesten. Master's thesis, Universitetet i Oslo.

Rikvoll, Monica and Wold, Vera (2012) "Naver" seg til skolefri. NRK, 28 March.

Rostad, Kristian (2012) Å nave er årets nyord. NRK, 5 December. www.nrk.no/kultur/a-nave-er-arets-nyord-1.9411357.

Rothstein, Bo (1998) *Just Institutions Matter: The Moral and Political Logic of the Universal Welfare State*. Cambridge: Cambridge University Press.

Rothstein, Bo (2001) The Universal Welfare State as a Social Dilemma. *Rationality and Society* 13 (2): 213–233.

Rothstein, Bo (2015) The Moral, Economic and Political Logic of the Swedish Welfare State. In: Jon Pierre (ed.), *Oxford Handbook of Swedish Politics*. Oxford: Oxford University Press.

Skånland, Øystein Haga (2010) "Norway Is a Peace Nation": A Discourse Analytic Reading of the Norwegian Peace Engagement. *Cooperation and Conflict* 45 (1): 34–54.

Sørensen, Aage B. (1998) On Kings, Pietism and Rent-Seeking in Scandinavian Welfare States. *Acta Sociologica* 41: 363–375.

Soss, Joe, Fording, Richard S. and Schram, Sanford (2011) *Disciplining the Poor: Neoliberal Paternalism and the Persistent Power of Race*. Chicago: University of Chicago Press.

Statistisk sentralbyrå (2016) Økonomisk sosialhjelp, 2015. www.ssb.no/sosiale-forhold-og-kriminalitet/statistikker/soshjelpk.

Statistisk sentralbyrå (2017) Gjennomføring i videregående opplæring. www.ssb.no/utdanning/statistikker/vgogjen.

Svallfors, Stefan, Halvorsen, Knut and Andersen, Jørgen Goul (2001) Work Orientations in Scandinavia: Employment Commitment and Organizational Commitment in Denmark, Norway, and Sweden. *Acta Sociologica* 44 (2): 139–156.

Tvedt, Terje (2003) *Utviklingshjelp, utenrikspolitikk og makt: Den norske modellen*. Oslo: Gyldendal Akademisk.

van der Wel, Kjetil A. and Halvorsen, Knut (2015) The Bigger the Worse? A Comparative Study of the Welfare State and Employment Commitment. *Work, Employment & Society* 29 (1): 99–118.

Wilson, David Sloan, Ostrom, Elinor and Cox, Michael E. (2013) Generalizing the Core Design Principles for the Efficacy of Groups. *Journal of Economic Behavior and Organization* 90.

Witoszek, Nina (2011) *The Origins of the "Regime of Goodness": Remapping the Cultural History of Norway*. Oslo: Universitetsforlaget.

8 Challenges to the Nordic work model in the age of globalized digitalization

Atle Midttun

From industrial to service economy

Solidly grounded in the industrial economy, the classical Nordic work model has been characterized by coordinated wage setting – forged by strong, responsible trade unions and employers' organizations. The model is couched in a negotiating culture that developed while the Nordics built up mature industrial societies in the second half of the 20th century. This culture was founded on an understanding of the merits of a well organized labour market, with the state playing a supporting role.

Both the legitimacy and functioning of the model have been underpinned by a high organization rate by international standards, on both the employee and the employer side. As argued by Nielson (2016) this organizational capacity and the negotiating culture that has accompanied it have established a "compromise competence" that stands in contrast to more contrarian relations between labour and capital in many other regions of the world.

As argued in the introduction to this book, and corroborated by Nielson (2016), cooperation in the arena of work in the Nordic region has been characterized by a comprehensive and multi-faceted network of relations on many levels. The negotiated wage settlements in the labour market chime with Nordic political negotiating culture, where a system of proportional representation has fostered a practice of pragmatic compromise between opposing interests and parties.

These small, homogeneous societies, with their cooperative culture, have also fostered political mobilization around the welfare state. The Nordic work model thus also rests on the basic social security provided by numerous pro-social arrangements that provide workers and their families with a guaranteed livelihood under turbulent market conditions. This allows the Nordics to practise their so-called "flexicurity", which facilitates flexible and productive industrial adaptation to market demands, while retaining security for the worker. At the same time the state harvests the benefits of increased productivity and competitiveness, upon which the high level of Nordic welfare ultimately depends.

Challenges of the service economy

Major challenges to the Nordic work model are shaped by the shift from an industrial economy based on mass production towards an increasingly digitalized service economy characterized by flexible specialization. This transition has been going on for decades. Industrial employment peaked in Sweden in 1965 and in Norway 10 years later. By the turn of the century, industrial employment in both countries had been reduced by about one-third, while the service economy's share of GNP had risen to more than 60 per cent[1] (Skoglund 2005). The extent of the impact on work life increased over the early decades of the 21st century, as global outsourcing and digitalization gained momentum.

Many features of the classical Nordic model under industrial mass production are challenged by the transition to the service economy with its strong pressure for flexibility. Service businesses are now moving away from the normal working day, with fixed long-term work contracts, in the direction of less standardized working time and labour contracts (Sennett 2009). Such flexibility is considered essential to their business model. For instance, a Norwegian study of retailers (Gulbrandsen 2016) shows that store managers regard flexible labour as fundamental and see current operations as impossible without part-time employment. Gulbrandsen argues that part-time employment seems to embody both the flexibility and stability that these retail organizations need to adapt to as they navigate a changing competitive landscape. A study of the new features of working life in Sweden also documents developments towards flexibility, individualization and heterogenization of employment (Allvin et al. 2011). The study points to a movement away from the industrial workplace, with its standardized and sub-divided tasks, towards a post-industrial workplace that is goal- and task-oriented – one that requires a high degree of flexibility on the part of both the company and the worker (Allvin et al. 2011).

The shift towards flexibility in work comes as businesses themselves are feeling the pressure from increasing deregulation and international competition. As firms become exposed to growing financial risk, they limit their exposure to fixed costs through flexible working arrangements such as the use of part-time employees, overtime, temporary employment, lay-offs, and calling on temporary staff recruitment agencies and subcontractors. More and more, such modifications of working conditions stretch beyond the service economy and into the industrial economy.

Such "atypical" work arrangements have been opposed by Nordic trade unions, in spite of their readiness to contribute to the increased productivity upon which their welfare ultimately depends. While Nordic collaborative industrial arrangements have traditionally allowed considerable reorganization of the business model within the firm (functional flexibility), the Nordic work model has been less open to quick and easy increases or decreases in staff in line with short-term changes in demand for labour (numerical flexibility) (Atkinson 1984). However, outsourcing labour to so-called staffing companies has implanted such flexibility into the system. As, these practices are becoming more and more common, and the Nordic work model has had to adjust in order to give such practices a more "responsible" form.

Digitalization, sharing and robotization

The so-called "sharing economy" amplifies flexibility and individualization of work to its very limit. Exemplified by sharing platforms such as Uber, Haxi and Airbnb, new commercial configurations are taking the transport and housing capacity owned by private individuals onto the market. In such business models, traditional employment relations disappear, as most sharing economy companies define themselves as platforms for intermediation – where service providers on the platform are independent contractors, not employees.

The rapid expansion of the sharing economy is driven by powerful technology trends, such as high internet adoption, easily accessible payment systems, advanced mobile telephone technology and user-friendly applications. In the second decade of the 21st century, the sharing economy is just beginning in the Nordic countries. Estimates by Vista Analyse for the Norwegian Government suggest 60 per cent annual growth in Norway over the next 10 years (NOU 2017:4).

Given its rapid expansion and its competitive advantage, the sharing economy has considerable potential for disrupting traditional business models and work relations. Technology-driven reduction of transaction and information-gathering costs may lead firms to make less use of permanently employed labour and instead recruit labour in the various markets supplied by sharing economy companies. While this may create new employment opportunities for people with weak labour market affiliation, it leads individuals to perform tasks for companies without any regular employment relationship being established (NOU 2017:4). Self-employed people in the sharing economy therefore typically lack security in basic aspects of work, such as guarantees of employment, pensions, parental leave, holiday pay and other rights that are established in regular employment relationships (Nielson 2016).

As this way of organizing economic activity extends inexorably, it has the potential to change the labour market and ultimately threaten Nordic welfare societies. These societies have relied on a pragmatic settlement between socially responsible business and productivity-oriented labour. Growth in the sharing economy may weaken the company's role as a place of production, and thus also impair the functions now attended to by the firm as an employer. As jobs previously carried out by permanent employees are increasingly being outsourced to independent contractors, the bargaining position of many workers will suffer. In a tight labour market, a single worker who is forced to register as an independent contractor does not have the same bargaining power as a large, multinational group enjoying monopolistic power.[2]

Accepting a model where individual workers stand alone as independent contractors, or "freelancers" may eventually threaten the balance in the labour market upon which many Nordic welfare arrangements have been built. It will likely also push down the salary levels of low-income groups. As seen by the trade unions, this could create adverse effects for many workers with regard to earnings, social welfare benefits and general working hours. Furthermore, without the security that a classic organization gives the members of a trade union, this growing group of self-employed people will over time create an overload on the public social security system (Nielson 2016). This overload is aggravated by the ability of the core players in the multinational virtual economy to avoid taxation.

Beyond the sharing economy comes robotization, where workers are substituted by software-driven machines (Brynjolfsson and McAfee 2016). While the sharing economy may marginalize labour, robotization disrupts work altogether. It either forces labour into new sectors that robotization has not yet conquered or out of the labour market altogether.

Liberalization and Europeanization

The commercial and technological challenges to the Nordic countries have been institutionally facilitated by market liberalization, and largely promoted under EU regulation. The Nordics have thereby had to tailor their approaches to meet these challenges within a wider European market context, where EU harmonization has imposed significant restrictions on Nordic work practices. In this respect EU participation – despite all its other opportunities – also becomes a challenge.

Negotiation versus regulation

The Nordic countries differ from most of the other EU Member States[3] in that their labour market has well defined and representative actors on both the employers' and employees' sides, and the agreements negotiated by the parties are respected (Nielson 2016). This is in contrast to many other European countries, which are characterized by fragmented and weak organizations on both sides of the labour market or an imbalance in the relationship between them. And while many labour conditions in the Nordic countries are determined through negotiations between employer organizations and the trade unions, in other European countries the legislature decides these issues.

From the point of view of countries with weak labour organizations, legislative processes in the EU aimed at upgrading labour conditions may come as a welcome intervention to secure balance between business and worker interests. Seen through Nordic eyes, however, these processes are perceived as a threat to core elements of established bargaining models, as EU law overrides national tradition. Paradoxically, this impingement of EU legislation comes in spite of the fact that work and social policy are supposed to be policy domains under national prerogative. In reality, however, EU directives aimed at market liberalization are increasingly affecting working conditions, and their applicability is often defined by the European Court of Justice.

Work as shaped by EU courts

As cases are brought before the European Court of Justice, whose rulings ultimately determine the content of the EU's policy in the labour market arena, the balance between the parties' freedom of contract and the role of the state as legislator is shifting as the judiciary gains a central role in defining applicable law (Nielson 2016).

A case in point is the so-called Posting Directive (European Commission 2017), which has granted extended rights to service companies to override Nordic wage-bargaining agreements when delivering services in Nordic countries. Two cases – the Swedish Laval case and the Norwegian Holship case – serve as illustrations.

The Laval case: Having won a public tender in Sweden to renovate a school near Stockholm, the Riga-based construction company Laval posted workers to Sweden. Estimates suggest that these posted workers earned around 40 per cent less than their Swedish counterparts (Whittall 2008). Concerned that the posting of cheaper labour to Sweden threatened the position of Swedish construction workers, their trade union, Byggnads, encouraged Laval to comply with the local terms and conditions of employment laid down in the collective agreement. But Laval refused to sign the existing collective agreement and Byggnads, supported by the Swedish Electricians' Union (Svenska Elektrikerförbundet, SEF), started picketing Laval building sites in November 2004 (Whittall 2008). In response the company took the case to the Swedish Labour Court, where the company demanded that the action be ruled unlawful. The national court sided with the workers and dismissed Laval's request that the collective action to be brought to an end.[4] However, the case was subsequently brought before the European Court of Justice, which took a different position, and ruled, in 2007, that to force a foreign undertaking which posts workers to Sweden to abide by a Swedish collective agreement was illegal. The decision undermined the right of Swedish trade unions to make collective agreements valid for foreign workers posted in Sweden (European Court 2007).

The Holship case: The December 2016 Supreme Court decision in a case brought by the Danish shipping company Holship against Norwegian port workers and their union provides another example of a setback for Nordic negotiated pro-social agreements. The conflict with Holship arose when the company's business grew significantly in the port city of Drammen in 2013 and the Norwegian Transport Workers' Union subsequently required the company to recruit its dock workers through the system of port offices, which it had established to avoid social dumping. Holship rejected the Union's demands, believing that the practice the Union and the Confederation of Norwegian Enterprise (NHO) had agreed among themselves led to unfair competition and was an obstacle to the free right of establishment. Holship therefore decided to counter the Union's boycotts in spring 2013 in court. The company fought a legal battle against LO (the Norwegian Confederation of Trade Unions) and the Norwegian port monopoly for three years, claiming the right to use their own staff. In December 2016 the Danish company emerged victorious from a supportive decision in the Norwegian Supreme Court (Lorentzen 2016). A central premise for this conclusion was a previous judgment in the EFTA court (EU court for EES matters) that gave full support to Holship's position.

In both the Laval and Holship cases, local, prosocial negotiated agreements were overrun by European market regulation, in spite of the fact that the subjects of wages and strike action are explicitly excluded from the EU's competences. It appears that the Posting Directive has allowed the European Court of Justice to bring the subject of strikes in by the back door, requiring that the exercise of the right to strike comply with the neoliberal principles of the Maastricht and Lisbon Treaties (Veldman 2013). The unions have defended the principle that cross-border business should adhere to local labour standards so as not to undermine the employment conditions of the workers already present, but extended EU market regulation is starting to erode this in practice. The Nordic tradition of building prosociality on the basis of tripartite negotiated settlements is particularly vulnerable in the encounter with more formal and legalistically oriented EU culture.

The question of legislation versus negotiation goes beyond a matter of principle about institutional power relations. As Nielson (2016: 28) has pointed out:

> At the workplace, it makes a real difference whether an employee can get support and assistance for mediation from his or her shop steward and trade union, or is forced to seek legal counsel and go to court, with the negative consequences this will inevitably have, both for the continued employment of the person concerned and for the company.

Given the existence of a well organized work model, with trust between the parties, the agreement system also has considerable advantages for employers in the form of low conflict and stability in return for upgraded work conditions. As extended European market liberalization and rulings of the EU/EFTA courts directly or indirectly affect the Nordic balance between the state and the social partners, the core of the model is coming under threat.

The Eastern European ascension

The EU challenges to the Nordic work model have emerged more clearly with the Eastern European ascension. With respect to both wage levels and work organization, the Nordics and the Eastern Europeans find themselves at opposite ends of the scale. With average salaries around 8 euro/hr in Poland and 40 euro/hr in Norway (EUROSTAT 2017), Eastern European workers have naturally flocked to richer regions like the Nordic countries, and particularly to Norway with its low unemployment and wages propped up by the petro-economy. Furthermore, in terms of work organization, the Nordics and the Eastern Europeans stand miles apart (OECD Stat 2017). Trade union membership stands at between 85 per cent and 50 per cent in the Nordic nations but between 15 per cent and 5 per cent in most Eastern European countries.

The Eastern European labour force has clearly filled labour shortages in countries like Norway, where the booming economy of the early 2000s was in need of labour immigration to prevent inflationary pressure. However, the downturn of the European economy following the financial crisis in 2007/2008 created a more precarious employment situation in the Nordic countries as well. Even in Norway, with its booming petroleum economy, the unprecedented volume of immigration from Eastern Europe – rising from under 6,500 in 2003 to around 160,000 in 2014 (Eldring 2015) – challenged the country's egalitarian wage policies.

Until more equalization of wages and working conditions takes place in Europe, the common labour market will continue to exert a downward pressure on Nordic work arrangements. The Nordics are, however, revising their working practices, organization, legislation and institutions to meet this pressure. The generalization of tariff agreements to apply to whole industries is one of their major approaches. It is an attempt to bridge the gap between the Nordic culture of negotiation and the EU culture of regulation.

Industrial organization

The combination of liberalization and availability of cheap labour has facilitated new modes of industrial organization that entail atypical work relations, at odds with mainstream Nordic working traditions. Staffing companies have been central to this development. They have become an important resource for flexibility as employers increasingly turn to part-time, freelance and temporary workers to fill gaps in their workforce. The temporary hires provided by staffing companies have been attractive to many Nordic companies because they have offered flexibility – employers are provided with a workforce that is fluid and can be dynamically adjusted to meet their hiring needs on an ongoing basis. This development has also offered reductions in the legal responsibilities of being an employer. Staffing firms often take on important liabilities such as the payment of certain taxes, insurance coverage and adherence to labour laws.

The Norwegian airline company Norwegian may serve as an example. The company was founded in 1993 and recast as a low-cost carrier in 2002. It has been listed on the Oslo Stock Exchange since 2003, and has grown considerably in recent years, becoming the sixth largest budget airline in the world with around 6,000 employees and offering over 450 routes to more than 150 destinations in Europe, North Africa, the Middle East, Thailand, the Caribbean and the United States (Norwegian.no n.d.). This expansive growth has been accompanied by major restructuring that now includes:

- Transfer of aircraft leases and ownership to the Dublin-based asset group Arctic Aviation Asset Ltd.
- Hiring of employees through country-specific staffing companies that offer employment locally.

In 2015 Norwegian took a majority stake in the Cyprus-based staffing company OSM Aviation, which offers employment for airline staff. OSM Aviation already employed more than 1,000 crew members for Norwegian in Sweden, Finland, the UK, Spain and the United States and offered recruitment, training, crew management and in-flight services to several international customers besides Norwegian.

The aviation company has in fact adopted different versions of business models from international shipping, where tax and labour outsourcing has been routine for many years. Many companies do not go as far as Norwegian, but maintain traditional work relations for a diminishing core of workers on regular work contracts, and supplement them with workers on short-term contracts in order to maintain flexibility to match fluctuations in their product or service markets.

With respect to the Posting Directive, Nordic use of staffing companies has grown in response to general international trends, preceding European legislation. Denmark was the first of the Nordic countries to deregulate the public employment exchange monopoly in 1990, followed by Sweden in 1993, Finland in 1994 and lastly Norway in 2000 (Eklund 2017). The European Directive on Temporary Agency Work (2008/104/EC) came later and sought to consolidate this practice by establishing a general framework applicable to the working conditions of temporary workers in the European Union. The Directive aimed to "contribute to the development of the temporary work sector as a flexible option for employers and workers", while guaranteeing a minimum level of effective protection to temporary workers.

Nevertheless, as with the Posting Directive, staffing agencies and the flexible employment they entail pose a challenge to Nordic working traditions. Commercial reconfiguration amplifies this challenge by including outsourcing and the decomposition of enterprises to optimize on tax and labour costs and facilitate flexible adaptation to market dynamics. With workers employed in staffing companies, while other strategic resources reside in a completely different organization, the classical, pragmatic and collaborative work model loses some of its organizational integrity.

The combination of staffing agencies, short-term contracts and the posting of workers across EU borders has placed Nordic working traditions under pressure. The volume of these challenges is large: in 2010, EurWORK (2010) indicated that even prior to the financial crisis more than a quarter of European employees had atypical employment arrangements. Among the Nordics, temporary work has been most widespread in Sweden and Finland, followed by Norway and Denmark (Svalund 2011). Should such business models become predominant, they might erode not only Nordic working patterns but also the egalitarian wage structure, thus undermining the tax revenue of the Nordic welfare states.

Scenarios

How can the Nordic countries meet the current challenges? Are they able to reform/reinvent the Nordic work model for the modern age? Will the recipe for their *competitive advantage of collaboration*, with high-productivity/high-inclusiveness and high-egalitarian societies, still work under extended marketization, increased migration, digitalization and the emerging sharing economy? And will the Nordics be able to carry on their special working arrangements under the massive legislative intervention of the European Union?

It would be premature to give definite answers to these questions. Instead we will sketch three scenarios that explore the possible trajectories of the Nordic work model. The first, *dualization*, explores a neoliberal development in the Nordic region. The second, *resilience*, outlines a path where the Nordics manage to cope with their challenges while retaining their formula of socio-economic sustainability. The third, *transformation*, depicts a deeper change in the Nordic model, in response to profound structural challenges.

Dualization

Dualization is a scenario where the Nordic model is gradually overrun by its surroundings. This implies that Nordic work standards and other welfare arrangements migrate towards a European average, turning the Nordic countries into less egalitarian and more class-divided societies.

Increased globalization and liberalization under EU directives are strong drivers in this direction. But drivers towards dualization are also to be found within the Nordic countries themselves. Conservative-dominated governments have become much more frequent since the 1980s and have been active promoters of liberal policies. Yet market-oriented efficiency policies have also been introduced by social democratic parties, often framed as measures to enhance the performance of the welfare state. Furthermore, digitalization and the sharing economy have put Nordic-style work relations under pressure, while robotization is threatening industrial jobs.

As these processes take hold, the formula of inclusive wage policies, embodying commitments to moderation in high-wage segments in return for an uplift in wages for lower-paid work, cracks. As a result, elements of the class society re-emerge, although along different dividing lines than under the mass production economy of much of the 20th century. Researchers like Standing (2014) have talked about a growing "precariat", which may have disruptive political and social consequences.

Even if the welfare state still has a stronger equalizing effect than in most other countries, increased privatization, including private health services, creates alternative fast-track and high-quality options for corporate elites as well as for wealthier parts of the population. The extensive privatization of schools (Chapter 4) also supplies a clear basis for segregation and class divisions in Swedish society.

To take Norway as an example, by the end of 2015 more than 850,000 inhabitants out of a total population of 5 million had an immigrant background – three times as many as in 2000. Around half of these had backgrounds from Asia and Africa (NOU 2017:2). The extensive increase in refugees in 2015 put the Nordic immigration regimes under strong pressure. Even Sweden, which until autumn 2015 had represented a European exception with a liberal and positive view of refugee-immigration, was overrun by more than 160,000 refugees that year, and had to impose restrictions (NOU 2017:2).

While the refugees enter under different conditions than EU/EEA labour migrants, the two groups meet in the labour market, where they find themselves competing for the same low-cost jobs with European jobseekers. This reinforces low-wage competition.

Since work migrants and refugees alike tend to flock towards certain sectors, such as construction, services such as hotels and restaurants and the informal economy, there is a trend towards lower wages and less orderly work conditions in these parts of the economy. Other sectors, where entry barriers are higher, remain dominated by ethnic Nordics and embody more of the Nordic working traditions. These divergent recruitment processes thus serve to increase inequalities in Nordic societies, and stimulate the formation of ethnic-cultural class divisions, which replace the classical labour–bourgeoisie divide that the Nordics have struggled to overcome. One can observe increased ghettoization in Nordic societies, especially in Sweden, where parts of larger cities such as Malmö, Gothenburg and Stockholm, with extensive youth unemployment, are struggling to uphold law and order.

Groups falling behind

In addition to the downward pressure on wages and working conditions exerted by immigrants and refugees, who are willing to work for lower pay than the domestic work force, there are concerns about rising disability among the younger population, possibly indicating difficulty in finding jobs. To again take Norway as an example: while work participation by older employees has been stable – and for the oldest groups clearly falling – the opposite trend can be observed for groups in the 25–44 age group (Figure 8.1). Should this trend

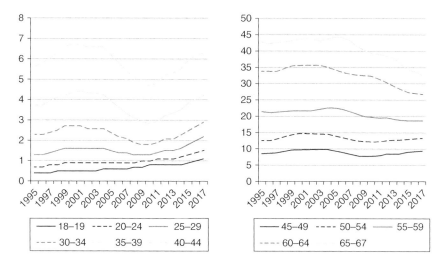

Figure 8.1 Disabled as a share of the population by age groups
Source: Statistics Norway

continue, we could be seeing increasing work exclusion, thereby creating an additional class-like divide.

Challenges to egalitarian society

But even before the massive immigration, there were signs that Nordic egalitarianism was weakening. Taking Norway as an example, Aaberge et al. (2013) have pointed to a persistent trend from the end of the Second World War until the late 1980s, when top income shares declined steadily. The lowest point was reached in 1989, when it took less than 2 per cent of the population to match the wealth of the richest 0.5 per cent. This was down from around 5 per cent in the late 1960s. This period was characterized by high economic growth, an extension of the social security system and improved access to education, combined with relatively tightly regulated capital markets. The financial deregulation initiated in 1984 did not lead immediately to a rise in top shares, since its distributional impact was probably postponed by economic recession and the related Norwegian banking crisis of 1988 to 1992. However, as the economy picked up speed from around 1990, there was a steep increase in top income shares. Tax reforms from 1986 to 1992 reduced the marginal tax on capital income, which increased incentives to realize dividends and capital incomes and led to a rise in the top income shares (Figure 8.2). Except for the distributionally turbulent years of 2000/2001 and 2005/2006, top income shares appear to have stabilized at the levels of the 1950s.

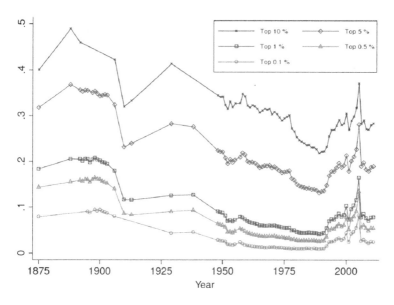

Figure 8.2 Top income shares 1875–2011
Source: Aaberge et al. (2013)

A similar pattern can be observed in Sweden (OECD 2015). The country still belongs to the group of most equal OECD countries, despite a rapid surge of income inequality since the early 1990s. The growth in inequality between 1985 and the early 2010s was the largest among all OECD countries, increasing by one-third. In 2012, the average income of the top 10 per cent of income earners was 6.3 times higher than that of the bottom 10 per cent. This is up from a ratio of around 4 to 1 during much of the 1990s (OECD 2015).

The dualist formula

The traditional Nordic model relied on a social contract that established a collaborative bond between elites and broader society, to secure productive inclusiveness and fair distribution. The dualist scenario assumes that this contractual bond erodes. It erodes because the Nordics find themselves entrenched in a more invasive EU and global economy, one where the EU also increases its control over social and work policy, often channelled through the European Court of Justice. While the Nordics, as small open economies, have a long tradition of managing exposure to international markets, their negotiated social market arrangements crack when they are overridden by EU regulation. Under extensive labour and refugee migration, and novel business configuration, such as staffing companies and posting arrangements, the prosocial Nordic institutions and work culture may be too weak to withstand the pressure.

Resilience

As indicated in the dualism scenario, major shifts in the economy are putting the Nordic model on trial. However, the Nordic ability to negotiate and adapt to changing circumstances since the Nordic model's origin in the mid-1930s suggests its resilient nature. Contemporary challenges are similarly surmountable. First, the Nordic countries are gradually finding new alternatives to old working arrangements that have been overrun by deregulation or technological innovation. Second, elements of Nordic work organization are effective and represent a competitive advantage in certain sectors of the economy. Third, the welfare state – although it comes with a cost – also represents an invaluable resource in a modern economy. Finally, a number of indicators still rank the Nordics as high performers, in terms of both economic productivity and socio-economic welfare. Against this background, the resilience scenario focuses on how the Nordics may deploy their collaborative capital as an asset towards achieving a productive and inclusive economy under 21st-century conditions.

Finding new forms for Nordic prosociality

The Nordic countries have followed different strategies to counter pressure on wages and work conditions in the labour market. They have generally been reluctant to establish state-defined minimum wages, because of the downward pressure this might have on wages. Denmark and Sweden have therefore been reluctant to move very far towards regulation, and the trade unions, acting through boycotts and sympathy actions, have remained the main anchor for fair wages (Dølvik and Eldring 2008).

Striking a compromise between EU regulation and the Nordic bargaining culture, Finland, Iceland and, increasingly, Norway have built on a generalization of tariff agreements and reinforced government control. This meets the EU's demand for formal state regulation, but automatically adjusts wage levels to bargaining results. In Norway, for example, generalized collective agreements imply that pay and working conditions apply to all who perform work within a specific sector, even if they are not part of the agreement (Norwegian Labour Inspection Authority [Arbeidstilsynet] 2017). In the second decade of the 21st century, the following sectors have general tariff agreements: the construction industry (for those who do construction work), electro-work, the ship and shipbuilding industry, freight transport by road, agriculture and horticulture, passenger transport by coach, cleaning, and fish manufacturing. Compliance is supervised by the Norwegian Labour Inspection Authority.

152   *Midttun*

According to Dølvik and Eldring, the Nordic countries have been able to develop efficient regulatory regimes for wage and working conditions that reduce loopholes and limit the inflow of workers. The greatest challenges have been in securing adequate registration and control (Dølvik and Eldring 2008).

The competitive advantage of Nordic work organization

While the Nordic model has come under pressure to change, its heritage also contains important inspirations for creative adaptation. Innovative vanguard firms have found Nordic workinge traditions conducive to dynamic participation in the global economy. The Nordic tradition of worker co-determination and flat organization apparently pays off in facilitating learning organizations characterized by autonomy, and the capacity to handle task complexity (Lorenz and Valeyre 2003).

The welfare state as an asset

Moreover, the welfare state itself, with its generous education and health and welfare services, as well as security under unemployment, creates a basis for coping with the dynamic experimentation of the international economy. By providing basic health care and social security for individuals and families, the welfare state may allow workers and companies to engage in dynamic adaptation to new market conditions, without worrying about the potential negative impacts.

Furthermore, the welfare state facilitates more active participation in the innovation economy. Nordic countries offer their citizens much more equal educational opportunities and equip a larger proportion of the population with educational experiences than most other countries do. Additional resilience is provided through the Nordic welfare states' engagement in basic retraining for new job qualifications, as part of an active "flexicurity" policy.

Nordic performance

Measured by several indicators, the Nordics seem to have maintained their resilience (Table 8.1).

The Nordic countries are in the top league in Europe when it comes to work productivity, and they have demonstrated the ability to hold unemployment at a substantively lower level than the EU in general, in the aftermath of the financial crisis in 2008. The exception is Finland, where unemployment is closer to the EU average.

The Nordics still boast some of the most inclusive economies when it comes to participation in the economy. Around 75 per cent of the population, as opposed to 67 per cent in the EU as a whole, participate in the economy. Part of the explanation behind the higher share of population at work in the Nordic countries is the wide participation of women. Norway, Sweden

Table 8.1 Nordic performance

Country	Labour prod. (2016)	Unemployment (2016)	Employment % of pop. (15–64) (2016)	Female employment % of pop. (15–64) (2016)	Gini Index (2015)	Human Dev. Index (2015)	Public spending on disability % of GDP (2013)
Denmark	63.5	6.2	74.9	72.0	0.256	0.925	4.732
Finland	51.4	8.8	69.1	67.6	0.260	0.895	3.827
Norway	79.1	4.7	74.3	72.8	0.257	0.949	3.690
Sweden	56.3	7.0	76.2	74.8	0.274	0.913	4.254
Benchmarks							
EU28	47.7	8.5	66.6	61.3	–	–	–
USA	62.89 (2015)	4.9	69.4	64.0	0.390	0.920	1.421
Germany	59.5	4.1	74.7	70.8	0.289	0.926	2.055

Sources: OECD, UNDP

and Denmark top the list, with Finland lagging slightly behind, together with other north-western European countries.

In spite of trends noted under "Dualization", the Nordics still get top scores on egalitarianism as measured by Gini coefficients. And towards the end of the second decade of the 21st century, the Nordic countries continue to be ranked at the summit of the Human Development Index.

Furthermore, the Nordics have apparently managed to avoid overload on their social security systems. The number of Danes on disability pensions has been going down, from close to 6 per cent in 1998 to around 4 per cent in 2015. Sweden experienced a rise from under 5 per cent in 1998 to over 6 per cent in 2005, but the proportion of claimants fell to close to 3 per cent in 2015 (OECD 2015).

To sum up, the resilience scenario is more optimistic than the dualist scenario with respect to preserving Nordic prosociality. This optimism is based on a stronger belief in the persistence of Nordic prosocial provisions, not least in the ability of the Nordic countries to find functional equivalents to replace the institutional arrangements that have been undermined by the EU's liberal deregulation. Furthermore, high scores on core productivity and welfare indicators suggest that the battle for prosociality is far from lost.

Transformation

The transformation scenario goes beyond the dualism and resilience scenarios by including the Nordic model's exposure to radical technological innovation. The characteristics and consequences of the radical technology shift awaiting us have been described as "the Second Machine Age" by Erik Brynjolfsson and Andrew McAfee (2016). They argue that the automation of a lot of cognitive tasks means that software-driven machines are replacing humans, rather than acting as complements. They contrast this with what they call the "First Machine Age", or the Industrial Revolution, which helped make labour and machines complementary. Klaus Schwab (2017) has described a similar technology shift under the heading of the "Fourth Industrial Revolution", which is marked by emerging technology breakthroughs in a number of fields, including robotics, artificial intelligence, nanotechnology, quantum computing, biotechnology, The Internet of Things, 3D printing and autonomous vehicles. Carlota Perez's (2009) take on the current technology shift focuses on the transition from the era of mass production to the era of ICT-driven flexible specialization. This era, she argues, will demand new modes of work organization, but potentially represents a new golden era of sustainable growth, if properly regulated.

All three perspectives on disruptive technological transformation concur in highlighting tremendous potentials for productivity and welfare increases. However, they point out that delivering the necessary societal innovation for these potentials to be broadly and inclusively realized in society is a tall order. The transformation scenario explores the assets and capabilities of the Nordic model to meet this challenge, and points to both advantages and limitations.

The Nordic model as an asset in the innovation economy

First, it is worth noting that although digitalization and robotization have put the Nordic model under pressure, advanced segments of Nordic industry have thrived. They have done so in part due to the compatibility of Nordic work organization and welfare arrangements with the need for flexible specialization under the new innovation economy.

An increasing body of literature has highlighted how inclusive or participatory organizational practices have strong links with both product and process innovation (Eurofund 2007). As already mentioned under the *Resilience* scenario, the Nordic tradition of worker co-determination and flat organization seems peculiarly well equipped to create learning organizations characterized by autonomy, the ability to handle task complexity, and skill in problem solving (Lorenz and Valeyre 2003). When this translates into advanced functional flexibility and teamwork capability, it puts Nordic high-performance firms in an advantageous position in the innovation economy (Figure 8.3).

A set of case studies of innovative Nordic firms documents their agility in the innovation economy, based on Nordic work attributes. According to Kristensen and Lilja (2011) a predominant feature of several of these cases is their ability to flexibly engage with their customers in creating innovative products and solutions. By working across numerous customer firms the Nordic companies increased their knowledge assets, enabling them to continuously improve and innovate. The pace and complexity of these innovations entailed the decentralization of strategic power to project teams. By acquiring such capacities, Kristensen and Lilja argue, the teams were able to take on a

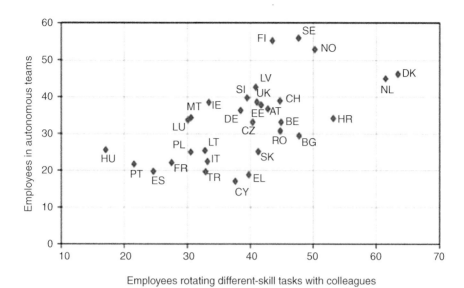

Figure 8.3 Advanced functional flexibility and teamwork, by country
Source: Eurofund 2007

more strategic role including innovation, searching for complementary technology and detecting new opportunities. In her study of the Kongsberg group (one of Norway's major engineering groups) Eli Moen (2011) points out how the group erased the social division of the workforce in order to create project teams. Their achievements relied on a work organization where employees enjoyed a high degree of autonomy, were less exposed to formalized forms of control, learnt continuously and were able to apply their own ideas at work.

The insights from Kristensen and Lilja and Moen are corroborated by the findings of innovation researcher Bengt Åke Lundvall (Lundvall et al. 2002). Based on the example of Danish firms, he concluded that features such as autonomy in work, training, cross-unit teams and job rotation were positively linked to innovation. Lundvall has also pointed to the interaction between technical innovations and organizational cooperation between firms ("networking"), which he claims is crucial for transforming innovation into economic performance. As pointed out by Lorenz and Valeyre (2003), the Nordic success cases presuppose a work organization that is not beholden to stiff bureaucracy, or to a strong, lean approach, but rather thrives in a working tradition characterized by co-determination and flat organization.

Furthermore, the Nordic model has a capacity to let this mode of flexible flat organization interplay dynamically with welfare arrangements. The "flexicurity" model, mentioned under the *Resilience* scenario, may be geared up from its traditional function as an employment facilitator, to take on a stronger role in industrial transformation. As parts of the economy devolve through disruptive innovative technological change, advanced welfare arrangements may facilitate the upgrading of human capabilities and provide guarantees for decent living.

Challenges to social inclusion

However, there are also issues of major concern: Brynjolfsson and McAfee are worried about technology creating a strong divide between the included and excluded – between experts and less competent workers, whose jobs are expropriated by robotization. Perez is more optimistic and expects massive job-creation in caring, health and other service industries. However, should Brynjolfsson and McAfee be right, there would be a need for the expansion of current Nordic welfare buffers, which are already among the most generous in the world.

A next step could be further development of a citizen's wage model, which is already being tried out in Finland, although on a very limited scale (Henley 2017). The citizen's wage model, or universal basic income, would provide a guarantee of inclusiveness, in a less stigmatizing way than a fall-back on social security. However, it raises complicated issues around motivation and incentives.

Without successful social organization, we could experience the paradox that technology and robotization allow us all to enjoy unprecedented welfare, with less work. We could all be like free Athenians, with robots substituting for slaves as workers, enabling us to enjoy free thinking, the arts and politics. Yet if we cannot organize technology in a socially inclusive way, we may instead end up with a severe version of the *Dualist* scenario, where all the benefits accrue to elites and global monopolies harvesting their oligopoly positions in markets characterized by network-economics.

Nordic societies and the Nordic model have several attributes that make it likely that a socially inclusive organization of the disruptive technological shift could take place in the region. They have high state capacity and well organized administrative apparatuses and are fairly transparent, with low corruption. Nordic societies have a strong capacity for reaching societal consensus around common policies in a way that reaches across class divides. They host populations with high welfare expectations, and focus on egalitarian values.

Furthermore, the Nordic countries have traditionally had strong taxation regimes with fairly advanced capabilities to tax national players, and might, therefore, be capable of financing advanced welfare reform. However, as business extends internationally and engages in advanced tax planning, the model is coming under pressure. Socially inclusive policies are therefore dependent on innovative approaches to taxation in the international economy – as major actors in the digital world seek to confine the enormous value they create to tax havens, with minimal payback to the societies where the money was made.

While attempts are made to grant tax authorities better insight, and to achieve fairer taxation of real value creation, the Nordics are generally too small to act alone in the global arena. They are therefore dependent on pushing this agenda at the European level. This comes on top of innovation incentives built into Nordic wage bargaining. Barth, Moene and Willunsen (2015) thus argue that Nordic solidaristic wage bargaining, with its high wages for unskilled workers, motivates investment in work-saving innovation, while the relatively low wages for skilled workers add additional bonus to such investments.

Going forward

As I see it, the Nordics have several options on the table. With their strong and competent states and pragmatic prosocial culture, they are better positioned than most other countries to undertake even transformative transition in a fairly inclusive way. The populist reactions to liberalist globalization and Euro-liberalism may, interestingly, have paved the way for stronger national leverage in economic policy, and thus for Nordic prosocial initiatives. This is on the condition that EU elites recognize that they have to allow for more autonomy at the national level.

The question is, however, whether the Nordics themselves are ready to use the opportunity to reconsolidate their prosocial arrangements. Increased propensity to vote for liberal/conservative governments may indicate that Nordic societies are changing from within. Paradoxically, successful welfare policies have fostered a growing middle class with increasing liberal inclinations. Should this trend grow stronger, we may come to see more conspicuous dualist elements penetrating Nordic societies. Should integration of sizeable immigrant populations fail, the middle classes may feel further encouraged to support mechanisms of segregation, such as private schools and more restrictive welfare provisions.

While much of the debate about the future of Nordic work organization has concentrated on its exposure to outside pressure, there has been less focus on its challenges from within. The Nordic societies have shown a remarkable ability to orchestrate a commitment to a common prosocial future under 20th-century industrial organization. Their transformation into middle-class societies in the 21st-century digital service economy raises questions about the degree of commitment to prosocial values.

Notes

1 Corrected for the effect of the petroleum economy, Norway's share was around 65 per cent in 2000 (Skoglund 2005).
2 As many of the new digital business models are based on network economics, monopoly power is an increasing problem in the modern economy.
3 With three Nordic countries being EU members, and two (Iceland and Norway) associated through the European Economic Space, EU policies and regulation directly affect their economies.

4 The Court had sought guidance from the European Court of Justice (EC), and the EC's legal advisor Paolo Mengozzi gave statements supportive of the Swedish trade union's position.

References

Aaberge, R., Atkinson, A. B. and Modalsli J. (2013) The Ins and Outs of Top Income Mobility. *Discussion Paper Statistics Norway.* Research department 762, October.

Allvin, M., Aronsson, G., Hagström, T., Johansson, G. and Lundberg, U. (2011). *Work without Boundaries: Psychological Perspectives on the New Working Life.* Oxford: John Wiley & Sons.

Atkinson, J. (1984) The Flexible Firm and the Shape of Jobs to Come. *Labour Market Issues* 5: 26–29.

Barth, E., Moene, K., and Willumsen, F. (2015) The Scandinavian Model – An Interpretation. *Journal of Public Economics* 117: 60–72.

Brynjolfsson, E. and McAfee, A. (2016) *The Second Machine Age: Work, Progress, and Prosperity in a Time of Brilliant Technologies.* New York: Norton.

Dølvik, J. E. and Eldring, L. (2008) *Mobility of Labour from New EU States to the Nordic Region: Development Trends and Consequences.* Nordic Council of Ministers.

Eklund, R. (2014) Temporary Employment Agencies in the Nordic Countries. Available at: http://arbetsratt.juridicum.su.se/filer/pdf/ronnie%20eklund/eklund-bemanningsforetag.pdf (accessed 5 October 2017).

Eldring, L. (2015) Tåler den norske modellen arbeidsinnvandring? In: B. Bungum, U. Forseth and E. Kvande (eds), *Den norske modellen: Internasjonalisering som utfrdring og vitalisering.* Bergen: Fagbokforlaget.

EUROSTAT (2017) Wages and Labour Costs. http://ec.europa.eu/eurostat/statistics-explained/index.php/Wages_and_labour_costs (accessed 5 October 2017).

European Commission (2017) Posting Directive. http://ec.europa.eu/social/main.jsp?catId=471 (accessed 5 October 2017).

European Court (2007) Grand Chamber Judgment of 18.12.2007, Case c-341/05.

Eurofund (2007) Fourth European Working Conditions Survey. www.eurofound.europa.eu/sites/default/files/ef_publication/field_ef_document/ef0698en.pdf

EurWORK European Observatory of Working Life (2010) www.eurofound.europa.eu/observatories/eurwork/comparative-information/flexible-forms-of-work-very-atypical-contractual-arrangements (accessed 14 December 2017).

Gulbrandsen, Å. P. (2016) Fleksibilitet eller stabilitet? Butikklederes vurderinger av deltid i varehandel. Master's thesis.

Henley, J. (2017) Finland Trials Basic Income for Unemployed. The Guardian 3 January. www.theguardian.com/world/2017/jan/03/finland-trials-basic-income-for-unemployed (accessed 5 October 2017).

Kristensen, P. H. and Lilja, K. (eds) (2011) *Nordic Capitalisms and Globalization: New Forms of Economic Organization and Welfare Institutions.* Oxford: Oxford University Press.

Lorentzen, M. (2016) Havnearbeiderne tapte på alle punkter [The Dock Workers Are Losing on All Fronts]. *E24* published 10:01 – 16/12/2016, updated 14:30 – 16/12/2016. http://e24.no/lov-og-rett/ny-dom-om-havnemonopolet-holship-vant-i-hoeyesterett/23874638 (accessed 5 October 2017).

Lorenz, E. and Valeyre, A. (2003) Organisational Change in Europe: National Models of the Diffusion of a New 'One Best Way'?. *Danish Research Unit for Industrial Dynamics (DRUID) Working Paper* 04-04.

Lundvall, B-Å., Johnson, B., Andersen, E. and Dalum, B. (2002) National Systems of Production, Innovation and Competence Building. *Research policy* 31 (2).
Moen, E. (2011) Raw Material Refinement and Innovative Companies in Global Dynamics. In: P. H. Kristensen Lilja (eds), *Nordic Capitalisms and Globalization: New Forms of Economic Organization and Welfare Institutions*. Oxford: Oxford University Press.
Nielson, P. (2016) Working Life in the Nordic Region: Challenges and Proposals. *Report to Nordic Council of Ministers*.
Norwegian Labour Inspection Authority (2017) Webpage. www.arbeidstilsynet.no/fakta.html?tid=90849/ (accessed 5 October 2017).
Norwegian.no (n.d.). Webpage. www.norwegian.no (accessed 5 October 2017).
NOU 2017:2. Integrasjon og tillit – Langsiktige konsekvenser av høy innvandring (Integration and Trust – Long-term Consequences of High Immigration). White Paper to the Norwegian Ministry of Justice and Security.
NOU 2017:4. Delingsøkonomien – muligheter og utfordringer (The Sharing Economy – Possibilities and Challenges). White Paper to the Norwegian Ministry of Finance.
OECD (2015) OCED Income inequality data update: Sweden (January 2015). www.oecd.org/els/soc/OECD-Income-Inequality-Sweden.pdf (accessed 5 October 2017).
OECD (n.d.) OCED Data. https://data.oecd.org/ (accessed 10 September 2017).
OECD.Stat (2017) Trade Union Density (OECD). https://stats.oecd.org/Index.aspx?DataSetCode=UN_DEN (accessed 5 October 2017).
Perez, C. (2009) Technological Revolutions and Techno-economic Paradigms. Working Papers in Technology Governance and Economic Dynamics. TOC/TUT Working Paper 20. The Other Canon Foundation, Norway; Tallinn University of Technology, Tallin. Available at: www.idunn.no/lor/2017/02/holship_hoeyesterett_om_haandhevelse_avinternasjonale_forpl (accessed 5 October 2017).
Schwab, K. (2017) *The Fourth Industrial Revolution*. New York: Crown Business.
Sennett, R. (2009) *The Craftsman*. London: Penguin Books.
Skoglund, T. (2005) 100 års ensomhet? Norge og Sverige 1905–2005: fra jordbruk til olje og tjenester (A Hundred Years of Loneliness? Norway and Sweden 1905–2005: from Agriculture to Oil and Services). Available at: www.ssb.no/nasjonalregnskap-og-konjunkturer/artikler-og-publikasjoner/fra-jordbruk-til-olje-og-tjenester (accessed 5 October 2017).
Standing, G. (2014) *The Precariat. The New Dangerous Class*. London: Bloomsbury.
Svalund, J. (2011) Undersysselsetting og ufrivillig deltid. Varighet og veien videre (Underemployment and Involuntary Part Time), *Faforapport* 2011: 34. Oslo: Fafo.
Veldeman, A, (2013) The Protection of the Fundamental Right to Strike within the Context of the European Internal Market: Implications of the Forthcoming Accession of the EU to the ECHR. *Utrecht Law Review* 9(1): 104–117.
Whittall, M. (2008) Unions Fear ECJ Ruling in Laval Case Could Lead to Social Dumping. EurWORK European Observatory of Working Life. Published on: 24 February. www.eurofound.europa.eu/observatories/eurwork/articles/unions-fear-ecj-ruling-in-laval-case-could-lead-to-social-dumping (accessed 5 October 2017)

9 Between individualism and communitarianism

The Nordic way of doing politics

Nik Brandal and Dag Einar Thorsen

> A state without the means of some change is without the means of its conservation.
>
> Edmund Burke (2004 [1790]: 106)

According to former United States Senator and Director of the Institute of Politics at Harvard University's John F. Kennedy School of Government Alan K. Simpson, politics rarely provides an outcome that is clearly right or wrong. Rather, he sees politics as a "continuing flow of compromises between groups, resulting in a changing, cloudy and ambiguous series of public decisions where appetite and ambition compete openly with knowledge and wisdom" (Simpson 1998). What Simpson captures in his description is that the political sphere is a multi-tiered system of units where conflict seems to be the default position. At a higher level are the conflicts between ideological units: socialists, libertarians, conservatives and so forth. At an intermediate level are political parties that may or may not subscribe to similar ideological units, but compete for a shared voter base and differ with regard to which policies or politics are more likely to bring about a desired result. At a lower level are the different units within the political parties, for example local and regional chapters, and organized factions such as feminists, environmentalists and religious groups. All these political units will have divergent self-interests and different priorities on how to advance their own preservation. Individual party members can rise to a position of power only at the expense of other party members, political parties can access power only at the expense of opposing parties, and ideologies can triumph only at the expense of rival ideologies.

There are numerous studies on how such conflicts shape the political system. A factor that has often been overlooked, however, is the way in which these conflicts resemble and share a basic evolutionary feature found throughout the biological world, namely the struggle between lower-level selfishness and higher-level welfare. If left unchecked, the individual units associated with a political system are prone to act as "cancer cells", destroying the body in favour of their own short-term gain (Wilson and Hessen 2014). The question is then how to make the different units stop acting in a self-serving manner and cooperate in a non-selfish and prosocial way, denying what is their immediate individual self-interest in favour of the maintenance and renewal of the larger social body?

We will argue that the success of the Nordic countries – commonly attributed to the somewhat elusive "Nordic model" – is derived from the way in which the Nordic countries have been able to overcome the inherent tribal conflicts between different levels and different units, and instead promote prosocial behaviour in their political system. Furthermore, we will argue that the individual parts making up the Nordic model(s) are by no means exclusive to the Nordic countries. Rather, the model comprises the totality of agencies, policies, traditions and institutions, developed – at times incidentally, at times purposefully – through a constant process of adaptation, changing and tweaking. The Nordic political model is grounded in a particular mix of individualism and communitarianism, which has led to a closer alignment of moral values between the Nordic right and left than is normally found elsewhere. This shared value basis has in turn lent itself more easily to political compromises, even when the end results have been radical deviations from the past. Our contention is that, rather than being a fixed set of policies and institutions from the first half of the 20th century, the Nordic model has come about gradually as a way of doing politics, where the actual outcome in terms of policies and institutions can vary between the individual Nordic countries and over time. Thus, rather than one Nordic model, what we are in reality talking about is several Nordic models, all of which have gone through a constant process of change and adaptation. While the models have proven to be resilient to broad international trends in the past, they also show themselves to be vulnerable to potential future changes that might at first seem to be rather insignificant.

In the following, we will discuss the roots and development of the Nordic way of doing politics, its key features and its mechanisms for maintenance and renewal. We will then highlight three major political trends that are currently facing not only the Nordic countries, but all nations, and discuss how these relate to the Nordic way of doing politics and its possibilities for continued success in the 21st century.

Political culture in the Nordic countries

In our conceptualization, the Nordic way of doing politics involves general and fundamental features of the political culture and traditions of the Nordic countries, which have been developed through competition and cooperation between social units at different levels, and have been able to adapt and renew themselves amidst international currents and changes. Viewed in this way, the Nordic model – or, as we say, the Nordic way of doing politics – is a way of organizing society, shaped by a number of mechanisms for maintenance and renewal. It has come about partly as a compromise between political actors and the gradual diffusion and absorption of values and political ideas, and partly because this way of doing politics has been so successful.

An instructive starting point for understanding this development is the transition from authoritarian rule to democracy in the Nordic countries in the early 19th century. Unlike France's, Germany's or Italy's, for example, the Nordic transition to a mass-based liberal democracy took place in a literate, moderate, compromise-oriented society that was rather well equipped for such a political system.[1] A contrast might even be drawn to Britain, a country often held up as exemplifying the preferred political development path. While the Glorious Revolution of 1688 brought about institutions that limited the powers of the king, increased those of the parliament and laid out important civil rights, the benefits of this development were restricted to a narrow elite. Up through the early 20th century, Britain was an aristocratic oligopoly where power was concentrated in the hands of an Anglican landowning elite that dominated high-status positions in politics and society, controlled local politics and law-making and was immensely wealthy. As Sheri Berman has pointed out, up through the 19th century British liberalism did not prevent its elite from enjoying a combination of economic wealth, social status and political power that would make today's plutocrats blush (Berman 2017). It was only as pressure built during the 19th century for democratization that the full "benefits" of liberalism were extended to the entire population. According to Berman, the trajectory of the United States is similar, in as much as for most of the country's history, liberal rights were restricted to white, male Americans. It took the bloodshed of the Civil War to begin to change this, and then another century before basic civil rights could be enjoyed by all citizens.

From the available research, it is possible to identify some key features of the Nordic way of doing politics, which has been prevalent in developing the political model found in the Nordic countries, and which we believe to be crucial for its upkeep and renewal. While the longevity and relative strength of the individual features have varied between the Nordic countries – for example, the role of social democratic thought is a feature of the 20th century and the policies aimed at facilitating public spheres has been significantly different across the Nordic countries – they themselves have been developed over time through adaptations and integration.

The first is the Nordic Sonderweg model, put forward by historians Bo Stråth and Øystein Sørensen. This model sees the political process in the Nordic countries as chiefly characterized by the way in which vested interests are included in drawn-out political discussions, tying stakeholders to an eventual outcome. This primes the participants towards cross-political, cultural and social compromise favouring evolution and cooperation, rather than revolution and confrontation (Stråth and Sørensen 1997; Witoszek 2011). Political processes have also tended to include a much broader range of organizations than political parties *sensu stricto*. Instead, we see in the Nordic countries that inclusion (and co-option) into the political process has been extended to an array of stakeholders within civil society, especially, but not exclusively, the social partners in the tripartite concertation (*trepartssamarbeidet*) between the state, labour unions and business associations. While the negotiated or "corporatist" economy means that political decision-making often takes time, the end result has been a high level of transparency, a high level of legitimacy and a high level of political trust (see especially Trägårdh 2007).

While this negotiation-centric approach has disadvantages – namely it is time- and resource-consuming – its advantages have been significant. The slowness of the process has meant that it is hard to push through rash decisions or implement policies or institutions on a whim based on short-term trends. In addition, the involvement of multiple stakeholders means that the eventual outcome will inevitably be an imperfect compromise. By including a large number of stakeholder competencies in the process, however, the end result will seldom result in bad policies. Like any policy that has come about as a cross-political compromise, it is also likely to be stable and lasting even after a change of government. The Nordic welfare state would seem to be a case in point. It was introduced gradually by the social democratic parties across the Nordic countries, but in the Norwegian case prosocial key parts of the system – such as the National Insurance Act of 1966 – were implemented by the conservative Borten government.

Second, the Nordic political model is underpinned by a belief in the primacy of politics; the idea that politics shape the world – at least more than the "blind" forces of history or the market economy – and that the community, the country or the world at large can and will change for the better through consciously enacted policies. Another feature of the political model is its communitarianism, or the idea that a functioning political community is dependent on individual members who strongly believe in its efficacy and potential for positive change. According to Sheri Berman, this particular form of communitarianism, balancing individual needs and liberty with the needs of the community, is a defining feature in the Nordic version of social democracy, which developed in the first half of the 20th century. This was made possible through a conscious decision to forge a strong, national community to undergird the political processes and the nation state, which included all adult members of society, rather than just the social and economic elites in a "people's home" (in Swedish *folkhemmet*) (Berman 2006).

Third, the political model is grounded in what the Norwegian political scientist Øivind Bratberg has called "solidarity by default": rather than trying to increase its return by picking social winners – as in the process promoted by Anthony Giddens and New Labour in Great Britain, for example – the Nordic states have invested universally in their populations (Brandal and Bratberg 2015). Through its social investments, the state carries the responsibility of maintaining human rights in a broad sense, including economic, social and cultural rights such as access to work, education, health and a minimum of material wealth.[2] The state thus guarantees the freedom of the individual. The negotiated economy also ensures a degree of social equality through equitable conditions in the labour market, while social investment is encouraged through the welfare state (Brandal and Bratberg 2015). Furthermore, the model is robust across party political divides: it is supported by social democrats because they subscribe to equality, and by conservatives and liberals because they promote the productivity that is inherent in the model. A case in point would be how the emerging socialist movement adapted to, and was changed by, participating in the Nordic way of doing politics in the 19th century. In turn, the social democratic dominance in the 20th century and the success of the Nordic model led to conservative and liberal groups, within both politics and the business sector, absorbing and adapting to social democratic values (Brandal and Bratberg 2015; see also Berman 2006). This also chimes well with the assumption that social investment is most effective if supplemented by a social structure with limited inequality and strong social actors.

A fourth and final key feature has been the quite general acceptance of state responsibility for facilitating a critical public sphere in an almost ideal-type Habermasian sense (Habermas 1962). The creation of a deliberative and communicative public sphere through the state, subsidizing small-scale public spaces within and across associations, has been a necessary bulwark against the disenfranchising effects of the market economy, as well as facilitating the creation of a public opinion necessary for the Nordic way of doing politics to function. This is perhaps most directly seen in the way in which the state in the Nordic countries has subsidized both local and national newspapers in various ways. A more subtle way in which the state in these countries has facilitated open-ended public debates, in which relatively many people can participate, has been in organizing small municipalities with directly elected politicians who have extensive responsibility for the practical implementation of state policies. When there are many elected politicians residing in practically all communities, the result tends to be a high level of political literacy and understanding of political processes in the population in general, as well as elected officials developing more personal acquaintances among the population.

The resulting political process, while fiercely competitive in its initial stages, is geared towards eventual cross-political, cultural and social compromise, leading in turn to a high level of social and political trust (Listhaug and Ringdal 2007). The ideal end-type result is a "decent" and "civilized" society, tying stakeholders at different levels to the eventual outcome, while reducing the risk of escalating conflicts, and avoiding a situation in which minorities rightly feel humiliated by the state or the majority (Margalit 1996; see also Rawls 1993). The importance of these features in how the Nordic way of doing politics has evolved becomes even more apparent when you separate general ideas about how society ought to be organized from features of the political system grounded in more or less coincidental traditions. The former has to some extent shaped the latter, but influence has also gone the other way.

A prominent example of this development path is the growth of the social democratic movement in the Nordic countries. While social democracy began towards the end of the 19th century as a small political sect on the outskirts of polite society, with foreign political ideas imported from Germany and even further afield, it was gradually integrated into the local political sphere (Brandal et al. 2013; Sejersted 2011). As social democrats garnered ever more support, especially, but not exclusively, from the industrial proletariat, they gradually became a political force to be reckoned with. When they finally, in the 1920s, formed their first governments, they had already for some time been integrated into a pre-existing political system. The social democrats changed the political system in various ways even before they entered government for the first time, but they themselves were also changed by their participation in the political system (Brandal et al. 2013, Berman 2006). Almost a century later, we can perhaps see these effects of reciprocity (*vekselvirkninger*) from the gradual entry into the political sphere of a new political movement. Interbellum social democrats had to adapt to pre-existing political conditions, and change them only gradually, from the inside, or else face perpetual powerlessness and perhaps gradual extinction. It has been partly due to sheer luck that the social democrats of the Nordic countries, at a pivotal point in their history, had leaders who successfully made the case that some gradual change was better than no change at all, and better than a revolutionary confrontation with the better established elements of society.

However, access to political power also changed the social democrats themselves. They, or at least their leaders, quickly became used to discussing political matters with politicians from other parties, as well as business leaders and the upper echelons among bureaucrats. That became the beginning of a shared sense of trust between new and old components of the political elite, and made it possible to use negotiations to hammer out consensus-based solutions to common challenges. For both the social democrats and the old bourgeoisie, that led to the ritualization of class conflict, while leaders from all camps developed answers to common problems in negotiations that emphasized the importance of consensus building.

After World War II, this pattern of broad-based and consensus-oriented policymaking became a staple feature of politics in the Nordic countries, with some local variations. Policy formation was for the most part driven by an appeal to shared values such as freedom, solidarity and community. Abstract ideologies or political theories, which attracted the support of only some sections of society, played a less important role (Brandal et al. 2013). While specific policies have tended to change and mutate over time, political processes and the values underpinning them have been more stable and, in a sense, have functioned like a cultural programme or *genome*, which has been able to adapt to changing social and economic circumstances.

It is also important to note that the political culture has been process driven, based on knowledge, deliberation and inclusion, which has tended to defuse polarization between different political parties and ideologies. That is not to say that the political sphere has not been competitive. Rather, the default position has been to seek compromises across the political spectrum, and the process has to a high degree been self-correcting, developing gradually by testing and adapting to what works and what does not, into what may be described as a "kinder and gentler democracy" (Lijphart 2012). The Nordic preference for universal benefits rather than means testing is a case in point, in as much as the latter has been tried, tested and discarded on account of being expensive, inefficient and bureaucratic, and not because of ideological preferences. In fact, the social democrats of the Nordic countries were originally among the champions of means testing, but gradually changed their perspective as they collected practical experience with universal benefits (see e.g. Esping-Andersen 1990).

As the evolutionary biologist David Sloan Wilson has pointed out, a prerequisite for such a high level of generalized trust is mechanisms such as the political culture that rewards altruism and punishes selfishness (Wilson et al. 2013; Wilson and Hessen 2014). This idea is supported by the German-Norwegian social psychologist Evelin Lindner, who, on the basis of her studies of societies that have succumbed to genocide and mass violence, has pointed out that a democracy can function and survive only if its citizens are willing to bend to the common will without viewing a political defeat as a humiliation that needs to be avenged. Lindner sees democracy as a traffic light, where all drivers of all cars, small and large, must abide by the same rules: at a red light, you stop; at a green, you go. Everyone has to bend equally to the neutral authority of the traffic light without experiencing it as degrading. Such a system – Lindner's contrasting example to genocidal societies is Norway – can function only when the power of the state and its institutions are able to guarantee this neutrality (Lindner 2013). A functioning democracy thus requires a level of faith. To engage with others, you must believe that if you lose, the winner will treat you equitably, the resulting institutions will be fair and the new leaders will act in the country's best interest. In other words, it necessitates some form of social control mechanisms that prevent exploitation and create the foundation on which generalized trust is built. However, while it is easy to observe that such mechanisms must be in play in the Nordic countries – for example, when a change of government does not lead to major upheavals in policies or state institutions – it is much harder to pin down from the existing research exactly what these mechanisms or agencies are.

Within party units, the mechanisms of reward and punishment are, of course, obvious: prosocial behaviour is rewarded by access to positions of power and the ability to implement policies and share political influence in general, while antisocial behaviour is punished by exclusion from positions of political power. These mechanisms also hold true, at least to some extent, for coalition partners, whether in government or in opposition. The more difficult question is why thy have also applied across the ideological blocks. A long-term explanation going back to the Enlightenment would stress the importance of education, where literacy was common in the population as early as the mid-18th century. This was important for the emergence of a public sphere for critical discourse and the way in which democracy developed in the Nordic countries. An educated population made it easier to press for and expand voting rights, leading to a higher degree of political participation, through both political parties and social movements. A critical public sphere of enlightened voters also necessitated that politics be fact-based rather than driven by ideology or values, and therefore lend itself more easily to broad compromises.

A similar argument can be made from the prominence of a particularly individualistic and egalitarian culture found in the Nordic countries, which simply does not lend itself easily to political tribalism between party units. For example, the Norwegian social anthropologist Halvard Vike has pointed out that "equality as sameness" has been constituted by the formalization of social relations, where formal areas for participation in popular movements have contributed to shape the citizens' idea of "the state" (Vike 2013; Bendixen et al. 2017). From his studies in cognitive anthropology and political culture in the Nordic countries, Vike understands this as a form of "bureaucratic individualism, which denotes a form of individuality that arises from a tendency to use formalization as a way to undermine personal dependency" (Vike 2013: 181). Egalitarianism in the Nordic countries is then "an emergent property of strong, formally organized collectives in which conformity turns out to serve as a useful tool for protecting the collective good", which Vike captures in the concept "the morality of membership" (Vike 2013: 181). A similar argument has been made by the Swedish historian Bo Stråth, who finds that the Nordic countries have managed to keep the tension between freedom and equality under better control than elsewhere in Europe. They have therefore become, in some sense, more equal than many other societies, and the ideals of equality have, then, been connected to ideals of positive freedom in the sense suggested by the British philosopher Isaiah Berlin (Stråth 2017). According to Berlin, positive freedom was a state of affairs in which the citizens have a role in choosing who governs the society to which they belong (Thorsen 2012: 59–73; see also Berlin 1958, 2002; Lijphart 2012). In the Nordic context, the development of a strong welfare state since the end of World War II, based around universal coverage and an egalitarian distribution of rights and duties alike, has strengthened the formal, politically constituted collectives. At the same time in real terms, it has undoubtedly strengthened the freedom of individuals to do what they please, including choosing who is to govern. This development has, however, weakened more informal collectives at the intermediate level, such as family or locally based associations, neighbourhoods and village communities. These intermediary collectives have fewer responsibilities than they used to, such as caring for children or the elderly, and have become less important in the lives of individuals as more and more basic needs for care in certain phases of life have been met by the state.

Drawing on the arguments put forward by Vike and Stråth, it would then seem that conservatives in the Nordic countries have developed and internalized a moral foundation that is much closer to that of their liberal opponents.

Unlike conservatives elsewhere, who, according to the American social psychologist Jonathan Haidt, tend to value sanctity, loyalty and authority (Haidt 2013), Nordic conservatives have – like their liberal counterparts – largely assumed care and fairness as the most important moral values.[3] This also holds true to some degree for the right-wing populist parties that emerged in the Nordic countries from the 1970s onward. Even if they are closer to their non-Nordic conservative brethren with regard to minorities, migration, foreign aid and so on, they have adapted to and accepted many specifically Nordic values and political traditions, as exemplified by their continuing support for the welfare state. Rather than making a fundamental break with the Nordic conservative tradition, populists tend to question who should be included in the nation's "universe of moral obligations" (Glover 2012), and therefore be subjected to the ideals of care and fairness.[4]

These ideas may suggest that the mainsprings of the political model found in the Nordic countries are to a large extent anchored in Nordic culture and traditions, as Chapter 3 suggests. For our further enlightenment, we might turn to the American cognitive linguist and philosopher George Lakoff. He has argued that the lives of individuals are significantly influenced by the central metaphors they use to explain complex phenomena, and that people with opposing political viewpoints therefore tend to think differently at a quite fundamental level (Lakoff 1996). According to Lakoff, the most deep-seated philosophical divisions between right and left in politics are founded in different grasps of human nature. The right – ranging from libertarian proponents of a minimal state to fascists who believe in a totalitarian state – tends to perceive of human nature as a rigid, stable and inevitable entity. The left, on the other hand – ranging from left-leaning liberals and social democrats to anarchists and communists, also believing in a totalitarian state – tend to understand human nature as an entity that is malleable by social circumstances. Perhaps with a nod to the British economic historian R. H. Tawney (1920), Lakoff makes the argument that while an unregulated market economy will make the acquisitive side of human nature more pronounced, a well regulated economy will promote a sense of community and solidarity within a given social group. This basic understanding of human nature is instrumental in understanding how the Nordic way of doing politics developed. In the same way that conservatism in the Nordic countries is based on a moral foundation close to liberal ideals and values, the basic understanding of human nature among Nordic conservatives would also appear to correspond more closely to views that are elsewhere normally associated with the political left. This peculiarity of Nordic conservatism might then provide an explanation for why the Nordic countries have been able to transcend not only the *me vs. us* conflict, but also – more importantly – the *us vs. them* conflict, which often leads to disruptive tribalism even within democratic nation-states.

Following Lakoff's and Tawney's arguments, one might then contend that a more egalitarian, yet prosperous, society will also reap the good fortune of a mentally better adjusted populace. Moreover, when thus constituted, such a society is in turn predisposed to behave, rationalize and empathize in a certain way, further reinforcing a pro-social biological reproduction. Going from this premise, one might say that happiness reproduces itself in the collective, reifying direction because of the way in which our biology has evolved. This becomes even more apparent if we contrast the Nordic countries to societies that have been subject to more market-based, neo-liberal structures. A case in point would be the Nordic welfare state. As the Norwegian historian Øystein Sørensen has argued (1993), for example, the Nordic welfare state was originally based on an Anglo-American model of welfare policy developed before and during World War II in Great Britain and the United States that for various reasons was later rejected in these countries (see also Brandal et al. 2013). The Nordic welfare state was then implemented over decades by social democrats with conservative parties initially in fierce opposition. However, it was passed as a negotiated multi-partisan legislation and not subjected to major changes as the political winds shifted. Over time, the success of the welfare state has meant that the populace in the Nordic countries, as a result of their circumstances, have also come to think differently about taxation and public redistribution of economic resources than people in many other countries. The contrasts between the bipartisan approach to the welfare state that has developed among voters and political ideologies alike in the Nordic countries, and the growing political divide apparent in the debates over health reform in the US and the National Health Service in the UK could not be more stark. It would therefore appear that the more societies adopt a market-based, neo-liberal order, the greater will be the challenge to advance prosocial policies. Even if vested interests, "power" or institutions have played a role in the decline in broad compromises, they are not the root causes of this decline. Rather, as Lakoff and Tawney have suggested, its origins are to be found in the fact that the economic systems of the US and UK have become more likely to produce a competitive, non-empathic and acquisitive type of political ideology, at least among a significant proportion of the populace.[5]

This would then appear to put the Nordic way of doing politics at a crossroads between culture and economics. Though culture plays a definitive part, one cannot neglect the role of geopolitics and economic circumstances. The distinctive political features of the Nordic countries are also likely to have derived from the fact that the nations in question have small and open economies, depending on international trade and interaction with the surrounding world through commerce, migration, cultural exchanges, etc. Even if institutions, means and agencies have been different in the individual nation-states and subject to change over time, the geopolitical and economic circumstances have undoubtedly contributed greatly to the development of similar values, institutions and agencies across the region, which in turn have produced economic growth, employment and equality (Dølvik et al. 2014). The Competitive Partnership (*konfliktpartnerskapet*), forged in the first half of the 20th century between the social partners and between the labour parties and the conservatives, was an acknowledgement of interdependence and the need to find a common ground on which to base conflict resolution.[6] Combined, these agreements created a framework of institutions, rules and regulations that promoted broad political participation, but also peaceful bipartisan solutions to social conflicts. The institutionalization of conflict through the representation and inclusion of affected parties and vested interests thus became a key feature in the political process from the inter-war period onwards.

The Nordic approach to politics is also likely to have derived from the small scale of the Nordic states. Like most successful small states, they have over the centuries based their political model on their ability to build internal competence and provide external shelter (Baldersheim and Keating 2015). If the Nordic countries needed a sharp warning of the consequences of failing to do so, the Icelandic banking crisis of 2008–2011 was it (Thorhallsson 2015).

Returning to Lakoff, it is clear that the cost–benefit analysis in the Nordic countries has been shaped over time both by individuals' expectation of making a return on their tax investment through the universal welfare state, and by their willingness to make sacrifices to the improvement of the collective. For most of the past century, the Nordic countries have had political and economic systems characterized by a high degree of political control over the market, a high level of taxation and a high degree of redistribution. These in turn have shaped the preferences of the population who, unlike people in the US, for instance, no longer experience the tax burden as unduly high.

Challenges to the Nordic way of doing politics

The Nordic countries are certainly not immune to international trends and challenges. Rather, due to their small and open economies relying heavily on foreign trade and access to the global marketplace, successful adaptation to these trends and challenges is a key feature of the Nordic model, as well as the maintenance of the model itself. On the potentially negative side, we see three main challenges to the Nordic model, namely *globalization*, *technocratization* and *mediatization*, which we will discuss further, below. While it should be noted that these challenges are certainly not unique to the Nordic countries, and could also be viewed as possibilities for redevelopment of the model, the early signs of adaption to changing circumstances have not been entirely promising – especially with regard to the prevalent norms of participation and inclusion, the promotion of competence, and the basic prosocial values underpinning the Nordic way of doing politics.

Globalization

For the Nordic countries, globalization is nothing new. They have for centuries, out of necessity, had open economies and a global approach to commerce and economic development. Indeed, one could argue that this approach has been an important feature in developing the Nordic model, in as much as the relatively modest size of their domestic markets has fostered a positive attitude towards international trade and cooperation (Keating 2015). The ability to roll with the punches of globalization is therefore critical and vital to the maintenance and redevelopment of the Nordic model. Furthermore, as Wilson and Hessen (2014) have argued, the solution to the challenges posed by environmental changes necessitates that the Nordic nation-states participate in institutions promoting prosocial policies at a global level, where the social control mechanisms and institutions are relatively weak compared with the Nordic way of doing politics.

Again, the need to adjust to external circumstances in the 21st century is not a novel phenomenon for the Nordic countries. Much of the post-war prosperity of the Nordic countries has been due to a successful adaptation to the Western and global economic system put in place towards the end of the World War II, with the implementation of the Bretton Woods agreements and the General Agreement on Tariffs and Trade. The countries have also, albeit in slightly different ways, adapted successfully to the change of environment delivered by intergovernmental and supranational organizations such as the United Nations, NATO and the European Union.

While most of the current debate on the impact of globalization on the Nordic model has focused on its effect on specific policies, especially concerning the ability to protect national industries and reduce welfare export and welfare tourism, it is our contention that a far more serious challenge is to its political processes. This takes place in at least two ways: (i) the making of political decisions is increasingly taken out of the traditional institutions of the nation-state; (ii) new groups emerge – in the aftermath of increased migration across borders – with a low level of political participation, causing an intensification of uncertainty among the general population.

On the political left, neoliberal ideology has been seen as the root cause of these "deplorable" developments, leading towards an increasingly unhinged form of capitalism. At the opposite side, on the political right, blame for negative changes is placed on a leftist ideology increasingly influenced by multiculturalism and identity politics. This has led to a growth of political polarization and tribalism. As Jonathan Haidt (2013) has pointed out, politics has always been about competing factions and groups. However, the new conflict lines have tended to become more about values and identity, which do not easily lend themselves to compromises in the same way as, for example, the conflict between workers and business interests. Compared with the United States, for example, the increase in political polarization and tribalism is still at a low level in the Nordic countries. However, the development is cause for concern for a model based on the ability to reach bipartisan political compromises.

The increased focus on identity and values is also, undoubtedly, closely linked to increasing levels of international migration, which might change the political culture of the Nordic countries in adverse ways. Taking the Norwegian voting population as an example, the number of eligible voters with an immigrant background has more than doubled over the past decade, up from 6 per cent in 2003 to 14 per cent in 2015 (of which 6 per cent have gained Norwegian citizenship).[7] The turnout is, however, considerably lower among the immigrant population as a whole and even among Norwegian-born descendants of immigrants. The participation in national elections is somewhat higher than in local elections, 53 per cent and 40 per cent, respectively, but shows a significantly lower participation than among the general electorate (78 per cent in national and 62 per cent in local elections). The contrast is even starker when looking at elected officials. In the most recent local elections in 2015, only 3 per cent came from an immigrant background (NOU 2017:2: 136f.). While there are both regional and national nuances, these numbers do not seem to vary significantly across the Nordic countries.

While the available research suggests that there is a strong correlation between the level of social interaction with the majority population and voting patterns among immigrants, it shows a weak correlation between voting and affiliation with religious or immigrant organizations (NOU 2017:2; see also FAFO 2012: 26). As the Norwegian government commission on the long-term consequences of immigration (the Brochmann II commission) has pointed out, participation in democratic processes brings a sense of community, trust and support for democratic principles, and a low voter turnout can be interpreted as a lack of engagement and identification with the democratic system (NOU 2017:2: 137). In relation to our starting point, that high levels of participation are important both to channel competence into the political process and to generate trust in the eventual outcome, this obviously represents an important challenge for the Nordic model.

Assembling a functioning multi-ethnic society is difficult and its potential for breaking down will be a constant challenge, but it is by no means impossible. Our argument, building on Haidt (2013) is that the solution to the challenges posed by globalization lie in tackling increased migration through integrating the migrant population in the Nordic way of doing politics, where society and political interaction are organized in a way in which reason and intuition interact in healthy ways. Taking this as a starting point, the Nordic countries need to find new ways to facilitate the development of sympathetic relationships between citizens of differing backgrounds, where they can seek to understand one another instead of using reason to parry opposing views. The emphasis should therefore be on creating spaces for contemplation of opposing arguments to avoid the creation of ideological segregation, which has permeated the political debate in the UK and the US. Increased political interaction across racial, ethnic, social and political boundaries at local and national levels in the Nordic countries would also have the potential effect of generating greater understanding and trust, which are necessary for making global politics work.

Our suggestion, based on the Nordic experiences of the 19th and early 20th centuries, would then be to build social cohesion from the local level upwards, based on a pragmatic justification for Nordic communitarianism. Rather than trying to re-establish the state–citizen relationship eroded by neo-liberalism, the effort should be made to establish and nourish various forms of local and intermediary social organization. Through inclusion at these levels, migrants' participation in the political system can be increased more easily, and their competences and experiences can thus be channelled into the political process. This would in turn promote a better understanding of the Nordic way of doing politics and its prosocial benefits among migrants, and in turn generate a higher level of general trust across social, cultural and ethnic cleavages. Moreover, such an interaction would be expected to increase trust between the majority population and the minorities.

While this may seem like a tall order, recent experiences show that relatively low-resource policies can have a great impact. In the run-up to the Norwegian national election of 2013, researchers sent a package of election information either through the post or by SMS to selected groups among the electorate who had tended to be underrepresented, such as migrants and young people. The results showed a significant increase in participation, especially among migrants (Bergh et al. 2016;NOU 2017:2: 136), which implies that there are still fairly simple solutions to waning levels of political participation available to authorities in the Nordic countries.

Technocratization

The Nordic countries have been characterized by a high degree of correlation between political aims and actual results, and the ability to maintain and re-create these results through various social, political and economic crises. In much of the current literature, the success stories of the Nordic countries have been attributed to their system of tripartite concertation between the state and social partners, i.e. trade unions and employers' associations (Katzenstein 1986; Keating 2015). The main explanation for this is that, rather than relying on a limited set of means or institutions, the Nordic countries have based their policymaking on powerful agencies – the social partners, non-governmental organizations and government institutions. These have had a mutual understanding, institutional manoeuvrability and capacity for strategic thinking, which in turn have facilitated collective competence building and action (Dølvik et al. 2014). Going back to the maintenance and redevelopment mechanisms described above, this process has several advantages, such as bringing an array of competences, stability and legitimacy to a deliberative type of political process.

However, although the institutional features may be path-dependent, in the sense that they are built upon pre-existing traditions and arrangements, they are not permanent or perennial. Within the Nordic countries there has been a tendency, especially among conservative governments, to weaken the direct influence of the social partners in shaping policy, as tripartite concertation and negotiations have given way to expert committees, often without the social partners and even without participation from civil society (Dølvik et al. 2014: 92). There is also a question whether this is a prefiguration of greater ideological misgivings about the Nordic model, in as much as it does appear to be the preference of conservatives and liberalists, but not social democrats, that broad negotiations ought to be replaced by a more technocratic, expert-dominated approach to the making of political decisions.

This tendency will most likely have adverse consequences both for the legitimacy of the processes themselves and for the outcomes they will eventually produce, especially as the conditions for political action are also changing. The traditional bonds between parties and voters have declined, as the social and cultural background of voters has become less important and as values and individual preferences have taken a more central role in determining their choice of political party. The mutation of political parties from broad, mass-based membership organizations to more professional organizations could also weaken both the transparency and the competence-building component of the Nordic model of society and politics (see e.g. Katz and Mair 2009; Hagevi 2014).

A case in point is the development of the Norwegian Labour Party. Since the 1990s, electoral support for the party has been slowly declining, with particularly weak showings in the general elections (held every four years) of 2001, 2013 and 2017. Interestingly, the decline in electoral support has coincided with a radical transformation of political parties in Norway, from mainly voluntary associations whose economy was based on donations and membership fees, to entities almost wholly dependent on transfers of public funds. Increased funding from public sources has in turn been used to employ a larger number of political staff, which in the case of the Norwegian Labour Party has led to a weakening of the relationship between party leaders and ordinary members, and to a general professionalization of the party apparatus. In addition, the bi-annual national party conference morphed from being the Labour Party's main political workshop into a public relations event staged for the Norwegian media (see e.g. Thorsen 2017).

As Brandal and Bratberg (2015: 127) have argued, the small-state character of the Scandinavian countries has served to their advantage when it comes to addressing swift changes in their environment, requiring a refitting of the policy toolkit while permitting the basic structure of the model to remain. The Nordic development model thus seems to illustrate what Pierson (2000) refers to as the 'increasing returns' of a given institutional settlement, where the trajectory of the model is difficult to change because the actors have adapted to it and tend to expand rather than reverse established policies. However, several trends currently point to a weakening of the institutions that have traditionally been the basis of the model. One, which has already been discussed, is the decline of participation in party politics. Whereas the level of social and political activism and engagement seems to hold, it tends to be channelled more through ad hoc organizations and single-issue movements rather than stable civil society organizations (Brandal 2005). These trends apply to the political parties as well as to the social partners – both trade unions and employers' associations.

It is still not clear what the result of this will be for the Nordic model. However, it would seem that, combined with a growing number of rules and regulations being negotiated at a supra-national level, the model runs the risk of a decline in democratic participation, a loss of transparency and reduced general trust in both individual policies and arrangements, and the political system as a whole. What is clear, however, is that whenever traditional structures are weakened, power vacuums emerge that are quickly filled with new actors and new priorities. In the case of the Nordic countries, this means that if political parties and membership in interest-based organizations decline any further, both administrative and corporate leaders are in a position to assume a more proactive role in political processes, and thus remove the effective point of political decision-making further away from the individual citizen. If this premise is correct, the end result could very well be an evolution towards a more tribal political system with a lower level of participation – one more prone to embrace neo-liberal policies, as has been seen in the US and the UK since the 1970s.

However, it is our contention that this development is not inevitable, nor is it caused by globalization itself. Rather, it is due to the lack of knowledge and understanding among the political and financial elites of the Nordic way of doing politics and how it evolved in the 19th and 20th centuries. The solution is, then, to remain faithful to the configuration of the political process and trust it to deliver prosocial policies also in the 21st century.

Mediatization

Traditionally, the mass media have been seen as having three basic functions in a democracy: to act as a watchdog over the state, like an independent fourth estate; to act as an agency of information and debate for citizens to participate in their democracy; and to represnt the voice of the people vis-à-vis the state (Butsch 2007: 7). Free and independent mass media thus facilitate political debate and make elites accountable to the voting public, and have indeed been a key feature in the development of a public sphere underpinning the Nordic democracies for more than a century (Dahl et al. 2010). The notion that increased media involvement in the political sphere could pose a challenge to the traditional ways in which political processes have been structured may therefore sound surprising, but it could make it harder for actors and organizations with different vested interests to reach compromises on broad and often complex issues.

Mediatization is defined as the process in which non-media social institutions conform to an increasing degree to the logic and values of the media. In short, society comes to act through technology and the symbolic worlds of the media, which then constitute the reality with which people interact (Hjarvard 2008). The mediatization of politics is then a process in which political institutions adapt to and become dependent on the media and media logic. On the one hand, this entails the integration of media in the day-to-day political activity of parties and individuals, shaping both the content and the form of politics. On the other hand, it is a process in which the media are also autonomous social institutions that contribute to the establishment of public consent to political decisions and in setting the political agenda. In this way, mediatization necessitates that political agencies must adhere to media norms and standards of newsworthiness and forms of expression, as well as the self-understanding of the media in relation to other social institutions and the public at large. At the same time, the media are driven by a logic that is both outside and different from the logic and norms of the political sphere.[8]

Mediatization poses challenges to the Nordic way of doing politics both through its values and its logic. Starting from the positive functions for the media in a democracy as described above, by stressing the role of the media as a counter-power to the state, the media are more likely to value and protect the rights of the individual over the common good. A case in point would be the issue of taxation. The Nordic countries have through cross-political compromises agreed to pay for a generous welfare state through a high level of taxation. While it may be necessary to pay for publicly provided goods which the citizens have come to take for granted, there is still the issue of who ought to pay the most, and taxes will in any case burden some individuals more than others. Both on the basis of its values and its logic, the media are then more likely to side with those worst affected by taxation than to argue for the common good.

However, as the decline of the party system and the reconfiguration of civil society have weakened the arenas for voluntary work, the media have become more influential in the political process. It has become increasingly difficult for the actors in the political sphere to pass legislation that increases the level of taxation. As we have seen in a number of countries throughout the Western world in the past decade, deficiently financed tax cuts leading to an underfunding of welfare arrangements pose the greatest risk for the modern welfare states and their long-term sustainability (Brandal et al. 2013; Brandal and Bratberg 2015). While this has as yet not been visible at the central level in the Nordic countries, it is a growing conflict at the local level, which has increasingly been made responsible for carrying out national welfare policies. For instance, in Norway, a majority of local councils have had to introduce local property taxes to make up for lost revenues and increased expenditure, leading to an enhanced media scrutiny focusing on individual suffering rather than prudent public finances. At the same time, the very same media also offer enhanced scrutiny on behalf of citizens denied public services due to an impoverishment of the public sector. Viewed in this way, the media contribute to higher levels of public spending, while at the same time encouraging forces that want to cut the actual incomes needed to finance such spending.

One might say that the value basis of the media is based on the freedom of the individual from government and authority, and not freedom through community and solidarity. The competence it brings to the political process is derived from this value basis, and it is indeed an important corrective on its own, but a problem if, and when, it becomes dominant. Furthermore, it runs the risk of feeding into a neoliberal view of the state as the problem. In the Nordic countries, where the state is the main guarantee of individual freedom, undermining the role of the state will inevitably lead to the individual becoming more exposed to the powers of market capitalism. If this erosion of state power is not stopped or state power is replaced by new and similarly powerful forms of social organization, the end result will be a reduction in the freedom of the individual.

Added to this is the media logic of favouring conflict over cooperation in choosing which issues to cover, and how to cover them. Whereas competition is an important part of the multi-level deliberative political process found in the Nordic countries, the political end goal is a broad compromise tying the stakeholders to the outcome. The media, on the other hand, are likely to see political conflicts as more worthy of coverage and as preferable to agreement. While this may lead to a misconfiguring of the political process, it also leads to some issues being given more scrutiny and other issues less, based on their conflict potential (see e.g. Allern 2001; Slaatta 2005). There is therefore a question of whether the values and logics of the media are wholly compatible with the prosocial and conciliatory value basis of the Nordic political model.

The flip side is of course the way in which the political elites have, if not embraced the mediatization process, then certainly been willing to adapt to it. We have increasingly seen the political parties replacing communication through the party system by mass-media communication. The result is decreased opportunities for political participation, which in turn, quite naturally, leads to a decrease in the level of political participation. The long-term risks are obviously decreased trust in the political system, as well as a lower level of competences brought to the table.

The challenges posed by mediatization through the traditional media, however, are miniscule in comparison with those posed by social media. While social media is still relatively new, there is a distinct possibility that the social impact of online social media in the 21st century will be as large as that of traditional media in the past. Just as the development of the printing press meant that information could be transmitted across space and time at a greatly enhanced pace, online social media have given nearly every human being the tools of instant worldwide mass communication. In the pre-20th-century world, the traditional media became the foundation for the scientific and industrial revolutions, which in turn became a key factor in bringing down authoritarian regimes and instigating a transition to democratic rule. The question is whether social media and mobile communication have the potential to become to become an equally corrosive power to the dominant institutions of the 21st century. While the traditional media developed alongside and in symbiosis with democratic institutions in the 19th and early 20th centuries, the libertarian and almost anarchistic leaning of internet media came about almost in direct opposition to them.[9] This development is certainly not unique to the Nordic countries, but it does pose particular challenges to a political system relying on the involvement of mass-membership social and political movements. First and foremost, the increasing role of the internet in politics has further enhanced a changing mode of social organization, from one of stable, long-term structures to one that favours ad hoc movements and short-term mobilization to promote singular causes. This development has had at least two important consequences. On the one hand, such movements have less impetus either for taking a broad, longer-term view or for reaching short-term compromises. Their approach to politics then runs the risk of becoming expressive rather than incremental and instrumental (Lipset 1971). On the other hand, the growth of social media has shifted the power from the traditional political leaders, in as much as their ability to mediate and control connections between the parties and the voters has been weakened. As we saw in the last US election, Donald Trump through his Twitter feed was able to short-circuit the electoral process of the Republican Party, and Bernie Sanders, through his followers' use of online media, came very close to doing the same to the Democratic Party. Before Trump and Sanders, activists' use of online media was a key factor in the election of Jeremy Corbyn as the leader of the British Labour Party.

However, there is some evidence that the Nordic way of doing politics may also withstand the challenges posed by online media. If we take the development of the environmental movement as a case in point, the facilitation of a public sphere (i.e. rather generous funding schemes for NGOs) has meant that the Nordic green movements have developed stable organizational structures. Over time they have evolved into political parties that are currently in the process of being socialized into the Nordic way of doing politics through participating in coalitions with the established parties, mainly on the left. While this is certainly not a novel feature in the Nordic countries – the German Green Party became a coalition partner in a social democratic government as early as the late 1990s – it is more consequential in the Nordic countries due to the nature of the political model. The result is that, rather than remaining as protest movements, the overwhelming majority of green organizations, both inside and outside of the political sphere, have come to take an incremental view and have shown themselves capable of joining in negotiated compromise solutions.

The challenges posed by the weakening of party structures, however, have become more serious with the advent of social media. According to Jonathan Haidt (2013), the growth of social media has been the major driving force behind political tribalism in the US, immersing citizens in "a constant stream of unbelievable outrages perpetrated by the other side" and making it increasingly difficult to trust and work together towards common goals (Illing 2017). This view is supported by the American legal scholar Nathaniel Persily (2017), who argues that the rise in power of the internet has accelerated the decline of institutions that once provided a mediating force in political campaigns. Neither the traditional media nor the established political parties exercise the power they once had as referees, particularly in helping their members and sympathisers to assess the quality of information. Beyond that, the traditional media, which once helped set the agenda for political conversation, now often take their cues from new media. Social media often determine what the old media talk about, and what transforms issues into trending topics is often determined by unknown, but by no means disinterested, forces such as the algorithms of Google, Twitter and Facebook, to name but three. As we have seen recently in the referendum on Brexit in the UK and the US presidential election, the end result can have seriously adverse consequences for the political system, in terms of building majorities for clearly irresponsible alternatives (Grassegger and Krogerus 2017; Cadwalladr 2017). As the African-American poet and actor Theo Wilson has noted, social media are showing signs of becoming to politics what a car is to road rage: the glass and steel create a bubble of perceived safety, which amplifies people's rage, but keeps them from having to deal with the consequences of that rage (Holley 2017). While there were anonymous political forms of communication and false or misleading stories in the media before the internet, social media have characteristics that can heighten their disruptive and damaging influence on political campaigns. According to Persily, one such characteristic is the speed with which news, including fake news, moves, expands and is absorbed. Viral communication can create dysfunction in campaigns and within democracies. Another is the pervasiveness of anonymous communication, facilitating a coarsening of speech on the internet. It has become more and more difficult to determine the source of such information.

Available research from the Nordic countries would seem to support Persily's warnings. Social media have become an important news source, but are consumed and interacted with differently across various social groups. A major divide seems to be between the educated and non-educated, where the educated tend to have greater variety in their news consumption. Ytre-Arne et al. (2017: 31) have described the different approaches and possibilities for information accrual as a divide between "news-omnivores" and "news-monovores". This leads to increased differences in accumulation of *public capital*, understood as the sum of everything that touches on the ability and desire to participate in the public debate, as well as the ability to make oneself heard and make use of available information. Furthermore, instead of using social media as a new way of opening up and "re-democratizing" the political process to a broader spectrum of participants, the political parties have preferred to use it as a one-way stream of information.

It is far from clear how the current media trends will change and shape the Nordic way of doing politics. Will important discussions be removed from a critical discourse, or will the possibilities for participation be further enhanced? Will mediatization lead to enhanced conflict and polarization as the algorithms of social media lock the participants into political and social bubbles or echo chambers? And what will this development mean for the possibilities of maintaining a shared moral value foundation based on mixing individualism and communitarianism in the future? One thing is clear: if the Nordic countries are to maintain the prosocial approach in, and to, politics, they will require political leadership that is able and willing to counterbalance the power of the media and rejuvenate the faith in the embodied and personalized political processes that have shaped the Nordic way of doing politics.

Conclusion: the future of the Nordic way of doing politics

There is no one, single feature found in the Nordic way of doing politics that is unique to the Nordic countries. Its uniqueness is rather found in the complex make-up of its policies, institutions, traditions and processes. As we have argued in this chapter, the key feature of the Nordic way of doing politics is therefore the way in which the political processes have been structured. Furthermore, broad political compromises, which have proven to be stable over time, have been possible due to a closer alignment in both values and basic view of human nature across the political spectrum, grounded in a peculiarly Nordic mix of communitarianism and individualism, where the state has been the key guarantor of the freedom of the individual. The key example is how the government-run welfare state frees up individual citizens to be the masters of their own destiny. They have the security to exchange a low-paying job for a better paying one without having to worry about their retirement funds or health insurance, or about finding good schools and kindergartens near the new workplace. However, one might argue that dependency on the state and the relative weakness of more informal collectives at the intermediary and local level mean that the Nordic countries are more vulnerable to the forces of neoliberalism. When the role of the state is weakened, it leaves the individual more exposed, as the main bulwark against the disenfranchising effects of market capitalism is also weakened.

Furthermore, while the conditions for political action will inevitably change, and necessitate an ever-changing process of adaptation and renewal, the decline of the traditional bonds between parties and voters that was developed alongside democratic institutions in the 19th and 20th centuries is also a worrying sign for the Nordic way of doing politics. The social and cultural background of voters has become less important in determining their political choices, while values, opinions and individual preferences have taken centre stage. As we have outlined in this chapter, this development means that the uniquely Nordic way of doing politics faces serious challenges both in the present and in the near future, and its continued success rests on its ability to adapt to the changing environment. Globalization is certainly a challenge to specific welfare policies based on some form of universal coverage (NOU 2017:2). However, a deeper challenge for the Nordic countries is the way in which it has moved political processes from the national to the supra-national level, and to political and economic institutions with less democratic transparency and legitimacy (Berge et al. 2009; NOU 2011:7). Likewise, increased complexity disfigures existing political processes by placing more of the opportunities for deliberation in the hands of expert committees, professional politicians and bureaucrats. That way, political decisions increasingly stem from deals being made between national and international political elites, rather than from broad-based negotiations (Berge et al. 2009; Dølvik et al. 2015). Finally, round-the-clock media coverage of politicians and their initiatives makes fast communication through social media attractive to the political elites, as opposed to the more demanding and drawn-out forms of deliberation and negotiations between stakeholders and broad-based interest groups (Hjarvard 2008).

Far from being merely a mechanical process, the development of the political model in the Nordic countries has been due to mechanisms in the political culture that reward altruism and punish selfishness, thus ensuring that the principal agencies have the necessary legitimacy and power to initiate and implement comprehensive prosocial policies. Currently, only one major political party – the Danish Liberal Alliance – could with some justification be said to explicitly challenge the core values and organizational basis of the Nordic model (Hedegaard 2016; see also Jupskås 2015: 53f.). However, the lack of policies to counter the challenges discussed above poses a risk to the legitimacy of both specific policy outcomes and the high level of trust that has been the hallmark of policy formation in Scandinavia for some time. Sustained collective action has already become more difficult, and, as groups and associations based on traditional social identities dwindle, they are replaced by "event communities", temporary gatherings that come and go without long-term commitment. Partly as a response to this development, and partly as an adaptation to the media logic, we have seen signs of political parties mutating from broad, mass-based membership organizations into more professional, cartel-like organizations. These developments could adversely affect the transparency and participation-inducing components of the Nordic model. At the same time, the adaptive mechanisms built into the Nordic model have been put under pressure by ideologies and new political movements which do not see thorough deliberation and the capacity for compromise as a strength, at least not necessarily so (e.g. Andersen et al. 2009).

The overall impact of these challenges moves the point of effective political decision-making away from locally and nationally constituted interest groups, concentrating power among economic and administrative elites. On the other hand, it also weakens the power of the state to ensure the freedom of the individual. Political power is thus moved to groups and institutions that do not necessarily share all the prosocial values, nor appreciate and facilitate the participation and transparency underpinning the model, nor contribute the same broad level of competence to the political process. The end result could then be an erosion both of the prosocial mechanisms and of trust in the political system among the population at large, leading to more tribalism within the political system.

In our view, the main answer to the challenges is to maintain the deliberative and prosocial competence-building process of negotiated solutions between units at different levels. As we have argued, the social mediatization of politics poses a particular threat of polarizing the Nordic political system. As yet, it is not possible to identify political tribalism that matches the level seen in many other countries, but recent developments within information technology have undoubtedly put the traditional Nordic arrangements for deliberation and conflict management under pressure. A prerequisite for a competitive political discourse to function in a non-harmful way is that its leaders both within the political sphere and in civil society make it a priority to persuade citizens to accept the legitimacy of political perspectives they themselves do not share. In other words, the future of the Nordic way of doing politics is dependent upon a leadership that appreciates the benefits of prosocial behaviour with regard to both political process and policies, and is determined to avoid the temptations presented by new technology and international trends to short-change the system. As in the 19th and 20th centuries, this will require a leap of faith and belief in the self-correcting ability of Lijphart's "kinder and gentler democracy".

On the other hand, the cornerstones of the support for the Nordic model, i.e. the power relations and institutionally anchored interest patterns in the Nordic countries, mean that any political agencies attempting to fundamentally alter the Nordic model must be prepared to suffer severe political costs (Berge et al. 2009: 76). As mentioned above, even the populist right parties in Norway and Sweden have embraced the cornerstones of important policies such as the welfare state arrangements, and thus internalized important prosocial values of caring and fairness more commonly associated with the left in Haidt's moral foundation theory.

Both in the present and in the future, there are serious questions to be asked about whether the Nordic way of doing politics is suitable for solving the conflict between selfishness and mutual benefits beyond the national level. However, it is our contention and conclusion that, while the entrenched traditions play a significant role in making the Nordic model resilient, ultimately it is the democratic citizens in Scandinavia who will decide whether to maintain or dismantle the model that made them thrive and prosper.

Notes

1 While the reduced political role of the nobility in the 18th and early 19th centuries undoubtedly played an important role in the democratization of the Nordic countries, this happened for very different reasons across the individual countries, and cannot thus be attributed to a particular feature or culture in the Nordic model.

2 The German political scientist Thomas Meyer has seen this as a specific feature of social democracy (Meyer 2011).
3 While some have argued that the prevalence of coalition governments in the Nordic countries is an expression of this shared value basis, there is little evidence to support this. Rather, as the Norwegian political scientist Kaare Strom has shown, it seems to be the result of an electoral system geared towards producing such coalitions, which is not unique to the Nordic countries. The prevalence of minority governments, however, seems to be a Nordic feature. (Strom 1990).
4 One should note, however, that the experience of right-wing populist parties in a coalition government – namely that of the Norwegian Progress Party (FrP) in a centre-right minority government – is somewhat mixed. Rather than being forced by the weight of governing into adapting to rules and procedures, individual ministers have been allowed to act as an external opposition with regard to immigration and integration. Thus, the Progress Party has been able to avoid bearing the political costs of becoming a responsible governing party.
5 The argument has been developed by the Welsh political theorist Christopher White.
6 A basic agreement between the social partners was made in Denmark as early as 1899, in Sweden (the Saltsjöbaden Agreement) in 1938 and in Norway (Hovedavtalen) in 1935. Similarly, the Kanslergade Compromise (Kanslergadeforliget) in Denmark was made in 1933 and the Crisis Compromise (Kriseforliket) in Norway in 1935.
7 While only Norwegian citizens get to vote in national elections, citizens of foreign countries with at least three years of continuous legal residence are allowed to participate in local elections. Citizens of other Nordic countries, with which Norway has a shared labour market, may participate in local election after less than three months of continuous residence in Norway.
8 The operationalization of the concept for the purpose of this chapter is derived from Mazzoleni and Schultz (cf. Hjarvard 2008: 29), who links mediatization directly to the problematic aspects of media influence on the political sphere.
9 For example, the GOP operative and former chief of staff to President George W. Bush, Karl Rove, has argued that the interactive nature of digital communication promotes a feeling of individual agency among users. It thus leads them to question the importance of a large central government, and nudges them toward libertarianism (Goldberg 2007).

References

Allern, Sigurd (2001) *Flokkdyr på Løvebakken: søkelys på Stortingets presselosje og politikkens medierammer*. Oslo: Pax.
Andersen, John, Larsen, Jørgen Elm and Møller, Iver Hornemann (2009) The Exclusion and Marginalisation of Immigrants in the Danish Welfare Society: Dilemmas and Challenges. *International Journal of Sociology and Social Policy* 29 (5/6): 274–286.
Bendixsen, Synnove, Bringslid, Mary Bente and Vike, Halvard (eds) (2017) *Egalitarianism in Scandinavia: Historical and Contemporary Perspectives*. Basingstoke: Palgrave Macmillan.
Berge, Øyvind, Christensen, Johan, Dølvik, Jon Erik. Fløtten, Tone. Hippe, Jon M. Kavli. Hanne and Trygstad, Sissel (2009) *De nordiske modellene etter 2000 – en sammenliknende oppsummering*. Fafo-report 2009: 11. Oslo: Fafo.

Bergh, Johannes, Christensen, Dag Arne and Matland, Richard E. (2016) *Getting Out the Vote. Experiments in Voter Mobilization among Immigrants and Natives in Norway*. Report. Oslo: Institutt for samfunnsforskning.

Berlin, Isaiah (1958) *Two Concepts of Liberty: An Inaugural Lecture Delivered Before the University of Oxford on 31 October 1958*. Oxford: Clarendon Press.

Berlin, Isaiah (2002) Two Concepts of Liberty. In: Henry Hardy (ed.), *Liberty: Incorporating Four Essays on Liberty*. Oxford: Oxford University Press.

Berman, Sheri (2006) *The Primacy of Politics: Social Democracy and the Making of Europe's Twentieth Century*. Cambridge: Cambridge University Press.

Berman, Sheri (2017) *The Pipe Dream of Undemocratic Liberalism. Journal of Democracy* 28 (3): 29–39.

Brandal, Nik. (2005) Mellom staten og samfunnet: LNUs nasjonale arbeid frå 1980 til idag. In: Unni Kvam (ed.), *Frå byrjinga ... og fram til idag: Landsrådet for Norges barne- og ungdomsorganisasjonar (LNU) 25 år*. Oslo: LNU.

Brandal, Nik and Bratberg, Øivind (2015) Small-state Scandinavia: Social Investment or Social Democracy? In: Harald Baldersheim and Michael Keating (eds), *Small States in the Modern World. Vulnerabilities and Opportunities*. Cheltenham: Edward Elgar Publishing.

Brandal, Nik, Bratberg, Øivind and Thorsen, Dag Einar (2013) *The Nordic Model of Social Democracy*. Basingstoke: Palgrave Macmillan.

Burke, Edmund (2004[1790]) *Reflections on the Revolution in France*. Edited by Conor Cruise O'Brien. London: Penguin.

Butsch, Richard (ed.) (2007) *Media and Public Spheres*. Basingstoke: Palgrave Macmillan.

Cadwalladr, Carole (2017) *The Great British Brexit Robbery: How Our Democracy Was Hijacked*. The Guardian May 7th. Available at: www.theguardian.com/technology/2017/may/07/the-great-british-brexit-robbery-hijacked-democracy (accessed 17 December 2017).

Dahl, Hans Fredrik, Eide, Martin Ottosen, Rune, Hjeltnes, Guri and Flo, Idar (eds) (2010) *Norsk presses historie*, Vols 1–4. Oslo: Norwegian University Press.

Dølvik, Jon Erik, Fløtten, Tone, Hippe, Jon M. and Jordfald, Bård (2014) *Den nordiske modellen mot 2030. Et nytt kapittel?* Fafo-report 2014: 46. Oslo: Fafo.

Dølvik, Jon Erik, Fløtten, Tone, Hippe, Jon M. and Jordfald, Bård (2015) The Nordic Model Towards 2030: A New Chapter? Fafo report 2015: 07. Oslo: Fafo.

Esping-Andersen, Gøsta (1990) *The Three Worlds of Welfare Capitalism*. Cambridge: Polity.Tronstad, Kristian Rose and Rogstad, Jon (2012) *Stemmer de ikke? Politisk deltakelse blant innvandrere og norskfødte med innvandrerforeldre*. Fafo-report 2012: 26. Oslo: Fafo.

Glover, Jonathan (2012) *Humanity: A Moral History of the 20th Century*. 2nd ed. New Haven: Yale University Press.

Goldberg, Jeffrey (2007) *Party Unfaithful: The Republican Implosion*. The New Yorker June 4th 2007. Cf. www.newyorker.com/magazine/2007/06/04/party-unfaithful (accessed December 17th 2017).

Grassegger, Hannes and Krogerus, Mikael (2017) *The Data That Turned the World Upside Down*. Motherboard January 28th 2017. https://motherboard.vice.com/en_us/article/mg9vvn/how-our-likes-helped-trump-win (accessed August 21st 2017).

Habermas, Jürgen (1962) *Strukturwandel der Öffentlichkeit: Untersuchungen zu einer Kategorie der bürgerlichen Gesellschaft*. Neuwied am Rhein: Luchterhand.

Hagevi, Magnus (2014) *Förändrade villkor för riksdagens partigrupper. Statsvetenskaplig tidskrift* 116 (1): 5–20.

Haidt, Jonathan (2013) *The Righteous Mind: Why Good People Are Divided by Politics and Religion*. New York: Vintage Books.
Hedegaard, Troels Fage (2016) *Neo-liberalism and the Nordic Welfare Model: A Study of the Liberal Alliance and Ideological Adaptation in Denmark*. Nordic Journal of Social Research 7. Available at: https://journals.hioa.no/index.php/njsr/article/view/2099 (accessed 28 September 2017).
Hjarvard, Stig (ed.) (2008) *En verden af medier – Medialiseringen af politik, sprog, religion og leg*. Copenhagen: Samfundslitteratur.
Holley, Peter A. (2017) *A Black Man Went Undercover Online as a White Supremacist. This is What he Learned*. Washington Post, 24 August. Available at: www.washingtonpost.com/news/the-switch/wp/2017/08/24/a-black-man-went-undercover-as-a-digital-white-supremacist-this-is-what-he-learned/?utm_term=.5eb581f893fe (accessed 17 December 2017).
Illing, Sean (2017) *Why Social Media Is Terrible for Multi-ethnic Democracies*. Vox, 18 June. Available at: www.vox.com/policy-and-politics/2016/11/15/13593670/donald-trump-jonathan-haidt-social-media-polarization-europe-multiculturalism (accessed 20 June 2017).
Jupskås, Anders (2015) *Persistence of Populism: The Norwegian Progress Party, 1973–2009*. Oslo: University of Oslo.
Katz, Richard S. and Mair, Peter (2009) *The Cartel Party Thesis: A Restatement*. Perspectives on Politics 7 (4): 753–766.
Katzenstein, Peter J. (1986) *Small States in World Markets. Industrial Policy in Europe*. Ithaca; London: Cornell University Press.
Keating, Michael (2015) *The Political Economy of Small States in Europe*. In: Harald Baldersheim and Michael Keating (eds), Small States in the Modern World. Vulnerabilities and Opportunities. Cheltenham: Edward Elgar.
Lakoff, George (1996) *Moral Politics: What Conservatives Know that Liberals Don't*. Chicago, IL: University of Chicago Press.
Lijphart, Arend (2012) *Patterns of Democracy: Government Forms and Performance in Thirty-Six Countries*. 2nd ed. New Haven: Yale University Press.
Lindner, Evelyn (2013) Ydmykelse, ydmykhet, og demokrati. In: Bernt Hagtvet, Nik Brandal and Dag Einar Thorsen (eds), *Folkemordenes svarte bok*, 2nd ed. Oslo: Norwegian University Press.
Listhaug, Ola and Ringdal, Kristen (2007) *Trust in Political Institutions: The Nordic Countries Compared with Europe*. Paper prepared for the Norwegian Political Science Meeting, NTNU, Trondheim, 3–5 January.
Margalit, Avishai (1996) *The Decent Society*. Trans. Naomi Goldblum. Cambridge, MA: Harvard University Press.
Meyer, Thomas (2011) *Theorie der sozialen Demokratie*, 2. Durchgesehene und aktualisierte Auflage. Wiesbaden: VS Verlag für Sozialwissenschaften.
NOU 2011:7 (2011) *Velferd og migrasjon – den norske modellens framtid* (the Brochmann I Commission). Oslo: Ministry of Children and Equality.
NOU 2017:2 (2017) *Integrasjon og tillit – Langsiktige konsekvenser av høy innvandring* (the Brochmann II Commission). Oslo: Ministry of Justice and Public Security.
Persily, Nathaniel (2017) *Can Democracy Survive the Internet?* Journal of Democracy 28 (2): 63–76.
Pierson, Paul (2000) *Increasing Returns, Path Dependence, and the Study of Politics*. American Political Science Review 94 (2): 251–267.

Rawls, John (1993) *Political Liberalism*. New York: Columbia University Press.
Reinemann, Carsten (2010) *Medialisierung ohne Ende? Zum Stand der Debatte um Medieneinflüsse auf die Politik*. Zeitschrift für Politik, Neue Folge, 57 (3): 278–293.
Rosenberg, Paul (2017) *Don't Think of a Rampaging Elephant: Linguist George Lakoff explains how the Democrats helped elect Trump*. Salon.com, 15 January. Available at: www.salon.com/2017/01/15/dont-think-of-a-rampaging-elephant-linguist-george-lakoff-explains-how-the-democrats-helped-elect-trump (accessed 17 December 2017).
Sejersted, Francis (2011) *The Age of Social Democracy: Norway and Sweden in the Twentieth Century*. Princeton: Princeton University Press.
Simpson, Alan K. (1998) That's Politics. Ubben Lecture, Meharry Hall, 11 June. Available at: www.youtube.com/watch?v=7YBrskGpAag (accessed 17 December 2017).
Slaatta, Tore (2005) *Makt og demokrati i den norske medieorden*. Nytt Norsk Tidsskrift 22 (1): 79–91.
Sørensen, Øystein (1993) *Verdenskrig og velferd: britiske, tyske og norske sosialpolitiske planer under annen verdenskrig*. Oslo: Cappelen.
Stråth, Bo (2017) The Cultural Construction of Equality in Norden. In: Bendixen, Synnove et al. (eds), *Egalitarianism in Scandinavia: Historical and Contemporary Perspectives*. Basingstoke: Palgrave Macmillan.
Stråth, Bo and Sørensen, Øystein (eds) (1997) *The Cultural Construction of Norden*. Oslo: Scandinavian University Press.
Strom, Kaare (1990) *Minority Government and Majority Rule*. Cambridge: Cambridge University Press.
Tawney, R. H. (1920) *The Acquisitive Society*. New York: Harcourt Brace.
Thorhallsson, Baldur (2015) *Do Small States Need Shelter? The Economic and Political Turmoil in Iceland*. In: H. Baldersheim and M. Keating (eds), *Small States in the Modern World: Vulnerabilities and Opportunities*. Cheltenham: Edward Elgar.
Thorsen, Dag Einar (2012) *The Politics of Freedom: A Study of the Political Thought of Isaiah Berlin and Karl Popper, and of the Challenge of Neoliberalism*. Oslo: University of Oslo.
Thorsen, Dag Einar (2017) *Rådgiverpartiet*. NRK Ytring 13 September. www.nrk.no/ytring/radgiverpartiet-1.13687433 (accessed September 28th 2017).
Trägårdh, Lars (ed.) (2007) *State and Civil Society in Northern Europe: The Swedish Model Reconsidered*. New York: Berghahn Books.
Vike, Hallvard (2013) *Egalitarianisme og byråkratisk individualisme*. Norsk antropologisk tidsskrift 24 (3–4): 181–193.
Wilson, David Sloan and Hessen, Dag O. (2014) *Blueprint for the Global Village*. Social Evolution Forum. https://evolution-institute.org/focus-article/blueprint-for-the-global-village (accessed August 14th 2017).
Wilson, David Sloan, Ostrom, Elinor and Cox, M. E. (2013) *Generalizing the Core Design Principles for the Efficacy of Groups*. Journal of Economic Behavior & Organization 90: 21–32.
Witoszek, Nina (2011) *The Origins of the Regime of Goodness: Remapping the Norwegian Cultural History*. Oslo: Universitetsforlaget.
Ytre-Arne, Brita, Hovden, Jan Fredrik Moe, Hallvard, Torgeir Uberg, Nærland, Sakariassen, Hilde and Johannesen, Ingrid Aarseth (2017) *Mediebruk og offentlig tilknytning. Delrapport fra Mecin-prosjektet*. Bergen: University of Bergen.

10 Civilising global capitalism
Aligning CSR and the welfare state[1]

Atle Midttun

Introduction

There have been arguments to the effect that the predominantly business driven CSR agenda is antithetical to the politically driven welfare state tradition. The Nordic deployment of CSR, however shows otherwise. The chapter demonstrates that, while solid domestic welfare state arrangements are certainly not substituted by CSR, Nordic companies and Nordic state governments have appropriated CSR pragmatically in areas where traditional welfare state policies lack resources or outreach. One of these areas is the international economy, where CSR becomes part of what can be called a tacit strategy for "civilizing global capitalism". This chapter shows how CSR may be part of a 'soft law' approach, where the Nordics and like-minded countries push an institutional agenda for social and environmental upgrading of the international economy. The soft CSR approach could be seen as a stepping stone towards hard law. However, the chapter also shows how the Nordic political embrace of CSR may in itself be an emerging modality of international governance – a 'partnered governance' where sustainability-oriented states and businesses, seconded by civil society-organizations work together, challenging each other in a normative space in brand-sensitive markets in a communicative society.

Accommodating CSR in welfare states

Over the last couple of decades, corporate social responsibility (CSR) has risen steadily on the international agenda. Large western European and North American multinational companies have found it necessary to develop CSR programmes and initiatives to comply with ethical expectations voiced by well organized interest groups, often in the media spotlight.

The inclusion of CSR in advanced welfare states' public policies, however, involves reconciling two starkly different traditions. The Nordic welfare state tradition emphasizes universal rights and duties, extensive state engagement in the economy, and negotiated agreements to regulate labour relationships. In contrast, the CSR tradition originated in a neoliberal, Anglo-American context and emphasizes corporate discretion, voluntarism and market-based policy solutions.

The welfare state tradition

Fundamental to advanced welfare state policy is the idea of policy implementation through public regulation and "economic tripartism", where business, labour and state interact to establish economic policy. A central feature of the welfare state is the high degree to which social policy transfer payments are "decommodified", that is, made independent of the market mechanism and the degree of stratification they produce in society (Esping-Andersen 1990).

Nevertheless, despite the central role of public policy and negotiated agreements, the Nordic model is also known for its ability to deliver market results. In a comparative study of European political economy, Sapir (2005) praises the Nordic welfare states for delivering both efficiency and equity. The Nordic model's proposed "double dividend" has continued to attract both popular and scholarly attention. It was hailed as "the future of capitalism" (Milne 2009) and was highlighted in the Davos World Economic Forum in both 2011 and 2012 for its resilience to the European economic crisis.

The CSR tradition

As opposed to the welfare state tradition, with its strong reliance on public policy, the CSR tradition assumes that open societies with competitive markets and free media can drive businesses to adopt strong, voluntary self-regulation to enhance social and environmental performance. In other words, CSR delegates key welfare issues to the discretion of businesses and private actors.

The business-driven CSR agenda in many ways complements political liberalism, with a strong emphasis on individual freedom and the doctrine of limited state interference, which subscribes to a small public sector and larger reliance on corporate and civil society initiatives. Essentially, CSR builds on a state–market–civil society model in which business and civil society are the main actors in securing decent social and environmental conditions. Thus, CSR draws the boundaries between state, market and civil society in a fundamentally different way than the advanced welfare state model, indicating that CSR has a close affinity to neoliberal ideals. As Sadler and Lloyd (2009) argue, it is no coincidence that CSR debates have been most prevalent in those societies at the forefront of neoliberalization: the United Kingdom and the United States.

Compatibility and contradiction

The welfare state and CSR literatures leave considerable ambiguity regarding the relationship between CSR and the advanced welfare state. With respect to goals, the CSR agenda, with its emphasis on fostering socially and environmentally responsible business practices, resonates well with the ethos of the Nordic welfare states. For example, the CSR idea of the "triple bottom line" (Elkington 1999), securing balanced development whereby financial, social and environmental elements are all are factored in, compares well with

Nordic welfare state policies whereby business development is regulated and/ or negotiated to take into account distributive and ecological concerns. The CSR tradition's idea of commercial responsibility for development in regional clusters (Porter and Kramer 2006) apparently fits well with the Nordic states' emphasis on regional welfare and development. Furthermore, CSR's focus on socially responsible investments fits the advanced welfare state ambitions of socially motivated economies.

At the level of *means*, however, the two traditions differ. As opposed to the advanced welfare state model, CSR relies primarily on voluntary business initiatives. CSR is traditionally industry-driven and delegates key welfare issues to business discretion. Consequently, the representation of stakeholder interests in CSR is not related to numerical democracy, traditional political bargaining or corporatist structures. In contrast, advanced welfare states emphasize that the responsibility for social and environmental concerns lies with government, and even the business sector in the Nordic countries is sceptical about voluntary solutions in securing key welfare goals (Lindell and Karagozoglu 2001).

The apparent compatibility between the CSR tradition and the advanced welfare state tradition is therefore conditional, and might depend on whether one is speaking of *goals* or *means*.

Strategies for accommodation

Although goal compatibility offers the promise of extending the welfare state programme into the global economy, the conflict in means among the four Nordic states threatens to prevent that extension. The question is if, and how, CSR can be translated into welfare-state-compatible forms, where either contradictions are softened or CSR engagements are focused on policy fields where tensions are less likely to arise. To explore these questions, this chapter draws on a study that examines government CSR engagement in Denmark, Finland, Norway and Sweden and investigates their respective policy formulation and operational implementation of CSR in its formative years in the first decade of the 21st century (Midttun et al. 2015).[2]

The study found that Nordic CSR policy practices, with potential conflicts at the operational level, were largely resolved by introducing CSR policy as a supplement to the old welfare state agenda. However, tailoring CSR policy to supplement the welfare state agenda involved specific applications in each country and entailed careful accommodation of CSR policies to national institutions and traditions. The interviews and the policy documents collected for this analysis indicate that there are three main strategies of accommodation, as illustrated in Figure 10.1:

1. *Externalizing* potential conflicts by confining CSR policies to a foreign policy for international welfare capitalism.
2. *Supplementing* welfare state protection, but only in times of obvious welfare state limitations.

190 *Midttun*

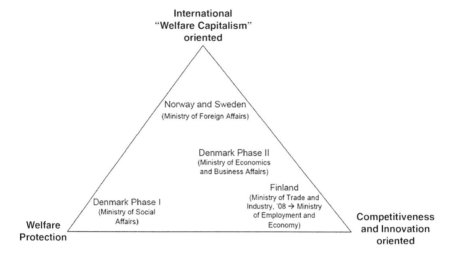

Figure 10.1 Government strategies to increase compatibility between CSR and advanced welfare states' policies

Note: "08 ->" indicates a shift of the political anchoring of CSR from one ministry to another in 2008.

3. *Compartmentalizing CSR* by confining it to a field less amenable to traditional regulation, namely, competitiveness and innovation.

Externalizing CSR: the international welfare capitalism model

The Norwegian and Swedish solutions of focusing CSR abroad are the most obvious cases of externalization, with CSR filling a regulatory gap in the global market economy that has not been amenable to traditional regulatory governance. In Sweden and Norway, known for their high international ambitions, CSR is thus aligned with strong Nordic political engagement for a socially responsible welfare model in the global economy. This effort to shape the global market arena in accordance with Nordic standards is couched in rhetoric of moral obligation; the aim is to increase social welfare, environmental protection and economic prosperity in developing countries, as opposed to merely promoting the interests of domestic business communities. For such reasons, an interviewee from the Swedish Ministry of Foreign Affairs disliked the "Eurocentric focus on CSR as competitive advantage" as opposed to CSR as a means to improve social and environmental standards in developing countries. This humanitarian justification of and motivation for political engagement in CSR is mirrored in the Norwegian White Paper on CSR:

> Just as politics is not an end in itself, but a means of promoting social change for the benefit of the people and the environment, a company's profits or activities are not goals that can be viewed in isolation from

other considerations. Economic activities also require an ethical foundation that puts people, the environment and broader social considerations centre stage.

(Norwegian Government, 2008–2009, p. 6)

Using CSR to promote international welfare capitalism ties in with Nordic foreign policy goals generally, which, in Kuisma's (2007) words are strongly influenced by an internationalist, normative project of "spreading the good message of [...] social democracy to the world". Promoting global welfare capitalism through CSR can be seen as a logical counterpart to, and extension of, the welfare state at home, in what Bergman (2007) terms a "co-constitution of domestic and international welfare obligations". Correspondingly, CSR in both Norway and Sweden has been firmly led by the Ministries of Foreign Affairs, with the Ministries of Trade and Industry taking a second seat. Some interviewees even perceived CSR as a clever tool to bypass traditional politics by going straight to the corporate level, especially in countries like China, where, for instance the Swedish government has had limited success in raising certain issues through the ordinary political channels: "CSR is used to promote politically sensitive issues such as labour rights and human rights, without any links to the political level".[3]

Elements of the international welfare capitalism model of CSR were, however, not only confined to Norway and Sweden, but also present in the other Nordic countries, as they all emphasize multilateral solutions and institutions in their CSR policies.

Supplementing CSR: the domestic welfare protection model

The early Danish CSR policy model, with its focus on domestic labor market issues, contrasts with the Norwegian and Swedish CSR approaches and reflects the extraordinarily high Danish public unemployment expenses in the 1990s. Denmark has the most extensive practice of the so-called Nordic flexicurity model, with higher benefits and payments for retraining than elsewhere in the Nordic countries (Nørgaard 2007). The Danish government creatively included CSR in the labour market policy arena, traditionally dominated by regulations and tripartite agreements – between government, civil society and industry – thereby implementing CSR and encouraging voluntary industrial engagement to supplement the welfare state by way of confronting extraordinary socio-political challenges early in the 1990s. However, several interviewees question whether the Danish government's use of CSR in flexicurity really amounted to anything new and claim that these CSR initiatives were in fact traditional incentive schemes that merely used "CSR" as a fashionable label. After unemployment was reduced, flexicurity issues were again dealt with via traditional welfare state policies and tools, whereas CSR was reconceptualized to conform to a more mainstream CSR approach, as discussed in the next section.

The early Finnish debate on CSR and outsourcing is also best understood in the context of securing domestic welfare state foundations following Finland's loss of economic arbitrage opportunities when the communist block transitioned to a market economy. CSR has occasionally been invoked in Norwegian debates about industrial outsourcing and layoffs, but Norwegian, and particularly Swedish, interviewees seem sceptical of introducing voluntary CSR tools in a domestic welfare state domain.[4] As illustrated, the scope for using CSR in domestic policies that are close to the kernel of the welfare state seems quite limited in the Nordic countries, and using CSR domestically in key welfare state areas seems legitimate only in times of welfare state crisis.

Compartmentalizing CSR: the international competitiveness and innovation model

The most recent Nordic policy trend in CSR focuses on CSR as a competitive advantage in international trade. This competitive advantage view is the dominant trend in both Denmark and Finland and stands in stark contrast to the humanitarian, international welfare capitalism model of CSR favoured by Norway and Sweden. Instead, the international innovation and competitiveness model favoured by Denmark and Finland focuses on using CSR to further the domestic business community's interests. The core idea is that the high Nordic social and environmental standards constitute a comparative advantage for success in CSR that should be used more actively to increase international competitiveness – as expressed in the Danish government's action plan for CSR (Danish Government 2012),

> It is the goal of the government to develop and to utilize this comparative advantage so that Danish companies can profit in the global market from being responsible [...] The government wishes to promote and support CSR and to enable Danish companies to derive advantage from being global frontrunners in CSR.

In particular, interviewees from both the Danish Ministry of Economy and the Danish Confederation for Small and Medium-size Enterprises (SMEs) reported explosive growth in the need for CSR-related assistance among Danish export-oriented SMEs at the turn of the millennium. The interviewees therefore saw a greater need for government initiatives and practical advice, as reflected in the large-scale SME-oriented CSR initiatives from the Danish government.

In Finland, the framing of CSR in a competitiveness and innovation perspective fits the larger Finnish economic policy paradigm launched in 2003, the "New Industrial Strategy". This comprehensive government programme, based on rapid liberalization and a clear orientation toward the EU, transformed Finland's former raw material-based economy into a knowledge economy based on innovation, technology and R&D and seems to have motivated the convergence of CSR with these goals. Given the strong industrial reorientation with radical and active public policies to increase innovation when CSR entered the agenda, public policies for CSR were largely absorbed by the innovation paradigm.

The Finnish government's lower CSR engagement mirrors its generally weaker welfare state and lower foreign policy ambitions, as well as the difficult economic times after the Soviet Union's fall, when Finland lost its most important trading partner. Thus, this strategy for accommodation avoids conflicts by compartmentalizing CSR to areas less amenable to traditional regulation. There is no strong collision with traditional welfare state measures because innovation policy is typically pursued in a complex market network approach rather than by strong regulation.

CSR as a tool for "upgrading" global markets

While Nordic-style CSR may have an important role in stimulating domestic innovation and competitiveness, its main focus and application remains in international markets. As small, open economies, the Nordic countries are highly dependent on foreign trade under fair market conditions. They are therefore established multilateralists, supportive of the UN and international institution-building, and promoters of development aid and social and ecological issues through international institutions. But they still have a long way to go in bringing international market regulation up to the social and environmental standards of their advanced welfare states. In this context, CSR has stood out as an attractive option. Although Nordic welfare states may favour legislative or negotiated strategies for improving social and environmental conditions at home, CSR emerges as a good second best when traditional governance cannot be mobilized internationally.

With respect to the apparent contradiction between CSR and the Nordic welfare state, it is interesting to note that the concept of 'stakeholdership' – a core element in modern CSR – usually attributed to the American business strategy thinker, Edward Freeman (1984), originated in Scandinavia. The Swedish management theorist, Eric Rhenman, used the concept to argue for more democracy in industrial organizations (Rhenman 1968).[5] Both in CSR and in the welfare state, stakeholder dialogue and negotiations create enhanced capacity to orchestrate collaborative strategies for sustainability.

Engagement with Nordic front-runner companies

As opposed to US-style CSR, where corporations run the show alone, CSR in the Nordic context is a joint project promoted by industry and the state alike, and Nordic governments have engaged in CSR with advanced policy agendas alongside Nordic firms that hold front-runner positions in the global economy. This Nordic formula has apparently worked quite well. Studies of Nordic companies' CSR performance, as ranked in major CSR and sustainability indexes and participation in CSR fora, do indeed rank them in leading positions, together with Swiss, and to some extent UK and Dutch, companies in the formative years of CSR (Midttun et al. 2006; Gjølberg 2013) (Figure 10.2).

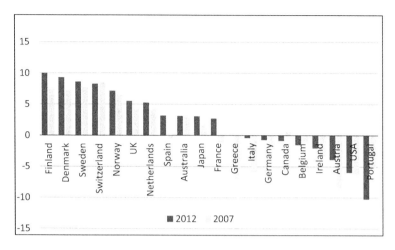

Figure 10.2 Cross-national CSR performance in 2007 and 2012
Source: Gjølberg 2011 and 2013

Six indicators[6] are standardized and aggregated into an index, where a score of 1 represents a perfect proportion of companies active in CSR, relative to the size of the economy. A score higher than 1 equals over-representation and a score lower than 1 equals under-representation.

The Nordic companies' inherent comparative advantages in CSR appear to be rooted in the strong Nordic institutions for social and environmental governance of the economy, and the common engagement by business and government seems to strengthen both sides. In a study of CSR front-runnership among Nordic companies, Gjølberg (2013) found that in the Nordic setting, the dialogue- and consensus-building effect of tripartite arrangements is most likely the primary cause of companies' CSR success. Cooperation with labour unions has taught, or even forced, companies to integrate broader societal concerns into their business operations. Such traditions may enhance corporate competence in dialogue and consensus-oriented strategies, which are important "CSR-skills".

Vibrant civic engagement

The Nordic CSR approach encompasses not only business and trade unions, but also civil society organizations in a broader sense. The Nordic countries are characterized by vibrant civil societies, and the extent of voluntary engagement in society is greater than in most other countries (except the Netherlands), regardless of whether one focuses on formal membership, active membership or on volunteer work (Strømsnes 2010). And civil society is actively supported by public policy, while respectful of the need to allow civic independence. The Norwegian government, thus, states that:

> The government will facilitate a strong civil society that may be a counterbalance to the power of the state. At the same time, there are long traditions for cooperation between the voluntary and public sector
> (Norwegian Government 2017) (my translation).

Strong nature conservation, human rights and business-watch organizations, as well as national chapters of major international civil society organizations characterize the Nordic CSR scene, and are essential promoters of social and environmental sustainability. Nordic companies are under continuous scrutiny from media and NGO watchdogs, and consequently have a strong incentive to engage in CSR.

Partnered governance

The Nordic attempts at social and environmental upgrading of the international economy thus builds on a compact between government, business and civil society in what can be called *partnered governance* (Midttun 2008), where the Nordics creatively attempt to expand governance beyond their national borders. By doing so under the CSR label, they may legitimately transcend the lock-in to the territorial limitations of the nation-state, and thereby gain far greater regulatory out reach. However, they do so at the cost of leaving the authoritative mode of governance of domestic welfare policy, which rests on tripartite bargaining under the auspices of sovereign welfare states. The tripartite compact between government, business and society in international CSR policy is of a looser, and partnered kind.

The logic of partnered governance

Conceptually, partnered governance and its interfaces with conventional political government on the one side and industrial self-regulation on the other may be graphically displayed in a two-dimensional matrix. Conventional political governance, under the assumption of strong state capacity, is displayed in the upper part of Figure 10.3 (quadrants I and II), while the lower part (quadrants III and IV) represents the space where the strong governance assumptions do not hold because of failed states or lack of efficient international institutions. This domain is largely left to CSR-based industrial self-regulation.

Much of the traditional political debate in the Nordic countries, as well as elsewhere, has concentrated on planning (quadrant I) versus markets (quadrant II), under the assumption that there would be access to an efficient regulatory state. With globalization and de-regulation, however, an increasing

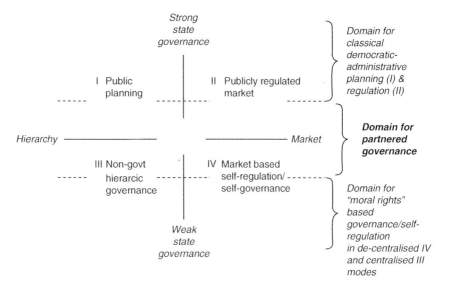

Figure 10.3 Partnered governance
Source: Midtttun 2008

share of the economy has moved into the lower part of the figure, where governance at best is limited to individual companies' self-regulation (quadrant IV), or private/industrial regulation by industrial associations (quadrant III).

The broad Nordic compact between government, industry and civil society represents an attempt at strengthening governance from the middle, where the two spheres interface. By partnering policy-initiatives with complementary business strategies and in active interplay with civil society – the Nordics have sought to pressure actors in the global economy towards classical welfare state goals of environmental and social sustainability.

Such partnered governance has forced Nordic governments to engage beyond traditional roles. They have had to move out of traditional mandating strategies based on command and control legislation to facilitating, partnering and endorsing strategies (Fox et al. 2002).

In the facilitating role, Nordic and like-minded public authorities have stimulated industrial action by developing or supporting appropriate CSR management tools and mechanisms, including voluntary product labeling schemes, benchmarks and guidelines for company management and reporting systems, thereby supporting self-regulatory initiatives. Nordic and like-minded governments have also facilitated CSR orientation by creating fiscal incentives through their own procurement and investment practices.

In the partnering role, Nordic governments have brought in complementary competencies and resources to tackle social and environmental issues outside their unilateral authoritative control. By acting as participants, conveners or facilitators, they have stimulated complementary self-regulatory engagement and thereby achieved effects that go far beyond what they might have achieved through unilateral action when operating under conditions of limited authoritative control.

Furthermore, Nordic and like-minded governments have engaged in endorsement through the effects of public procurement and public sector management practices as well as through direct recognition of the efforts of individual enterprises. In this process, civil society organizations have been active promoters, acting in a combination of watchdog, partner and consultant roles.

Like the welfare state, Nordic engagement in CSR and partnered governance is not unique. Rather, the Nordic countries have picked up models from other front-runner nations, such as the UK and the Netherlands, and tailored them to a Nordic context. This context, with its tradition of social dialogue and strong egalitarian values, has often proven to be fertile ground for further stimulus of partnered governance arrangements. The Extractive Industries' Transparency Initiative (EITI) and the Ethical Trade Initiative are good examples. Both originated in Britain, under Tony Blair's "New Left" agenda, and both were subsequently warmly taken over in the Nordic countries in a partnered governance mode.

EITI – the extractive industries' transparency initiative

The process that led to EITI was pioneered by civil society organizations, including Global Witness, Human Rights Watch, Oxfam and Transparency International in a campaign against British Petroleum and the Angolan government under the slogan, "Publish What You Pay". The campaign challenged British Petroleum to publish the revenue transferred to the Angolan government. BP was eventually pressured to publish the signature bonus of USD111 million it paid to Angola for an offshore licence. However, the threat from the Angolan government to bar BP from further licences led it to back down. Therefore, in the first, round, the campaign failed as a pure CSR initiative, and where civic pressure alone forces business to shape up.

Subsequently, Publish What You Pay mobilized to bring the government of the UK – BP's home base – on board. And under the British Labour Party's New Left agenda, the initiative found support. The "Extractive Industries Transparency Initiative" (EITI) was thereafter launched in September 2002 by UK Prime Minister Tony Blair at the World Summit on Sustainable Development in Johannesburg, and formally founded at a conference in London in 2003, where delegates from government, companies and civil society agreed on 12 principles to increase transparency over payments and revenues in the extractives sector. The British government provided seed funding and secretarial support through its Department for International Development (DFID). The EITI thus took the civic initiative into a broader partnered governance mode.

Still under British hosting, the second EITI Conference in 2005 in London set out the minimum requirements for transparency in the management of resources in the oil, gas and mining sectors, reflecting the wide differences experienced in the four countries that by then had piloted the EITI. By this time, transparency in natural resource development has also been championed at a series of G8 Summits. The G8 subsequently called on the International Monetary Fund and the World Bank to provide technical support to governments wishing to adopt transparency policies. This led to the establishment of the World Bank-administered Multi-Donor Trust Fund (MDTF) for the EITI in 2004. Partnered governance was thus also established on the international arena.

The third EITI conference, held in Oslo, Norway, in 2006, marked the Norwegian take-over as host country for the EITI secretariat, with the support of the Ministry of Foreign Affairs. With its new base in a considerable petroleum-exporting nation with an ambitious development agenda, the EITI provided a welcome opportunity to extend Norway's prosocial resource-management policy in the international arena. As in the case of the UK, the Norwegian government's motivation for engagement with the EITI was strengthened by the embarrassment of seeing "their" oil companies' international operations getting into trouble as host-countries were suspected of diverting oil revenues to illegitimate private pockets.

The tripartite governance modality – balancing government, industry and civil society – makes the EITI a classic example of partnered governance. The EITI is organized as a non-profit association under Norwegian law, and the membership of the board reflects its multi-stakeholder nature: it has several government representatives both from countries implementing the EITI and from supporting countries. There is strong Nordic buy-in beyond Norway, from Denmark to Sweden, the latter represented by the prominent board chairmanship of ex-Prime Minister Fredrik Reinfeldt and the leadership of the Secretariat. The participation of government is checked and challenged by participation from civil society organizations across the world as well as balanced by solid industrial attendance.

With this tripartite format, the EITI has attempted to support public insight into revenue streams and facilitate public enquiry into their distribution in society. By providing civil society a place at the table – not only on the international board, but also in the fora involved with the EITI implementation at the national level – the organization is contributing a democratic impulse through Nordic and north-west European-style stakeholder dialogue.

The "Publish What You Pay" movement was instrumental in triggering self-regulation and recruiting inside agency by involving civil society organizations in the target countries in local rule-making – that Nordic welfare states could not have achieved through traditional international political negotiations. The EITI was also ingenious in that implementation was staged through stakeholder conferences with broad societal representation.

However, a hard set of sanctioning mechanisms has been difficult to put in place. The EITI has therefore been caught between the desire to expand the number of signatories and the potential hardships the sanctions will cause for its signatories when the time to implement rolls around. This illustrates the dilemma of spreading Nordic-style prosociality through soft power, even if strongly assisted by civic engagement and considerable industrial buy-in partnered governance mode.

Following a critical evaluation in 2011, the EITI has re-oriented itself towards establishing a standard, which, if successful, may drive the EITI certification through market pressure. If important financial institutions make extractive industry investments conditional on EITI certification, and banks providing loans to host governments see EITI implementation as risk reduction, money may eventually provide enforce compliance.

ETI – the ethical trading initiative

The Ethical Trading Initiative (ETI) is another example of partnered governance initiated in the UK under Tony Blair's New Left government. Like the EITI, the ETI started with civic action. In the mid-1990s, several well orchestrated trade union and NGO campaigns and media exposés highlighted the exploitation of people making clothes, shoes and other products for major global brands and retailers. In response, the companies started to adopt labour codes governing the working conditions of the people in their supply chains.

But the codes were widely criticized for lacking credibility, and although companies started to invest in "monitoring" programmes, aimed at checking supplier workplaces for code compliance, these were criticized as piecemeal and insufficient to promote real change.

In 1997, a group of companies, trade unions and NGOs followed up on this critique and began a discussion about how codes could be made more effective. Eventually, these discussions were backed up by the Secretary of State for International Development, head of the DFID, which resulted in a pioneering group of companies joining the trade unions and establishing the ETI in 1998. From this pioneering group, the ETI has grown into a major success, which in 2017 included companies with a combined turnover of GBP166 billion, and union members representing nearly 160 million workers around the world. Moreover, it is now involved with the DFID in a long-term commitment for strategic support (ETI 2017).

The UK initiative was soon picked up in Norway, where it fitted nicely into the Nordic model of tripartite negotiated governance, and complemented the welfare state with international outreach to facilitate social and environmental policy upgrading. As in the UK and other Western economies, Nordic companies got caught in the embarrassing situation of neglecting to secure decent labour conditions and allowing environmental pollution to wreak havoc in their increasingly outsourced supply chains.

Again as in the UK, the Norwegian initiative came from civil society, more specifically from The Norwegian Church Aid, trade unions and the Enterprise Federation (VIRKE). However, it soon recruited broadly among firms, civil society and public agencies, municipalities and counties, which had been struggling to find solutions to their commitment to tackle environmental and social concerns in their procurement of goods and services. The central government has also played an active role in supporting the initiative through major grants from the Norwegian Development Agency (NORAD). Furthermore, the government stimulates engagement in ethical trading through legislation that calls for the reduction of environmental pollution and enhancement of climate-friendly solutions, as well as respect for human rights in acquisition and production processes.

Following Norway's model, Denmark developed its ETI in 2008, and it includes a multi-stakeholder alliance that seeks to create real improvement in businesses' global supply chains.

The ETIs offer their members courses, fora for dialogue and tools to meet challenges in the supply chain, that stretches across business, government and civil society. Furthermore ETI extends initiatives for social and environmental upgrading across regions beyond the outreach of both Nordic and other European welfare states, for instance through courses on supply chain management in China, Vietnam, India and Bangladesh (ETI Norway 2017; ETI Denmark 2017).

Beyond EITI and ETI, the CSR agenda counts numerous other initiatives, such as sustainable investment strategies, triple bottom line reporting, the United Nations' Global Compact and sustainable development goals, which I cannot deal with within the scope of this chapter. The Nordic countries, together with other like-minded nations, are engaged in many of these initiatives, which invite partnered governance across government, business and civic domains. The flourishing of such initiatives from the end of the 20th century and in the beginning of the 21st reflects the need for socially and environmentally ambitious nation-states to scale up influence beyond their borders to keep up with globalizing business.

CSR and prosocial governance beyond the welfare state

As indicated in the EITI and ETI cases, the combination of broad international engagement and a vibrant civil society under Tony Blair's New Left government provided an advantageous setting for innovative global governance initiatives. In this sense the Nordic countries are not unique as international CSR champions. They were furnished with several international initiatives that they could join (ETI) or take over (EITI) and evolve.

However, the Nordic countries have had a persistent engagement in global social and environmental sustainability at a scale relative to the size of their economies, that few other nations can match. This may reflect the fact that stakeholder dialogue and tripartite negotiations (state, business and civil society) in many CSR and partnered governance initiatives resonates so well with the welfare state tradition, where similar dialogue is of central importance. CSR, in partnered governance mode, therefore, provides Nordic and like-minded societies a chance to expand such ideas beyond territorial boundaries.

What the Nordic CSR engagement implies may, however, be seen in a double light. Firstly CSR is a vehicle for governance promotion on the road from soft to hard law. From this perspective, CSR and partnered governance allows Nordic states and companies to promote governance innovation in early-stage non-binding versions as a stepping stone towards institutional consolidation. The strategy is to strengthen the Nordics' bargaining position by forging solid alliances with global industrial players and civil society with strong moral appeal on the global arena, and thereafter to negotiate hard law and institutionalization as momentum weighs in on their side. Forging alliances with like-minded nations and their industrial players, and expanding civil society buy-in is part of this approach.

The second perspective sees CSR as part of a more permanent, novel governance approach where government and industry, strongly supported by civil society organizations, forge partnered governance to jointly enhance social and environmental sustainability in weakly-regulated global markets. Intriguingly, the prosociality of Nordic societies, kept up by tripartite bargaining under adherence to strong law at home, may necessitate extensive use of looser polycentric governance to support global diffusion. CSR-based partnered governance could therefore be a new hybrid mode for complementary stakeholder-based governance where consensus on hard law is impossible, or even undesirable.

Notes

1 This chapter builds on research reported in several articles and underlying working papers, including Midttun (2008, 2010, 2013) and Midttun et al. (2006, 2015).
2 The study is based on 55 interviews with Nordic public administration, industry, union and NGO representatives, conducted by researchers at business schools in Copenhagen, Helsinki, Oslo and Stockholm. In each country the interviews were led by national CSR researchers with knowledge of national contexts relevant to CSR policy. First interviewed were representatives of the main ministries in charge of CSR in each country: the Norwegian and Swedish Ministries of Foreign Affairs, and the Danish and Finnish Ministries of the Economy. These interviews were supplemented by interviews of representatives of other relevant ministries, mainly those of the environment and social affairs. Interviews with NGOs, labour unions, and employer associations were chosen depending on CSR engagement, which varied significantly across the four countries. The interviews were supplemented by studies of public policy documents from each country.
3 Interview with Ambassador Dahlin, Swedish Ministry of Foreign Affairs, October 2007.

4 A Norwegian interviewee even claimed that invoking CSR in relation to domestic business issues was a misuse of the term that "destroys the CSR debate".
5 Strand and Freeman (2012) clarify the historical roots of stakeholder theory to establish that a much larger role was played by Scandinavian thinkers in its development than is currently acknowledged.
6 The six indicators are the Dow Jones Sustainability Index, FTSE 4 Good Index Series, KMPG International Survey of CSR Reporting, ISO 14001, and membership of the Global 100 and World Business Council for Sustainable Development (WBCSD).

References

Bergman, A. (2007) Co-constitution of Domestic and International Welfare Obligations. The Case of Sweden's Social Democratically Inspired Internationalism. *Cooperation and Conflict: Journal of the Nordic International Studies Association* 42 (1): 73–99.

Danish Government (2012) Danish Action Plan for CSR. http://csrgov.dk/danish_action_plan_2012 (accessed 5 October 2017).

Freeman, E. (1984): *Strategic Management: A Stakeholder Approach*. Boston: Pitman.

Esping-Andersen, G. (ed.). (1990). *The Three Worlds of Welfare Capitalism*. Cambridge: Polity.

ETI (2017) Ethical Trading Initiative. Webpage. www.ethicaltrade.org/

ETI Denmark (2017) *Annual Report 2016*. Available at: www.dieh.dk/dyn/Download/6/126/Download_Files/file/1068/1/1492678160/dieh_aarsrapport2016_web.pdf (accessed 5 October 2017).

ETI Norway (2017) *Annual Report 2016*. Available at: http://etiskhandel.no/Publikasjoner___Rapporter/_rsrapporter_2016_2001/index.html (accessed 5 October 2017).

Fox, Tom, Ward, Halina and Bruce, Howard (2002) Public Sector Roles in Strengthening Corporate Social Responsibility: A Baseline Study. Corporate Responsibility for Environment and Development Programme; International Institute for Environment and Development (IIED), The World Bank.

Gjølberg, M. (2011) Explaining Regulatory Preferences: CSR, Soft Law, or Hard Law? Insights from a Survey of Nordic Pioneers in CSR. Business & Politics 13 (2): 1–31.

Gjølberg, M. (2013) Nordic Companies – Global Pioneers in CSR. In: A. Midttun (ed.), *CSR and Beyond: A Nordic Perspective*. Oslo: Cappelen Damm.

Kuisma, M. (2007) Social Democratic Internationalism and the Welfare State after the "Golden Age". *Cooperation and Conflict: Journal of the Nordic International Studies Association* 42 (1): 9–26.

Lindell, M. and Karagozoglu, N. (2001) Corporate Environmental Behaviour: A Comparison between Nordic and US Firms. *Business Strategy and the Environment* 10: 38–52.

Midttun, A. (2008) Partnered Governance: Aligning Corporate Responsibility and Public Policy in the Global Economy. *Journal of Corporate Governance* 8 (4): 406–418.

Midttun, A., Gautesen, K. and Gjølberg, M. (2006) The Political Economy of CSR in Western Europe. *Corporate Governance – The International Journal of Business in Society* 6 (4): 369–385.

Midttun, Atle et al. (2015) Public Policies for Corporate Social Responsibility in Four Nordic Countries: Harmony of Goals and Conflict of Means. *Business & Society* 54 (4): 464–500.
Milne, R. (2009) Nordic Model is "Future of Capitalism". *Financial Times*, 22 March. Available at: www.ft.com/intl/cms/s/0/2a0ffc30-170c-11de-9a72-0000779fd2ac.html#axzz1zpT4kRoS
Nørgaard, E. (2007) Nordisk sosialstatistikk i 60 år – Flere ulikheter enn du tror [Nordic Social Statistics over the Last 60 Years – Larger Inequalities than You Expected]. Retrieved from www.ssb.no/ssp/utg/200701/06/
Norwegian Government (2008–2009) Corporate Responsibility in a Global Economy. White Paper 10. Oslo: Author.
Norwegian Government (2017) Prop. 1 S (2016–2017) ch. 7. Available at: www.regjeringen.no/no/dokumenter/prop.-1-s-kud-20162017/id2514232/sec3(accessed 9 September 2017).
Porter, M. E. and Kramer, M. R. (2006) Strategy and Society: The Link between Competitive Advantage and Corporate Social Responsibility. *Harvard Business Review* 84 (12): 78–92.
Rhenman, E. (1968) *Industrial Democracy and Industrial Management*. Tavistock: London.
Sadler, D. and Lloyd, S. (2009) Neo-liberalising Corporate Social Responsibility: A Political Economy of Corporate Citizenship. *Geoforum* 40: 613–622.
Sapir, A. (2005) Globalisation and the Reform of European Social Models. Background document for presentation at ECOFIN informal meeting in Manchester. Brussels: ECOFIN.
Strand, R. and Freeman R. E. (2012) The Scandinavian Cooperative Advantage: Theory and Practice of Stakeholder Engagement in Scandinavia. Working Paper 01-2012, CSR & Business in Society CBS Working Paper Series. Copenhagen Business School.
Strømsnes, Kristin (2010) Betydningen av sosial kapital og frivillighet. *Innlegg på Christiekonferansen* 26 April.

11 Eco-modernity Nordic style

The challenge of aligning ecological and socio-economic sustainability

Atle Midttun and Lennart Olsson

Introduction

Since the 1970s, the Nordic countries have engaged forcefully in environmental policy – locally, nationally and internationally. They have taken leading positions in promoting environmental issues on the international stage and launched a number of worldwide initiatives to deal with specific environmental challenges.

Their early and strong environmental engagement may have something to do with how environmental issues have been reinforced by the evolution of the welfare state. Worker health and safety was always of central concern to the labour movement and was gradually integrated into legislation and industrial practice. With the growth of broad health care programmes in the second half of the 20th century, environmental issues affecting public health became a priority of Scandinavian welfare states. Furthermore, the founding tradition of the Nordic countries admitted a strong dependence on – and interaction with – the natural environment; and until the 21st century, nature-informed narratives, habits and practices dominated Nordic national memory and cultural heritage (Witoszek 1998, 2012). The Nordics apparently have the potential to become the birthplace of eco-modernity, where concerns for economic productivity and social well-being could align with concern for the environment.

Yet climate challenge and global warming – the new overarching themes on the environmental agenda – have proved difficult to handle, and the Nordic countries can no longer stand out as the best in the class. As argued in the first chapter of this book, the hallmark of the Nordic welfare states is their socio-economic compact, whereby economic productivity is prioritized under collaborative work–life relations and a redistributive and inclusive welfare society. This compact requires a highly productive growth economy to allow both high wages and welfare benefits.

Many of the earlier environmental challenges were met without seriously hampering economic growth, because they affected only specific sectors, and alternative environmentally friendly solutions could be found. In some cases, the absorptive capacity of the vast Nordic territories could be relied upon to provide the solution. The climate agenda was seen at an early stage, however, as threatening industrial growth across numerous sectors of the economy and therefore jeopardizing the socio-economic basis of the Nordic welfare societies. The Nordic economies, after all, relied heavily on the extraction of natural resources, which entailed extensive ecological footprints.[1]

To the extent that environmental and socio-economic sustainability collide, the Nordics face a dilemma. Their inherent prosocial orientation supports strong collective action in both domains, yet when realities are seen as not permitting the pursuit of the one without undermining the other, short-term socio-economic, rather than long-term ecological, sustainability prevails.

However, two developments have helped resolve this dilemma. First, as the Nordic countries have evolved from industrial to service and knowledge economies, their reliance on industry, with its high CO_2 emissions, has declined. Second, as the climate agenda evolves from austerity approaches to green growth, the Nordics hope to reconcile socio-economic and ecological sustainability in a pragmatic reorientation towards eco-modernity. In this endeavour, their collaborative capability represents a potential for driving transition in the same way as it had previously been mobilized to support inclusive competitiveness. We show how this reorientation may help the Nordics regain their position as environmental front-runners.

The Nordic cases demonstrate, however, that environmental leadership cannot be built on a "one size fits all" approach. While all the Nordic countries experience the effect of the climate challenge on their socio-economic compact, their exposure to dilemmas and potential solutions varies. Due to differing industrial bases, they may share strong collective engagements for ecological upgrading, yet must address substantially different industrial contexts that underpin their socio-economic welfare. This, we argue, may explain Nordic diversity in climate-related performance, in spite of strong common climate policy engagement. Nevertheless, urban greening is widely shared, and the Nordic capitals top European green city rankings. Based on a green growth agenda, the urban greening may provide an attractive opportunity for bridging ecology and economy, and allow the Nordics to transcend their ecology versus growth dilemma.

Nordics as front-runners

Over the last quarter of the 20th century, the Nordics presented themselves as environmental front-runners. Through numerous initiatives, they signalled, from an early stage, the desire to champion environmental sustainability on the international stage, usually in close collaboration with the United Nations or other multilateral organizations. To mention but a few of the most important initiatives:

- In 1972 the UN Conference on the Human Environment, hosted in Stockholm, was an early attempt to place environmental issues on the international agenda; it was followed by massive international engagement.

- The 1972 Oslo Convention on dumping waste at sea, which later merged with the 1974 Paris Convention on land-based sources of marine pollution, was another early Nordic initiative to promote international environmental policy. The Oslo and Paris conventions later merged into the OSPAR Commission, which established the legislative instruments that regulate international cooperation.
- The Helsinki Convention, which was signed in 1974 and came into force in 1980, was the first multilateral agreement signed by countries on both sides of the Iron Curtain during the Cold War. It promised to clean up the Baltic Sea, which at that time was considered one of the most polluted seas in the world. The Convention was agreed on after persistent and skilled negotiations in which Finland managed to cross the political divide between the Soviet Union and the West, and was subsequently re-negotiated in 1992 following the collapse of the Soviet Union (Hassler 2003; Räsänen and Laakkonen 2008).
- The 1985 Helsinki Protocol on the Reduction of Sulphur Emissions represented a Nordic-initiated first step to deal with long-range, transboundary air pollution. It was followed by another Nordic initiative – the 1994 Oslo Protocol on Further Reduction of Sulphur Emissions. Both conventions were successful in achieving their goals.
- Nordic policy-makers have also championed early environmental policies. The Norwegian Prime Minister Gro Harlem Brundtland's chairing of the 1987 report on sustainable development, *Our Common Future*, set the stage for fusing environmental policy with core welfare state values. The publication of *Our Common Future* and the work of the World Commission on Environment and Development laid the groundwork for merging the development and environmental agendas and linking them to fair distribution and political democracy.
- The 1990s saw Norwegian-led, policy-oriented international conferences on biodiversity in Trondheim in 1993 and 1999. Both conferences were held in close cooperation with UN agencies.
- In 1996, the Swedish Prime Minister Göran Persson announced Sweden's ambition to green the welfare state. Sustainability was incorporated into the long-standing "people's home" concept of consensus politics aimed at reducing economic disparities, redistributing wealth and carrying out welfare reforms. This initiative integrated environmental policy into the core of the "Nordic model".
- In classic Nordic participatory style, the 1998 Aarhus Convention on Access to Environmental Information and Public Participation in Environmental Decision-Making introduced a directly democratic element into environmental policy.
- Another major Nordic initiative was the 2001 Stockholm Convention on Persistent Organic Pollutants, a global treaty to protect human health and the environment from chemicals that remain intact in the environment for long periods.

Ecological and socio-economic sustainability 207

- One year later, in 2002, Denmark adopted a national sustainable development strategy to be presented to Parliament every four years and followed up by sectoral plans and a range of indicators. Denmark's high-profile sustainability policy culminated in its hosting in 2009 of a conference of parties to the United Nations Framework Convention on Climate Change (UNFCCC).
- The Finnish government also promotes sustainable development as part of its diplomacy, including it in its relations with the East, with the Nordic countries, and as part of the European Union. Together with the other Nordic countries, it has taken initiatives to integrate environmental concerns with trade policy so that both fields have equal status in international law.

Early environmental administrations

One reason for why the Nordics have successfully managed to present themselves as ecological/environmental front-runners is that they have backed up their strong environmental policy engagement by early establishment of environmental administrations (Midttun and Kamfjord 1999).

In 1971, the establishment of the Danish Ministry of Pollution Abatement marked the beginning of the Nordic foundation of ministries with an environmental focus. The ministry's name was changed in 1973 to the Ministry of Environment, after the passing of a series of environment-related laws. A strong environmental focus in Danish energy policy later led to the 1994 merger between the Ministry of Energy and the Ministry of the Environment, reflecting the pioneering role of Denmark in wind energy under its dynamic minister Svend Auken. In 2005, the energy sector was detached again and the ministry reverted to the old name.

Norway was also quick to establish a Ministry of the Environment in 1972, and has, through one of its most famous ministers, Gro Harlem Brundtland, who later became Prime Minister, established a profile as an international champion of environmental policy. The Ministry came as a reinforcement of environmental policy that had been spearheaded by the Committee for Resources (Ressursutvalget) since its establishment in 1968. Both the Committee and the Ministry reflected an increasing concern over the use of natural resources and pollution.

Swedish environmental policy gained momentum in the aftermath of the 1980 nuclear referendum, when a majority voted for the gradual discontinuation of Swedish nuclear power generation. The strong relation between energy and environmental policy led to the creation in 1987 of a joint ministry: the Ministry of the Environment and Energy. The Ministry went through several transformations, only to revert to a pure Ministry of the Environment a couple of years later.

The Finnish Ministry of the Environment was established in 1983 in spite of strong opposition from the Ministry of Trade, the Ministry of Industry and the Ministry of Agriculture and Forestry. In 1995, the Environmental Administration was created in order to tackle pivotal cross-cutting issues between these three ministries.

Welfare states as high-consumption states

Building on rich resource endowments, including forestry, hydropower, petroleum, minerals and rich farmland, the Nordic countries built up advanced industrial economies during the second half of the 20th century – a process which involved considerable ecological footprints. In this way, they moved away from being primarily exporters of raw materials with little industrial processing – such as fish from Norway, iron from Sweden, timber from Norway, Sweden and Finland, and agricultural products from Denmark – to producing more sophisticated and value-added products, such as canned and frozen seafood, electro-metallurgical products, paper, pulp and biochemical products, machinery and electronics, as well as agro-industrial products. Their productive resource economies allowed them to build up advanced welfare states, underpinned by a social contract that focused on egalitarian distribution, high productivity and social security.

On the basis of this industrial transformation, the Nordic countries today enjoy some of the world's highest living standards – widely distributed among the population. Their high productivity has allowed them to embrace high material consumption. Together with Luxemburg, Switzerland and Ireland, Norway, Iceland, Denmark and Sweden top the European GDP per capita league table, with Finland following close behind (Table 11.1).

Table 11.1 GDP per capita, 11 highest European countries

Country	GDP per capita nominal	Rank GDP per capita nominal	GDP per capita ppp	Rank GDP per capita ppp in Europe
Luxembourg	105,829	1	101,936	1
Switzerland	79,578	2	59,376	5
Norway	71,497	3	69,296	3
Ireland	65,871	4	69,375	2
Iceland	57,889	5	48,070	9
Denmark	53,243	6	46,603	11
Sweden	51,604	7	49,678	7
San Marino	49,579	8	64,444	4
Netherlands	45,210	9	50,846	6
Austria	44,561	10	47,856	10
Finland	43,492	11	41,813	15

Source: International Monetary Fund: World Economic Outlook (October 2016)

As indicated in Figure 11.1, the Nordics' high consumption and prosocial inclusive economies have affected ecological sustainability. In terms of global hectares[2] per person (see light grey columns under the 0.0 line), Sweden, Denmark, Norway and Finland are among the highest footprint societies with high carbon emissions (all), high pressure on fish resources (Norway), high pressure on cropland (Denmark) and high pressure on forest products and grazing land (Finland, Norway and Sweden).

Footprints and biocapacity

Given their high per capita ecological footprints, can the Nordic economies be characterized as ecologically sustainable? The answer depends – as nearly always – on the perspective applied. From a territorial perspective, the answer is yes. Three of the four major Nordics are capable of absorbing their footprints within their territorial boundaries, and the fourth is not (Figure 11.1).

As displayed by the thick rugged line in Figure 11.1, Finland, Sweden and Norway have excess biocapacity[3] to handle their ecological footprints (the dark columns [biocapacity] are higher than the light grey [ecological footprint]). As measured by the Ecological Footprint Network, Finland, with a footprint of 6.7 global hectares (light grey column) has a biological credit of 6.6 (surplus biocapacity illustrated by the dark column under the thick rugged line), which means that the country could more or less double its footprint and still claim ecological sustainability. Sweden's biological credit is 3.9

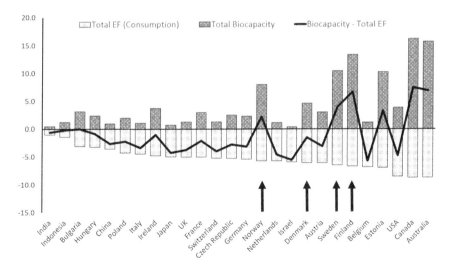

Figure 11.1 Ecological footprints in 2013 of selected industrial countries (in global hectares)

Source: Global Footprint Network (2017) National Footprint Accounts

global hectares and Norway's is 2.1. Population densities of 16.1 persons/km^2 (Norway), 16.2 (Finland) and 21.8 (Sweden) allow above average per capita footprints to be levelled out. Denmark, with a similar ecological footprint, and an equally small population, but with a much smaller territory, comes out with an ecological deficit of -1.5 (light grey column over thick rugged line). The population density of 135 persons/km^2 puts Denmark on a par with much of continental Europe.

From an ethical point of view, it is of course questionable whether citizens in a large country can be allowed a more wasteful lifestyle than citizens in a small one. Australians and Canadians, for example, have among the highest ecological footprints in the world, primarily due to their heavy dependence on very dirty fossil fuel (coal in Australia and tar sands in Canada), but their biocapacity is still larger.

Footprints and the climate challenge

Seen from a climate change perspective, however, the ecological sustainability of the Nordic countries is less convincing. Except for Sweden, the four Nordic countries have CO$_2$ emissions above, or on par with, the rest of the EU, as seen in Figure 11.2. Even though, since about 2005, all four countries have started to reduce their emissions, the reduction rate is insufficient to reach their ambitious political targets, except perhaps for Denmark.

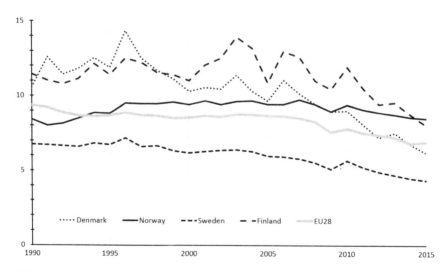

Figure 11.2 Territorial emissions of CO$_2$ (tonnes/capita) of four Nordic countries and the EU from 1990 to 2014

Source: Global Carbon Budget (wwwglobalcarbonprojectorg/carbonbudget) and World Bank development indicators. Original data source for Global Carbon Budget data is Peters et al. (2012)

Assuming common responsibility for climate change across nations and populations, a globally sustainable per capita level of CO_2 emissions should be around 2 tonnes – on the condition of a 2 degree warming limit – according to the Paris Agreement.

Admittedly, most of the Nordic countries have embarked on a path towards lowering emissions. However, their trajectories have varied extensively, reflecting differences in their industrial economies and resource bases. Sweden's CO_2 emissions peaked as early as 1970, reflecting the country's early industrialization and early development towards a service economy. Furthermore, the country expanded its electricity supply beyond hydropower through a massive engagement in nuclear power, thereby avoiding energy-related CO_2 emissions. In spite of a referendum in 1980 to discontinue nuclear power, Sweden pursued the completion of plants under construction, and implemented a slow phase-out as plants approached the end of their lifespan.

Denmark's CO_2 emissions peaked more than 25 years later, reflecting the country's later industrialization and hence later transition to a service economy, as well as its massive reliance on coal-based electricity, which gave it the highest Nordic per capita CO_2 emissions. Only when Denmark embarked on its strong wind-energy programme did it gradually move to a downward CO_2 emission trend. The move into wind energy was motivated as much by the need for energy self-sufficiency as by ecological concerns.

The peak in Finnish CO_2 emissions occurred almost 10 years after Denmark's, reflecting both Finland's late industrialization and its belated transformation into a post-industrial economy. Both its move into consumer electronics and the engagement of its massive forestry industry in bioenergy helped to set Finland on a declining CO_2 emission path.

Norway is clearly the most problematic case. The country benefited from abundant hydropower resources in its industrial development, and could build up a massive electro-metallurgical and electro-chemical industry while retaining the lowest Nordic CO_2 emissions. Norway saw a first peak in CO_2 emissions around 1990, after which industrial emissions were considerably reduced. However, this reduction was soon negated by the rapid rise in emissions from a massive engagement in petroleum production, which did not peak until around 2010. The country has subsequently become the heaviest per capita Nordic CO_2 emitter.

Trade and climate change

Because climate change is a global challenge and the world economy is highly integrated in terms of manufacturing, trade and transport, it makes sense to consider not only emissions within the borders of countries but also external emissions embedded in the consumption of goods and services. In Figure 11.3, we show the trade-related emissions of the four Nordic countries and the average for EU countries. While Denmark, Finland and Sweden score

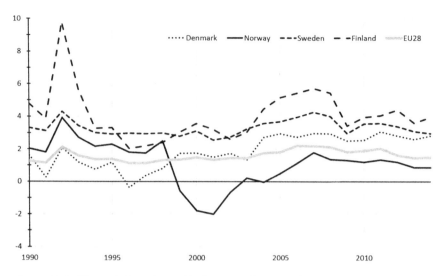

Figure 11.3 CO₂ emissions from the four Nordic countries and the average of EU countries (tonnes/capita)

Source: Global Carbon Budget (wwwglobalcarbonprojectorg/carbonbudget) and World Bank development indicators. Original data source for Global Carbon Budget data is Peters et al. (2012)

significantly higher than the EU average, Norway ranks below this and is even negative in some periods.[4]

As indicated in Figure 11.3, the Nordics have achieved reductions in domestic CO_2 emissions, to some extent, by outsourcing the CO_2-intensive products that they rely on in their own consumption, to other nations. And they do so to a greater degree than other European nations, probably as a result of the higher/faster-than-average transition to service and digital economies. The exception is Norway, which has included more of its carbon consumption in its domestic petro-economy.

Nordic and EU climate change policies

In the 21st century, Nordic climate policies have increasingly veered towards teamwork with other European players in a common EU approach. The three Nordic EU members have tuned their climate policy closely to EU frameworks, while Norway has signed on to EU policy through its membership in the European Economic Area. This does not, however, preclude active Nordic engagement *within* the EU to strengthen the EU's climate policy. Under the EU/EEA framework, the Nordics have thus consistently positioned themselves in the avant-garde and have sometimes taken steps to exceed EU standards. Indeed the Danish leadership of the 2009 Copenhagen climate summit is an example of engaged Nordic backing for EU climate leadership, even if the summit partly failed.

EU climate policy, to which the Nordics have actively aligned themselves, hinges on two mechanisms, the European Emission Trading Scheme (ETS) and the Effort-Sharing Decision (ESD), and is set up with goals for 2020 and 2030, plus a long-term vision for 2050. The ETS covers around 45 per cent of the EU's greenhouse gas emissions and sets targets for reductions in emission-intensive sectors such as power and heat, cement and lime, and pulp and paper. The remaining 55 per cent of total EU emissions, under the ESD, includes sectors such as housing, agriculture, waste and transport (excluding aviation). For these sectors binding national emission reduction targets have been set by the Renewable Energy Directive, differentiated according to national wealth (EU 2009).

The EU framework contains a binding target to cut emissions in EU territory to at least 40 per cent below 1990 levels by 2030. This is translated into a reform to strengthen the ETS, whereby the sectors covered would have to cut emissions by 43 per cent (compared with 2005). However, so far, the ETS has been without much effect,[5] and will continue to be so until 2025 because of the surplus of emission certificates, which were allocated over-generously, and the industrial downturn after the financial crisis (Hu et al. 2015).

Non-ETS sectors, under the ESD mechanism, are set to cut emissions by 30 per cent by 2030 (compared with 2005) for the EU as a whole, but translated into different individual binding targets for Member States. For the non-ETS sectors, the Nordics have taken a leading role – like they did for the 2020 emission cuts[6] and top the list of emission reduction targets, together with Luxembourg (Table 11.2). Norway has signed up for a 40 per cent reduction under the EEA agreement.

In the longer run, the European Commission has spelled out its policy in a low-carbon economy roadmap (EU 2017), suggesting that the EU should cut greenhouse gas emissions to 80 per cent below 1990 levels by 2050. Milestones to achieve this comprise 40 per cent emissions cuts by 2030 and 60 per cent by 2040. Some of the Nordics aspire to surpass these goals and aim at even higher cuts.

Table 11.2 EU Member States' GHG reduction targets

Top countries	2030 target compared with 2005
Luxembourg	- 40%
Sweden	- 40%
Denmark	- 39%
Finland	- 39%

Source: EU (2017a, b)

Sweden stands out as the most climate-conscious Nordic country, outlining a climate agenda way beyond the EU's. Sweden's Climate Policy Act (Government of Sweden 2017) specifies that emissions in the country in the sectors that will be covered by the EU regulation on the division of responsibilities (ESD) should be at least 63 per cent lower than in 1990 by 2030, and at least 75 per cent lower by 2040. The Act does, however, specify that the goals may partly be achieved through supplementary measures, such as increased uptake of carbon dioxide by forests or by investing in various climate-related projects abroad. The Act also commits Sweden to have net zero emissions of greenhouse gases by 2045 and thereafter to achieve negative emissions.[7]

Danish climate policy has also been closely aligned with the EU's (Danish Ministry of Energy, Utilities and Climate 2016). Given its strong early engagement in wind power, the country has found it a fairly easy task to match the 2020 goals. Following procedures established under the Danish climate law (Energistyrelsen 2017), the government announced that it will live up to the EU's high climate policy expectations but foresees that they will be harder to meet (Energistyrelsen 2017). With respect to the long term, the government has committed Denmark to be independent of fossil fuels – coal, oil and natural gas – by 2050. This means that Denmark will produce enough renewable energy by 2050 to cover total Danish energy consumption (Energistyrelsen 2017).

Finland specified its climate commitments in a national Climate Change Act (609/2015) (Finnish Ministry of the Environment 2017). The goal is to ensure that Finland fulfils its binding targets and objectives for reducing and monitoring greenhouse gas emissions, and implements national measures for the mitigation of climate change and adaptation to it. Finland is the least ambitious of the Nordic countries, with no ambitions to move beyond the EU's targets.

Norway joined the EU emission trading scheme from the beginning in 2008, and also joined the ESD for non-ETS sectors, imposing a target of a 40 per cent reduction by 2030, in line with the most ambitious other Nordics (see Table 11.2). Given Norway's growing CO_2 emissions from petroleum extraction, the country has not managed to reduce its territorial emissions. In fact, projections made by the Ministry of the Environment estimate that emissions in Norway will rise slightly by 2020 and then decline until 2030 (Norwegian Environment Agency 2016). Norway has therefore engaged extensively in buying credits generated by emission-saving projects around the world – notably investments in forest preservation in developing countries. Regarding long-term reductions, Norway also subscribes to a long-term low carbon economy, with 80–95 per cent CO_2 emission reductions compared with 1990. In order to retain focus on climate policy and its implementation, in 2017, the Norwegian Government passed a new climate law to this effect (Stortinget 2017).

In spite of their position as top performers under the EU EDS scheme, Denmark and Finland are rated as mediocre climate performers under the broader metrics deployed by Carbon Market Watch (2017), and there is reason to believe that Norway's performance would be rated even lower. Sweden, however, scores high also on this scale, and thus remains the only real Nordic climate performance star.

Eco-modernity and green growth

From front-runner positions in environmental policy in the international arena, the Nordics have moved into the climate avant-garde within the EU. However, as implementation becomes more demanding, the Nordics are faced with reconciling ecological sustainability with their acclaimed economic and social agendas. The strong productivity needed to support high welfare aspirations implies reluctance to support ecological measures that would limit economic growth[8], and may explain the fact that the Nordics have lagged behind in translating their high aspirations into operative practice. However, with the emergence of green growth opportunities in more and more sectors of the economy, there is greater potential for a broader synthesis, fusing socio-economic and ecological sustainability into what we call *eco-modernity*.[9]

In this particular context, we define eco-modernity as the coupling of ecological sustainability to industrial development and welfare creation in order for a country to benefit from its resources and capabilities, while also furthering green growth. In this perspective, the Nordic climate approaches must vary according to resources and existing industrial bases. Each of the Nordic countries will have to develop green growth strategies and accompanying mobilizing narratives that align environmental goals with national potentials (Jerneck 2014).[10]

While the Nordic countries share a number of common features, such as the wish to combine ecological, welfare and industrial front-runnership, their mobilizing narratives differ. Sweden has chosen to frame eco-modernity in terms of decarbonization (with a focus on reducing the carbon content of energy) as part of a transition out of nuclear power and towards a green high-tech society. Denmark has emphasized energy independence with a focus on replacing foreign fossil sources of energy with domestic renewable sources, while building a competitive eco-efficient economy. Norway has struggled to balance its massive petroleum economy with ecological modernization, and has opted for achieving carbon neutrality within a story of eco-efficient petroleum production combined with international offsetting to balance its emissions. Finland has pledged to fulfil its commitment to the Paris Agreement by means of its vast forest resources, balancing emissions by forest uptakes, and strong engagement in bioenergy.[11] These features are to be supplemented by an expansive nuclear power programme.

Swedish green transition

More specifically, Sweden, as the most mature and diversified industrial economy among the Nordics, has the potential for mobilizing a broad spectrum of capabilities and resources towards green growth. The country boasts a long history of sustainable transport and has dedicated resources to the development and implementation of electric car technologies, batteries, charging infrastructure and fuel cells. Volvo's announcement of a shift to electric or hybrid passenger car models from 2019 is an example of Swedish industry (although with Chinese owners) taking eco-modern front-runner positions. Swedish companies are also at the cutting edge of energy efficiency and Sweden has overtaken Denmark as the Nordic wind-energy champion in terms of total installed capacity (according to data from the Global Wind Energy Council and national energy agencies). In addition, Swedish firms offer innovative solutions in heating and cooling, energy storage systems and smart grid technology. However, after a long period of declining emissions, Sweden's emissions have started to increase again during 2015 and 2016 (Statistics Sweden 2017). Emissions from households are still declining, but they are increasing from the transport, manufacturing and the energy sectors.

Sweden harbours innovative solutions and extensive know-how in waste collection and recycling. The country is a global leader when it comes to dealing with and recycling waste. This includes the world's highest utilization of biogas from waste and waste-water as vehicle fuel (IEA 2017). Swedish companies in the field of green buildings and infrastructure enjoy a global reputation for their methods and use of innovative technologies. Wooden building technology and low-energy housing solutions are also areas where Sweden is at the forefront.

Last but not least, the combination of Sweden's chemical industry experiences and knowledge of chemical products on the one hand, and the forestry industry's resources and materials on the other, has allowed Swedish industry to take front-runner positions in bio-based chemicals and sustainable materials. Sweden's largest chemistry and materials cluster has espoused a collective ambition to work towards fossil-independence by 2030 and the production of sustainable products.

Danish green transition

The Danish green transition strategy draws on its leading position in wind energy, and encompasses the ambitious climate goal of becoming independent of fossil fuels by 2050. The country has already taken advantage of the demand for renewable energy and has become a world leader in wind turbines. By further expanding the share of renewable energy, Denmark will strengthen its industrial competencies in wind turbines and related technologies[12] (Lewis and Wiser 2007; Lund, P. 2009; Moe 2015), while coal power – based on imported feedstock – and remaining petroleum production will be phased out, the latter due to resource depletion.

Denmark has also focused its climate action on bioenergy from its large agricultural sector. A government-commissioned study has sparked off major bio-refinery initiatives, whereby perennial crops and secondary crops are combined with conventional crops for fodder and biomass and for energy production as biogas (Biovalue 2016).

In addition to its energy initiatives, Danish climate policy encompasses greening initiatives within transport, housing, public procurement and the cyclical economy – where Danish firms like Velux and Danfoss hold leading international positions. The Danish building code is among the strictest in the world and is being revised to stimulate green innovation. Furthermore, Denmark aspires to strengthen its competence in advanced information technology by an ambitious policy to increase energy efficiency, and by driving the development of an intelligent energy system capable of managing the fluctuations of renewable energy (a policy known as "State of Green").[13]

Norwegian transition: a study in duality

The Norwegian climate strategy combines a number of green industrial initiatives and active financial engagement in international climate mitigation with the development of forest sink capacity. Given a fully hydro-powered electricity system, further Norwegian green transition in energy must largely take place in transport. Norway holds the world record in electric car density, following strong state support policy for electric vehicles. In addition, zero- and low-emission solutions are being promoted at sea through public contracting for ships and ferries.

The Norwegian Government has also focused on green transition in the building sector, where requirements for the carbon footprinting of building materials and building solutions are being promoted. This is expected to facilitate increased use of the vast Norwegian wood resources, and is additional to an escalation plan for the use of advanced biofuels.

To compensate for the high CO_2 emissions of the petroleum sector, the Norwegian government has come to rely strongly on offsetting domestic carbon emissions through international carbon compensation schemes (Climate Action Tracker 2017).[14] Norway is to buy 30 million climate quotas in the period 2013–2020 (Friends of the Earth Norway 2017; Norwegian Government 2014). Long-term plans are emerging for gas-to-hydrogen production, with carbon capture and storage, which would push Norway's main CO_2-emitting industry towards carbon neutrality. This project remains at an early piloting stage, however, and is dependent on further breakthroughs in carbon capture and storage technology. An equally controversial part of Norway's carbon neutrality is the massive reliance on forest management. Predictably, while the government claims success, the scientific community is sceptical (Eilenberg 2015) or guarded (Lund, J. et al. 2017; Seymour et al. 2015).

Finnish forest-based transition

The Finnish approach to climate mitigation is closely aligned with the capabilities and resources embedded in its extensive forest industry, and the country's ambitious plans for expansion of nuclear energy. This is in addition to high competences in mechanical engineering and information technology, as well as extensive infrastructure in central heating.

The cleantech sector, including advanced energy efficiency, water management and bioenergy technologies, has been growing at a spectacular rate, and Finnish climate policy is stimulating the public sector to develop cleantech even further (Niinistö 2014).

The expansion of forest-based bioenergy may threaten CO_2 sequestration, however. In Finland, forests annually sequester around 30–60 per cent of greenhouse gas emissions (Finnish Ministries of the Environment; Agriculture and Forestry; and Employment and the Economy 2015). Finnish climate policy will therefore attempt to limit the decline of carbon sinks in Finnish forests by fortifying the growth and carbon-binding capacity of forests over the long run. This will be done by mapping out the afforestation of treeless areas, and reducing the clear-cutting of forests in connection with infrastructure and transport construction.

At the forefront of urban greening

In spite of industrial differences, the Nordics do share some CO_2-reducing green growth approaches. One of them is the mobilizing narrative of urban greening, widely shared in the Nordic countries. The European Green City Index ranks Copenhagen first, Stockholm second and Oslo third in a comprehensive study of multiple indicators (Economist Intelligence Unit 2009). Helsinki occupies seventh place. These cities have all taken bold steps to drive ambitious green transition, in part ahead of their national governments, and hence are able to contribute extensively to fulfilling national climate ambitions. The mobilization of the massive public procurement behind the green policy turn of large cities has extensive industrial implications, and creates room for new green product development.

Carbon neutrality and energy efficiency

All these cities have ambitious carbon emission reduction plans: Copenhagen intends all heating and cooling in the city's districts to be carbon-neutral by 2025 and all commercial, household and public buildings to drastically lower their energy consumption (C40 Cities 2012). Stockholm aims to be fossil fuel free by 2050 (WWF 2014; LSE Cities 2017).[15] The city already has one of the lowest levels of per-person annual emissions in Europe. Oslo has decided to cut carbon emissions by 50 per cent by 2020 and by 95 per cent by 2030, compared with 1990 levels (Røsland 2013), and plans to fit carbon capture technology to a waste incineration plant in a joint project with the government. Helsinki is striving to reduce greenhouse gas emissions by 30 per cent by the year 2020 compared with 1990, and is following the other Nordic capital cities by aiming to become carbon-neutral by 2050. A central part of the green transition is envisaged to come from the greening of district heating and electricity generation (City of Helsinki 2017).

Ambitious transport systems

Emissions from the transport sector are the most difficult to reduce in most countries; therefore, transport is an area of focus for all cities. Copenhagen will encourage its citizens to take three-quarters of all trips by bicycle, on foot or by public transport by 2025 (and 50 per cent of trips to work or school will be by bike, up from 36 per cent in 2012). This will be achieved through still better biking infrastructure and better public transport, as well as through implementing a congestion charge for road transport in the city. Copenhagen also intends to replace the municipality's vehicle fleet with hydrogen cars and electric cars. The Environment and Health Administration of the city of Stockholm has been running the "Clean Vehicles in Stockholm" programme since 1994. The scheme aims to accelerate the transition to clean vehicles and renewable fuels – including biogas, ethanol and electric vehicles. The main objective in the early years was to improve air quality in the city. However, increased awareness about climate change, carbon emissions and security of energy supply has led to a shift in focus during the lifetime of the programme.

A key part of Oslo's green transition plan has been to prioritize pedestrians, cyclists and public transport ahead of car traffic, with the intention of making the city centre car-free by 2019. The plan is to have all public transport powered by renewables by 2020, and at least 20 per cent of heavy transport running on renewable fuels by the same year. By 2030, the city plans to have all heavy transport equipment operating on renewable fuel. In Helsinki, the greening of transport is included in a climate partnership or a cooperative network between the city of Helsinki and the business sector, whereby both parties are committed to promote the use of low-emission vehicles.

Greening buildings

All four Nordic capitals have tried to upgrade building standards as part of their green transition.

For new urban development areas, Copenhagen's city authorities have required that new buildings comply with very strict energy standards, way ahead of national legislation. According to the climate plan, the city will derive all its electricity consumption from renewable sources.

The city of Stockholm has stimulated innovation by developing eco-districts. The eco-districts at Hammarby Sjöstad and Royal Seaport are clean technology demonstrator projects delivered through public–private partnerships. These eco-districts have made Stockholm one of the leading cities in the world for developing and demonstrating innovative green solutions at the district level (Sweden.se 2017). Helsinki has promoted the upgrading of building standards through a combination of municipal energy efficiency agreements, a green focus on planning and land use and a climate partnership between the city of Helsinki and the business sector. These are intended to turn the city into a pioneer of environmental housing, including renovation to promote energy efficiency and energy saving (City of Helsinki 2017). Oslo's climate plan includes an ambition to achieve increases in energy efficiency of 1.5Twh by 2020. These efficiency gains will be promoted by a Climate and Energy Fund, which will stimulate the implementation of cost-efficient measures such as solar panels, heat pumps and isolation (Oslo Municipality n.d.).

Towards eco-modernity

Our analysis has shown how mediocre Nordic practice – as far as CO_2 emissions are concerned – does not live up to the Nordic avant-garde tradition in environmental policies. The Nordics have prided themselves for decades on being environmental front-runners and have largely succeeded in establishing an international reputation for this. Given their high governance capacity and sensitivity to broad welfare concerns, the Nordics have been motivated to engage and deal with environmental issues that did not fundamentally challenge economic growth. However, CO_2-reduction policies were seen to limit growth and therefore run counter to their high consumption/high welfare formula. Therefore, the Nordics were hesitant to move too fast.

The transition towards "green growth", whereby the CO_2 agenda is transformed from an austerity to a growth policy, carries a stronger appeal. Embedding climate policy in the green growth agenda resonates well with Nordic pragmatic, productivity-oriented welfare engagement. As we have shown, this shines through in the Nordic enthusiasm for green cities, where the benefits from green transition are felt more directly than at the national level. Furthermore, urban politics has been more decoupled from vested interests in CO_2-emitting industries than national policy. The contrast between Oslo's urban greening and Norway's petro-economy is a case in point.

Given the maturation of the Nordic economies into modern service economies and the emergence of the green growth approach to CO_2 mitigation, the tension between socio-economic and ecological sustainability experienced by the Nordic societies may be reduced. In accomplishing this task, public policy-makers are mobilizing support from both trade unions and industry.

Thus SAMAK, the Cooperation Committee of the Nordic Social Democratic parties and trade union confederations, stated in 2014:

> Our green perspective will be wide. It's about good environment and good living conditions locally, nationally and globally, in the short and long

term. This includes efforts to save the global climate, but also the effort for good local and working environments, more equal life chances and equality.

(SAMAK 2014) (authors' translation)

The inclusion of the external environment in the HSE (health, safety and environment) field is now becoming standard practice. For example, the HSE specialist Bjergene in Unio (The Confederation of Unions for Professionals) believes that the climate crisis is a matter for cooperation in the Norwegian labour market and that Norwegian HSE representatives will have key roles: "The country's 20,000 HSE representatives are important forces in their efforts to make Norwegian businesses more environmentally friendly" (quoted in Arntsen 2014). Similarly, Virke, the Enterprise Federation of Norway, emphasizes that health, safety and environment includes "Minimizing the strain on both inner and outer environment (Virke 2017). Nordic industry, as expressed through its industry associations, the Nordic chapter of Global Compact and individual companies, is strongly engaged in climate mitigation.

In Sweden, several large firms are at the forefront of climate change action and are very visible in the public media. These include Hagainitiativet, a lobby organization comprising 14 large companies. In February 2017, it had an op-ed in the leading Swedish daily newspaper *Dagens Nyheter* in which the 14 firms pledged to become fossil free by 2030, 15 years ahead of the government strategy target (Hagainitiativet 2017). Swedish steel manufacturing companies have also promised to try to develop the first carbon-neutral steel. If successful, this would give them a significant competitive advantage over the coming decades (DN Debatt 2017).

Similarly, the Norwegian Commission on Green Competitiveness has elicited advanced plans for ecological modernization from several sectors of the Norwegian economy. In its Green Costal Programme, the Norwegian Shipowners' Association, together with a number of shipping and supply companies, outlines an ambition to achieve zero emissions by 2050, while also seeing opportunities for the export of Norwegian environmental technology and green transport services (Grønn konkurransekraft n.d.). Another example is the Norwegian process industry, which envisages the possibility of becoming carbon-neutral, or even carbon-negative, by 2050, while at the same time doubling production from its 2017 level. An important condition is that the industry receives adequate access to sustainable biomass and infrastructure for the transport and storage of CO_2.

Denmark has many leading companies pioneering circular economy solutions (Kalundborg Symbiosis), where the by-product or residual product of one firm is used as a source by another firm. With firms like Grundfos and Vestas in the driving seat, Denmark also has a long-term strategic commitment to energy efficiency and renewable energy (Stateofgreen 2017). Danish industry topped the 2017 Green Innovation Index, based on strong scores in both inputs to innovation and outputs of innovation. The key cleantech drivers that have contributed to this performance include the amount of capital raised by cleantech funds and the number of cleantech organizations. Denmark also shows strong evidence of commercialized cleantech, as shown by the level of cleantech exports, the number of public cleantech companies and the number of renewable energy jobs (Cleantech Group 2017).

In Finland, globally operating forest industry companies, such as UPM, StoraEnso, Metsä Group, SCA and Sappi, are spearheading the forest-based bioeconomy with ostensibly large climate benefits. Finland is already a pioneer in the development of new technologies to turn various biomasses into gaseous and liquid biofuels, and intends to increase the share of low-emission, renewable energy to 50 per cent by 2030 (Investinfinland.fi n.d.).

Our analysis shows how the Nordics are developing considerable momentum behind a broadening of the socio-economic compact towards eco-modernity, and are regaining momentum in climate issues, towards environmental front-runnership. The strong and pragmatic governance capacity of the Nordic welfare states, together with Nordic traditions for forging collaborative strategies across interests and social divides, implies that the Nordic model may also develop considerable momentum behind a triple sustainability agenda (economic, social and ecological).

The Nordic ambition for climate front-runnership is not unique in Europe, however. It is shared with other small north-west European states like Switzerland and the Netherlands. The Nordics' position as climate policy leaders will therefore be contested.

Furthermore, the measurement of climate performance will influence the ranking of the climate front-runners. The Nordics are thus stepping up their efforts to include the climate-sink effects of their vast forests in the emission calculations, an addition which is far from uncontroversial (Körner 2017). Their problem, however, is that they also have plans for extensive expansion of forest-based bioenergy, and there is considerable uncertainty about how this will add up.

Another point of contention is the role of "financial greening" or the purchase of offsets against domestic emissions through financial investment in green projects abroad. Norway's ability to handle emissions from its vast offshore petroleum production, while at the same time figuring as a climate front-runner, hinges on the ability to buy climate offsets around the world – the argument being that since the climate challenge is global, the location of climate mitigation is irrelevant. In the longer run, attempts at commercializing gas-to-hydrogen solutions with carbon sequestration – if successful – may turn the Norwegian petro-economy into a cleantech solution. However, this pilot initiative still has a long way to go.

Finally, an important question is whether the Nordic countries manage to maintain and develop the welfare state without outsourcing emissions to other parts of the world. Most mature European nations do in fact achieve their CO_2 reductions by outsourcing production to developing countries.

Measured by consumption, their CO_2 performance is far less impressive, and the Nordics are no exception.

What the Nordics have in common is eco-modernity with a strong social dimension. Their concern with tailoring the economy and society towards spreading welfare broadly across society clearly includes both healthy work environments and clean livelihoods. The climate agenda, with its global dimension and long-term focus, becomes a more problematic affair, particularly when it challenges the strong extractive elements of some Nordic economies. Green growth has, however, opened a gateway to rapid improvement. The promise of a triple win–win solution (economic, social and environmental) has created an attractive synthesis whereby the Nordics can capitalize on all three fronts without having to sacrifice one against the other. At this point, the high state capacity and preparedness for collective action, which are characteristic of the Nordic model, click in, and may become an asset for eco-modernity, just as they proved to be assets in forging the Nordics' earlier social and economic compact for productive and prosocial societies.

When it comes to the specific development of their climate strategies, however, the Nordics will differ according to their natural resources and industrial competences. While one may expect them to compete over front-runner status – as illustrated by their climate commitments under the EU's Effort Sharing Decision scheme – their different industrial strengths will lead them to come up with divergent solutions.

Notes

1 For example, from about 1870 to 1970 Swedish economic growth was the highest of all the industrialized countries (Maddison 1990). This growth was primarily based on iron and lumber and the extraction was far from environmentally benign (see e.g. Blomström and Kokko 2001).
2 Global hectare (gha) is a measurement unit for quantifying both the ecological footprint of people or activities and the biocapacity of the earth or a region.
3 A city's, state's or nation's biocapacity represents the productivity of its ecological assets (including cropland, grazing land, forest land, fishing grounds and built-up land). These areas, especially if left unharvested, can also absorb much of the waste we generate, especially our carbon emissions. www.footprintnetwork.org/our-work/ecological-footprint/
4 We have checked for Norwegian hydropower exports/imports, but there is no co-variation with Norway's CO_2 emissions. This may have to do with the acquisition of climate quotas abroad.
5 When the scheme was introduced, the emission levels for 2020 under the ETS were set 21 per cent lower than in 2005. This scheme entails similar obligations for industry in all the EU and EEA. The ETS has, however, come under strong criticism. Price levels for CO_2 emissions during the first 10 years fluctuated enormously, between almost €30 in 2005 to zero in 2007 and 2008 (Karpf et al. 2016). Then the price stabilized at a level much lower than the reference level of €30, and then plummeted to between €4 and €6, reflecting the downturn of the industrial economy following the financial crisis.

6 Under the ESD the obligations for 2020 were differentiated – from a 20 per cent cut for the richest EU countries to a maximum 20 per cent increase for the least wealthy. The Nordics were among the front-runners. Together with Ireland and Luxembourg, Denmark took on the most ambitious target of a 20 per cent reduction; Sweden followed with a slightly less ambitious 17 per cent and Finland with 16 per cent (on a par with Austria, the Netherlands and the UK) (EU 2017).
7 Negative emissions mean that greenhouse gas emissions from activities in Sweden are, for example, less than the amount of carbon dioxide absorbed by nature as part of the ecocycle, or less than the emissions Sweden helps to reduce abroad by investing in various climate projects. However, the remaining emissions from activities on Swedish territory will be at least 85 per cent lower than in 1990.
8 The Nordic model has traditionally focused on a socio-economic synthesis of economic productivity and social inclusion, a formula which, at its best, engenders a competitive advantage of collaboration.
9 Eco-modernity refers to a triple paradigm shift in culture, economy and politics to further pro-environment, pro-climate and pro-social measures combined with high productivity and innovation (Midttun and Witoszek 2016).
10 A mobilizing narrative is a coherent frame for thinking and acting, and, according to Jerneck (2014), it must include direction (towards a climate change goal), distribution (global inclusiveness) and diversity (multiple approaches, methods and solutions).
11 This statement was contested by the Finnish Green Party and environment organizations, who claimed that Finland's aggressive forestry policy will effectively nullify any emission cuts (Yle Uutiset 2017).
12 The Danish wind turbine industry accounts for over 5 per cent of Denmark's exports and employs almost 30,000 people, almost 30 per cent of whom live in the western rural part of Denmark.
13 Stateofgreen (2017) is a public–private partnership founded by the Danish Government, the Confederation of Danish Industry, the Danish Energy Association, the Danish Agriculture & Food Council and the Danish Wind Industry Association. H.R.H. Crown Prince Frederik of Denmark is the patron of Stateofgreen.
14 Already in 2008, when Norway set the ambition to become carbon-neutral by 2030, conditional upon a global agreement at the COP15, international offsets were a major premise, and they have remained integral to Norwegian policy ever since.
15 Early infrastructure investment such as building the city's metro system in the 1950s, and the development of district heating following the 1970s oil shocks have helped lay the foundations of today's lower carbon economy. The city now benefits from a low-carbon energy system, a relatively compact centre with good public transport, and an innovation-led economy primed for developing smart city solutions and export markets of the future (LSE Cities 2017).

References

Arntsen, E. (2014) Arbeidstakerorganisasjoner vil ha miljø i arbeidsmiljøloven. Available at: www.arbeidsrettsadvokaten.no/arbeidstakerorganisasjoner-vil-ha-miljo-arbeidsmiljoloven/ (accessed 5 October 2017).

Biovalue (2016) New Report Boosts Denmark's Green Transition. Available at: http://biovalue.dk/new-report-boosts-denmarks-green-transition/ (accessed 5 October 2017).
Blomström, M. and Kokko, A. (2001) From Natural Resources to High-tech Production: The Evolution of Industrial Competitiveness in Sweden and Finland. Working Paper, Stockholm School of Economics. Available at: http://web.worldbank.org/archive/website00895A/WEB/PDF/BLOMSTRO.PDF (accessed 5 October 2017).
C40 Cities (2012) Copenhagen: CPH Climate Plan 2025. Report. Available at: www.c40.org/profiles/2013-copenhagen (accessed 4 October 2017).
Carbon Market Watch (2017) EU Climate Leader Board – Where countries stand on the Effort Sharing Regulation. Available at: http://carbonmarketwatch.org/eu-climate-leader-board-where-countries-stand-on-the-effort-sharing-regulation/ (accessed 4 October 2017).
City of Helsinki (2017) Environmental Protection Programmes. Available at: www.hel.fi/helsinki/en/housing/environmental/programmes/climate-action# (accessed 5 October 2017).
Cleantech Group (2017) The Global Cleantech Innovation Index 2017. Report. Available at: www.wwf.se/source.php/1706406/global_cleatech_innovation_index_2017_final_web.pdf (accessed 4 October 2017).
Climate Action Tracker (2017) Online database. Available at: http://climateactiontracker.org/countries/norway.html (accessed 29 September 2017).
Danish Ministry of Energy, Utilities and Climate (2016) Klimapolitisk redegørelse 2016 (Presentation of Climate Policy 2016). Report. Available at: http://efkm.dk/media/8113/klimapolitisk-redegoerelse-2016.pdf (accessed 4 October 2017).
DN Debatt (2017) Svensk stålproduktion kan bli avgörande för klimatet (Swedish Steel Production May Become Crucial for the Climate) (published 19 July). Available at: dn.se/debatt/svensk-stalproduktion-kan-bli-avgorande-for-klimatet/ (accessed 5 October 2017).
Economist Intelligence Unit (2009) European Green City Index. Report. Available at: www.siemens.com/entry/cc/features/greencityindex_international/all/en/pdf/report_en.pdf (accessed 4 October 2017).
Eilenberg, M. (2015) Shades of Green and REDD: Local and Global Contestations over the Value of Forest versus Plantation Development on the Indonesian Forest Frontier. Asia Pacific Viewpoint 56 (1): 48–61.
Energistyrelsen (2017) Dansk Klimapolitikk (Danish Climate Policy). Available at: https://ens.dk/ansvarsomraader/energi-klimapolitik/fakta-om-dansk-energi-klimapolitik/dansk-klimapolitik (accessed 5 October 2017).
EU (2009) On the Promotion of the Use of Energy from Renewable Sources. Directive 2009/28/EC of the European Parliament and of the Council of 23 April 2009.
EU (2017a) Greenhouse Gas Emissions 2005–2009. Report. http://ec.europa.eu/regional_policy/sources/docoffic/official/reports/interim7/greenhouse_gas_en.pdf (accessed 5 October 2017).
EU (2017b) Effort Sharing Regulation, 2021–2030 Limiting Member States' Carbon Emissions. (www.europarl.europa.eu/RegData/etudes/BRIE/2016/589799/EPRS_BRI(2016)589799_EN.pdf) (accessed 5 October 2017).
Finnish Ministry of Environment (2017) Mitigation of Climate Change. Available at: www.ym.fi/en-US/The_environment/Climate_and_air/Mitigation_of_climate_change/. (accessed 5 October 2017).

Finnish Ministries of the Environment; Agriculture and Forestry; and Employment and the Economy (2015) Finnish Climate Policy – Towards a Low-carbon and Energy-efficient Future. Report. Available at: https://ilmasto-opas.fi/ilocms-portlet/article/8a54c390-fed4-42da-a2c2-4bab74993ebd/r/b844a8fb-f69d-4c20-a506-cf17ac9f5a9e/suomen_ilmastopolitiikka_rgb_en.pdf (accessed 4 October 2017).

Friends of the Earth Norway (2017) Available at: https://naturvernforbundet.no/?lang=en_GB (accessed 4 October 2017).

Global Footprint Network (2017) National Footprint Accounts. Webpage. www.footprintnetwork.org/ (accessed 5 October 2017).

Government of Sweden (2017) Lagrådsremiss om ett klimatpolitiskt ramverk för Sverige. Available at: www.regeringen.se/48fe4b/contentassets/7b33bbdda7e24f54b86c09c4463b826d/faktablad-lagradsremiss-om-ett-klimatpolitiskt-ramverk-for-sverige.pdf (accessed 3 January 2018).

Grønn konkurransekraft (n.d.) Roadmaps for Expert Committee on Green Competitiveness. Webpage. www.gronnkonkurransekraft.no/linker/ (accessed 4 October 2017).

Hagainitiativet (2017) Companies go Further than Swedish Government – Toward Zero Net Emissions in 2030. Electronic newsletter. www.mynewsdesk.com/se/hagainitiativet/pressreleases/companies-go-further-than-swedish-government-toward-zero-net-emissions-in-2030-1792542 (accessed 4 June 2017).

Hassler, B. (2003). Protecting the Baltic Sea: The Helsinki Convention and National Interests. In: O. Schram Stokke and O.B. Thommesen (eds), Yearbook of International Co-operation on Environment and Development, 2003–04. London: Earthscan.

Hu, Jing et al. (2015) Ex-ante Evaluation of EU ETS during 2013–2030: EU Internal Abatement. *Energy Policy* 77: 152–163.

IEA (2017) IEA Bioenergy Member Country Reports. Available at: http://task37.ieabioenergy.com/country-reports.html (accessed 5 October 2017).

Investinfinland.fi (n.d.) www.investinfinland.fi/

Jerneck, A. (2014) Searching for a Mobilizing Narrative on Climate Change. *The Journal of Environment & Development* 23 (1): 15–40.

Karpf, A., Mandel, A. and Battiston, S. (2016) A Network-based Analysis of the European Emission Market. *Proceedings of ECCS 2014*. Springer International Publishing. 283–295.

Körner, C. (2017) A Matter of Tree Longevity. *Science* 355 (6321): 130–131.

Lewis, J. I. and Wiser, R. H. (2007) Fostering a Renewable Energy Technology Industry: An International Comparison of Wind Industry Policy Support Mechanisms. *Energy Policy* 35 (3): 1844–1857.

LSE Cities (2017) Stockholm|Green Economy Leader Report. Available at: https://lsecities.net/publications/reports/stockholm/ (accessed 5 October 2017).

Lund, J. F., Sungusia, E., Mabele, M. B. and Scheba, A. (2017) Promising Change, Delivering Continuity: REDD+ as Conservation Fad. *World Development* 89: 124–139.

Lund, P. D. (2009) Effects of Energy Policies on Industry Expansion in Renewable Energy. *Renewable Energy* 34 (1): 53–64.

Maddison, A. (1982) Phases of Capitalist Development. Oxford: Oxford University Press.

Midttun, A. and Kamfjord, S. (1999) Energy and Environmental Governance under Ecological Modernization: A Comparative Analysis of Nordic Countries. *Public Administration* 77 (4): 873–895.

Midttun, A. and Witoszek, N. (2016) *Energy and Transport in Green Transition: Perspectives on Ecomodernity*. London: Routledge.

Moe, E. (2015) Renewable Energy Transformation or Fossil Fuel Backlash: Vested Interests in the Political Economy. Basingstoke: Palgrave Macmillan.

Norwegian Environment Agency (2016) Norske utslipp av klimagasser (Norwegian Climate Gas Emissions). Available at: www.miljostatus.no/tema/klima/norske-klimagassutslipp/ (accessed 4 October 2017).

Norwegian Government (2014) Statens kjøp av klimakvoter (The State's Acquisition of Climate Qotas). Available at: www.regjeringen.no/no/tema/klima-og-miljo/klima/innsiktsartikler-klima/Statens-kjop-av-klimakvoter/id2005479/ (accessed 5 October 2017).

Niinistö, Ville (2014) Finland – Creating a Low-carbon Industry. *Climate Leader Papers*. Available at: www.climateactionprogramme.org/climate-leader-papers/finland_creating_a_low_carbon_country (accessed 4 October 2017).

Oslo Municipality (n.d.) Energiforbedring i privatboliger (Energy Improvements in Private Residences). Available at: www.oslo.kommune.no/politikk-og-administrasjon/tilskudd-legater-og-stipend/energiforbedring-i-boliger/#gref (accessed 4 October 2017).

Peters, G. P., Davis, S. J. and Andrew, R. (2012) A Synthesis of Carbon in International Trade. Biogeosciences 9: 3247–3276.

Räsänen, T. and Laakkonen, S. (2008) Institutionalization of an International Environmental Policy Regime: The Helsinki Convention, Finland and the Cold War. In: M. Joas, D. Jahn, and K. Kern (eds), Governing a Common Sea. Environmental Policies in the Baltic Sea Region. London: Earthscan, pp. 43–59.

Røsland, Stian B. (2013) Urban Ecology in Oslo, *Climate Leader Papers*. Available at: www.climateactionprogramme.org/climate-leader-papers/urban_ecology_in_oslo (accessed 4 October 2017).

SAMAK (2014) Vi bygger Norden (We Build the Nordics). Declaration from Nordic Worker's Congress. Available at: http://samak.info/wp-content/uploads/2015/11/Sormarka-erklaringen_Norwegian.pdf (accessed 5 October 2017).

Seymour, F., Birdsall, N. and Savedoff, W. (2015) The Indonesia–Norway REDD+ Agreement: A Glass Half-Full. Policy Center for Global Development Policy Paper 56, February.

Stateofgreen (2017) Discover Denmark's Solutions for a Greener Future. https://stateofgreen.com/en (accessed 5 October 2017).

Statistics Sweden (2017) Utsläppen av växtuhusgaser fortsätter att öka (Emission of Greenhouse Gasses Continues to Increase). Available at: www.scb.se/hitta-statistik/statistik-efter-amne/miljo/miljoekonomi-och-hallbar-utveckling/miljorakenskaper/pong/statistiknyhet/miljorakenskaper--utslapp-till-luft-tredje-kvartalet-2016/ (accessed 4 October 2017).

Stortinget (2017) Vedtak til lov om klimamål (Decision on Law of Climate Targets). Available at: www.stortinget.no/no/Saker-og-publikasjoner/Vedtak/Beslutninger/Lovvedtak/2016-2017/vedtak-201617-095/ (accessed 4 October 2017).

Sweden.se (2017) Sweden Tackles Climate Change. Available at: https://sweden.se/nature/sweden-tackles-climate-change/ (accessed 4 October 2017).

Virke (2017) Handel og Miljø (Trade and Environment). Report from Hovedorganisasjionen (Main Organisation). Available at: www.virke.no/globalassets/var-politikk/andre-dokumenter/handel-og-miljo.pdf (accessed 10 October 2017).

WWF (2014) Stockholm Climate Plan. Report. Available at: http://wwf.panda.org/?229202/Stockholm-climate-plan (accessed 5 October 2017).

Yle Uutiset (2017) Environment Minister: Finland Carbon Neutral by 2045. Available at: http://yle.fi/uutiset/osasto/news/environment_minister_finland_carbon_neutral_by_2045/9469850 (accessed 5 June 2017).

Afterword

Lessons from the Nordic model – the US perspective

Jerome Lieberman and Pamela Izvanariu

The 2016 Presidential election campaign in the United States will be indelibly remembered for the surreal rise to power of the scapegoating and warmongering Donald Trump. But one of its great ironies is that it also witnessed the unexpected ascendance of Trump's mirror opposite. Bernie Sanders, an avowed "socialist" senator from rural Vermont, rose from virtual oblivion to become a very viable candidate and was almost nominated to represent the Democratic Party in the general election. A core part of Sanders's appeal was his explicit endorsement of Nordic means to overcome America's deep scars of inequality and poverty. Nor was Sanders's popularity the fleeting outcome of election fever. According to opinion polls, he is, and has been for some time, the most popular politician in the country (*Newsweek* 2017).

"I think we should look to countries like Denmark, like Sweden and Norway and learn from what they have accomplished for their working people", Sanders proclaimed during a CNN primary debate with Hillary Clinton in October 2015. His was not a last-minute conversion either. In the spring of 2013, following a visit from the Danish ambassador, Sanders elaborated on the elements of the Danish "solidarity system" he thought the US could learn from. These included free health care and cheap prescription drugs, affordable child care, free tuition in higher education, training programmes for workers, paid maternity and paternity leave, more paid vacation time, generous unemployment and disability benefits and strong trade unions with large memberships (*Huffington Post* 2013). Sanders's interest is not in Denmark alone – at other times he has admired similar qualities across Scandinavia, "where government works for ordinary people" rather than "the billionaire class".

For years Sanders has ploughed a lonely furrow in American politics. He is disdained by much of the media as an isolated "far left" senator from the liberal enclave of Vermont. But that his comparison of the Nordic states with contemporary American realities touched a nerve was evident not just in the 13 million votes he received in the Primaries. Many media commentators were intrigued by Sanders's novel invocation of the Scandinavian alternative. A good many dismissed out of hand the suggestion that the US should try to emulate the Nordic states. But others pondered whether, in reality, Norway, Sweden, Denmark and Finland were proving better at realizing the American Dream than America itself.

Part of the reason was the universal nature of Scandinavian welfare states. "In the Nordic countries," wrote the Oslo-dwelling American author Ann Jones in *The Nation*, "democratically elected governments give their population freedom *from* the market by using capitalism as a tool to benefit everyone" (Jones 2016). And at the heart of Scandinavian democracy, said Jones, was equality between men and women. The state had decided to assume the unpaid household duties of women – care of children, the elderly, the sick – "freeing women in the workforce to enjoy both their jobs and their families."

Then there was the crucial difference between collective and individual bargaining at work. National agreements between trade union and employer bodies play a large part in determining wages and conditions and, as a result, income inequality ranks among the lowest in the world.

Indisputably the contrast between the Nordic countries and the US is stark. According to the US Labor Department, unionization of the American workforce hit a historic low in 2016. It stood at just 10.7 per cent, down from 11.1 per cent in 2015 and roughly half the level of the early 1980s. In Norway, by contrast, unionization stands at nearly 52 per cent. In Denmark, it is 67 per cent and in Sweden 70 per cent. Since the 1970s, the US labour market has taken a dramatic turn. As unions have declined, so have the benefits, job security, wage levels, humane labour practices and decent working conditions that they helped to secure. The quality of jobs in manufacturing and service industries has been eroded, spurred on by an insatiable demand among employers for temporary, mobile, flexible and exploitable workers. Meanwhile, economic inequality and insecurity have spiralled. And the "massive amount of economic anxiety" that Bernie Sanders has discerned in the United States is beginning to have tangible effects. Life expectancy for Americans *declined* in 2015, a reversal thought to be linked to "nationwide trends in obesity and opioid abuse, plus socioeconomic conditions" (Ars Technica 2016).

However, the irony is that, although commentators muse on the disparities between the US and the Nordics and the difficulty of importing such an "alien" model, the two once had a great deal in common. Before the Second World War, it was the United States that had led the charge towards a more cooperative and group-focused approach. In the 1930s, in the teeth of the Great Depression, the US embarked on a major programme to reform the free market capitalist system. Known as the New Deal, this bevy of laws addressed head-on the economic crisis, unemployment, economic inequity and poverty that had taken hold of the country. New programmes and federal agencies were created, such as the National Labor Relations Act, the National Labor Relations Board, the Social Security Act and the Works Progress Administration. Benefits for retirees and the unemployed were introduced. President Franklin Roosevelt, the New Deal's architect, called for a "permanent readjustment of many of our ways of thinking and therefore many of our social and economic arrangements" (Roosevelt 1938).

The response of the Nordic countries, particularly Sweden, to the depression of the '30s displayed a remarkable kinship with America. Public works programmes were enacted for the unemployed and social insurance schemes, including old age pensions and unemployment insurance, were introduced. Laws banning strike-breaking were passed and Keynesian deficit spending became the norm. In 1936, the young American journalist Marquis Childs published a book called *Sweden: The Middle Way*. Based on his own visits to Sweden, Childs asserted that the country had ensured full employment, social security and equality without sacrificing individual rights and democracy. Active government involvement in the economy allied to a strong cooperative movement had created a model that worked, in both human and economic terms.

Sweden: The Middle Way had a palpable influence on Roosevelt. Inspired in part by the book, he developed a strong interest in cooperative developments in Europe, dispatching a commission in June 1936 to examine the cooperative economy across the continent, Sweden in particular. "I was tremendously interested in what they had done in Scandinavia along those lines". Roosevelt revealed. "They have these cooperative movements existing happily and successfully alongside of private industry and distributions of various kinds, both of them making money." (Roosevelt 1936).

Over 80 years later, a renewed spirit of two-way collaboration between Scandinavia and the United States is again gestating, formed around the benefits of cooperatives, worker centres and strong labour unions. The advantages of the Nordic model are falling on fertile ground in America, while, in turn, Scandinavian unions are realizing they have something to learn from the innovations of the labour movement in the US. There are, undeniably, significant institutional, social and political differences that inhibit a simple adoption of the Nordic model in America. However, recent experiences indicate the feasibility of embracing and employing the underlying framework at the organizational, institutional and national levels in the US. This is an achievable feat, the promise of which can be seen in the American public's embrace of Bernie Sanders.

There are more than 230 worker centres in the US, organizations which Janice Fine describes as "community-based mediating institutions that provide support to low-wage workers"(Fine 2006: 2). In Scandinavia, little is known about them, but they have become crucial support organizations for low-wage workers and, in particular, to immigrants and blacks, who face limited employment opportunities and potential for advancement, as well as poor job quality, and suffer extreme discrimination inside and outside the workplace (Cordero-Guzmán et al 2013). The centres are generally organized along the lines of racial and ethnic identification, although some group around a particular occupation or industry. These centres have developed networks and partnerships at the regional and national level and work together to build and strengthen multi-ethnic organizing efforts and address labour market segmentation and racial prejudice (Fine 2006: 61, 66).

In their role as service providers, worker centres provide legal advocacy and representation, English language classes, worker rights education and access to health clinics, bank accounts and loans (Fine 2006: 73). They also conduct legal research and litigate on behalf of their worker clients, inform the public about the atrocious conditions of low-wage industries and lobby for relevant legal reforms in labour and immigration law (Narro 2005; Fine 2006; Milkman 2008). Worker centres have also engaged in collaborative efforts with government agencies to enforce existing labour and employment laws and ensure compliance with and enforcement of labour regulations (Fine 2006: 157). They have also succeeded in establishing new public policies at local and state-wide levels regarding issues of worker exploitation and lack of corporate responsibility (Narro 2005).

Worker centres and their networks have also played a critical role in recent immigration reform efforts, which seek to combat federal immigration policy and enforcement that make it nearly impossible for low-wage immigrant workers to adjust their status or procure jobs with better working conditions or wages (Fine 2006: 180). These advocacy efforts include public and political educational efforts to counter anti-immigrant rhetoric, litigation and advocacy for policy reform at the national and state levels, and efforts to build solidarity between immigrant workers, black communities, and other poor and marginalized groups in American society (Fine 2006: 182). Additionally, worker centres have served as a vehicle for these excluded workers to articulate oppositional accounts of racial experiences that document the particular harms low-wage workers, especially immigrants and blacks, have suffered.

What occurs in worker centres can be understood as an exemplar of the ways in which the principles of the Nordic model can be applied in a larger society like the United States – a place where de-unionization is rampant and many unions are either unwilling or unable to shift their focus to racial justice, anti-subordination, social justice and well-being. Traditional labour unions have failed, over a significant period of time, to address the needs of these workers (Crain and Matheny 2001). Importantly, the genesis of organizations like the worker centres has begun to move the United States in this direction. Their existence and exuberance suggest that it is these types of organizations that retain the capacity not only to mobilize the model and scale it for adaptation to the United States, but also to ensure that it is appropriate, inclusive and representative.

Since 2007, the US Federation of Workers of Co-ops (USFUC) has established and supported a Union Cooperative Council (UCC). Together, they envision a democratic society in which workers are in control of the management and ownership of their work. There is nothing comparable to this in Norway. The UCC strongly believes that there are many advantages to worker cooperatives. They can add to union membership and allow the labour force to respond to economic downturns with greater flexibility. Workers are empowered through ownership and control of management, and the business is less susceptible to attack and decimation of capital. Other considerations include building membership wealth in the form of enterprise ownership and sustainable and liveable wages. Labour unions are directed towards more democratic practices, and organized labour has a greater opportunity to be involved in a constructive approach to bringing about these transformations from capital to worker ownership.

The disparity in income that is already wide in the United States and growing in Norway requires serious consideration of alternative business and economic practices. What these are will have a direct impact on workers. Greater democratization in the workplace can directly contribute to reducing income disparity.

A strong relationship exists between the USFUC and the Cooperative Development Institute (CDI), the oldest and most effective regional organization of its kind in the United States, and together they are forging a relationship with the Evolution Institute (EI) think tank.[1] One outcome of this is that a director of the CDI from Maine joined the EI think tank in meetings with Norwegian labour leaders and representatives of a Norwegian organization involved with cooperatives, in 2015. Important and highly relevant connections were made, and the stage is set to capitalize on these in more tangible ways. For example, many agree that Norway can serve as an example of a cooperative economy/ecosystem and that Maine – because of comparable industries (fishing and forestry) and climate, and its sparsely populated rural regions – is a good place for components of the Norwegian model to be adopted in the United States. We have also identified blighted neighbourhoods in the Tampa Bay area of Florida that would benefit from the development of worker cooperatives. The initiative will include deeper research into cases where much richer cooperative structures exist, particularly in Norway, and local US unions will be engaged in all phases.

All these burgeoning and long-standing institutions – worker centres, labour unions, cooperatives and similar social justice organizations – can create the conditions for change in the United States. These organizations can be informed by the Nordic model in their work to effect lasting reform, especially at the highest levels of government. While sceptics might argue that the political climate suggests otherwise, these recent events in the United States can be seen as representing what Moghaddam and Breckenridge (Moghaddam et al. 2011) refer to as an "opportunity bubble" – a "promising, yet fleeting, time to shape the course of subsequent events". The hope is that the aforementioned long-standing institutions take this opportunity seriously, and use these recent events to inspire a dialogue about the promise of the Nordic model, and a rediscovery of its roots in the United States, in a way that leads directly to collective mobilization.

Conversely, these organizations have the potential to cross-fertilize and address growing inequality and the overrepresentation of immigrants in

Norway's poorest population, as Norway experiences an increasing influx of immigration and diversity, and subsequent social and political resistance as a result.

Such cross-fertilization depends on active collaboration between US unions and their Scandinavian counterparts. Jerry Lieberman – the co-author of this afterword – initiated a concrete project in 2012 to encourage sustained contact between the labour movements of Norway and the US. Using the concept *labour representatives* as a springboard – and organizing meetings between US union leaders and their Norwegian equivalents to discuss their experiences and strategies – the study is "work in progress". It focuses on building a transnational alliance of trade unions to combat virulent and destructive forms of competition that result in greater inequality, political instability and distrust of government. The first step was to schedule meetings with Norwegian labour unions – including local and national unions as well as confederations, the largest being LO (the Norwegian Confederation of Trade Unions), with its headquarters in Oslo.

But what possible benefit would the unions derive from collaborating? There was no history of engagement in Norway or an incentive to prove credibility. What could those labour union representatives from the United States possibly offer to Norwegian unions, when the latter already had their own domestic think tanks with leadership and staff, often with extensive labour union experience? How could Norwegian incredulousness towards working with people from the United States be overcome? Why look to help from the Americans when that country has experienced an enormous decline in unionization and retreated from the paths of the New Deal and the Great Society?

Five years of deep, comprehensive and ongoing engagement in Norway provides the reason why some Norwegians have come to see a real benefit of working with their American colleagues. American labour unions, their hand forced by an unremittingly hostile political and economic environment, have shown the value of experimenting and treading new paths. Such innovations, worker centres in particular, demonstrate to Scandinavian unions the value and potential of multi-ethnic organizing; a feature of growing relevance since all of the Nordic countries have experienced significant increases in immigration over the past 20 years. A continuing relationship exists with Norwegian think tanks, local and national unions, youth groups, political party leaders, and faculty, administrators and students at Oslo University and other academic institutions. We have built a viable relationship and we see its continuance well into the future.

We envision some practical steps that will help strengthen the well-being of Norway and move the United States closer to adapting some beneficial tenets of the Norwegian model. This will engage Norwegian and US unions in growing collaboration and incorporating worker centres and cooperative enterprises. Initially it will involve one union at a time from the United States and Norway – beginning with a union that includes nurses. This choice is based on the fact that the union representing nurses in the United States is highly progressive and strongly supported Bernie Sanders in the 2016 Democratic Primaries – consequently, it is likely to be open to learning more about Norway and meeting with its counterpart there. There is already growing interest in advancing beyond the conceptual stage. Direct and formal contacts have already been made between the Florida Public Service Employees International Union and Norwegian unions, including two visits to Norway for meetings with unions there – hosted by the Norwegian unions in their local and national offices in Oslo.

There is a profound opportunity and benefit to both US and Norwegian unions to become more involved in developing and expanding cooperative enterprises and considering whether there is also a role for worker centres. Presently, interest is greater in the United States than in Norway. This can be partly accounted for by the fact that unions in Norway are in a much stronger position and therefore not as motivated to seek alternatives to private ownership.

Despite disparate levels of interest in worker centres and cooperatives, Norway represents something of a promised land to US activists. Trade unions there have large memberships and exert a significant influence in the Labour Party (in contrast to US unions' marginal role in the Democratic Party). Moreover, other political parties are broadly sympathetic and there is a relative balance of power and respect between labour and employers, embodied in national collective bargaining arrangements. That the Nordic model is exerting an increasing pull on US public opinion can be seen in Bernie Sanders's pithy response to the suggestion that Republicans would attack him for wanting to make the US more like Scandinavia: "And what's wrong with that?".

However, Norway is not immune to the neoliberal drift. According to *Norway Today* (18 February 2017), since 2006 income inequality increased by 14 per cent. Consequently, the dynamic between cooperation and competition is tilting more visibly in the direction of the latter.

But the source of the value shift is deeper than globalization or the ubiquity of neoliberal policy prescriptions. At its root lies a growing emphasis on America's geopolitical role – partly legitimized by Norway's dependence on NATO – and the iconic status of the United States as a cultural and educational model. A crucial question then is: Will the present trends continue? Will it be Norway that finds itself adapting to the US model or the other way around? Given the results of the US election in 2016 and the subsequent, more hostile, attitude toward unions, there is a high risk that Norway will be influenced by more neoliberal American policies. Strong, dialogue-orientated unions and their value-charged narratives of social solidarity have been essential safeguards against virulent competition in Scandinavia. Now those safeguards need to be exported. The best protection for the Nordic model is for the United States itself to radically change tack in favour of a cooperative, egalitarian, collective and fair economy.

Note

1 The Evolution Institute aims to connect scientists with public policy in order to solve the world's most pressing social problems (https://evolution-institute.org/).

References

ABC News (2015). Bernie Sanders Interviewed by George Stephanopoulos, 3 May. Available at: http://abcnews.go.com/ThisWeek/video/sen-bernie-sanders-us-scandinavia-30770990

Ars Technica (2016) Americans' Life Expectancy Dips as Middle-aged See Uptick in Death Rates. 8 December. Available at: https://arstechnica.com/science/2016/12/americans-life-expectancy-dips-as-middle-aged-see-uptick-in-death-rates/

Cordero-Guzmán, Héctor R., Izvanariu, Pamela A. and Narro, Victor (2013) The Development of Sectoral Worker Center Networks. The Annals of the American Academy of Political and Social Science 647 (1): 102–123.

Crain, Marion and Matheny, Ken (2001) Labor's Identity Crisis. *California Law Review* 89 (6). Available at: http://scholarship.law.berkeley.edu/californialawreview/vol89/iss6/3/

Fine, Janice (2006) *Worker Centers: Organizing Communities at the Edge of the Dream*. Ithaca, NY: Cornell University Press.

Huffington Post (2013) Senator Bernie Sanders: "What Can we Learn from Denmark?". 26 May.

Jones, A. (2016) After I Lived in Norway, America Felt Backward. Here's Why. *The Nation* 28 January. www.thenation.com/article/after-i-lived-in-norway-america-felt-backward-heres-why/ (accessed 26 August 2017).

Milkman, Ruth (2008) Putting Wages Back into Competition: Deunionization and Degradation in Place-Bound Industries. In: Annette Bernhardt, Heather Boushey, Laura Dresser and Chris Tilly (eds), *The Gloves-off Economy: Problems and Possibilities at the Bottom of America's Labor Market* (pp. 65–89). Champaign, IL: Labor and Employment Relations Association.

Moghaddam, Fathali M. and Breckenridge, James N. (2011) The Post-tragedy "Opportunity Bubble" and the Prospect of Citizen Engagement. *Homeland Security Affairs* 7: 1–4.

Narro, Victor (2005) Impacting Next Wave Organizing: Creative Campaign Strategies of the Los Angeles Worker Centers. *New York Law School Law Review* 50: 470–471. Available at: www.nylslawreview.com/wp-content/uploads/sites/16/2013/11/50-2.Narro_.pdf (accessed 3 January 2018).

Newsweek (2017) Bernie Sanders is Still the Most Popular Politician, Even as Senate Approval Ratings Plunge. Newsweek 11 July. Available at: www.newsweek.com/senate-approval-ratings-bernie-sanders-mitch-mcconnell-634882 (accessed 26 August 2017).

Roosevelt, Franklin D. (1936) Presidential Press Conference, 23 June. Available at: www.presidency.ucsb.edu/ws/?pid=15310

Roosevelt, Franklin D. (1938) Annual Message to Congress, 3 January 1934. In: Samuel I. Rosenman (ed.), *The Public Papers and Addresses of Franklin d. Roosevelt, Vol. 8*, p. 8.

Index

Aaberge, R. 149
Aasen, P. 60, 61, 63, 65
Acemoglu, D. 6, 38
across-domain sustainability 5–6
AFDC (Aid to Families with Dependent Children, US) 132
altruism 20, 36
Andersen, B. R. 124, 125, 127, 130
Anglo-American feminism 103, 104, 105, 107–108, 111, 113
animateurs 39, 50
Atkinson, A. B. 149
Averaging Fallacy 20–21

Baudet, T. 98
Berman, S. 162, 163
Bjørnson, B. 46–48, 50, 53
Boehm, C. 22–23
Britain 96, 162, 169, 172, 179, 197, 199
Brynjolfsson, E. 153–154, 156

carbon emissions 8, 205, 210–212, 213, 219, 220–221, 222–223; Denmark 210, 211, 213, 215, 219; EU 214, 215–216; Finland 210, 211, 213, 214, 215, 216, 218, 219; Norway 30, 210, 211, 212, 214–215, 216, 218, 219, 222, 223; Sweden 210, 211, 213, 215, 216, 219
CDPs (Core Design Principles) 12, 27–28, 31, 32, 51
Childs, M. 2, 79, 231
China 191, 200
citizenship 88–89, 92, 93, 94, 95, 120
citizen's wage model 156
civic statism 97
civil rights 84, 89, 91, 97
climate change 9, 14, 30, 204, 210–212, 214, 221

climate policies 8, 10, 204, 212–213, 214–215, 223; Denmark 213, 214, 215, 217; EU 212–214; Finland 213, 214, 215, 218; Norway 212, 214–215, 217–219; Sweden 213, 215, 216–217; *see also* green growth
collaboration 5–6, 193
collective wage bargaining *see* negotiated settlements
collectivism 8, 59
common-pool resources 5, 27, 28, 123
communitarianism 161, 163, 173, 180
competition 5–6, 8, 24–26, 51–52, 177
competitive advantage 5, 192
Competitive Partnership 169–170
consensus-making institutions 111–112
cooperation 3, 6, 7, 8, 23, 25, 26, 27, 31, 51–52, 139, 177
Core Design Principles *see* CDPs (Core Design Principles)
cosmopolitization 9, 14, 51, 95, 96, 113
Cox, M. 5, 27, 79, 99
crimmigration 93
CSR (corporate social responsibility) 7, 10, 187, 188–189, 193, 200; domestic welfare protection model 191–192; EITI 197–199, 201; ETI 197, 199–200; international competitiveness and innovation model 192–193; international welfare capitalism model 189–191; Nordic companies 7, 10, 193–197, 200
cultural diversity 64
cultural evolution 23–24, 29
cultural innovation 7, 38, 41, 46, 52

Darwin, C. 19
Davy, U. 92

Dawkins, R. 18
Denmark 3, 7, 9, 14, 37, 43–44, 79, 151, 153, 230; carbon emissions 210, 211, 213, 215, 219; climate change 210, 211, 214; climate policy 213, 214, 215, 217; CSR 189, 191, 192; deregulation 62, 67; ecological footprints 209–210; eco-modernity 216; education 43–44, 61, 62, 68; education policies 66–67, 68; environmental policy 207; ETI 200; gender equality 102, 103, 107, 114; green growth 217, 219, 220, 222; happy Christianity 38, 43, 44; national curriculum 65, 72; private schooling 66, 67; sex work 107
deregulation 62, 67, 68, 72
digitalization 9, 10, 140, 154
Dølvik, J. E. 122, 152
domestic welfare protection model 191–192
dualization 147–151, 156
Dubois, V. 131

Eastern European workers 144–145
ecohumanism 53
ecological footprints 208–210
ecological sustainability 10, 205, 209–210, 215–216
eco-modernity 2, 3, 8–9, 10, 204, 206, 215–216, 220–223
economic theory 26, 28
education 59–65, 67, 68–70, 71–73; Denmark 43–44, 61, 62, 68; Finland 61, 62, 68, 69, 72; Iceland 61; national curricula 63, 64–65, 71, 72; Norway 52, 61, 62, 67–68, 69–70, 71–72; Sweden 59, 61, 62, 68, 69–70, 71–73; *see also* private schooling
educational values 63–65, 71
education policies 65–67, 68, 71, 72; Denmark 66–67, 68; Finland 66, 68; Iceland 66, 68; Norway 66, 68; Sweden 66, 67, 68
effective groups 107, 110, 112, 115
Effort-Sharing Decision, EU *see* ESD (Effort-Sharing Decision, EU)
egalitarianism 113, 149, 153, 167
EITI (Extractive Industries' Transparency Initiative) 197–199, 200
Eldring, L. 152
Emission Trading Scheme, EU *see* ETS (Emission Trading Scheme, EU)
Entzensberger, H. M. 13

environmental policies 200, 204–208; *see also* climate policies
environmental sustainability 3, 53–54, 205–210
equality feminism 108
ESD (Effort-Sharing Decision, EU) 213, 215, 223
Esping-Andersen, G. 102, 120
ETI (Ethical Trade Initiative) 199–200
ETS (Emission Trading Scheme, EU) 213
EU (European Union) 10, 88, 93, 98–99, 142, 150; carbon emissions 212, 213–214; climate policy 212–214
European Court of Justice 143, 144, 150
Evolutionary Game Theory 20, 21
evolutionary theory 12, 18, 19, 26, 32, 103

feminism 7, 103–105, 106, 111, 112, 113–114, 115; equality feminism 108; liberal feminism 7, 103, 104, 105, 108; radical feminism 108–109, 110
feminism of difference 108, 109, 110, 114
Finland 3, 9, 39, 54, 64, 79, 87, 151, 152, 153, 156; carbon emissions 210, 211, 213, 214, 215, 216, 218, 219; climate change 211, 214; climate policy 213, 214, 215, 218; CSR 189, 191, 192; deregulation 62, 67; ecological footprints 209; eco-modernity 216; education 61, 62, 68, 69, 72; educational values 63, 64; education policies 66, 68; environmental policy 206, 207–208; gender equality 102; green growth 218, 220, 222; national curriculum 63, 64, 65, 71; private schooling 59, 62, 66
flexibility 8, 53, 140, 141, 145
flexicurity model 8, 29, 139, 152, 155–156, 191
Fløtten, T. 122
folkhemmet (people's home), Sweden 13, 38, 44, 46, 48–50, 51, 82, 83–84, 85, 163
France 89, 131, 161; feminism 103, 104, 108
Fukuyama, F. 11

Geijer, E. G. 84
gender equality 102–103, 104, 113; Denmark 102, 103, 107, 114; Finland

102; Iceland 102; Norway 102, 103, 105, 106, 111; Sweden 102, 103
Gender Equality Act (Norway, 1979) 105
generalized trust 82, 166
genetic evolution 22–23
Germany 48, 83, 84, 86, 90, 161
global civil society 97, 99
global economy 30, 152, 190, 196, 200, 201
globalization 11, 12, 96, 97, 170–173, 181
global market society 96
global warming *see* climate change
good governance 8, 12, 28, 32
good society 11, 12–13, 43, 46
governance 18, 28, 32, 72
Gray, J. 11
green growth 8, 10, 12, 205, 215–220, 221, 223; Denmark 217, 219, 220, 222; Finland 218, 220, 222; Norway 3–4, 217–218, 219–220; Sweden 4, 30, 216–217, 219, 220
greenhouse gas emissions *see* carbon emissions
green movements 178
group-level selection 19, 20–21
groups 5–6, 12, 19, 21, 28–29, 99; effective 107, 110, 112, 114
group selection 18, 20–21, 22, 23, 24, 25–26
Grundtvig, N. F. S. 43–44, 50, 62

Haidt, J. 168, 171, 172, 178–179, 182
Hamilton, W. D. 21
Hammerskjöld, D. 49, 50, 86
happy Christianity, Denmark 38, 43, 44
Hartberg, Y. 37
Hauge, H. N. 40, 41, 50
Haugianism 40–41
Hernes, H. 107, 113
Hessen, D. 12, 171
high-trust societies 8, 82–83, 98
Hippe, J. M. 122
Holm, G. 63, 64
Holship case, Norway 143–144
human evolution 5, 39
humanism 37, 38, 44, 46, 48, 50, 51, 52, 53
human rights 29, 50, 51, 88–89, 91–92, 93, 95, 96, 97

Iceland 39, 67, 151; education 61; education policies 66, 68; gender equality 102; private schooling 66

ICESCR (International Covenant on Economic, Social and Cultural Rights) 92
immigration 29, 92–93, 132, 148, 171–172; Norway 132, 145, 148, 172, 233–234; Sweden 29, 51, 80–82, 95; United States 232
Inclusive Fitness Theory 20, 21
individualism 59, 112, 125, 161, 167, 180
industrial economies 2, 125, 139, 140, 213
innovation economy 152, 154–155
international competitiveness and innovation model 192–193
International Covenant on Economic, Social and Cultural Rights *see* ICESCR (International Covenant on Economic, Social and Cultural Rights)
internationalism 83, 87, 96–97
international welfare capitalism model 189–191

Jordfald, B. 122

Kristensen, P. H. 154–155

Labour and Welfare Administration, Norway *see* NAV (Labour and Welfare Administration, Norway)
labour force 10, 148, 230, 231–233
labour market 114, 131, 141–143; EU 142–144, 145; unemployment 119, 123, 131; women 46, 102, 114
Labour Party, Norway 174, 235
Lagerlöf, S. 45, 53
Lakoff, G. 168, 169, 170
Laval case, Sweden 143
liberal feminism 7, 103, 104, 105, 108
liberalism 105, 106, 107, 114, 162
Lilja, K. 154–155
Lindbeck, A. 122
Lindner, E. 166
Lorenz, E. 155
Lundvall, B. Å. 155

McAfee, A. 153–154, 156
major evolutionary transitions 22–23
Marshall, T. H. 89, 90
Maynard Smith, J. 22
Mediås, O. A. 60, 61, 63, 65
mediatization 170, 175–180, 181; social media 52, 177–179, 181

methodological individualism 18
migration *see* immigration
Modalsli, J. 149
modernity 2, 4, 11–12, 13, 15, 36, 39, 51, 52
Moen, E. 155
Multi-level Selection (MLS) theory 5, 18, 19, 20, 21–22, 24, 25, 28, 30
Myrdal, A. 48
Myrdal, G. 48

Nansen, F. 15, 46–48, 50, 51, 53
national community 37, 43–44, 51, 90, 93, 113, 163; Sweden 83, 84–85, 95
national identity 39, 50, 64; Sweden 64, 80, 82, 86, 87, 94
nationalism 9, 83, 86, 96
nation-states 79, 83, 88, 92, 93, 94, 96, 97–98, 99, 113, 168
natural selection 19
NAV (Labour and Welfare Administration, Norway) 119
navers 121, 123, 125–126, 130, 131, 133, 134; Norway 119–120, 121, 124, 126, 127–129, 130, 132, 133, 134
negotiated settlements 10, 143–144, 151, 187, 230
negotiating culture 139, 143–144, 145, 151
Nielson, P. 139, 144
Nordic companies 145–147, 154–155; CSR 7, 10, 193–197, 200; ETI 199
Nordic countries 2–8, 9–15, 29, 31, 38–39, 53–54, 60, 88, 90, 230, 231; carbon emissions 8, 205, 210–212, 220–221, 222–223; climate change 9, 210–212; climate policies 212–213, 214–215; eco-modernity 215–216, 220–223; environmental policies 204–208; green growth 8, 10, 12, 205, 216–219, 221; labour market 142–143; social contract 91, 208
Nordic development model 174–175
Nordic education model 70–72, 73
Nordic political model 29, 161–168, 169–170, 180–182; globalization 171–173, 181; mediatization 175–180, 181; technocratization 173–175
Nordic societies 9, 29, 148, 156–157, 174
Nordic Sonderweg model 162–163
Nordic welfare model 2–5, 3–10, 12–15, 31–32, 52, 79, 120–121, 122, 187, 231

Nordic welfare societies 2–3, 37, 70, 141, 205
Nordic welfare states 3, 10, 12, 14, 29, 38, 51, 60, 152, 163, 167, 169, 176, 206; CSR 187, 188, 189, 193
Nordic work model 139, 140–142, 144–145, 146–147, 154–157; dualization 147–151; resilience 151–153; transformation 153–154
Norway 1, 7, 9, 13, 14–15, 30–31, 87, 149, 176–177, 233–235; carbon emissions 30, 210, 211, 212, 214–215, 216, 218, 219, 222, 223; climate change 14, 30, 211, 221; climate policy 212, 214–215, 217–218; CSR 189–190, 191, 194; deregulation 62, 67; ecological footprints 209; eco-modernity 216; education 52, 61, 62, 67–68, 69–70, 71–72; educational values 64; education policies 66, 68; EITI 198; environmental policy 206, 207; ETI 199, 200; feminism 103, 104–105, 106, 108, 109, 110, 112–113, 114; gender equality 102, 103, 105, 106, 111; green growth 3–4, 217–218, 219–220; Haugianism 40–41; humanism 53, 54; immigration 132, 145, 148, 172, 233–234; labour force 148, 230; national curriculum 65, 71; national identity 64; *navers* 119–120, 121, 124, 126, 127–129, 130, 132, 133, 134; negotiated settlements 151; petroleum production 30, 198, 216, 218, 223; political parties 174, 182, 237; private schooling 59, 62, 66; regime of goodness 8, 36–37, 38, 41–43, 120; resilience 152–153; sex work 107; social policies 131, 132, 133, 134; universal welfare state 123, 124, 126–127; welfare state 110, 120, 121, 130, 134, 163
Norwegian (airline company) case 145–146

Österlind, E. 70
Ostrom, E. 5, 27, 28, 50, 51, 79, 99, 103, 123

Palme, O. 86, 87–88
particularized trust 82–83
partnered governance 195–197, 198, 200
patriarchy 105, 108–109

Paulsrud, B. 63, 64
people's home (*folkhemmet*) *see folkhemmet* (people's home)
Perez, C. 154, 156
Persily, N. 179
petroleum production, Norway 30, 198, 216, 218, 223
Polder model, Netherlands 32
political parties 91, 102, 160, 165, 167, 174, 175, 177, 178, 179, 182; Labour Party, Norway 174, 235
political processes 9, 111, 162–163, 164–166, 170, 171, 173, 175, 180, 181–182; mediatization 176, 177, 179
political systems 98–99, 108, 160–161, 162, 164–166, 175, 177, 178, 181–182
politics 96–97, 160, 168, 171, 176, 178
polycentric governance 12, 28
Posting Directive (European Commission, 2017) 143, 144, 146
Price, G. 21
private schooling: Denmark 66, 67; Finland 59, 62, 66; Iceland 66; Norway 59, 62, 66; Sweden 29, 59, 62, 72, 73, 148
productivity 8, 29
prosociality 5, 7–8, 10, 11, 13, 39, 51, 120, 144, 153, 157
public sphere 13–14, 162, 164, 166–167, 175; Sweden 9, 48–49, 178

radical feminism 108–109, 110
reductionism 18
refugees 51, 80–82, 92, 93, 95, 148
regime of goodness, Norway 8, 36–37, 38, 41–43, 120
resilience 147, 151–153, 154, 167
reverse dominance 23
Robinson, J. A. 6, 38
robotization 142, 147, 154, 156
Rothstein, B. 123, 132

Sanders, B. 97, 178, 229, 231, 235
Scandinavia 1–2, 37, 106–107, 111–112, 113, 125; feminism 103, 110, 111, 112, 113–114, 115; gender equality 102–103, 106, 114
School for All, A 60, 64, 65, 70, 71
Selfish Gene Theory 20, 21
self-limiting modernity 4
Sen, A. 91, 92
sex work 107

sharing economy 141–142
Simpson, A. K. 160
social adaptations 19–20
social contract 52, 90, 91, 96, 98, 99, 208; Sweden 79, 82, 84, 85, 86, 98, 99
social cooperation 4, 8
social democracy 7, 11, 46, 97, 107, 109, 110, 111, 113, 163, 164–166
social groups 5, 21, 22, 23
social investments 90, 163–164
social media 52, 177–179, 181
social partners 3, 144, 163, 169–170, 173–174, 175
social policies 89, 130–131, 132–133, 134
social rights 89–91, 92, 94–95, 96, 98
social sustainability 2, 3, 6, 7–9, 39
societies 5, 12, 18, 23–24, 29, 32, 38, 115, 168–169, 201–203; Nordic 9, 29, 148, 156–157, 174
socio-economic sustainability 4, 10
Sørensen, A. 124–125, 127, 130
Sørensen, Ø. 169
stakeholdership 201
statist individualism 49, 85
Stråth, B. 162, 167
sustainability 3, 4, 5–6, 10; ecological 10, 205, 208–210, 215–217; environmental 3, 53–54, 205–210; modernity 2, 3, 4, 5, 8, 9, 11, 79; social 2, 3, 6, 7–9; welfare state 120, 121, 124
sustainable development 3, 53–54
sustainable modernity 2, 3, 4, 5, 8, 9, 11, 79
Sweden 3, 7, 14, 37, 44–46, 79–80, 86–88, 95–96, 98, 99, 149–150, 231; carbon emissions 210, 211, 213, 215, 216, 219; climate change 211, 221; climate policy 213, 215, 216–217; CSR 189–190, 191; deregulation 67; ecological footprints 209; eco-modernity 216; education 59, 61, 62, 68, 69–70, 71–73; educational values 63, 64; education policies 66, 67, 68; environmental policy 206, 207; feminism 109; *folkhemmet* 13, 38, 44, 46, 48–50, 51, 82, 83–84, 85, 96, 163; gender equality 102, 103; green growth 4, 30, 216–217, 219, 220; humanism 53, 54; human rights 92, 95, 99; immigration 29, 51, 80–82, 95; internationalism 86, 87–88; labour force 230; national community 83, 84–85, 95; national curriculum 63, 64–65, 71, 72; national identity

64, 80, 82, 86, 87, 94; nationalism 83, 86; negotiating culture 151; political parties 182; private schooling 29, 59, 62, 72, 73, 148; public sphere 9, 48–49, 178; refugees 51, 80–82, 93, 95, 148; resilience 167; sex work 107; social contract 79, 82, 84, 85, 86, 98, 99; social rights 90–91, 92, 94–95; welfare state 79, 82, 85–86, 94, 95; work life 140
symbotypes 37–38, 39, 48, 52
Szathmary, E. 22

Tawney, R. H. 168, 169
technocratization 170, 173–175
techno-economic modernity 2, 3
technology 52, 141, 156
Telhaug, A. O. 60, 61, 63, 65
Tocqueville, A. de 6, 48
Trägårdh, L. 49
transformation 147, 153–154, 157
Trump, D. 96, 97, 178, 229
Turchin, P. 23, 24, 32
Tvedt, T. 36, 120

UDHR (Universal Declaration of Human Rights) 89
UK (United Kingdom) see Britain
unemployment 119, 123, 131
United States 32, 86, 90, 91, 162, 169, 179, 229–231, 234–235; feminism 104; immigration 232; labour force 230, 231–233; refugees 81; social media 178–179; social policies 132–133, 134

universal welfare state 121–122, 123, 124, 125, 126–127, 129, 130, 133–134, 170, 230
urban greening 218–219

Valeyre, A. 155
Vike, H. 167

Wallas, G. 1, 2, 3
welfare-claiming 124, 127, 131, 132; antisocial patterns 121, 122–123, 125, 129, 133
welfare states 8, 89–90, 96, 110–111, 122–124, 130–132, 180, 187; CSR 187, 188–189, 193, 201; modern 3, 13, 85, 90, 92, 176; Nordic 3, 10, 12, 14, 29, 38, 51, 60, 152, 163, 167, 169, 176, 204
welfare state sustainability 120, 121, 124
Wergeland, H. 41–43, 50, 53
Williams, G. C. 20
Wilson, D. S. 4, 5, 12, 37, 79, 99, 103, 166, 171
Wilson, E. O. 4
within-domain sustainability 5–6
women's shelter movement, Norway 105–106
worker centres, United States 231–232, 235
worker cooperatives, United States 232–233, 235
work life 7, 10, 29, 140

Zilliacus, H. 63, 64